THE NEW AMERICAN COMMENTARY

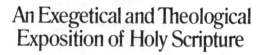

An Exegetical and Theological
Exposition of Holy Scripture

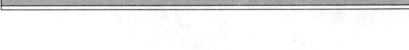

THE NEW AMERICAN COMMENTARY

Volume
23

MARK

James A. Brooks

BROADMAN PRESS

NASHVILLE, TENNESSEE

© Copyright 1991   Broadman Press
All rights reserved
4201-23
ISBN: 0-8054-0123-7
Dewey Decimal Classification: 226.3
Subject Heading: BIBLE. N.T. MARK
Library of Congress Catalog Card Number: 91-22704
Printed in the United States of America

Library of Congress Cataloging-in-Publication Data

Brooks, James A.
  Mark / James A. Brooks.
    p. cm. — (The New American commentary ; v. 23)
  Includes bibliographical references and indexes.
  ISBN 0-8054-0123-7
  1. Bible. N.T. Mark—Commentaries. I. Title. II. Series.
BS2585.3.B764 1991
226.3'077—dc20

To *Beverly*

Editors' Preface

God's Word does not change. God's world, however, changes in every generation. These changes, in addition to new findings by scholars and a new variety of challenges to the gospel message, call for the church in each generation to interpret and apply God's Word for God's people. Thus, THE NEW AMERICAN COMMENTARY is introduced to bridge the twentieth and twenty-first centuries. This new series has been designed primarily to enable pastors, teachers, and students to read the Bible with clarity and proclaim it with power.

In one sense THE NEW AMERICAN COMMENTARY is not new, for it represents the continuation of a heritage rich in biblical and theological exposition. The title of this forty-volume set points to the continuity of this series with an important commentary project published at the end of the nineteenth century called AN AMERICAN COMMENTARY, edited by Alvah Hovey. The older series included, among other significant contributions, the outstanding volume on Matthew by John A. Broadus, from whom the publisher of the new series, Broadman Press, partly derives its name. The former series was authored and edited by scholars committed to the infallibility of Scripture, making it a solid foundation for the present project. In line with this heritage, all NAC authors affirm the divine inspiration, inerrancy, complete truthfulness, and full authority of the Bible. The perspective of the NAC is unapologetically confessional and rooted in the evangelical tradition.

Since a commentary is a fundamental tool for the expositor or teacher who seeks to interpret and apply Scripture in the church or classroom, the NAC focuses on communicating the theological structure and content of each biblical book. The writers seek to illuminate both the historical meaning and the contemporary significance of Holy Scripture.

In its attempt to make a unique contribution to the Christian community, the NAC focuses on two concerns. First, the commentary emphasizes how each section of a book fits together so that the reader becomes aware of the theological unity of each book and of Scripture as a whole. The writers, however, remain aware of the Bible's inherently rich variety. Second, the NAC is produced with the conviction that the Bible primarily belongs to the church.

We believe that scholarship and the academy provide an indispensable foundation for biblical understanding and the service of Christ, but the editors and authors of this series have attempted to communicate the findings of their research in a manner that will build up the whole body of Christ. Thus, the commentary concentrates on theological exegesis, while providing practical, applicable exposition.

THE NEW AMERICAN COMMENTARY's theological focus enables the reader to see the parts as well as the whole of Scripture. The biblical books vary in content, context, literary type, and style. In addition to this rich variety, the editors and authors recognize that the doctrinal emphasis and use of the biblical books differ in various places, contexts, and cultures among God's people. These factors, as well as other concerns, have led the editors to give freedom to the writers to wrestle with the issues raised by the scholarly community surrounding each book and to determine the appropriate shape and length of the introductory materials. Moreover, each writer has developed the structure of the commentary in a way best suited for expounding the basic structure and the meaning of the biblical books for our day. Generally, discussions relating to contemporary scholarship and technical points of grammar and syntax appear in the footnotes and not in the text of the commentary. This format allows pastors and interested laypersons, scholars and teachers, and serious college and seminary students to profit from the commentary at various levels. This approach has been employed because we believe that all Christians have the privilege and responsibility to read and to seek to understand the Bible for themselves.

Consistent with the desire to produce a readable, up-to-date commentary, the editors selected the New International Version as the standard translation for the commentary series. The selection was made primarily because of the NIV's faithfulness to the original languages and its beautiful and readable style. The authors, however, have been given the liberty to differ at places from the NIV as they develop their own translations from the Greek and Hebrew texts.

The NAC reflects the vision and leadership of those who provide oversight for Broadman Press, who in 1987 called for a new commentary series that would evidence a commitment to the inerrancy of Scripture and a faithfulness to the classic Christian tradition. While the commentary adopts an "American" name, it should be noted that some writers represent countries outside the United States, giving the commentary an international perspective. The diverse group of writers includes scholars, teachers, and administrators from almost twenty different colleges and seminaries, as well as pastors, missionaries, and a layperson.

The editors and writers hope that THE NEW AMERICAN COMMENTARY will be helpful and instructive for pastors and teachers, scholars and students, for men and women in the churches who study and teach God's Word in various settings. We trust that for editors, authors, and readers alike, the commentary will be used to build up the church, encourage obedience, and bring renewal to God's people. Above all, we pray that the NAC will bring glory and honor to our Lord, who has graciously redeemed us and faithfully revealed himself to us in his Holy Word.

SOLI DEO GLORIA
The Editors

Author's Preface

During the first half of my Christian life, I probably had less interest in the Gospel according to Mark than in Matthew, Luke, or John. I now know that my attitude was similar to that of most Christians during most of Christian history. My interest in Mark was first aroused in 1975 when I was asked to conduct a doctoral seminar on that Gospel at New Orleans Baptist Theological Seminary, where I taught at that time. Since then I have frequently been drawn back to it. I have come to realize that although it is the shortest Gospel and has very little material which is not in Matthew and/or Luke, it has a unique point of view and a powerful message. Therefore when I was asked to write the commentary on Mark for *The New American Commentary*, I readily accepted.

I want to thank Mike Smith, the first editor of the series, and the consulting editors for the invitation. I want to thank the editors for their many helpful suggestions. I want to thank my wife, Beverly, who has a theological degree from Southwestern Baptist Theological Seminary and unusual insight into things spiritual and with whom I discussed many points of interpretation in the commentary, for her suggestions and encouragement. I want to thank Carlton Winbery, my student at New Orleans Seminary and now chairman of the religion department at Louisiana College, for his help with computer problems. I want to thank the librarians at Southwestern Baptist Theological Seminary and at Bethel Theological Seminary—two schools where I taught during the period of writing—for securing the necessary materials for me. And I want to thank you, dear reader, for considering what I have written. I ask not that you agree with me at every point. In fact, I believe that God will be most honored if you would consider my opinion and that of other commentators and then make up your own mind as did the Bereans long ago (Acts 17:11).

Abbreviations

Bible Books

Gen	Isa	Luke
Exod	Jer	John
Lev	Lam	Acts
Num	Ezek	Rom
Deut	Dan	1,2 Cor
Josh	Hos	Gal
Judg	Joel	Eph
Ruth	Amos	Phil
1,2 Sam	Obad	Col
1,2 Kgs	Jonah	1,2 Thess
1,2 Chr	Mic	1,2 Tim
Ezra	Nah	Titus
Neh	Hab	Phlm
Esth	Zeph	Heb
Job	Hag	Jas
Ps (*pl.* Pss)	Zech	1,2 Pet
Prov	Mal	1,2,3 John
Eccl	Matt	Jude
Song of Songs	Mark	Rev

Commonly Used Reference Works

AB   *The Anchor Bible*
CD   Cairo (Genizah text of the Damascus Document)
EBC   *Expositor's Bible Commentary*
Her   *Hermeneia*
Int   *Interpretation*
INT   *Interpretation: A Bible Commentary for Preaching and Teaching*
JSOT   *Journal for the Study of the Old Testament*
JTS   *Journal of Theological Studies [New Series]*

Contents

Mark

--------- **INTRODUCTION** ---------

Mark is the shortest of the Gospels. In one recent edition of the Greek New Testament, it consumes thirty-one pages as opposed to fifty-one for Matthew, fifty-four for Luke, and forty for John. It has less unique material than any other Gospel. About 92 percent of it is paralleled in Matthew, about 48 percent in Luke, and about 95 percent in Matthew and Luke combined. Even though Mark frequently mentioned that Jesus taught, this Gospel contains less of his teaching than any other. It records no resurrection appearances.[1] The quality of Mark's Greek is inferior to that of Matthew and Luke. Mark contains a number of candid statements about the humanity and self-imposed limitations of Jesus and the dullness of the disciples. These could be misunderstood and cause offense. Therefore, throughout most of Christian history, Mark has been the least popular of the Gospels. Popularity and importance, however, are not synonymous; and a purpose of this commentary will be to show that the importance of Mark is as great as that of the other Gospels.

---

[1] Assuming that the Gospel originally ended with 16:8 (see the commentary).

1. Mark in the Early Church

If indeed Mark was the first Gospel to have been written, Matthew and Luke quickly recognized its value as a source of information in writing their own Gospels. The first person to mention the Gospel of Mark was Papias about A.D. 120–130. His testimony is important enough to quote in full.

> The elder also said: "Mark was the interpreter of Peter and wrote accurately but not in order whatever he remembered about the things which were said or done by the Lord." He [Mark] neither heard the Lord nor followed him, but later, as I said, [he relied upon] Peter who adapted his teachings to the needs [of his hearers] without setting forth an orderly account of the Lord's sayings. Therefore Mark did not err in writing various things as he remembered them, for he made it his first priority not to omit or falsify anything which he heard.[2]

When making his canon list, Marcion (ca. A.D. 145) rejected Mark. But Tatian (ca. A.D. 170) employed Mark in constructing his *Diatessaron*, a new account of the life and teaching of Jesus that was made by weaving together the four individual Gospels. Justin Martyr (ca. A.D. 155) mentioned the Memoirs of Peter that contained the words "named Boanerges, which means 'sons of thunder.'"[3] These words are found only in Mark 3:17. Irenaeus of Lyons (ca. A.D. 180) wrote that Mark was the disciple and interpreter of Peter and that he wrote the Gospel after Peter's death.[4] Clement of Alexandria (ca. A.D. 200) said that the Gospels with the genealogies (Matthew and Luke) were written first and that Mark was a follower of Peter and wrote in Rome during Peter's lifetime at the request of the Christians there.[5] Tertullian (ca. A.D. 210) described Mark as an "apostolic man" who was the interpreter of Peter and who edited a Gospel.[6] Origen (d. 254) wrote: "The Second [Gospel] is according to Mark, who did as Peter instructed him."[7] The so-called Anti-Marcionite Prologue (ca. fourth cent.), which is found in various manuscripts of the Latin Vulgate, described Mark as the interpreter of Peter who wrote in Italy after Peter's death. The so-called Monarchian Prologue (also fourth cent.), which is found in other Vulgate manuscripts, stated that Mark was a disciple of Peter and bishop of Alexandria and that he wrote his Gospel in Italy. Jerome (d. A.D. 420) claimed that Mark was the interpreter of Peter and the first bishop of Alexandria.[8] Augustine (d. A.D. 430) believed that the order of writing was Matthew, Mark, Luke, and John. Concerning the second of

---

[2] Cited ca. A.D. 325 by Eusebius, *Church History* 3.39.15.
[3] Justin Martyr, *Dialogue with Trypho* 106.
[4] Irenaeus of Lyons, *Against Heresies* 3.1.1.
[5] Clement of Alexandria quoted by Eusebius, *Church History* 6.14.5–7.
[6] Tertullian, *Against Marcion* 4.2.5.
[7] Origen quoted by Eusebius, *Church History* 6.25.5.
[8] Jerome, *Commentary on Matthew*, Prologue 6.

these he wrote: "Mark followed him [Matthew] closely and appears to be his imitator or abstracter."[9]

Mark was the least quoted Gospel by ancient and medieval Christian writers, although it is often difficult to determine which Gospel is being quoted where parallel passages exist. No one appears to have written a commentary on the Gospel of Mark until the late fifth century when Victor of Antioch did so. Mark was used seldomly in the lectionary cycle. It was never placed first in the ancient manuscripts of the New Testament, and sometimes it was third or fourth rather than second.

2. Modern Study of Mark

About the middle of the nineteenth century, a great change took place in the status of Mark. Careful study of the interrelationships of the Gospels, i.e., study of the Synoptic problem, led most to the conclusion that Mark rather than Matthew was the first Gospel to have been written. With this claim came another, that Mark is the most historical of the Gospels. (The latter of these is often referred to as the "Markan hypothesis.") Late in the nineteenth century, therefore, Mark ostensibly became the basis of a rash of "lives of Jesus" by classic liberal scholars. About the turn of the century, however, A. Schweitzer, in his monumental work *Quest of the Historical Jesus* (1906), showed that these scholars had not based their "lives" on Mark but on their own preconceived notions of Jesus as a liberal, ethical teacher. Schweitzer claimed that the Gospels do not contain the right kind of and enough information to write a biography of Jesus. As a result the "old quest of the historical Jesus" ceased.[10]

About the same time, various attacks were made on the historicity of Mark, a prime example being W. Wrede, who claimed that Mark invented the idea of a "messianic secret" in order to explain the embarrassing fact that Jesus was not recognized as Messiah during his lifetime. About two decades later the form critics K. L. Schmidt, M. Dibelius, and R. Bultmann argued that Mark collected a number of short, independent accounts of the deeds and sayings of Jesus and invented a framework for them in order to produce a continuous account (form criticism is the analysis of a text according to typical and identifiable forms by which people express themselves linguistically). From their perspective, therefore, the Markan outline, which Matthew and Luke closely followed, has no historical or geographical value. As a result Mark was dethroned and had to take a place beside—but not below as in the ancient and medieval churches—the other three Gospels.

---

[9] Augustine, *Agreement of the Gospels* 1.2.4.

[10] Ironically Schweitzer's own view of Jesus as a fanatical preacher of the end of the world was no more satisfactory than the ethical "lives."

Radical form critics, such as Bultmann, were exceedingly skeptical about the historicity of all the Gospels. Bultmann even claimed that historical facts have no value because Christian commitment should not be to anything in the past but to "authentic existence" in the present. By the middle of the twentieth century, however, there was a reaction against such skepticism; and a "new quest of the historical Jesus" began. This quest attempted to determine which of the sayings and deeds ascribed to Jesus in Mark and the other Gospels were historical. Various criteria of authenticity were established, such as dissimilarity from Judaism and Hellenism, coherence, and multiple attestation. To say that the "new quest" is continuing probably is correct, although some speak of a "third quest."[11] In scholarly circles Mark continues to enjoy a status equal to that of the other Gospels; and in the new, three-year lectionary system it is given a rightful place.

The modern study of Mark includes some recent theories that deal with its occasion and purpose. S. G. F. Brandon claims that Jesus was a Zealot and that Mark was written just after the Jewish revolt to cover up that fact, to shift the blame of the crucifixion from the Romans to the Jews, and to show the Romans that the Christian community in Rome was not Jewish and had nothing to do with the revolt.[12] All the Gospels indicate, however, that Jesus tended to avoid the title Messiah or Christ. Inasmuch as the early church was not reluctant to ascribe that title to him (cf. Acts and the Epistles), the testimony of the Gospels must be accepted as historical. Jesus no doubt avoided the title because of its political overtones, and such avoidance is one indication that he rejected the nationalistic aspirations of the Jews. Likewise his preaching of nonresistance is firmly established by the critical criterion of dissimilarity from Judaism.

P. Carrington[13] and M. D. Goulder[14] think Mark was written to provide lectionary readings for use in public worship. Similar is the thesis of B. Standaert that Mark was written to be read on Easter eve to candidates for baptism.[15] Against these views there is no evidence that Christian writings were read as Scripture until the second century. This is not to imply that the Gospels or epistles were not read publicly as they were circulated.

---

[11] The "third quest," such as it is, employs historical and archaeological materials to show what Jesus must have been as a first-century Jew. Even Jewish scholars have engaged in this "quest" in an effort to reclaim Jesus for Judaism. One should realize, however, that Jesus transcended his national heritage.

[12] S. G. F. Brandon, *The Fall of Jerusalem and the Christian Church*, 2nd ed. (London: SPCK, 1957); "The Date of the Markan Gospel," *NTS* 7 (1961–62): 126–41; and *Jesus and the Zealots* (New York: Scribner's, 1967).

[13] P. Carrington, *The Primitive Christian Calendar: A Study in the Making of the Markan Gospel* (Cambridge: University Press, 1952).

[14] M. D. Goulder, *The Evangelist's Calendar* (London: SPCK, 1978).

[15] B. Standaert, *L'Evangile selon Marc: Composition et Genre Litteraire* (Nijmegen: Stichtig Studentenpers, 1978).

W. Marxsen, one of the earliest Gospel scholars to employ redaction criticism in the study of Mark, maintains that the Gospel was written in Galilee about A.D. 66 to persuade the Jerusalem church to flee the doomed city and go to Galilee to await the return of the Lord.[16] This theory is ingenious, but it is extremely doubtful that one would write a fully developed Gospel for such a purpose or that Matthew and Luke would have employed the Gospel if that had been its purpose.

T. J. Weeden argues that Mark was written ca. A.D. 80 to refute a false Christology and a false concept of the Christian life, namely that Jesus was a divine man similar to other such demigods in the Greco-Roman world and that the Christian life consists of following his illustrious example and triumphing over everything through the power of the Spirit. Mark supposedly did this by attributing the false Christology and false concept of discipleship of his opponents to the original disciples of Jesus and attacking them. Mark's own view was that Jesus and true discipleship are best understood in terms of suffering.[17] One may agree with the last claim without accepting the others. There is no evidence that the disciples ever claimed to be divine men. Some scholars now doubt whether there was a well-established concept of divine men in the first century or earlier.

In a similar way R. Martin maintains that Mark wrote to refute a Gnostic overemphasis on Paul's concept of a spiritual, divine Christ. He did so by emphasizing an earthly, human Jesus.[18] J. D. Kingsbury, however, denies that Mark wrote to correct a false Christology and argues that he conceived of Jesus as the Davidic Messiah-King. From Kingsbury's perspective the title "Son of God" should be interpreted as in the Old Testament to refer to a king of Israel. "Son of Man" is not a confessional title but a functional, public, polemical one.[19]

W. Kelber sets forth the thesis that Mark was written in Galilee shortly after the Jewish revolt to show that the family of Jesus, the original disciples, and Christian prophets in Jerusalem erred in associating the return of the Lord with the fall of that city. According to Kelber, Mark's own view was that Jesus would return later in Galilee.[20] If this is so, why is so much of Mark not related to eschatology?

---

[16] W. Marxsen, *Mark the Evangelist: Studies on the Redaction History of the Gospel,* trans. J. Boyce (Nashville: Abingdon, 1969).

[17] T. J. Weeden, "The Heresy That Necessitated Mark's Gospel," *ZNW* 59 (1968): 145–58; and *Mark—Traditions in Conflict* (Philadelphia: Fortress, 1971).

[18] R. Martin, *Mark, Evangelist and Theologian* (Grand Rapids: Zondervan, 1972). This book is also a good survey of the history of Markan studies. An even better one is S. P. Kealy, *Mark's Gospel: A History of Its Interpretation from the Beginning until 1979* (New York: Paulist, 1982).

[19] J. D. Kingsbury, *The Christology of Mark's Gospel* (Philadelphia: Fortress, 1983).

[20] W. Kelber, *The Kingdom in Mark: A New Place and a New Time* (Philadelphia: Fortress, 1974); and *Mark's Story of Jesus* (Philadelphia: Fortress, 1979).

E. Trocmé,[21] like Weeden and Kee (see below), thinks that Mark is polemical, but for him the issue is ecclesiology. Mark represented a progressive movement that had broken away from the conservative, self-centered Jerusalem church. Mark believed that a true disciple is not concerned with securing a place of prominence, as were the original disciples and the family of Jesus, but with following Jesus' example in missions and other kinds of service.[22] But there is no convincing evidence that Mark had any concern with the Jerusalem church. Other explanations are possible for his treatment of the disciples.

H. C. Kee employs modern sociology in his study of Mark and concludes that it was written in southern Syria shortly before the fall of Jerusalem for a charismatic, apocalyptic community that was estranged from society. A purpose was to promote itinerant evangelism in view of the approaching end.[23] There is much of value in Kee's study, and it is one of the more judicious of those being reviewed. Nevertheless the apocalyptic element in the Gospel is small, and this consideration raises serious questions about the theory.

E. Best has taken the position that Mark was written in Rome ca. A.D. 70 by someone named Mark, but not by the John Mark of Acts and the Pauline Epistles. The work was not polemical or apologetic and was not connected with any historical event, such as the Neronian persecution or the Jewish revolt. Rather, the Gospel was a pastoral adaptation of various traditions about Jesus, including some Petrine ones, to the needs of the writer's church. Mark was a conservative redactor who did not create traditions but adapted the ones he received. His main concerns were to show that true discipleship involves following Jesus in suffering and death and in mission.[24] We would question Best's position on authorship and date, and we would question the value of so much effort to distinguish Mark's own redaction from his sources.[25] Otherwise there is much value in his understanding of Mark.

D. Rhoads and D. Michie employ narrative analysis in their study of Mark, as do also the following studies. Above all else Mark is a story that is to be treated as a whole. The writer presents himself as an omniscient narrator who controls the material in order to get the "ideal reader" to respond properly by

---

[21] E. Trocmé, *The Formation of the Gospel According to Mark* (Philadelphia: Westminster, 1975). It may be a necessary part of his view that Trocmé believed that the original Mark consisted only of chaps. 1–13, which were written in the 40s or 50s. Chaps. 14–16 were added ca. A.D. 85.

[22] Ibid.

[23] H. C. Kee, *Community of the New Age* (Philadelphia: Westminster, 1977).

[24] E. Best, *Following Jesus: Discipleship in the Gospel of Mark* (Sheffield: JSOT, 1981); and *Mark: The Gospel as Story* (Edinburgh: T & T Clark, 1983).

[25] Redaction critics are far too optimistic about their ability to distinguish tradition (what the Evangelist received from his sources) and redaction (what he himself composed). As a result little effort is expended in the present commentary to isolate Mark's redaction.

seeing the advent of the reign of God in Jesus and by following him. The dominant motif in Mark's story is the journey of Jesus and his disciples. The book gives much attention to analyzing the characters (Jesus, the authorities, the disciples, and the "little people") and the conflict.[26] Mark is indeed a narrative and should be studied as such, but it is more than a narrative. It is also history and theology, which tend to be ignored by narrative criticism.

A. Stock argues that Mark is most closely related to the genre of Greek tragedy. Its purpose was to persuade the reader to identify with Jesus in his suffering.[27] That Mark has some points of contact with Greek tragedy few would deny, but it is most unlikely that one whose literary ability leaves something to be desired would have been influenced by a highly developed Greek literary form.

V. K. Robbins's thesis is that Mark is most closely related to Greco-Roman stories of disciple-gathering teachers whose integrity leads to their death but whose teaching is carried on by their disciples.[28] Jesus certainly was a teacher, but he was also a healer and a redeemer from sin. Nor does the gathering of disciples seem to have been his or Mark's major concern as Robbins would have us believe.

It should be obvious from this brief survey of some of the more important studies of the last forty years that modern scholarship has not come to a consensus about the authorship, date, place of writing, destination, occasion and purpose, and literary genre of Mark. Some of the studies have missed completely the meaning of Mark, but most have made some contribution to its understanding. A frequent fault has been to try to interpret the whole of Mark in terms of one theme or emphasis. Mark is too complex to permit that. Furthermore, the inability of contemporary criticism to agree suggests that traditional understandings of and approaches to Mark's Gospel remain valid. A presupposition of the present commentary is that the best in traditional interpretation and the best in modern, critical interpretation should be combined in a serious study of the Gospel.

3. The Priority of Mark?

The opinions of Clement (Matthew and Luke were written before Mark and John) and Augustine (the order of writing was Matthew, Mark, Luke, and John) have been noted. Augustine's view prevailed until the last half of the

---

[26] D. Rhoads and D. Michie, *Mark as Story: An Introduction to the Narrative of a Gospel* (Philadelphia: Fortress, 1982).

[27] A. Stock, *Call to Discipleship: A Literary Study of Mark's Gospel* (Wilmington: Michael Glazier, 1982). G. C. Bilezikian, *The Liberated Gospel* (Grand Rapids: Baker, 1977), had earlier identified Mark as an example of Greek tragedy. Both writers deny, however, that Mark deliberately wrote a tragedy.

[28] V. K. Robbins, *Jesus the Teacher: A Socio-Rhetorical Interpretation of Mark* (Philadelphia: Fortress, 1984).

nineteenth century when the priority of Mark was established by C. H. Weisse and H. J. Holtzmann. During the first quarter of the twentieth century, their arguments were reinforced by J. C. Hawkins and B. H. Streeter so that Markan priority became one of the "assured results" of biblical criticism.

Among the traditional arguments for the priority of Mark are the following. First, Mark is the shortest of the Gospels. It is much easier to conceive of Matthew and Luke expanding Mark by adding birth narratives, much more about Jesus' teaching, and accounts of resurrection appearances than to conceive of Mark abbreviating Matthew or Matthew and Luke by leaving out so much that is so appealing while at the same time expanding their individual accounts. Second, both Matthew and Luke occasionally differ from Mark's order, but they never agree against Mark in the order of the pericopes and only occasionally do they agree against him in their wording (a pericope is a term designating the self-contained literary units or sections of the Gospels). The best explanation for this phenomenon is that Matthew and Luke independently used Mark as a source. And third, Matthew and Luke appear to improve upon Mark in various ways. As already indicated, their language (vocabulary, style, grammar) is superior. Matthew especially compressed Mark's individual accounts, something that is often accomplished by rewriting. And Matthew and Luke do not have many of the candid statements of Mark that could be misunderstood and cause offense. Believing that Matthew and Luke improved upon Mark is much easier than thinking Mark impaired the account of Matthew alone or the accounts of Matthew and Luke.

Between the end of the nineteenth century and 1964, only an occasional objection was raised to the priority of Mark and to the two-document hypothesis of Synoptic relationships of which it is the foundation. (The two-document hypothesis holds that Mark wrote first and that Matthew and Luke independently used Mark and a collection of the sayings of Jesus usually referred to as Q as their most important sources.) Some of these objections were by Roman Catholic scholars who until 1943 were required to support Matthean priority. In 1964 W. R. Farmer published *The Synoptic Problem*. In it he attacked the traditional arguments for the priority of Mark and the two-document hypothesis, especially as summarized by Streeter, and in which he argued for the theory put forth late in the eighteenth century by J. J. Griesbach. The Griesbach or Farmer or two-Gospel hypothesis claims that Matthew wrote first, that Luke used Matthew, and that Mark used both Matthew and Luke.

The priority of Matthew is supported by ancient tradition and the reflection of Jewish Christianity in that Gospel. Furthermore, the theory best explains the so-called minor agreements in wording of Matthew and Luke against Mark. It cannot, however, explain two concerns. One is how Matthew and Luke could have so little in common if the latter was dependent upon the former. In fact, many indications are that Matthew and Luke worked independently.

The other concern is why Mark would have been written if only 5 percent of it was different from its sources, Matthew and Luke. Farmer and his growing number of followers have offered various explanations. One is that for the most part Mark accepted only those accounts found in both Matthew and Luke. This, however, implies a question in Mark's mind about the authenticity of the accounts that did not have dual support. Such doubts are most unlikely. Furthermore, in a number of instances Mark is paralleled by only Matthew or only Luke. Still another consideration that weighs against the Griesbach hypothesis is that redaction criticism has thrived on the assumption of Markan priority but has accomplished very little on the basis of Matthean priority (redaction criticism seeks to determine the theological concerns of an author by studying how he used and shaped his sources).

The question of Markan priority has not been settled, but to the present commentator it appears to be much more likely than Matthean priority. In fact, if Mark was the first Gospel, it ought to be interpreted with a minimum of references to the other two Synoptics. This will be the procedure of the present commentary.

4. A New Literary Genre?

Mark is not a biography or history in the modern sense. It does not deal exhaustively with such things as family background, influences on Jesus, psychological analysis of Jesus, or periods of his life. Mark's primary purpose was not to set forth historical facts as objectively as possible. His purpose was to describe Jesus in such a way as to promote loyalty to him and his teaching.

Although contemporary scholars are unanimous that Mark is not a biography or history, they are divided about whether it corresponds to any ancient genre of literature. It has something in common with ancient lives, acts, memoirs, and tragedies—especially the first—but it does not correspond exactly to any of them. Mark and the other Gospels represent a unique combination of the deeds and teachings of a great person, a combination that is not even paralleled in the later apocryphal gospels. It is probably correct, therefore, to claim that Mark created a new type of literature. If this is true, his literary accomplishment was great despite the fact that his work does not represent the highest quality of literature.

5. Authorship

The Gospel itself is anonymous. The *text* says nothing about the identity of the author. One must turn instead to ancient tradition. The title was attached to the Gospel probably about the middle of the second century when the Gospels were collected and a means of distinguishing them became necessary. The title indicates that someone named Mark was the writer. Because of its early date and universal acceptance, the title is a much more significant piece of evidence than is usually recognized.

By far the most important individual testimony is that of Papias, as has been noted. It requires several comments. The elder who was his authority cannot be identified, but he was an apostle or a disciple of the apostles. By citing and commenting on the statement of the elder, Papias seems to have been defending Mark against charges that he was not an eyewitness and that he did not write in chronological order. He did so by associating Mark with Peter. The statement amazingly anticipates by eighteen centuries the claims of form critics that the Gospels are not chronological and that the teachings of Jesus were adapted to the needs of the early Christian communities. For present purposes, however, the most significant point is that about A.D. 120–130 a churchman quoted an earlier authority to the effect that someone named Mark wrote the Gospel that bears that name.

Some modern critics have rejected the testimony of Papias as worthless and have claimed that all subsequent testimonies are dependent upon him. Some have claimed that Papias fabricated his attribution of the Gospel to Mark and Peter during the heat of battle with the Gnostics. It is doubtful, however, that Papias could have gained much by ascribing a Gospel to such an obscure person as Mark. The association of Mark with Peter is attested independently in 1 Pet 5:13. That Papias was the early church's only source of information about the Gospel is hard to believe, and that Papias was the only source for the title attached to all manuscripts is impossible to believe. Therefore the testimony of Papias remains a significant factor in the discussion of authorship.

The remainder of the external evidence can be summarized by saying that the early church was unanimous that Mark was the author of a Gospel. All but Augustine claimed further that Mark wrote in association with Peter. Some contemporary scholars are persuaded by the ancient tradition and embrace Markan authorship. A weighty consideration in their minds is that Mark was not a prominent person in the primitive church; indeed, he had tarnished his reputation by leaving Paul and Barnabas in the middle of a missionary campaign (Acts 13:13). It is most unlikely that the church would have attributed a Gospel to him without strong evidence that he wrote it. Other contemporary scholars, however, put no stock in church tradition and claim that the author cannot be known. A mediating position is that the book was written by someone named Mark, but not the John Mark of Acts. A major consideration in favor of this claim is that Mark was one of the most common Roman names.

Many contemporary scholars agree that Mark does not reflect any testimony of Peter. This conclusion grows out of the denial by form critics of any role of eyewitnesses in the Gospels. The claim is preposterous! Explaining the existence of the early church and the writing of the New Testament without any influence of eyewitnesses is almost as difficult as doing so without any influence of the earthly Jesus. Another reason for ruling out Peter is that Mark appears to have employed material that was handed down through various lines of oral tradition. Nevertheless, the large amount of concern for Peter and the less-than-flattering image of Peter in Mark may be an indication that Peter was one source among others. Various passages could be recollections of an eyewitness. Petrine influence cannot be proved or disproved, but it should be acknowledged as a possibility. Even if that part of the tradition were false, the part about Mark being the author could still be correct. Neither can that be proved or disproved; but when everything is considered, it appears to be the most probable view.

If the Gospel were written by the John Mark of Acts, what is known about him? We are uncertain whether he was the young man of 14:51–52. Acts 12:12 implies that his mother was a person of means who had a house large enough for a meeting of a group of Christians (many Palestinian houses had but one small room). Acts relates how Paul and Barnabas took him from Jerusalem to Syrian Antioch (12:25), how they included him on the mission to Cyprus (13:5), how he left them at Perga (13:13), and how Paul refused to take him on a second missionary endeavor and Barnabas took him instead back to Cyprus (15:37–39). Colossians 4:10 indicates he was Barnabas's cousin and that he was with Paul (in Rome?) at the time of writing. Philemon 24 indicates that he was with Paul (in Rome?) at the time of the writing of that letter. Second Timothy 4:11 expresses Paul's desire to have Mark join him in Rome. First Peter 5:13 associates him with Peter in Rome. The late tradition that he became bishop of Alexandria in Egypt has been mentioned. Hippolytus of Rome (d. A.D. 235) described him as "stump-fingered."[29] The *Paschal Chronicle* (seventh cent.) claimed that he died a martyr's death. The validity of the last three traditions is impossible to determine.

6. Place of Writing and Initial Audience

The early church located the writing and destination of the Gospel in Italy or more specifically Rome. The only exception was Chrysostom (d. A.D. 407) who opted for Egypt.[30] His view, however, probably represents a misunderstanding of the tradition that Mark once served as bishop of Alexandria. Various data seem to support a Roman setting. If in fact the Prison Epistles were written by Paul from Rome, Col 4:10 and Phlm 24 connect Mark with Rome in the early 60s. First Peter 5:13 connects Mark with Peter in Rome in the early 60s (assuming the word "Babylon" earlier in the verse is a code word for Rome and assuming Peter wrote or commissioned the letter). Second Timothy 4:11 suggests that Mark would soon be going to Rome. A comparison of Mark

---

[29] Hippolytus of Rome, *Refutation of All Heresies* 7.30.
[30] Chrysostom, *Homily on Matt.* 1.

15:21 with Rom 16:13 may connect the Gospel with Rome (assuming that the same Rufus is in mind in both passages and assuming that Rom 16 went to Rome and not Ephesus).

In addition to the tradition that connects Peter with Mark in Rome in the writing of the Gospel, additional independent tradition indicates that Peter died a martyr's death in Rome during the persecution of Nero (A.D. 64–65). Still further, a number of Latinisms in the book could favor Rome, although Latin was certainly spoken outside of Italy. The recent tendency to place the writing of Mark in Palestine or Syria is inseparably connected with particular theories about the occasion and purpose. Rome remains the most likely place for the origin and original readership of this work.

Quite aside from the geographical location of the recipients, something needs to be said about their ethnic background. Many indications exist that they were Gentile rather than Jewish Christians. The strongest evidence of this is that the writer often explains Jewish customs. The Gentile background of the recipients is an argument against a Palestinian setting for the writing and initial use of the book.

7. Date

The tradition that circulated in the early church dated the writing of Mark's Gospel either shortly before or shortly after Peter's death in A.D. 64 or 65. Although a large segment of contemporary scholarship disregards the tradition, there is widespread agreement that Mark was written between A.D. 65 and 75. Crucial in the minds of most is the relationship of Mark to the Neronian persecution in Rome during A.D. 64–65 and/or to the Jewish revolt against Rome between A.D. 66 and 70 (actually the last resistance at Masada was not crushed until A.D. 73 or 74). The Gospel mentions neither, but it is difficult to evaluate the significance of this because the remainder of the New Testament is silent also, even though some of the books almost certainly were written after these events.

This commentary regards the allusions to persecution (e.g., 8:34–38; 10:38–40) as too general for Mark to have been written in Rome after the outbreak of the Neronian persecution, an event that must have dominated the church there for at least a decade after A.D. 64–65. The Gospel reflects apprehension of persecution or other trouble, but it does not reflect a persecution in progress or one in the very recent past. Also, quite apart from any supernatural insight on his part, there is no reason Jesus could not have predicted the persecution of his followers. This commentary does not take chap. 13 to indicate that the Jewish revolt had begun. If these presuppositions are correct, and if Mark was written in Rome as seems most likely, it must have been written shortly before the beginning of the persecution of Nero and therefore in A.D. 63 or the first half of A.D. 64. If in fact Peter had any input, an earlier

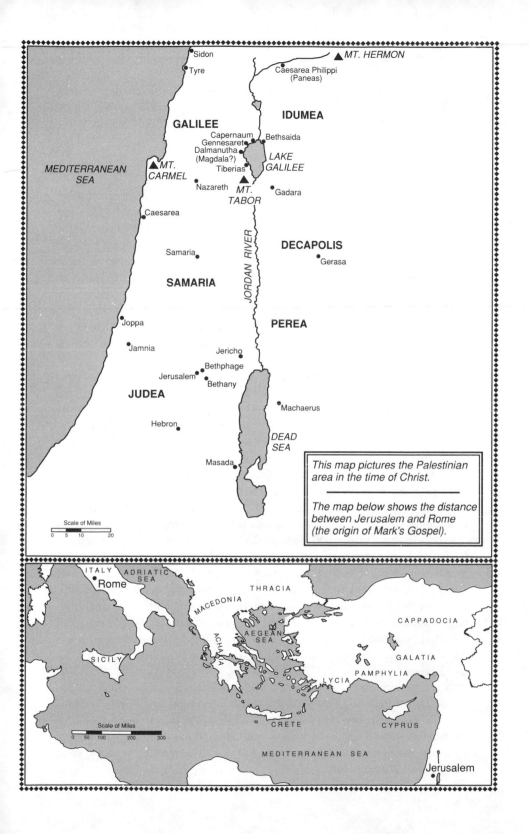

MT. HERMON

Sidon

Tyre

Caesarea Philippi
(Paneas)

GALILEE

IDUMEA

Capernaum
Gennesaret   Bethsaida
Dalmanutha
(Magdala?)   LAKE
Tiberias   GALILEE

MEDITERRANEAN
SEA

MT.
CARMEL

Nazareth   MT.
TABOR   Gadara

Caesarea

DECAPOLIS

Samaria   Gerasa

SAMARIA

Joppa

JORDAN RIVER

PEREA

Jamnia

Jericho

Bethphage

Jerusalem   Bethany

JUDEA

Machaerus

Hebron

DEAD
SEA

Masada

Scale of Miles
0   5   10   20

This map pictures the Palestinian
area in the time of Christ.

The map below shows the distance
between Jerusalem and Rome
(the origin of Mark's Gospel).

ITALY   ADRIATIC
SEA

Rome

THRACIA

MACEDONIA

CAPPADOCIA

ACHAIA

AEGEAN
SEA

GALATIA

SICILY

LYCIA   PAMPHYLIA

Scale of Miles
0   50   100   200   300

CRETE

CYPRUS

MEDITERRANEAN SEA

Jerusalem

date is not likely because it is improbable that he went to Rome before A.D. 62 (he is not mentioned in the Prison Epistles—Ephesians, Philippians, Colossians, and Philemon—which probably were written from Rome between A.D. 60 and 62; nor is he mentioned in Paul's letter to Rome about A.D. 56–57).

8. Occasion and Purposes

Assuming Mark was written about A.D. 63 or 64 from Rome, reconstructing its circumstances is difficult because so little is known about the Christian community there at the time. The expulsion of the Jews—and Jewish Christians—was a decade and a half in the past. Paul had recently been a prisoner in Rome but evidently had few contacts with synagogue or church, in part at least because associating with him was dangerous. Although the Neronian persecution had not begun, it is unlikely that it was the result only of the fire of the summer of A.D. 64. Quite likely the authorities already had been making hostile gestures toward Christians. As a result the church at Rome felt threatened. The threat of persecution may constitute the occasion for writing Mark.

Mark had more than one purpose in writing. The purposes can be inferred from the contents. Mark's first concern was simply to collect and arrange various individual traditions of the deeds and teachings of Jesus. A growing desire emerged for an orderly and connected *written* account. Isolated stories were no longer adequate. Oral tradition, although still preferred by some, was no longer satisfactory for others. Probably a broad outline—but not a full chronology—of the life of Jesus was available to Mark. If so, he may have arranged the various individual accounts into it in order to develop various themes.

Mark clearly was not content merely to give an account of the life and teaching of Jesus. He wanted to set forth his own understanding of Jesus and thus develop his Christology. He wanted to do so in such a way as to minister to the needs of his own church. He used and applied the accounts at his disposal—something Christian teachers and preachers have been doing ever since. Mark's concept of Jesus was that he was fully human and fully divine, both Son of Man and Son of God. Furthermore he was both the Jewish Messiah (Christ, Son of David) and the Lord of the Gentiles. Such a balanced Christology as Mark's weighs against the theory that he was battling a heresy. Mark was especially concerned to emphasize the suffering and death of Jesus as a ransom for sinners.

Mark is more than a book about Jesus. It is also a book about being a disciple of Jesus. For Mark discipleship was following Jesus in suffering and mission. He saw in the first disciples the same kinds of triumphs and failures that characterized the disciples in his own church, and therefore he set forth the former as examples of virtues to imitate and vices to avoid. The book therefore has a practical orientation.

The final major purpose for which Mark wrote was to clarify Jesus' teaching about the future. The crucial item is that no one can know when Jesus will return or when the end of the age will take place. One must not hasten to connect these things with any particular historical event, e.g., the past attempt of Caligula to set up his image in the Jerusalem temple, the past expulsion of Jews and Christians from Rome by Claudius, the coming persecution of Nero, or the coming Jewish revolt and destruction of the temple. Instead of preoccupation with the end, the faithful must devote themselves to discipleship in the present.

9. Structure

Traditional outlines of Mark use geographical terminology, e.g., Galilean ministry, ministry beyond Galilee, journey to Jerusalem, and last ministry in Jerusalem. From the perspective of form criticism, this approach makes primary what was secondary for Mark. If a redaction/composition critical perspective can be accepted in which Mark assembled independent units of tradition into a unified narrative in order to achieve a theological purpose, the divisions of his narrative must be related to that purpose. As already seen, however, contemporary scholarship has not been able to agree on the purpose. Nevertheless, a significant number of scholars have been able to agree on the approximate location of the divisions by using summary statements in the book.

First division:	1:1 or 1:14 through 3:6 or 3:19
Second division:	3:7 or 3:20 through 6:6, 6:13, or 6:29
Third division:	6:7, 6:14, or 6:30 through 8:21, 8:26, or 8:30
Fourth division:	8:22, 8:27, or 8:31 through 10:45 or 10:52
Fifth division:	10:46 or 11:1 through 13:37
Sixth division:	14:1 through 15:47 or 16:8.

Those who start the first division with 1:14 treat 1:1–13 as an introduction, and those who end the sixth division with 15:47 treat the remainder as a conclusion.[31] Despite the growing agreement about these divisions, the use of sum-

---

[31] Among those who adopt such a scheme are N. Perrin, *The New Testament: An Introduction* (New York: Harcourt Brace Jovanovich, 1974), 146–61; idem, with D. C. Dulling, 2nd ed. (1982), 239–54; F. G. Lang, "Kompositionsanalyse des Markusevangeliums," *ZTK* 74 (1977): 1–24; E. Schweizer, "The Portrayal of the Life of Faith in the Gospel of Mark," *Int.* 32 (1978): 387–99, who combined the last two, thus leaving five; D. J. Harrington, *Mark*, NTM (Wilmington: Michael Glazier, 1979), 4:1; L. Williamson, Jr., *Mark*, INT (Atlanta: John Knox, 1983), vii–ix; G. Mangatt, "The Gospel of Mark: An Exegetical Survey," *Bible Bhashyam* 9 (1983): 229–46; W. W. Wessel, "Mark," EBC, ed. F. E. Gaebelein (Grand Rapids: Zondervan, 1984), 8:615–17; and J. Carmody et al., *Exploring the New Testament* (Englewood Cliffs, NJ: Prentice-Hall, 1986), 107–08, who made chap. 13 a separate division, thus making seven. Perrin made his divisions where summary statements and geographical notices coincide, but his analysis has been criticized

mary statements seems arbitrary and selective, though it does give us some clue of the author's purpose and structure.

Somewhat different is the structure of V. K. Robbins.[32] Robbins's divisions are 1:14–3:6; 3:7–5:43; 6:1–8:26; 8:27–10:45; 10:46–12:44; 13:1–15:47. He argues that each of these is introduced by a three-step progression in which Jesus went to a new place with his disciples, engaged in interaction with the disciples or others, and as a result of the interaction summoned his disciples anew. The six introductory, three-step progressions are 1:14–20; 3:7–19; 6:1–13; 8:27–9:1; 10:46–11:11; 13:1–37. A question arises whether other instances of three-step progression are in Mark and whether chap. 13 is too long to serve as an introductory or transitional passage.

Still another approach is that of C. S. Mann.[33] He divides the book into two major units (1:16–8:21; 8:22–16:8) and each major unit into three segments. Each of the segments is divided on the basis of chiastic or inverted parallelism (e.g., a, b, c, b′, a′, in which a in some way corresponds to a′, etc.). The chiastic structure, however, will stand up only if one allows Mann's sometimes inaccurate description of the contents of the segments.

In my opinion Mark arranged his work into three major divisions by subject matter and by introducing and concluding the middle division with a giving-of-sight miracle. The middle division deals primarily with discipleship and more particularly with the "blindness" of the disciples who fail to see Jesus' role as a suffering and serving Messiah. The enclosure of this division with stories about Jesus healing blind men is highly significant, especially when one realizes that these are the only instances of curing blindness in Mark. Beyond the major divisions Mark apparently did not intend subdivisions other than the individual pericopes, which he arranged in a logical but not always chronological order. Also included are an introduction and conclusion.

Although Mark certainly did not intend it as a title in the modern sense, the statement in 1:1, "the gospel about Jesus Christ," is a summary of the contents of the book and therefore should be used as the theme on which to base the outline. For this purpose the word *gospel* should be translated "good news."

---

by C. W. Hedrick, "The Role of 'Summary Statements' in the Composition of the Gospel of Mark," *NovT* 26 (1984): 289–311, because many other summary statements and geographical notices do not happen to come together and because the "summary statements" do not summarize what precedes or follows.

[32] Robbins, *Jesus the Teacher*, 19–51.

[33] C. S. Mann, *Mark,* AB (Garden City, NY: Doubleday, 1986).

OUTLINE OF THE BOOK

I. Introduction: The Beginning of the Good News (1:1–13)
  1. The Preparation of John (1:1–8)
  2. The Baptism of Jesus (1:9–11)
  3. The Temptation of Jesus (1:12–13)
II. The Good News about Jesus' Proclamation of the Kingdom of God (1:14 – 8:21)
  1. Introduction (1:14–15)
  2. The Calling of the First Disciples (1:16–20)
  3. A Day of Ministry in Capernaum (1:21–39)
    (1) Teaching in the Synagogue and Exorcising an Evil Spirit (1:21–28)
    (2) The Healing of Simon's Mother-in-Law (1:29–31)
    (3) The Healing of the Crowds at Sunset (1:32–34)
    (4) The Departure from Capernaum and a Tour of Galilee (1:35–39)
  4. The Cleansing of a Leper (1:40–45)
  5. The Conflicts with the Scribes and Pharisees (2:1–3:6)
    (1) Over the Forgiveness of a Paralytic (2:1–12)
    (2) Over Associating with Tax Collectors and "Sinners" (2:13–17)
    (3) Over Fasting (2:18–22)
    (4) Over Picking Grain on the Sabbath (2:23–28)
    (5) Over Healing the Man with the Shriveled Hand on the Sabbath (3:1–6)
  6. The Popularity of Jesus (3:7–12)
  7. The Call of the Twelve (3:13–19)
  8. The Family of Jesus (3:20–21,31–35)
  9. The Accusation of Demon Possession and the Warning against the Unforgivable Sin (3:22–30)
  10. The Parable Discourse (4:1–34)
    (1) The Parable of the Soils and Its Interpretation (4:1–9,13–20)
    (2) The Purpose of Parables (4:10–12,21–25)
    (3) The Parable of the Seed Growing Spontaneously (4:26–29)
    (4) The Parable of the Mustard Seed (4:30–32)
    (5) Conclusion (4:33–34)
  11. A Collection of Miracle Stories (4:35–5:43)
    (1) The Stilling of the Storm (4:35–41)
    (2) The Exorcising of the Demons from the Wild Man of Gerasa (5:1–20)
    (3) The Raising of Jairus's Daughter (5:21–24a,35–43)
    (4) The Healing of the Woman with a Hemorrhage (5:24b–34)
  12. The Rejection at Nazareth (6:1–6a)
  13. The Mission of the Twelve (6:6b–13,30)

SECTION OUTLINE

I. INTRODUCTION: THE BEGINNING OF THE GOOD NEWS (1:1–13)
1. The Preparation of John (1:1–8)
2. The Baptism of Jesus (1:9–11)
3. The Temptation of Jesus (1:12–13)

I. INTRODUCTION:
THE BEGINNING OF THE GOOD NEWS (1:1–13)

The introduction presents Jesus, the main character of the following narrative, as an extraordinary person who was proclaimed by a prophet whose mission had been foretold in Scripture, who at the beginning of his own ministry was commended by a voice from heaven, and who withstood the assaults of Satan. The three items in the introduction are linked by references to the Spirit.

The introduction also establishes the two levels on which the narrative is written, that of the readers and/or hearers[1] and that of the characters. From the beginning the readers/hearers know things the characters—specifically the disciples—did not. They know the true identity of Jesus, that he is the Son of God (v. 1). This implies that they were already Christians, as does the emphasis on discipleship. The time line of the characters ends with 16:8, but, as we will see, that of the readers/hearers continues beyond the close of the book.

1. The Preparation of John (1:1–8)

[1]The beginning of the gospel about Jesus Christ, the Son of God. [2]It is written in Isaiah the prophet:

"I will send my messenger ahead of you,
who will prepare your way"—
[3]"a voice of one calling in the desert,
'Prepare the way for the Lord,
make straight paths for him.' "

[4]And so John came, baptizing in the desert region and preaching a baptism of repentance for the forgiveness of sins. [5]The whole Judean countryside and all the people of Jerusalem went out to him. Confessing their sins, they were baptized by him in the Jordan River. [6]John wore clothing made of camel's hair, with a leather belt around his waist, and he ate locusts and wild honey. [7]And this was his message:

---

[1]That most of the recipients were illiterate is highly probable. Therefore Mark was written more to be heard than read.

"After me will come one more powerful than I, the thongs of whose sandals I am not worthy to stoop down and untie. [8]I baptize you with water, but he will baptize you with the Holy Spirit."

1:1 "The gospel about Jesus Christ" well describes the entire work. Mark did not intend it as a title of his book, however, because until about A.D. 150 the word "gospel" was used to refer to the Christian message, not to books that contained one aspect of that message, and because he preceded the expression with the word "beginning." For Mark the beginning of the good news (the meaning of the Greek word *euangelion* translated "gospel") about Jesus Christ was the preaching of John,[2] who is alluded to in the quotation in vv. 2–3 and explicitly referred to in vv. 4–8 (cf. Acts 1:22). This could better be seen if the NIV had placed a comma rather than a period at the end of v. 1 and had translated the Greek word meaning *just as* (*kathōs*) at the beginning of v. 2. Mark may also have been thinking of a new beginning comparable to that of Gen 1:1. Of course the Greek words literally meaning *gospel of Jesus Christ* (*euangeliou Iēsou Christou*) could also refer to the message Jesus proclaimed, but there is comparatively little of that in Mark.

The "gospel" is an important subject in Mark. The word *euangelion* appears seven times (also 1:14–15; 8:35; 10:29; 13:10; and 14:9. Cf. also 16:15) versus only four times in Matthew and none in Luke and John (but Matthew has the cognate verb once and Luke ten times). By his frequent use of the term, Mark emphasized the freshness and even revolutionary character of the message of Jesus. This message offered hope to the neglected and oppressed.

The name "Jesus" is the Greek equivalent of the Hebrew "Joshua" (both words have been anglicized), which means *Yahweh* (or simply *God*) *saves*. As a common name in the first century, it was shared by two or three other persons who are mentioned in the New Testament: Barabbas (Matt 27:16–17, NRSV, NEB), Jesus Justus (Col 4:11), and Joshua (Acts 7:45; Heb 4:8, KJV; see explanation above). Josephus referred to about twenty different persons who had the name. Mark used it eighty times without stressing the theological significance of the name.

The Greek word "Christ" is the equivalent of the Hebrew "Messiah" (again both are anglicized) and is actually translated "Messiah" in some passages by the NRSV, NEB, REB, and GNB. Both mean *the anointed one*, i.e., a person commissioned by God for a special task. In the Old Testament priests (Exod

---

[2]An alternative interpretation is that v. 1 should be connected with vv. 14–15 (vv. 2–13 would then be looked upon as having been intercalated between vv. 1,14–15). Bracketing or intercalation is a frequent Markan literary device (cf. comments on 3:20ff.), but it is doubtful that he would have used it so early in the narrative or so clumsily as to leave vv. 2–13 without a context. Still another possibility is that the "beginning" consisted of Jesus' baptism and temptation as well as John's preaching.

29:7, 21), prophets (1 Kgs 19:16), and kings (1 Sam 10:1) were anointed for special tasks. Mark did not describe Jesus as a priest, and he said very little explicitly about him as a prophet (cf. 6:4,15; 8:28); but in 15:2,9,12,18,26,32 he described him as the king of the Jews/Israel. In the first century some Jews looked forward to an anointed king who, they hoped, would restore the kingdom of David and consummate the age. The term "Christ" or "Messiah" was originally a title, but by Mark's day it was on the way to becoming a proper name (cf. 9:41). The word appears only seven times in Mark (here; 8:29; 9:41; 12:35; 13:21; 14:61; 15:32; also 1:34 as a variant reading), probably reflecting accurately the reluctance of Jesus to employ it or to accept it when used by others because of its nationalistic connotations. The only instance where Jesus used it with reference to himself is 9:41 and there in an oblique way. For Mark and his readers/hearers Jesus was the one above all others who was anointed by God for the greatest task of all times. Evidently at his baptism (1:9–11) Jesus was formally anointed for his special mission.

The words "the Son of God" are omitted by one of the earliest and best Greek manuscripts, two other manuscripts of medium quality, two versions (translations) of medium value, and some nine early Christian writers who quote the verse. The textual evidence, however, heavily favors authenticity, and the omission may have been accidental due to six consecutive words in the Greek text having the same ending. Elsewhere Mark used the title at 3:11 and 5:7 in the confession of evil spirits and in 15:39 in the climactic confession of the centurion. To these ought to be added "Son of the Blessed One" in the question of the high priest in 14:61 and "Son" alone in the very important divine attestations of 1:11; 9:7.

Still further allusions to Jesus as Son occur in 12:6; 13:32. Although the demons confessed Jesus as Son of God in Mark, the disciples never did. Jesus did not explicitly refer to himself as Son, but the idea is implicit in 12:6; 13:32. Although not frequently used, the title comes at crucial points in the narrative and obviously is an important one, perhaps the most important one. That the title appears near the beginning and end of the Gospel, bracketing the entire book so as to emphasize this truth to the readers/hearers, is especially significant. Although used of angels (Job 1:6), the nation Israel (Hos 11:1), and Davidic kings (2 Sam 7:14) in the Old Testament and of rulers, deliverers, and healers in the Greco-Roman world, Mark doubtless used it to refer to the unique relationship of Jesus to the only true God.

The very first sentence therefore evidences that Mark's Gospel is more than a narrative of events. It is also a theology, primarily a Christology. Although the characters in the story struggle with Jesus' identity, the readers/hearers know from the beginning that he is the promised Messiah and the very Son of God.

1:2–3 "Isaiah the prophet" (40:3) supplies only that part of the quotation in v. 3. The part in v. 2 is from Mal 3:1, perhaps with an allusion to

Exod 23:20 as well (the same word means *angel* and *messenger*). As a result many medieval scribes substituted "in the prophets." This reading is found in the KJV and NKJV, which are based on the medieval Greek text rather than on the earliest and now regarded best manuscripts as is the NIV. Mark and other biblical writers simply did not employ the technical precision of modern research. It was not necessary for their purpose. Furthermore, both quotations are adapted in order to apply them to John. In Isaiah "the Lord" was God, but in Mark's quotation it is Jesus; Isaiah has "for our God," but Mark substitutes "for him," i.e., Jesus. Jesus and the New Testament writers often reinterpreted the Old Testament text in order to apply it to their own situation, in addition to quoting it loosely from memory. Malachi 4:5 probably identifies the "messenger" of Mal 3:1 as Elijah. Mark 9:11–13 almost certainly identifies John as the Elijah-like person who precedes Christ in his suffering. Also John's preaching of repentance in v. 4 (cf. 1 Kgs 18:37; Mal 4:6) and the description of him in v. 6 (cf. 2 Kgs 1:8) recall Elijah. The significance of the quotation is that both John and Jesus appeared as a result of divine providence. Mark quoted from the Old Testament infrequently, and elsewhere his citations are part of a quotation of one of his characters, usually Jesus.

"Lord" is not a major Christological title in Mark. Jesus is addressed as such only in 7:28, but there the word may mean nothing more than *Sir* (so NRSV, NEB, REB, GNB). Jesus probably alluded to himself as "Lord" in 11:3, although some think this refers to the owner of the colt or that the meaning there is *teacher*, and in 12:36–37, where he quoted and commented on Ps 110:1. The word also appears as a variant reading with fair attestation in 1:40 and 10:51. Mark's little use of the term probably indicates accurate reporting of the situation during Jesus' lifetime. Only after his resurrection was Jesus widely acclaimed as Lord. Elsewhere the word refers to God, various pagan gods, the master of slaves, managers, and the emperor. Therefore when Jesus is the referent, the term suggests his deity, dominion, and direction.

1:4 John is introduced abruptly. Certainly the original readers/hearers already knew something about him. The locale of his ministry was the "desert," more specifically the uninhabited, barren gorge of "the Jordan River" (v. 5). The "desert" is a major theme in the introduction (vv. 3,4,12,13). In the Bible it is more than a geographical place; it is the place where God meets, reveals himself to, tests, and saves his people. The most distinct aspect of John's ministry was his baptism or immersion of those who had repented of their sins, confessed them (v. 5), and as a result received forgiveness. Obviously the baptism symbolized the cleansing from sin that repentance effects. Evidently it was a new rite. Unlike the self-baptism of Jewish proselytes, it was administered to Jews by another person. Unlike the washings of the Essenes at Qumran, it was not self-administered, repeated, or confined to those who were already pious.

Baptism is not a major subject in Mark. Outside of the introduction, allusions to the baptism of John occur in 6:14,24,25; 8:28 (these allusions are clearer in Greek, where John is called "the Baptizer"), and a clear reference is in 11:30. The baptism of Jesus is briefly described in 1:9–10. Baptism symbolizes being overwhelmed by the Holy Spirit in v. 8 and by suffering and death in 10:38–39. But nothing corresponds to Matt 28:19 or John 4:1–2. Nor did Mark indicate how or when the prediction of v. 8 was fulfilled, though Mark's readers would recognize Jesus as the more powerful, coming one who baptizes with the Spirit.

John's message, like that of the prophets, consisted first of a call to repentance. The Greek word translated "repentance" literally means *change of mind*, but its New Testament meaning has been greatly influenced by that of several Old Testament words so that it refers to returning to God and changing one's whole course of life. The word translated "forgiveness" means *sending away* or *remission*.

1:5–6 The first sentence in v. 5 admittedly exaggerates, but it does accurately reflect the popularity of John. (No early Christian would have invented that.) As already suggested, v. 6 connects John with the prophets in general and Elijah in particular (cf. 2 Kgs 1:8). Mark wanted to suggest as early as possible that discipleship involves withdrawal from the world and sacrifice.

1:7–8 John's message concerned not only a way of life and a rite symbolizing that way of life but a person. The concepts of a coming one and a powerful one have messianic implications. The concept of baptism "with the Holy Spirit" (v. 8) fulfills Isa 32:15; 44:3; Ezek 11:19; 36:26–27; 37:14; Joel 2:28–29. Mark never described Jesus as baptizing with the Spirit and elsewhere said comparatively little about the Spirit. Outside of the introduction, where the Spirit is mentioned three times, the only references are 3:29 ("blasphemes against the Holy Spirit"); 12:36 ("David . . . by the Holy Spirit declared"); and 13:11 ("it is not you speaking, but the Holy Spirit"). Presumably the reader is left to understand that the baptism with the Spirit takes place after the close of the narrative. At various places Mark's account points beyond itself by leaving promises unfulfilled. Mark did not make a practice of reading into the life of Jesus things that took place or became prominent later.

2. The Baptism of Jesus (1:9–11)

[9]At that time Jesus came from Nazareth in Galilee and was baptized by John in the Jordan. [10]As Jesus was coming up out of the water, he saw heaven being torn open and the Spirit descending on him like a dove. [11]And a voice came from heaven: "You are my Son, whom I love; with you I am well pleased."

Mark said nothing about Jesus' ancestors, his family (but note 3:31–35; 6:3), or his childhood and youth. The Gospel is concerned only with Jesus' ministry and death.

The most striking aspects of Mark's account of the baptism are its brevity and lack of apology. Although classified as a legend by R. Bultmann and a myth by M. Dibelius, the historicity of this account cannot be reasonably doubted. So potentially embarrassing is the idea that the Christian Lord was baptized by a Jewish prophet in a rite that for others symbolized repentance for their sins that the early church would never have invented the story. Matthew (3:15) felt the necessity of making some explanation, and the second-century Gospel of the Nazarenes went even further by having Jesus say, "In what way have I sinned so that I should go and be baptized by him, unless what I have said is [the result of] ignorance?"[3] Mark evidently saw no problem, and this probably reflects the early date of his Gospel. Mark's primary purpose in recording the baptism appears to have been to show divine approval of Jesus. He said nothing about what the experience meant to Jesus. Was it the beginning of his messianic consciousness? Was it the occasion of his call? Most likely it signaled the beginning of his ministry. Nor did Mark indicate what the event meant to John. Did it confirm to him that Jesus was the more powerful one of v. 7?

1:9 "At that time" (cf. the similar expressions in 8:1; 13:17,24) is one of Mark's somewhat vague indications of chronology. Obviously it refers to the time when John was baptizing. "Nazareth" was such an obscure village it is not mentioned in the Old Testament, Josephus, or rabbinic literature. Matthew 2:23; Luke 2:39–40; 4:16 indicate it was Jesus' hometown. Mark probably implies that. The "Jordan" is one of the most overrated rivers in the world. Only a hundred and five air miles separate the river's sources in northern Palestine from where it empties into the Dead Sea. Even with its meandering between Lake Galilee and the Dead Sea, it is only a little over two hundred miles long. Only in flood stage is it more than a hundred feet wide or ten feet deep, and it can be forded easily in numerous places. None of the Gospels gives any indication where along the Jordan the baptism took place. The traditional site is near the southern terminus.

1:10 The NIV does not translate the word meaning *immediately* at the beginning of v. 10. Mark used this characteristic term forty-two times to heighten dramatic tension. Its omission in the NIV exemplifies a problem with "dynamic equivalence" translations where producing good English style is more important than word-for-word reproduction of the original.[4] Inasmuch as the word "baptize" means *to immerse*, the expression "coming up out of the water" almost certainly refers to *from beneath the water* rather than *upon the*

---

[3] As quoted by Jerome, *Against Pelagius* 3.2.

[4] A very literal translation (e.g., NASB) does not result in appealing English. Both careful reproduction of the original and idiomatic English are important, and a good translation keeps a fine balance between the two. In the present commentator's opinion the RSV does the best job of this.

bank. In the latter part of v. 10 and in v. 11 Mark's theological concern becomes apparent. First, by implying that Jesus alone saw and heard the supernatural manifestations, Mark provided the first intimation of his secrecy motif. The true identity of Jesus is concealed from the characters of the story, but not from the readers/hearers. Second, by using the expression "heaven being torn open," he suggested divine intervention and new revelation after a period of silence (cf. Isa 64:1). The expression seems to imply the advent of a new age in which things will be quite different from the old. The same word with the same implication is used again in 15:38 in connection with the tearing of the temple curtain. The dramatic opening of heaven may suggest further that God is accessible to an extent not previously known. The descent of the Spirit is suggested by Isa 61:1, but the source of the comparison of the Spirit to a dove is uncertain because the Old Testament never, and rabbinic literature but rarely, makes the association. Perhaps the source is meditation upon Gen 1:2.

1:11 Here the word "heaven" exemplifies the Jewish practice of using substitutes for the divine name. God himself spoke![5] The first part of the heavenly pronouncement reflects Ps 2:7, an enthronement psalm used for the coronation of kings of Israel. There may also be an allusion to the beloved son Isaac, who was intended for a sacrificial death (Gen 22:2). By identifying Jesus as God's Son, Mark recognized him as the true King of the new people of God, the new Israel, which was later called the church. The second part alludes to Isa 42:1, which is part of the first of the Servant Songs, the most famous of which is 52:13–53:12. Therefore Mark also recognized Jesus as the true Servant of the Lord.

Mark's treatment of the baptism, though very brief, is important from a theological standpoint. The Gospel opens with a statement that Jesus is the Son of God. At the baptism God himself affirmed that Jesus is his Son. The purpose of both passages—and especially the second—is to inspire the readers/hearers to acknowledge Jesus as Son of God and to love and take pleasure in him.

3. The Temptation of Jesus (1:12–13)

[12]At once the Spirit sent him out into the desert, [13]and he was in the desert forty days, being tempted by Satan. He was with the wild animals, and angels attended him.

Conflict between Jesus and various representatives of evil (Satan, the demons, nature, the Jewish leaders, and even the disciples) is a prominent

---

[5]Some, however, have claimed that it was the *Bath Qol*, the "daughter of the voice," a mere echo of the divine voice during the period after prophecy had ceased. With the appearance of John and Jesus, however, prophecy revived.

feature of Mark. Such conflict inevitably results from an attempt to establish the kingdom of God. Again one is astounded by Mark's brevity. Did Mark intend to contrast the testing of Jesus and that of Adam or of Israel in the desert? No confident answers can be given.

1:12 This time (contrast v. 10) the NIV translates the word meaning "at once" or "immediately" (*euthys*). Mark used the verb *ekballō* a total of seventeen times, most often about exorcisms so that something stronger than "sent . . . out" is needed, something like "drove . . . out" (RSV, NRSV, REB) or "impelled" (NASB). The idea is that of divine necessity, not that Jesus was reluctant to go. The "desert" was the place of John's preaching (vv. 3–4); it was also the place of Jesus' temptation.

1:13 The "forty days" recalls Moses on the mountain (Exod 24:18; 34:28), Elijah's journey to the sacred mountain (1 Kgs 19:8), Jesus' instruction of his disciples (Acts 1:3), and perhaps even Israel's forty years in the wilderness (especially Deut 8:2). The word translated "tempted" also means *tested*, and that is probably the primary idea here. "Satan" is the anglicized form of the Greek transliteration of a Hebrew word meaning *adversary*. Only Mark indicates that Jesus was "with the wild animals." Commentators divide over whether the animals were favorably disposed toward him and, therefore, symbolize the tranquility of the messianic kingdom after the defeat of Satan or whether they were hostile toward him and symbolize the forces of evil. Mark was concerned with the test itself, not its result. The intertestamental Jewish concept of the desert as the haunt of demons further supports the latter view. Mark did not indicate whether the angels "attended" or "ministered to" (RSV) Jesus during or after the temptation or whether they helped him resist, fed him, or witnessed what he did. Nor did Mark state that Jesus was victorious, perhaps because he looked upon Jesus' entire life as a continuing struggle with Satan. Perhaps the episode was recorded partly to encourage the original readers/hearers in their trials and temptations.

---------- *SECTION OUTLINE* ----------

II. THE GOOD NEWS ABOUT JESUS' PROCLAMATION OF THE
    KINGDOM OF GOD (1:14–8:21)
    1. Introduction (1:14–15)
    2. The Calling of the First Disciples (1:16–20)
    3. A Day of Ministry in Capernaum (1:21–39)
        (1) Teaching in the Synagogue and Exorcising an Evil Spirit (1:21–
            28)
        (2) The Healing of Simon's Mother-in-Law (1:29–31)
        (3) The Healing of the Crowds at Sunset (1:32–34)
        (4) The Departure from Capernaum and a Tour of Galilee (1:35–39)
    4. The Cleansing of a Leper (1:40–45)
    5. Conflicts with the Scribes and Pharisees (2:1–3:6)
        (1) Over the Forgiveness of a Paralytic (2:1–12)
        (2) Over Associating with Tax Collectors and "Sinners" (2:13–17)
        (3) Over Fasting (2:18–22)
        (4) Over Picking Grain on the Sabbath (2:23–28)
        (5) Over Healing the Man with the Shriveled Hand on the Sabbath
            (3:1–6)
    6. The Popularity of Jesus (3:7–12)
    7. The Call of the Twelve (3:13–19)
    8. The Family of Jesus (3:20–21,31–35)
    9. The Accusation of Demon Possession and the Warning against the
       Unforgivable Sin (3:22–30)
    10. The Parable Discourse (4:1–34)
        (1) The Parable of the Soils and Its Interpretation (4:1–9,13–20)
        (2) The Purpose of Parables (4:10–12,21–25)
        (3) The Parable of the Seed Growing Spontaneously (4:26–29)
        (4) The Parable of the Mustard Seed (4:30–32)
        (5) Conclusion (4:33–34)
    11. A Collection of Miracle Stories (4:35–5:43)
        (1) The Stilling of the Storm (4:35–41)
        (2) The Exorcising of the Demons from the Wild Man of Gerasa
            (5:1–20)
        (3) The Raising of Jairus's Daughter (5:21–24a,35–43)
        (4) The Healing of the Woman with a Hemorrhage (5:24b–34)

—— II. THE GOOD NEWS ABOUT JESUS' PROCLAMATION —— OF THE KINGDOM OF GOD (1:14–8:21)

The primary concern of the first major division in Mark is Jesus' proclamation and demonstration of the nearness of the kingdom of God. The proclamation was by preaching and teaching; the demonstration, by miracles. These further establish the identity and authority of Jesus. The first division is set in Galilee and the surrounding regions. Mark pictured Jesus as constantly moving from place to place, something that emphasizes the urgency of this message about the kingdom of God. Some of the travel was in Gentile territory, foreshadowing the Gentile mission that took place after the events of the narrative but before its writing.

1. Introduction (1:14–15)

14After John was put in prison, Jesus went into Galilee, proclaiming the good news of God. 15"The time has come," he said. "The kingdom of God is near. Repent and believe the good news!"

This statement, by far the most important summary statement in the book, introduces and summarizes the first division and perhaps the entire book.

1:14 Mark placed the beginning of Jesus' ministry after the imprisonment of John, although he did not describe John's imprisonment and death until 6:14–29. Actually the word Mark used (*paradidōmi*) means *to hand over* and is used to refer to the betrayal and arrest of Jesus in 9:31; 10:33; 14:21,41. Its use with reference to John suggests that his death foreshadowed that of Jesus.

The use of the passive voice implies that what was done was in accordance with God's purpose.[1]

Mark located the major portion of Jesus' ministry in Galilee, the northern part of Palestine, which had a larger Gentile element than did Judea. The word translated "went" could better be translated "came" (RSV, NRSV, NASB, NEB) because it identifies Jesus as the *coming one* of v. 7. The "good news [*euangelion*, the same word translated "gospel" in v. 1] of God" is a shorthand way of indicating the kingdom of God (v. 15). Indeed most later manuscripts add the words "of the kingdom" (KJV, NKJV)—a correct interpretation, but not the original text. God is the source of the gospel.

1:15 The word translated "time" (*kairos*) means a *favorable, opportune, or significant time* as opposed to mere *chronology*. Here Mark referred to the time appointed by God for the fulfillment of his promises. The period of preparation, that of ancient Israel and John, was complete. The divinely appointed time had come. The prophecies were being fulfilled in Jesus.

The expression "kingdom of God" appears fourteen times in Mark (also 4:11, 26,30; 9:1,47; 10:14,15,23,24,25; 12:34; 14:25; 15:43). According to the Synoptic Gospels, it was the major subject of Jesus' message. In first-century Judaism it described a future, earthly kingdom in which God through Israel would rule over the nations. With the possible exceptions of 14:25 and 15:43, however, in Mark it refers to a present, spiritual kingdom rather than a future, earthly one. Therefore the expression refers to the kingly rule, the reign, the dominion, the sovereignty of God in the hearts of people. "Realm" in the sense of sphere of influence might be a better translation, but it too is subject to misunderstanding. "Reign" probably is the best translation.

Jesus claimed that the kingdom, which to most Jews seemed far in the future, had drawn near with his appearance. On linguistic grounds either "is near" or "is at hand" (RSV, NASB) or "has come near" (NRSV) is a better translation than "has come" (cf. use in 14:42). One of the former alternatives is preferable on theological grounds as well. The reign of God began to take place in the life and ministry of Jesus, but it was not fully manifested then and will not be until Jesus returns. Therefore a present, mystical kingdom does not rule out the possibility of a future, earthly one. Mark, however, says little about that. Jesus, like John (cf. v. 4), preached repentance, but the distinctive element in his message was faith or commitment or trust. The necessity of faith is a major subject in Mark, underscoring the theological motivation of the writing. Note especially the commands to believe in 1:15; 5:36; 11:22,24 and the rebuke of unbelief in 4:40; 6:6; 9:19. Note also how faith is commended in 2:5; 5:34; 9:23; 10:52; 11:23.

---

[1]This use is called the "divine passive." It probably had its origin in the reluctance of the Jews to use the sacred name *Yahweh.* It was one of many substitutes for the divine name.

2. The Calling of the First Disciples (1:16–20)

[16]As Jesus walked beside the Sea of Galilee, he saw Simon and his brother Andrew casting a net into the lake, for they were fishermen. [17]"Come, follow me," Jesus said, "and I will make you fishers of men." [18]At once they left their nets and followed him.
[19]When he had gone a little farther, he saw James son of Zebedee and his brother John in a boat, preparing their nets. [20]Without delay he called them, and they left their father Zebedee in the boat with the hired men and followed him.

By beginning Jesus' ministry with this account, Mark showed that the disciples were qualified to be witnesses of his entire ministry. He showed the importance of discipleship. He showed the way in which all should respond to Jesus' summons: promptly and completely. He showed the inseparable relationship of discipleship and Christology. And he showed that Jesus takes the initiative in making disciples: they do not seek him, but he seeks them.

1:16 "Lake Galilee" (GNB) is a much more accurate description of the thirteen-by-eight-mile body of water than the traditional "Sea of Galilee." In fact, the same word near the end of the verse is translated "lake" in the NIV. Mark referred to the first of the two persons seen by Jesus as Simon six times, Peter eighteen times, and Simon Peter once. Mark contains more references to Peter in proportion to length than any other Gospel, perhaps showing a special interest in him, but not proving Peter was a source of information. Mark mentioned Andrew elsewhere only in 1:29; 3:18; 13:3.

1:17 The idea of following Jesus is frequent in Mark and denotes discipleship. Actually Mark used several different Greek words alone or in combination that are difficult to distinguish in translation. The idea is that of responding to a summons, attachment to a person, acceptance of authority, and imitation of example. The implication of continuation and pursuing a goal also is included. According to Acts, Christianity later came to be known as "the Way." The purpose of the summons was to make the two fishermen "fishers of men." The idea of God calling persons to fish for people is found in the Old Testament, most clearly in Jer 16:16; but there the purpose was to bring people to judgment. Here it was to escape judgment. Note that Mark pictured Jesus as an example of what he required of others.

1:18 Mark said nothing about any previous encounter; and even if he had known of one, he might not have recorded it. He showed the ideal response to the command of Jesus. It should be immediate. Here some intimation of the cost of discipleship is shown, for Simon and Andrew evidently left a lucrative business and perhaps also their families to follow Jesus (cf. 1:29).

1:19 James and John are mentioned together nine times in Mark with James's name appearing twice in two of the passages. John alone is mentioned in 9:38. They also were "called," another term closely related to discipleship.

Mark used it only once with reference to discipleship (2:17).

1:20 If the action of Simon and Andrew illustrates prompt response, that of James and John illustrates complete response. Following Jesus is costly and sometimes even involves severing family ties.

The disciples do not again appear in so favorable a light as they do here. The treatment here, however, is sufficient to refute the claim that Mark attacked his opponents by portraying the disciples as their representatives. A much more likely interpretation views his sometimes negative treatment of the disciples as for pastoral rather than polemical purposes, i.e., to show that even the original disciples had faults and yet were used by Jesus. The same is true of later disciples.

3. A Day of Ministry in Capernaum (1:21–39)

This section introduces the reader/hearer to some of the major elements of Jesus' ministry: preaching, teaching, exorcising demons, healing the sick, prayer, and instructing the disciples.

(1) Teaching in the Synagogue and Exorcising an Evil Spirit (1:21–28)

[21]They went to Capernaum, and when the Sabbath came, Jesus went into the synagogue and began to teach. [22]The people were amazed at his teaching, because he taught them as one who had authority, not as the teachers of the law. [23]Just then a man in their synagogue who was possessed by an evil spirit cried out, [24]"What do you want with us, Jesus of Nazareth? Have you come to destroy us? I know who you are—the Holy One of God!"

[25]"Be quiet!" said Jesus sternly. "Come out of him!" [26]The evil spirit shook the man violently and came out of him with a shriek.

[27]The people were all so amazed that they asked each other, "What is this? A new teaching—and with authority! He even gives orders to evil spirits and they obey him." [28]News about him spread quickly over the whole region of Galilee.

This typical exorcism story consists of an encounter with a demon (v. 23), the demon's defense (v. 24), the exorcism itself (vv. 25–26), and the effect on the observers (vv. 27–28).

1:21 There must be a period of time between vv. 20 and 21 because what is in vv. 16–20 could not have taken place on a Sabbath. Although not mentioned in the Old Testament, Capernaum, meaning *village of Nahum* or *village of consolation*, was an important town on the northwest shore of Lake Galilee. Capernaum was on the main road between Egypt and Mesopotamia, in the tetrarchy (*rule of a fourth part* or any petty kingdom) of Herod Antipas and near the border of the tetrarchy of Philip, and the site of a toll station. Jesus seems to have made Capernaum his headquarters during much of his Galilean ministry. Today some impressive ruins of a second- or third-century synagogue remain there. This synagogue may have been built on the same site as the one of Jesus' day, which probably was destroyed in the rebellion of A.D. 66–70. The synagogue was a place of informal worship and instruction. It may have originated during the Babylonian exile, but there is no archaeological evidence for synagogues until the third century B.C. and little literary evidence until the first Christian century (though one should see Deut 33:4, LXX; Ps 74:8; and *Pss. Sol.* 10:7).

It was a common practice for visiting teachers to be invited to read the Scripture and/or speak, a custom from which Paul as well as Jesus benefited. That Jesus was invited to speak indicates he had already established a reputation as a teacher and that this was not one of the first events in his ministry. Jesus was recognized as a teacher even by his opponents (cf. 12:19), although there is no evidence that he had received any formal training. Certainly he was not a typical rabbi.

Fifteen times Mark indicated that Jesus taught (also v. 22; 2:13; 4:1–2; 6:2,6,34; 8:31; 9:31; 10:1; 11:17; 12:14,35; 14:49), and twelve times he referred to him as a teacher (see references in comments on 4:38). He did not give much of the content of Jesus' teaching. Here Mark gave none.

1:22 The reason for the astonishment was that Jesus taught on the basis of his own authority and not by citing previous scholars as did the other teachers of that day. Mark used several different Greek words to indicate that Jesus made a profound impression by his teaching or miracles (a different word is used in v. 27 but is translated in the same way by the NIV). The combination of teaching and miracle in one account shows that Jesus was powerful in both word and deed.

The word usually translated "scribes" is found twenty-one times in Mark and is regularly translated "teachers of the law" by the NIV. They were not copyists but scholars and therefore experts in the interpretation of the law. Their interpretations, which in the time of Jesus existed only in oral form and are therefore called the oral tradition (cf. 7:5–13), constituted a second law that came to be as important as the written, or Mosaic, law. Ezra was the first such scribe mentioned in Scripture (Ezra 7:6,11,12,21).

1:23 Mark used the terms "evil [literally "unclean"] spirit" and "demon" to refer to the same entity. Demons were evil in themselves, and they made the persons they affected both ceremonially and morally unclean. As difficult as the concept of the demonic is for most people today, it cannot be satisfactorily treated as a primitive explanation for various kinds of physical and psychological illness. A better explanation is that there is much less evidence of the demonic today because Jesus won a decisive, although not yet total, victory over it. The Greek can be translated "he cried out" or "it cried out." Which one is chosen matters little because the man and the evil spirit had become identified.

1:24 The questions sought to put Jesus on the defensive and force him to justify his action (cf. Judg 11:12; 2 Sam 16:10; 1 Kgs 17:18; 2 Kgs 3:13; 2 Chr 35:21). The second sentence, however, could be an assertion rather than a question: "You have come to destroy us!" The demon tried unsuccessfully to oppose Jesus by employing his name. Note how the demon spoke through the man, sometimes for himself and sometimes for demons in general. "Holy One of God" probably is a messianic title, although there is very little attestation for that. In the Old Testament God is usually the Holy One. Here the title implies that Jesus has a special relationship with God. In v. 24 the demon acknowledged the true identity of Jesus (cf. v. 34)—something the disciples were slow to do. In fact, only at the crucifixion did a human being confess Jesus as the Son of God, and he was not one of the disciples (15:39).

1:25–26 Although silencing the demon was common in exorcisms, commands of silence are so prominent in Mark that v. 25 should be looked upon as the first intimation of the so-called "messianic secret." Where demons are involved, an adequate explanation might be that even true testimony from satanic beings could only discredit Jesus in the eyes of most.[2] Another explanation must be sought, however, where his disciples (8:30; 9:9) and those who had been healed or who had been witnesses of healings (1:44; 5:43; 7:36; and a variant reading at 8:26) were silenced. Jesus likely did not want to be known primarily as a wonder-worker or at all as a political or military deliverer because such a reputation would compromise his main mission of redemption (cf. 10:45). Even so the problem remains of why, if he did not want to be widely known for his miracles, he kept performing them in public and why the silence kept being violated (1:45; 7:24,36). In 5:19 Jesus even commanded a person to go home and tell how his demons had been expelled. A possible answer is that in the Bible generally and in Mark's presentation of Jesus specifically there is tension between the known and the unknown, between the revealed and the veiled. Until the cross and resurrection the true nature of Jesus could not be fully known.

1:27–28 As is typical of miracle stories, the effect on the witnesses is described. Again Mark stressed the authority of Jesus, a major reason for recording the event. Verses 16–20 emphasize the authority of Jesus' words; vv. 21–28, the authority of his deeds. Whether "with authority" goes with the preceding "new teaching" as in the NIV, NRSV, and NASB or with the following "He even gives orders" (cf. RSV, GNB) is uncertain.

Miracles obviously play an important role in this Gospel. Mark recorded seventeen individual miracles of Jesus and summarized others. In doing so he devoted more space in proportion to total length than any other Gospel. Nevertheless he did not attempt to employ them as compelling proof of the

---

[2] Cf. Paul's rejection of the testimony of the demon-possessed girl (Acts 16:16–18).

deity or authority of Jesus. They become "proof" only when accompanied by faith. They are signs of the advent of the kingdom of God. Especially do the exorcisms denote the breaking down of the reign of Satan and the establishing of the reign of God.

(2) The Healing of Simon's Mother-in-Law (1:29–31)

29As soon as they left the synagogue, they went with James and John to the home of Simon and Andrew. 30Simon's mother-in-law was in bed with a fever, and they told Jesus about her. 31So he went to her, took her hand and helped her up. The fever left her and she began to wait on them.

1:29–31   Here Mark set forth the shortest miracle story in the Gospels. As do most miracle stories, it indicates the setting, the nature of the disease, the request for healing, the healing itself, and the effect on the person healed; but it does not describe the symptoms, give any words of the healer, or describe the effect on the witnesses. Many traditional commentators think the story is a reminiscence of Peter. First Corinthians 9:5 also indicates that Peter (i.e., Cephas) was married and that he took his wife with him at church expense on his missionary journeys. Clement of Alexandria claimed that Peter's wife preceded him in martyrdom.[3] By indicating that Peter was married, Mark seems to have implied again that discipleship sometimes involves leaving one's family for a while at least. The account, however, primarily illustrates again the power and authority of Jesus. Verse 31 suggests the quickness and completeness of the cure. The mother-in-law is presented simply as a model of discipleship, which requires lowly service from all, male and female. By including accounts of the healing of women as well as men, Mark implied that Jesus was concerned about all people, including those who had a lowly place in society. What the NIV translates "helped . . . up" really means *raised* and often refers to the resurrection both of Jesus and believers. The early church may have seen in the story a foreshadowing of Jesus' power to raise from the dead at the last day.

(3) The Healing of the Crowds at Sunset (1:32–34)

32That evening after sunset the people brought to Jesus all the sick and demon-possessed. 33The whole town gathered at the door, 34and Jesus healed many who had various diseases. He also drove out many demons, but he would not let the demons speak because they knew who he was.

1:32–34   This Markan summary indicates that there were many other healings and exorcisms that are not described in detail. Both v. 32 and v. 34 distinguish between ordinary illnesses and demon possession—a further indi-

---

[3]Clement of Alexandria, *Stromata* 7.11.63, cited also in Eusebius, *Church History* 3.30. *Stromata* 3.6.52 merely indicates that Peter had a family.

cation that primitive, unscientific understanding is not a sufficient explanation of the latter.

Verse 32 accurately reflects that the Sabbath ended at sundown and that after that time it would have been lawful for Jews to walk any distance and to carry sick persons. The imperfect in v. 32 could be translated "kept on bringing." No distinction should be made between the "all" of v. 32 and the "many" of v. 34. The latter is a Semitism that means "all who were many." "The whole town" of v. 33 is a typical Markan hyperbole (cf. v. 5). The command to be silent is set forth again in v. 34 even more clearly than in v. 25.

(4) The Departure from Capernaum and a Tour of Galilee (1:35–39)

³⁵Very early in the morning, while it was still dark, Jesus got up, left the house and went off to a solitary place, where he prayed. ³⁶Simon and his companions went to look for him, ³⁷and when they found him, they exclaimed: "Everyone is looking for you!"

³⁸Jesus replied, "Let us go somewhere else—to the nearby villages—so I can preach there also. That is why I have come." ³⁹So he traveled throughout Galilee, preaching in their synagogues and driving out demons.

Obviously this account had no independent existence but depends on the three previous items. The four probably circulated as a unit before Mark's time. Here Mark established the autonomy of Jesus, who would not be controlled by the crowds or disciples.

1:35 The word translated "solitary place" (*erēmos*) is the same that is translated "desert" in 1:3,4,12,13 and perhaps suggests the same kind of spiritual testing described in the last two. There was no desert near Capernaum, and obviously Jesus wanted to find a secluded place apart from the crowds and even the disciples. The imperfect tense suggests prolonged prayer. In only two other places did Mark indicate that Jesus prayed, in 6:46 after walking on the water and in 14:32–42 in Gethsemane. All three were times of crisis when Jesus was tempted to take an easy way rather than that of suffering and death.

1:36 Mark perhaps referred to "Simon and his companions" (Andrew, James, and John? Cf. vv. 16–20) rather than the disciples because they did not act as disciples should (though Mark did not use the term disciple at all until 2:15). The verb translated "went to look for" usually means *to pursue with hostile intent*. Of course it reflects Mark's point of view, not that of the disciples.

1:37 Here Mark indicated the error of the disciples. They wanted Jesus to take advantage of his growing popularity and perform more miracles. However, Jesus' primary mission was not to be a miracle-worker but a redeemer. The disciples failed to understand that the popularity itself made Jesus want to withdraw. The people of Capernaum apparently had no interest in Jesus beyond his miracles or any interest in coming under the reign of God. The verb Mark chose near the end of v. 37 (*zētousin*) is filled with irony. Whatever Aramaic verb the disciples used, they meant it in a good sense. Everywhere else in Mark, however, the Greek verb, which is not the same as in v. 36, translated "looking for" means *to seek with evil or inappropriate intention.* Mark recognized that the acclaim of the crowd was not good. Verse 37 is the first instance in Mark where the disciples failed to understand the mission of Jesus.

1:38 Jesus' answer contains an ambiguity. The last statement could be translated literally, "For this [purpose] I have come out." The question is whether the reference is to leaving Capernaum, going into all of Galilee, or having come from God. Luke's parallel (4:43) takes the third possibility, and Mark probably meant the same thing (cf. Mark 1:24).

1:39 This Markan summary characterizes Jesus' ministry as one of synagogue preaching and exorcisms. "Their synagogues" possibly reflects the separation of the church and synagogue in the time of Mark, or it may have been a reference to Galilean synagogues.

4. The Cleansing of a Leper (1:40–45)

⁴⁰A man with leprosy came to him and begged him on his knees, "If you are willing, you can make me clean."

⁴¹Filled with compassion, Jesus reached out his hand and touched the man. "I am willing," he said. "Be clean!" ⁴²Immediately the leprosy left him and he was cured.

⁴³Jesus sent him away at once with a strong warning: ⁴⁴"See that you don't tell this to anyone. But go, show yourself to the priest and offer the sacrifices that Moses commanded for your cleansing, as a testimony to them." ⁴⁵Instead he went out and began to talk freely, spreading the news. As a result, Jesus could no longer enter a town openly but stayed outside in lonely places. Yet the people still came to him from everywhere.

The pericope on the cleansing of the leper combines a miracle and a pronouncement story (see vv. 43–44).[4] No reference is made to time and place, and it could have happened anytime during Jesus' ministry. Mark probably included it here to provide a climax to the preceding healing narratives and an appropriate transition to the five controversies that follow—appropriate in that it raises the question of the validity of the law.

1:40 Widespread agreement exists among commentators that in the Bible "leprosy" is a general term covering various chronic skin diseases and is not limited to Hansen's disease as is the contemporary use of the word ("a man suffering from a dreaded skin disease," GNB). Without treatment in a hot climate many skin diseases were vicious. Not only was the disease painful and

---

[4] A pronouncement story (V. Taylor's term) is a brief narrative the primary purpose of which is to provide a context for an important pronouncement of Jesus. M. Dibelius preferred the term "paradigm" and R. Bultmann "apothegm."

debilitating but it rendered the victims religiously and socially unclean. They were required to live outside of cities and towns, have no contact with anyone, and declare themselves unclean when anyone approached. The law regarding leprosy is found in Lev 13–14. The Bible never speaks of healing leprosy, always of cleansing it. Part of the reason may be the loathsome nature of the disease, but a more likely explanation is that leprosy is a symbol of sin that must be cleansed. The episode implies that Jesus can forgive sin and therefore prepares for 2:1–12.

The account further implies that, contrary to the law, the man approached very near to Jesus. By the statement "If you are willing," Mark probably did not intend to suggest any doubt on the leper's part. What probably is the best Greek manuscript of Mark, several other manuscripts of lesser value, and several ancient translations omit the words translated "on his knees," but this omission probably is a harmonization with Matt 8:2.

1:41–42 This verse contains a more important textual problem. The vast majority of textual witnesses, including those usually considered the most reliable, have a word meaning *filled with compassion*. Only one Greek manuscript, four Old Latin manuscripts, and one early Christian writer—all of medium value—have a word meaning *having become angry* ("In warm indignation," NEB; "Jesus was moved to anger," REB). Why scribes would have changed the latter to the former is easy to see, but that they would have changed the former to the latter is inconceivable. Despite the massive external attestation for "filled with compassion," internal considerations are so strong that "having become angry" probably is the original. Furthermore, several other references in Mark refer to Jesus being angry, although they use different words (see 3:5; 10:14). Whether Jesus was "filled with compassion" or "moved to anger," he displayed human emotion. Mark had no reservations about depicting the humanity of Jesus.

The question then arises, About what or with whom was Jesus angry? Was he angry with the leper? Most interpreters insist that such a thing would be out of character for Jesus, and certainly the idea that Jesus was angry with the leper for interrupting him or approaching him contrary to the law may be set aside. Most who adopt the variant reading take the position that Jesus was angry with the strangely unnamed religious authorities for being unable or unwilling to help the man or that Jesus was angry with the entire evil order in which suffering has such a prominent part. Before a decision can be made about the object of Jesus' wrath, the stern verbs of v. 43 need to be considered. Jesus was perhaps angered that the leper doubted that the God active in Jesus' ministry desired his cleansing (cf. Jesus' reaction to doubt in 9:22–23).

Before leaving v. 41 we should observe that even if "with compassion" is not the original reading, the compassion of Jesus comes out clearly in the fact that he touched the leper. Such a thing was unheard of and made Jesus ceremonially unclean. Ritual uncleanness, however, was of no consequence to Jesus in comparison with human need. At many points he is depicted as being indifferent to ritualistic prescriptions. To the Jewish leaders, however, such an attitude was a threat to the established order and could not be condoned.

1:43 The NIV and most translations obscure the problems in this verse. What the NIV translates "with a strong warning" (*embrimēsamenos*) is a verb that in classical Greek sometimes meant *to snort*. Etymologically it means *to have strong feeling within*. Among other possible translations are "to be angry," "to scold," and "to warn." The verb translated "sent . . . away" usually means *to cast out* and is often used with reference to expelling demons (vv. 34, 39). Unless Mark used the verbs in this verse with milder-than-usual meanings, it appears that Jesus was angry with the man and that he cast him out (of a house or synagogue?). It is highly probable therefore that v. 41 also indicates that Jesus was angry with the leper. If anyone except Jesus had been involved, few would ever have suggested any other interpretation. Why then was Jesus so angry with the man that he threw him out? Jesus may well have realized that the man would disobey his command to be silent and that this would greatly hinder his ministry. Furthermore Jesus—and Mark—wanted to make very plain that his primary ministry was not healing but redemption. This interpretation, as difficult as it may seem, is quite in keeping with the candor Mark displayed elsewhere.[5]

1:44 Here we find another example of the "messianic secret." In the last part of v. 44 Jesus is pictured as upholding the law, an appropriate balance to the subsequent conflict stories where he appears to have violated it. The early church may have found this account useful in disputes with Jews to show that Jesus did not indiscriminately violate the law. Whether the man had to go to Jerusalem is uncertain. Presumably a priest anywhere could declare him cleansed, but sacrifices could be made only in the temple.

Still another problem is the meaning of the last item in the verse. The word "them" probably refers to the priests, even though the word "priest" earlier in the verse is singular. Alternatively, it could refer to the people generally; but in this case there is no antecedent for the pronoun. In Greek the testimony can be either "to them" or "against them." If the former, evidence of the healing is presented; but this is so obvious that it need not be stated. If the latter, the priests who do not recognize the power of God at work in Jesus produce evidence against their worthiness to hold the office. In 6:11 the same three words certainly mean *against them*, and that is probably the idea here.

---

[5]Another interpretation is that the account has become jumbled in the course of transmission either before it came to Mark or after it left him, that originally Jesus was angry with a demon for oppressing the man and that he cast it out. Aside from the absence of any reference to a demon in the existing text, leprosy is not elsewhere ascribed to demons.

1:45 This verse contains the first instance of disobedience to the command to be silent, unless the word "he" refers to Jesus. The word "preach" (*kēryssō*, translated "talk freely" by the NIV) usually refers to the proclamation of the gospel, and the word "word" (*logos*, translated "news" by the NIV) often refers to the word of God; but they sometimes have a more general meaning as the NIV properly understands. The context requires that the reference be to the leper. Why would Jesus preach widely if the result were that he could no longer enter a city? No confident answer can be given. In any event the secret cannot be kept. So overpowering was Jesus that not even his own command could hide him!

5. Conflicts with the Scribes and Pharisees (2:1–3:6)

In this section Mark, or possibly some collector of tradition before Mark, brought together five conflict stories that introduce various opponents of Jesus and the early church. The arrangement is almost certainly topical rather than chronological. The encounters could have happened at any time during Jesus' ministry. Each contains an important pronouncement by Jesus (2:10,17,19,28; 3:4). Mark, first, prepared for his passion narrative by showing how the religious authorities opposed Jesus throughout his ministry (note especially 3:6) and, second, preserved material that was valuable in polemics with Jews and others in his own day. Christians of all ages have had opponents and have had to defend their beliefs. This passage has given and continues to give some direction in doing so.

(1) Over the Forgiveness of a Paralytic (2:1–12)

¹A few days later, when Jesus again entered Capernaum, the people heard that he had come home. ²So many gathered that there was no room left, not even outside the door, and he preached the word to them. ³Some men came, bringing to him a paralytic, carried by four of them. ⁴Since they could not get him to Jesus because of the crowd, they made an opening in the roof above Jesus and, after digging through it, lowered the mat the paralyzed man was lying on. ⁵When Jesus saw their faith, he said to the paralytic, "Son, your sins are forgiven."

⁶Now some teachers of the law were sitting there, thinking to themselves, ⁷"Why does this fellow talk like that? He's blaspheming! Who can forgive sins but God alone?"

⁸Immediately Jesus knew in his spirit that this was what they were thinking in their hearts, and he said to them, "Why are you thinking these things? ⁹Which is easier: to say to the paralytic, 'Your sins are forgiven,' or to say, 'Get up, take your mat and walk'? ¹⁰But that you may know that the Son of Man has authority on earth to forgive sins . . . " He said to the paralytic, ¹¹"I tell you, get up, take your mat and go home." ¹²He got up, took his mat and walked out in full view of them all. This amazed everyone and they praised God, saying, "We have never seen anything like this!"

Technical scholars differ as to whether this account consists of the combination of what originally had been two independent accounts, one a simple story of a healing and the other a story of the forgiveness of a sinner that resulted in conflict with the religious authorities, or whether it is a unity. The main problems are the relationship of healing and forgiveness and the broken grammar in v. 10. As for the former, forgiveness is irrelevant to healing only in the modern mind. In the Bible sickness and other kinds of suffering sometimes result from sin (John 5:14; Jas 5:15; cf. Job; John 9:2–3). Forgiveness and healing are sometimes treated as interchangeable (2 Chr 7:14; Pss 41:3–4; 103:3; Jas 5:15). Readers should have no difficulty believing that in a particular instance Jesus recognized that sin was the cause of illness or believing that all of Jesus' healings were symbols of forgiveness. As for the latter, there are other instances of unusual constructions in Mark where there is no question of multiple sources. When taken as a unit, the section shows the close relationship between healing and forgiveness and the authority (note the very word in v. 10) of Jesus not only to heal but also to forgive. The emphasis is on forgiveness, not healing. Again Mark emphasized that Jesus was mighty in both word and deed.

2:1   The Greek text states, "It was heard that he was in a house." Presumably it was the house of Simon Peter and Andrew (1:29).

2:2   Most Palestinian houses consisted of from one to four rooms and a courtyard. The "word" is the "good news" that God's reign has drawn near in Jesus' ministry (cf. 1:15).

2:3   The disease is not described beyond mere indication of a paralysis that prevented the man from walking.

2:4   This house like many in first-century Palestine evidently had an outside staircase leading to a flat roof made of branches and sod. To make an opening in such a roof was not difficult.

2:5   The reference to "faith" is significant. Several other times Mark associated it with miracles (5:34; 9:23; 10:52), and its importance in the Gospel generally has already been affirmed in the commentary on 1:15. Probably the reference is to the faith of the four who went to such lengths to get the paralytic before Jesus, although the faith of the paralytic himself should not be excluded. "Son" or "child" is a term of endearment and reveals nothing about the person's age. In view of the reaction of the teachers of the law, it should be noted that Mark did not claim Jesus said, "I forgive your sins." To indicate what God had done, the Jews often used the passive voice so they could avoid pronouncing his sacred name. The statement in v. 5 means no more than "your sins have been forgiven by God." Nevertheless the Jewish authorities understood Jesus to have forgiven the man's sins (v. 7), and in v. 9 Jesus seems to have admitted that he had forgiven the sins.

2:6   The "teachers of the law" were mentioned previously and commented on in 1:22. A literal translation of the Greek text is "reasoning in their hearts."

In Hebrew thought the heart was not so much the seat of the emotions as it is today but the seat of intellectual activity.

2:7 Blasphemy is irreverent, profane, impious speech about God; and its penalty in Old Testament times was death (Lev 24:16). Here the charge prepares the way for the same accusation at Jesus' trial (14:60–64). The scribes were certainly correct that the Scriptures everywhere teach that "God alone," or better "One, even God" or "the one God," can forgive sins. Nor did Jesus deny this. What they failed to recognize was that the reign of God had drawn near in Jesus and that he had authority to act on God's behalf.

2:8 Whether Mark intended to indicate supernatural knowledge on the part of Jesus is uncertain. Elsewhere he affirmed Jesus' limitations (13:32), and any person with insight could have surmised the thoughts of the scribes on this occasion. The word "spirit" almost certainly refers to Jesus' mind, not the Holy Spirit.

2:9 Ironically, the scribes evidently thought it was easier to affirm the forgiveness of sins than to heal because the former could not be verified and the latter could. For Jesus and Mark, however, the granting of healing and forgiveness are equally the work of God.

2:10 Here appears for the first of fourteen times in Mark the term "Son of Man." It is the most frequent Christological title in Mark, though "Son of God" is arguably more important (see the comments on 1:1). In the Gospels the term is always used by Jesus as a self-designation.[6] In the Old Testament it usually means simply *a man, a human being* (Pss 8:4; 144:3; 145:12 [obscured in NIV]; Ezek 2:1,3,6,8, etc.).[7] The plural "sons of men" in Mark 3:28 (RSV, NASB; NIV simply "men") reflects this usage. A possible exception to the Old Testament usage is Dan 7:13, where it may refer to a transcendent being or to the "saints of the Most High" (v. 18), i.e., Israel. In the apocryphal book 1 Enoch (chaps. 46–48; 62–71), it almost certainly refers to a supernatural being.

The question arises, Why did Jesus choose this term as his favorite self-designation? The best answer is its ambiguity. It could refer to an ordinary human being or to a supernatural being. It had overtones of both humanity and deity. By using it, Jesus forced persons to make up their own minds as to what kind of person he was. Was he a man or The Man? By using the term, Jesus further avoided the undesirable political connotations of the term Messiah/Christ.

---

[6]It appears elsewhere in the NT only in Acts 7:56, where Stephen used it to refer to Jesus, and in Rev 1:13 and 14:14, where it also refers to Jesus, even though its source is probably Dan 7:13 rather than the Gospels. But see the final comments on v. 10 and those on 2:28.

[7]"Son of" is a Hebraism meaning *characterized by.* A "son of destruction" (2 Thess 2:3, NASB) is one who is characterized by being "doomed to destruction" (NIV), and a "son of man" is one who is characterized by humanity.

60

Contemporary scholars, however, debate endlessly which if any of the "Son of Man" passages are authentic, i.e., go back to Jesus himself as opposed to having been placed on his lips by the early church. The lack of consensus after more than a century of such debate raises the question of the legitimacy of the whole endeavor. Even if some of the passages do not reflect what Jesus actually said, there is no certain way to determine which are genuine and which are not. The reports of the Evangelists should be accepted as accurate summaries but not necessarily the exact words of Jesus. How could they always be the latter when they are often highly condensed? Nevertheless, on rational grounds alone, it is virtually certain that Jesus did refer to himself as the Son of Man. Otherwise, how can one explain the absence of the expression from the Epistles that reflect the usage of the early church?

The "Son of Man" passages in Mark can be divided into those that deal with Jesus' authority during his earthly ministry (here, 2:28); his suffering, death, and resurrection (8:31; 9:9,12,31; 10:33–34,45; 14:21 [twice],41); and his glorious return (8:38; 13:26; 14:62). Therefore Mark's use of the term emphasizes not the identity but the destiny of Jesus. The one who is truly human must suffer and die. But this same person is more than a man, and he must also be raised from the dead and return in glory.

The NIV understands the first part of v. 10 to indicate what Jesus said to the scribes; but if so, the sentence is never completed, and there is an abrupt change of the persons being addressed. Alternately, the first part of the verse is Mark's parenthetical comment to his readers/hearers. Note how easy it is to read from v. 9 to the end of v. 10 without the first part of v. 10. A serious problem with this interpretation, however, is that Mark called Jesus the Son of Man, something that neither he nor any other Gospel writer did elsewhere. The NIV understanding is preferable.

2:11–12 As is typical of miracle stories, Mark indicated the immediacy of the cure (again the NIV does not translate "immediately" near the beginning of v. 12) and its effect on those who witnessed it. Whether the word "everyone" includes the scribes is doubtful. Mark had in mind the general effect on the crowd.

(2) Over Associating with Tax Collectors and "Sinners" (2:13–17)

¹³Once again Jesus went out beside the lake. A large crowd came to him, and he began to teach them. ¹⁴As he walked along, he saw Levi son of Alphaeus sitting at the tax collector's booth. "Follow me," Jesus told him, and Levi got up and followed him.

¹⁵While Jesus was having dinner at Levi's house, many tax collectors and "sinners" were eating with him and his disciples, for there were many who followed him. ¹⁶When the teachers of the law who were Pharisees saw him eating with the "sinners" and tax collectors, they asked his disciples: "Why does he eat with tax collectors and 'sinners'?"

[17]On hearing this, Jesus said to them, "It is not the healthy who need a doctor, but the sick. I have not come to call the righteous, but sinners."

This and the two following sections deal with the charge that there was a religious deficiency in the eating habits of Jesus and his disciples.

Mark or someone before him likely combined an account of the calling of Levi and one about Jesus eating with tax collectors and other outcasts because the former introduces the latter so well. Certainly the emphasis falls on the latter, which is another pronouncement story. Mark reaffirmed Jesus' ability to forgive sins and showed his acceptance of persons who were despised by many. Both truths were important to the early church (on the question of table fellowship cf. Acts 11:3 and Gal 2:12). Jesus and the early church were often criticized for associating with undesirable characters, and Mark justified Jesus' practice by showing how he changed the lives of such persons.

2:13–14 Levi is mentioned elsewhere only in the parallel in Luke 5:27,29. He is not on Mark's list of the Twelve in 3:16–19 or any of the other lists. In the parallel in Matt 9:9 the person is called Matthew, and the traditional view is that Levi and Matthew are different names of the same person. This may well be the case, but still it is strange for a person to have two *Jewish* names. In the four lists of the apostles including Mark's, the "son of Alphaeus" is identified as James; and some Greek manuscripts, ancient versions, and patristic quotations of medium value have "James" in the present passage. The words "son of Alphaeus" are omitted from the parallel in Luke 5:27. The circumstances of the call and the relationship of the present passage to 1:16–20 and 3:13–19 would seem to indicate that Mark considered Levi to be an apostle. If he did, why does not Levi's name appear in the list in the latter passage? It is barely possible to translate "a Levite, the son of Alphaeus." In such case the Levite could be either James or his brother, but one would not expect a Levite to be a tax collector. The problem is quite perplexing. While the traditional association of Matthew with Levi has merit, there is no altogether satisfactory solution.

Although Mark did not mention a place, the episode probably happened at Capernaum, where the first toll station would have been located for those coming from the tetrarchy (small kingdom) of Philip or the Decapolis (a league of Ten Cities) to the tetrarchy of Herod Antipas. Levi was a minor official of the Jewish client-king Herod Antipas and not a Roman tax collector. The tax collectors of Antipas, however, were probably as much despised as those of the Romans and for the same reasons: their dishonesty, use of intimidation and even force, and contact with Gentiles. Furthermore the Herodian rulers themselves were at best semi-Jews and were hated almost as much as the Roman governors. Like Peter, Andrew, James, and John (1:16–20), Levi responded to the call by leaving his secular work and following Jesus, i.e., becoming a disciple.

2:15 The NIV interprets the first part of the verse to mean that the dinner was in Levi's house, but the Greek text leaves it uncertain whether it was there or in Jesus' house. Some think that when vv. 15–17 circulated independently, the location was Jesus' house; but when the two accounts were combined, the location was shifted to Levi's house.

The word translated "was having dinner" (*synanekeinto*) literally means *to recline*. Apparently Jews sat at a table for ordinary meals but reclined on couches or carpets for formal meals. The NIV is quite correct to put the word "sinners" in quotation marks to indicate that it is being used with an unusual meaning. The reference is not to immoral or irreligious persons but to those who because of the necessity of spending all their time earning a bare subsistence were not able to keep the law, especially the oral law, as the scribes thought they should. As a result the scribes despised them. Perhaps a better translation would be "outcasts" (GNB).

The word "disciples" appears in v. 15 for the first of fifty-eight times in Mark, an indication of how important discipleship is in the book. Its etymological meaning is *a learner*, but the disciples of Jesus were more than pupils. They were devoted not just to his teaching but even more to him as a person. Furthermore, Jesus intended them to become ministers to the needs of others just as he was a minister.

The text and punctuation of the last part of v. 15 and the first part of v. 16 are in doubt. The alternative to the NIV is: "For there were many. And the teachers of the law who were Pharisees were following him, and when they saw him eating." The latter is improbable, however, because the verb "to follow" is usually a technical term for discipleship. Mark's point was that many so-called sinners and many tax collectors became part of the larger group of Jesus' disciples.

2:16 Those who live in modern, Western society with comparatively few social distinctions have difficulty realizing just how scandalous it was for Jesus to associate with outcasts. In Semitic society table fellowship was one of the most intimate expressions of friendship. For this reason the religious leaders could not understand how Jesus could be a religious person and dine with "bad characters" (v. 15, NEB). Jesus defied many of the conventions of his society. Ironically, throughout Christian history many have attempted to make Jesus conform to the conventions of their society and thus produce a folk religion.

Here Mark mentioned the Pharisees for the first of twelve times. They were a party of laymen that developed during the period of Hasmonean independence (142–63 B.C.) and devoted themselves to keeping the law, especially its oral interpretation, as taught by the scribes. The name probably means *separatists*, and they may have been called such because of their separation from the common people, the "sinners" of the present passage. Despite the very close relationship of the groups, not all scribes were Pharisees; and only a few Pharisees were scribes. Mark indicated that fact by his unique expression "scribes of the Pharisees," which the NIV renders "teachers of the law who were Pharisees."

2:17 Probably no scribes were at a banquet attended by "sinners," and their complaint was reported to Jesus. Jesus affirmed that his mission (note "I have . . . come") was to call sinners, not just to repentance as in the Lukan parallel and in a later copyist's addition here (KJV, NKJV), but to full acceptance in the kingdom of God. Therefore for Jesus to refuse to associate with sinners would have been as foolish as for a doctor not to associate with the sick. The word "righteous" is probably used ironically to mean *self-righteous*, for such were many of the scribes.

The love of Jesus for all kinds of sinners, his initiative in seeking them, his giving them full acceptance, and his desire to have close fellowship with them was a new and revolutionary element in religion and morals. Mark intended to convey the message that the disciples of Jesus should have the same attitude.

(3) Over Fasting (2:18–22)

> [18] Now John's disciples and the Pharisees were fasting. Some people came and asked Jesus, "How is it that John's disciples and the disciples of the Pharisees are fasting, but yours are not?"
> [19] Jesus answered, "How can the guests of the bridegroom fast while he is with them? They cannot, so long as they have him with them. [20] But the time will come when the bridegroom will be taken from them, and on that day they will fast.
> [21] "No one sews a patch of unshrunk cloth on an old garment. If he does, the new piece will pull away from the old, making the tear worse. [22] And no one pours new wine into old wineskins. If he does, the wine will burst the skins, and both the wine and the wineskins will be ruined. No, he pours new wine into new wineskins."

It is widely held that vv. 21–22 were originally independent from vv. 18–20 because they are very general and do not mention fasting. This may be, but certainty is impossible. Both parts contrast the old way (that of John and the Pharisees) and the new way (that of Jesus). It is also widely held that Jesus did not speak what is in vv. 19b–20 because it involves allegorization and a premature prediction of his death. The view that Jesus never employed allegory will be denied in the comments on chap. 4. As for the prediction of his death, it is characteristically veiled. Furthermore, since Mark's arrangement is obviously topical, the words may have been spoken late in Jesus' ministry. In recording the material in these paragraphs, Mark provided instruction about two issues in his church: fasting and the incompatibility of Christianity and Judaism.

2:18 If the tense Mark used is interpreted as a customary imperfect, a better translation might be "made a practice of fasting." The only biblically prescribed fast was on the Day of Atonement (Lev 16, especially vv. 29,31), although other fasts grew up late in the Old Testament period (Zech 7:5; 8:19). Furthermore, the Pharisees fasted every Monday and Thursday (cf. Luke 18:12). The Jews sometimes fasted as a result of personal loss, sometimes as an expression of repentance, sometimes as preparation for prayer, and sometimes merely as a meritorious act. The disciples of John may have been fasting because of the imprisonment or death of their leader, his ascetic life-style, or his emphasis on repentance. So important was fasting for ancient Jews that an entire tractate of the *Mishna, Taanith,* was devoted to it.

The expression "disciples of the Pharisees" is difficult because the Pharisees did not have disciples but were themselves disciples of the scribes. Perhaps the idea is "admirers" or "fellow travelers" who were sympathetic with but not members of the Pharisaic party. Although Jesus himself was not accused of failing to fast, he was held responsible for his disciples' failure in accordance with current practice.

Aside from this passage and its parallels in Matt 9:14–17 and Luke 5:33–39, the New Testament says little about fasting. The only passages are Matt 6:16–18; Acts 9:9; 13:2–3; and 14:23. Fasting is a matter of Christian freedom, not obligation. Therefore *Didache* 8.1 (early second cent.) is quite amiss in insisting that Christians fast on Wednesdays and Fridays instead of Mondays and Thursdays.

2:19–20 The use of a counterquestion was common in rabbinic disputes; and according to Mark, Jesus frequently used it. The statement in the first half of v. 19 is a simple analogy, but that in v. 20 allegorizes it by suggesting that Jesus is the bridegroom and his disciples the wedding guests. Some have denied that Jesus could have spoken v. 20 or that it was originally a part of the same piece as v. 19. Nevertheless only a preconceived notion of what is possible and impossible can rule out all allegorization on Jesus' part. Whether the disciples made the identification at the time is another matter. Inasmuch as the Jews never depicted the Messiah as a bridegroom,[8] the disciples probably did not understand the significance of the statement until later. The original readers/hearers of the Gospel, however, who were in on the "secret" from the beginning, could not have helped noticing this passage as the first allusion to the crucifixion, just as modern readers do.

Verse 19 seems to suggest no fasting at all; v. 20, that there may be occasions to fast. No contradiction exists. On some occasions fasting is inappropriate, and on others it is appropriate. The nearness of the kingdom of God in the person of Jesus was not a fitting time. During his absence fasting may be desirable now and then, but it is not a normative Christian practice as the paucity

---

[8]To the contrary the Old Testament sometimes pictured God as the "husband" of "adulterous" Israel: Isa 54:5–6; Jer 2:2; 3:14; Ezek 16–32; Hos 2.

of references in the New Testament shows. Christianity is characterized by joy, not mourning. Indeed a wedding is a symbol of the salvation associated with the kingdom of God. The passage further suggests that the way to God is not through religious practices but through joyful association with Jesus.

2:21–22 The twin parables here teach the incompatibility of the old (scribal Judaism) and the new (Christianity). Judaism is the old garment and the old wineskin. Christianity is the new garment (implied), the new wineskin, and the new wine (on the last cf. John 2:1–11, especially v. 10). The point is not that the "old" is wrong or evil but that its time has passed. As Acts shows, the Twelve were slow to learn this truth.

(4) Over Picking Grain on the Sabbath (2:23–28)

23One Sabbath Jesus was going through the grainfields, and as his disciples walked along, they began to pick some heads of grain. **24**The Pharisees said to him, "Look, why are they doing what is unlawful on the Sabbath?"

25He answered, "Have you never read what David did when he and his companions were hungry and in need? **26**In the days of Abiathar the high priest, he entered the house of God and ate the consecrated bread, which is lawful only for priests to eat. And he also gave some to his companions."

27Then he said to them, "The Sabbath was made for man, not man for the Sabbath. **28**So the Son of Man is Lord even of the Sabbath."

The last two of the five conflict stories Mark brought together deal with observance of the Sabbath, which was one of the most distinctive elements of Judaism. Not only did the Scriptures legislate about it, it was the subject of an entire tractate of the *Mishna*, namely *Shabbath*. Whether it should be observed by Christians was a problem throughout the apostolic era, and Mark needed to record pronouncements of Jesus on the subject. Many scholars argue that this section has been built up from two originally independent accounts, but they cannot agree on the content of the two parts. Such matters are always difficult to determine, and it is usually best to take the text as it stands.

2:23 The grain probably was wheat,[9] which ripens in Palestine in May and June. This event must have taken place about ten months before Jesus' death in March or April—possibly more if Jesus' ministry in this area lasted more than a year as John's Gospel seems to indicate. According to Deut 23:25, picking a little grain by hand from a neighbor's field was legal.

2:24 The Old Testament, of course, forbade work on the Sabbath (Exod 20:8–11). The scribes enumerated thirty-nine kinds of work that were prohibited, and the third of these was reaping.[10] The Pharisees interpreted picking a few heads of grain as reaping!

---

[9]The word "corn" in the KJV is the British word for grain. Corn in the American sense was unknown until the discovery of the New World.

[10]*M. Šabb.* 7.2; cf. Exod 34:21; *m. Sota* 5.3; also the "Sabbath day's walk" of Acts 1:12.

2:25–26 The reference is to the incident recorded in 1 Sam 21:1–6. The "consecrated bread" was twelve loaves that were put on a table in the tabernacle (the "house of God" of v. 26) each Sabbath, probably to symbolize God's presence and provision or to represent Israel before God (Exod 25:30; Lev 24:5–9), and which were eaten only by the priests at the end of the week. David and his men were not priests, but Jesus implied that what they did was justified because they were famished. Jesus set forth the basic principle that human need should take precedence over ceremonial laws. The Pharisees could have objected that Jesus' disciples were not starving, but the point remains that Sabbath observance should not be reduced to legalistic restrictions.

A difficult problem is in v. 26. According to 1 Sam 21:1–6, Ahimelech, not Abiathar, was high priest at the time. The most frequent explanation is that Mark's memory slipped. Such an explanation is impossible for those who embrace a concept of scriptural inerrancy as a result of their view of divine inspiration. The difficulty was felt even by ancient copyists, some of whom omitted "in the days of Abiathar the high priest,"[11] some of whom inserted an article in order to imply that Abiathar was not necessarily high priest at the time and some of whom substituted "priest" for "high priest." None of these variants has any claim to originality, nor do they solve the problem. The statement was perhaps a scribal gloss that later was accidentally taken into the text.

Another explanation is that the Greek construction that must mean "in the account of" in Mark 12:26 means the same thing here, i.e., in that portion of Samuel that deals with Abiathar. (In the first century there were no chapters and verses; thus such devices as the preceding were necessary to locate passages.) The absence of the Greek word for "days" in v. 26 supports this explanation. Abiathar, however, is not mentioned until the next chapter of 1 Samuel.

Another explanation, building upon the fact that the Aramaic word *abba* means *father* (cf. Mark 14:36), is that the original had *Abba-Abiathar* (i.e., "father of Abiathar," who was in fact Ahimelech). *Abba* was then accidentally omitted by an early copyist because its first two letters are the same as the first two of Abiathar. The last is perhaps the best explanation, though it apparently assumes an original Aramaic text. No explanation is completely satisfactory. The implied comparison between David and Jesus suggests that Jesus possessed authority similar to that of David and that in some sense he was David's successor. The idea is developed further in 11:10.

2:27–28 The introduction formula at the beginning of v. 27 may indicate that the pronouncements originally were independent of the preceding. Cer-

---

[11] The parallels in Matt 12:4 and Luke 6:4 also omit this phrase—one of many instances where they "improve" upon Mark and thereby show that they are later than Mark and that they used him as a primary source.

tainly they are more general. The statement in v. 27 is often compared to that of Rabbi Simeon ben Menasya (ca. A.D. 180): "The Sabbath is delivered over for your sake, but you are not delivered over to the Sabbath."[12] Jesus meant that human beings were not created to observe the Sabbath but that the Sabbath was created for their benefit. The Sabbath is not an end in itself or the greatest good. Jesus affirmed his right to determine Sabbath observance (v. 28), although some think this verse was Mark's comment rather than the words of Jesus. If the latter were true, Mark would have referred to Jesus as the Son of Man—something that neither he nor any other Gospel writer did elsewhere (but see the comments on 2:10). In the Synoptics "Son of Man" is always Jesus' self-designation. Most unlikely is the view that "Son of Man" here means *man* and that Jesus taught that human beings have authority to determine how the Sabbath is to be observed. That is the very thing he was protesting against!

(5) Over Healing the Man with the Shriveled Hand on the Sabbath (3:1–6)

¹**Another time he went into the synagogue, and a man with a shriveled hand was there. ²Some of them were looking for a reason to accuse Jesus, so they watched him closely to see if he would heal him on the Sabbath. ³Jesus said to the man with the shriveled hand, "Stand up in front of everyone."**

⁴**Then Jesus asked them, "Which is lawful on the Sabbath: to do good or to do evil, to save life or to kill?" But they remained silent.**

⁵**He looked around at them in anger and, deeply distressed at their stubborn hearts, said to the man, "Stretch out your hand." He stretched it out, and his hand was completely restored. ⁶Then the Pharisees went out and began to plot with the Herodians how they might kill Jesus.**

The account does not emphasize the healing but the question of Sabbath observance. Therefore it ought to be classified as a conflict and/or pronouncement story, although the pronouncement is cast as a question (v. 4). To understand the Pharisaic position, one must realize that Sabbath observance was one of the more important elements in Judaism and one noticeable distinction between Jews and Gentiles. Mark both gave further insight into Jesus' "liberal" attitude toward the Sabbath and showed how this attitude was a major factor in Pharisaic opposition that culminated in Jesus' death (v. 6). Likely Mark intended Jesus' freedom in observing the Sabbath to justify Christian freedom with reference to that day. Some think the vividness and detail of the account indicates eyewitness testimony, probably that of Peter. This could be, but it is beyond proof.

---

[12] *Mek.* 109b on Exod 31:14, cited by W. L. Lane, *Mark,* NIC (Grand Rapids: Eerdmans, 1974), 119.

3:1 Jesus and his disciples regularly worshiped in synagogues, as did Paul later (see the commentary on 1:21). Inasmuch as this is not really a healing story, the affliction is not described in detail. It probably was some kind of paralysis ("paralyzed hand," GNB).

3:2 The "some of them" are identified in v. 6 as the Pharisees (see comments on 2:16). The imperfect tense (*pareteroun*) is probably iterative: "they kept on watching" or "kept on lying in wait for." Apparently they were more concerned to accuse Jesus than to worship. The scribal rule the Pharisees followed permitted healing on the Sabbath only where life was in danger,[13] which certainly was not the present case.

3:3 The NIV's "stand up front" is a modernization. The Greek says "get up in the middle" because, in second- and third-century synagogues at least, the seats were stone benches around the walls.

3:4 By his question Jesus lifted the issue of Sabbath observance above a list of prohibitions to the higher general principle. No one would claim that it was "lawful" or right to do evil or kill on the Sabbath. The obvious alternative is that it must be right to do good and save life. To heal is to do good; to do nothing is to do evil. To heal is to "save" a life;[14] not to heal is the equivalent of killing.[15] For Mark merely not doing work and resting on the Sabbath or the Lord's Day was not enough. The day must be used for all kinds of good things.

The Pharisees were silent because whatever answer they gave to Jesus' question would have undermined their position on Sabbath observance.

3:5 Here is a certain reference to the anger of Jesus (see also 10:14 and compare the comments on 1:41 and the accounts of the expulsion from the temple). In their parallel accounts Matthew and Luke preferred not to attribute to Jesus an emotion that among humans is often sinful. Jesus' anger was not sinful, however, because it was directed toward evil and because it was controlled. Perhaps "with righteous indignation" would avoid the offense. "At their stubborn hearts" could be translated more literally "at their hardness of heart," but the word "hardness" often takes on the additional idea of willful "blindness." The NEB and REB have a striking rendition here: "Looking round at them with anger and sorrow at their obstinate stupidity." Jesus was angry not only at insensitivity toward suffering but at the entire system of legalism where the letter is more important than the spirit.

---

[13] *M. Yoma* 8.6; cf. *m. Šabb.* 18.3.

[14] The verb *to save* is used here in its nontheological sense of deliverance from any kind of harm. As previously indicated, all of Jesus' healings of the body are symbols of his healing of the soul, which is often referred to by the technical term "salvation." Jesus' healings were a sign of the nearness of the kingdom of God.

[15] Some think this is an allusion to the plot to kill Jesus mentioned in v. 6. The most natural interpretation, however, is that killing is set in contrast with healing.

3:6 In all of ancient literature the Herodians are referred to only here and in 12:13 (cf. Matt 22:16).[16] One can only surmise that they supported Herod Antipas, the tetrarch of Galilee and Perea (see the comments on 6:14–29). They may have further advocated restoration of Herodian rule of Judea, which was a Roman imperial province governed by a legate, or (as such officials were later called) procurator, during the ministry of Jesus. Ordinarily the Pharisees would have had nothing to do with the Herodians, but common enemies often make strange bedfellows. Perhaps the Herodians opposed Jesus because of his relationship to John the Baptist, who condemned Herod's divorce and remarriage (6:18).

The first explicit reference to Jesus' death is in v. 6. The verse concludes not only the present pericope but all five conflict stories. The Pharisees' plot to "kill" (*apolesōsin*, which literally means *destroy* as one would do to an animal) one who not only saved a life but who came to give life to all exemplifies Markan irony.

6. The Popularity of Jesus (3:7–12)

⁷Jesus withdrew with his disciples to the lake, and a large crowd from Galilee followed. ⁸When they heard all he was doing, many people came to him from Judea, Jerusalem, Idumea, and the regions across the Jordan and around Tyre and Sidon.

⁹Because of the crowd he told his disciples to have a small boat ready for him, to keep the people from crowding him. ¹⁰For he had healed many, so that those with diseases were pushing forward to touch him. ¹¹Whenever the evil spirits saw him, they fell down before him and cried out, "You are the Son of God." ¹²But he gave them strict orders not to tell who he was.

Many regard this paragraph as an editorial summary, i.e., an original composition of Mark rather than a piece of tradition he passed on with or without editing. A few argue for a traditional core, e.g., vv. 7,9–10, which Mark expanded. As usual unraveling tradition and redaction is difficult. The passage does not summarize the previous account but the following by introducing several items later dwelt upon. It shows the widespread appeal of Jesus' ministry and reaffirms his authority over the demonic.

3:7–8 The word translated "withdrew" can mean *flee from danger*, and therefore some have thought that Jesus was trying to avoid persecution (cf. v. 6). Others have suggested that it intimates his rejection of Judaism. Probably it refers to nothing more than Jesus' desire to extend his ministry beyond

---

[16] The references in Josephus, *War* 1.16.6 and *Antiquities* 14.15.10 are nontechnical and are associated with supporters of Herod the Great (40–4 B.C.).

the towns and their synagogues. The lake, of course, is Lake Galilee (see comments on 1:16). "Idumea" is the Greek name for Edom, but it refers not to ancient Edom but to the area to the south of Judea which the Edomites occupied in the sixth and fifth centuries B.C. after the Nabateans forced them out of their homeland east of the Dead Sea. The Herodian family was Idumean and at most was semi-Jewish. They were forced by the Maccabeans to adopt Judaism or face death.

The "regions across the Jordan" River were known at the time as Perea (from the Greek adverb *peran* meaning *across, beyond, on the other side*). "Tyre and Sidon" were to the north on the Phoenician coast (in modern Lebanon) and were not in Palestine. All three of the areas were largely Gentile and probably symbolize the world beyond the land of the Jews (Judea and Galilee). Mark seems to have been suggesting that all peoples should seek Jesus and that they may be assured of acceptance. Readers and hearers of his Gospel naturally think about the later Gentile mission.

The original text of vv. 7–8 is quite uncertain. Some textual witnesses omit "followed," some omit "Idumea," some omit "many people," and some make other changes. The NIV translated what probably is the original text, which distinguishes between two groups, one from Galilee, which had special importance for Mark, and one from the other places. The text, which omits "followed" and "many people," suggests only one group.

3:9–10 The scene is one of great commotion, involving pushing and shoving. Apparently the crowd sought Jesus because of his healings, not to submit themselves to the reign of God. Even so Jesus "healed many" (which probably means "all who were many"). Verse 9 is the first of eight passages that involve a boat; and whether Mark intended such an idea, ancient and medieval Christian artists used the boat to symbolize fellowship between Jesus and his disciples and by implication fellowship among Christians.

3:11–12 In 1:24,34 the demons knew who Jesus was, and in 1:24 one called him "the Holy One of God." Here they explicitly confessed that he is "the Son of God"—the ultimate Christological title. Theirs was, however, not a confession of commitment but of fear (cf. Jas 2:19) and even opposition—the latter because some thought that if one knew and used the name of a divine being, he or she could control that being. This is one reason Jesus refused to let the demons use an otherwise appropriate title. The account provides an example of Mark's irony. Another reason Jesus silenced the demonic confession is that the title they used can be understood properly only in light of his death and resurrection. Therefore the time for such explicit confession had not come. Only at the crucifixion did a human being confess Jesus as Son of God (15:39). Mark probably intended to contrast what the demons acknowledged as a fact with what the religious leaders were not willing to consider as a possibility.

7. The Call of the Twelve (3:13–19)

[13]Jesus went up on a mountainside and called to him those he wanted, and they came to him. [14]He appointed twelve—designating them apostles—that they might be with him and that he might send them out to preach [15]and to have authority to drive out demons. [16]These are the twelve he appointed: Simon (to whom he gave the name Peter); [17]James son of Zebedee and his brother John (to them he gave the name Boanerges, which means Sons of Thunder); [18]Andrew, Philip, Bartholomew, Matthew, Thomas, James son of Alphaeus, Thaddaeus, Simon the Zealot [19]and Judas Iscariot, who betrayed him.

The New Testament contains four lists of the twelve apostles: here; Matt 10:2–4; Luke 6:13–16; Acts 1:13. Peter is always first, Philip fifth, James the son of Alphaeus ninth, and Judas Iscariot twelfth. The order of the other names varies. Eleven of the names are the same. As for the other one, Matthew and Mark have Thaddaeus, but Luke and Acts have Judas the son (or brother) of James. The call of the Twelve is found at a different place in each of the Synoptic Gospels. The term "the Twelve" is also found in John 6:67,70–71; 20:24, but that Gospel has no list. Outside of the Gospels the term appears only in Acts 6:2 and 1 Cor 15:5. The lack of references has led some to deny the historicity of the stories about the appointment of this group. Historicity is guaranteed, however, by the independence and early date of 1 Corinthians, the embarrassing presence of Judas Iscariot on the lists, and the absence of a record of most of the persons ever doing anything significant. The appointment of the Twelve was the first step in the establishment of a new people of God, the church.

3:13 Whether Mark intended the mountain to symbolize something such as revelation or nearness to God or whether it is merely a place cannot be determined. Whether those who were called and came are synonymous with the Twelve or a larger group from whom the Twelve were chosen is also unclear. Mark emphasized the freedom of Jesus in choosing those he wanted and the immediate response of those so chosen.

3:14–15 The number twelve recalls the twelve tribes of Israel and therefore symbolizes the new or restored people of God, which later came to be known as the church. The Twelve were the nucleus of this new creation. A new creation is suggested by the use of a verb that usually means *to make* but that is translated "appointed" in the NIV. The clause "designating them apostles" is probably a scribal assimilation to Luke 6:13, where it is an authentic reading. Apparently Mark did not call the Twelve "apostles" (the word in 6:30 probably is used in its nontechnical sense of "a missionary"). The last part of v. 14 and the first part of v. 15 indicate the two purposes of Jesus' summons: that they might be with Jesus (one of the most important elements in being a disciple) and that they might be sent on a mission to proclaim the advent of the kingdom of God and demonstrate it by exorcising demons (cf. 6:7–12).

3:16 The statement "These are the twelve he appointed" may also be a scribal addition. (Interestingly it is not in the text translated by the KJV and NKJV.) Something else may have originally stood at this point because the list begins awkwardly: "And he gave the name Peter to Simon" (literal translation). One would expect Simon to have been mentioned before it is said that he was given another name. Of course the calling of the first four persons on the list was related in 1:16–20. *Petros* is the Greek equivalent of the Aramaic *kepha* (cf. Cephas in John 1:42 and four times each in 1 Corinthians and Galatians) and means *a rock*. Except for 14:37 Mark used it from this point on, a total of nineteen times. Peter's character in the Gospels is not comparable to a rock, and Jesus either symbolized his leadership role or his character after the resurrection.

3:17 Mark said that "Boanerges" means "Sons of Thunder," but linguists are unable to confirm this. It is reasonably certain that *boane* represents *bene*, which means *sons of;* but what Hebrew or Aramaic word *rges* represents is uncertain. In any event the reference may be to their thunderous preaching or perhaps to a trait of character such as that reflected in 9:38 or Luke 9:54. The parenthetical statement is peculiar to Mark.

3:18 "Bartholomew" is not a proper name but a patronymic and means *son of Talmi.* He is often identified with the Nathaniel of John's Gospel, but this is mere conjecture. Matthew is a shortened form of Mattathias (1 Macc 2:1ff.; 2 Macc 14:19; Luke 3:25–26). By adding "the tax collector" Matt 10:3 seems to identify Matthew with the Levi of Mark 2:14,[17] but Mark seemingly makes no such association (cf. the comments on 2:14). "James the son of Alphaeus" is sometimes identified with James the younger (15:40) and even with Levi. Instead of "Thaddaeus" some representatives of the Western type of text in both Mark and Matt 10:3 have "Lebbaeus," and the Byzantine type of text in Matthew has "Lebbaeus who is called Thaddaeus" (cf. KJV, NKJV). As previously indicated, "Judas the son of James" stands in Luke 6:16 and Acts 1:13 in the place of Thaddaeus. In the Greek text "Simon the Cananaean" (RSV, NRSV) does not refer to a resident of Canaan or Cana but reflects the Hebrew word *kana*, which means *a man of zeal.* Indeed, the Greek text of Luke 6:15 and Acts 1:13 has "Simon the Zealot." Whether the reference is to a person characterized by religious zeal or to a member of the nationalistic, revolutionary party is uncertain.

3:19 "Iscariot" probably means *man of Kerioth*, a village south of Hebron (Josh 15:25), rather than *assassin, man of Issachar, man of falsehood*, or *man of red hair*, etc.

---

[17] A few Greek manuscripts of Mark do this also.

8. The Family of Jesus (3:20–21,31–35)

[20]Then Jesus entered a house, and again a crowd gathered, so that he and his disciples were not even able to eat. [21]When his family heard about this, they went to take charge of him, for they said, "He is out of his mind. . . . "

[31]Then Jesus' mother and brothers arrived. Standing outside, they sent someone in to call him. [32]A crowd was sitting around him, and they told him, "Your mother and brothers are outside looking for you."

[33]"Who are my mother and my brothers?" he asked.

[34]Then he looked at those seated in a circle around him and said, "Here are my mother and my brothers! [35]Whoever does God's will is my brother and sister and mother."

Mark 3:20–35 is the first clear instance in the Gospel of intercalation or bracketing or sandwiching, a literary and theological device used to indicate a lapse of time, heighten tension, draw attention to, contrast, and most importantly to use two accounts to interpret each other. In other words, the purpose of intercalation is primarily theological.[18] Other examples are 4:1–20; 5:21–43; 6:7–29; 11:12–25; 14:1–11; 14:53–72 (or 14:53–15:15; possibly 14:17–31; 15:40–16:8.

In 3:20–35 a story about the scribes accusing Jesus of being possessed by a demon (vv. 22–30) has been inserted into a story about Jesus' family in order to allow for the family's travel time from Nazareth (cf. 1:9) to wherever Jesus was and—more importantly—to show that Jesus' family as well as the religious authorities misunderstood and opposed him. Mark portrayed opposition by one as serious as opposition by the other. Both stories contrast those who opposed Jesus and those who embraced his teaching. Both are pronouncement stories (vv. 28–29,34–35, respectively).

The story about Jesus' family redefines who constitutes his family. Jesus' true family consists of those who respond positively to him rather than those who are physically related to him. The story also suggests that being a part of Jesus' family may require adjusting or even severing relationships with an earthly family.

3:20 The material in vv. 20–21 is not found in another Gospel. Locating the house was not important for Mark's purpose. It may have been that of Simon and Andrew in Capernaum (1:29). As in 3:7–10 a large, demanding, unruly crowd is depicted.

3:21 In the Greek text the subject of the first two clauses is literally "those with him." The KJV and RSV (1st ed.) interpret this to mean "his friends," the NASB and NKJV "his own people," and the RSV (2nd ed.), NRSV, NEB, REB, and NIV "his family." In view of vv. 31–32 the last of these is certainly

---

[18]An especially helpful treatment of this matter is J. R. Edwards, "Markan Sandwiches: The Significance of Interpolations in Markan Narratives," *NovT* 31 (1989): 193–216.

correct. The idea that Jesus' family opposed him troubled some ancient copyists who changed the text to read, "When the scribes and the rest heard." The concern of Jesus' family was not likely limited to his physical needs (v. 20); they probably were more concerned about the family's reputation because in their estimation Jesus was acting in a fanatical and even insane way. The same verb is used in Acts 26:24 and 2 Cor 5:13 and means literally *to stand outside of oneself*. The verb translated "to take charge" means *to arrest* in 6:17; 12:12; 14:1, etc. Evidently they intended to seize Jesus and force him to return to Nazareth with them.

3:31–32 Jesus' mother is named "Mary" in 6:3, and these are the only references to her in Mark. The most natural understanding of the word *adelphoi* is that it refers to the physical brothers of Jesus.[19] Belief in the virginal conception, of which Mark says nothing, may modify the meaning to halfbrothers. Those, however, who embrace the idea that Mary remained a virgin, about which the New Testament says nothing, argue that the reference is to Jesus' cousins or step-brothers. It is true that *adelphoi* may refer to other kinds of relationships; and even if Mary had normal sexual relations after Jesus' birth, the preceding view is possible—but not probable. Lack of mention of Joseph is usually thought to imply that he was dead. Mark evidently intended a contrast between the family standing outside and the crowd including the disciples who were sitting around Jesus inside the house. Therefore it probably was a case of not wanting to go in rather than not being able to get in as in 2:2.

3:33–35 "Those seated in a circle around him" obviously are Jesus' disciples. Despite all their failures, Jesus acknowledged them as those who did God's will and therefore his true family. Mark's Gentile readers/hearers and modern Christians (the "whoever" in v. 35) have been encouraged that relationship with God is not a matter of genetics but of obedience to God's will. It is difficult to conceive of a more meaningful symbol than being a part of the family of God and his Son. Of course Jesus did not teach that physical relationships have no value, only that they must be subordinated to spiritual relationships. Even so, his teaching was radical. It seemed to threaten the most important human institution. The difference of Jesus' teaching and that of Judaism and Hellenism guarantees its authenticity.

9. The Accusation of Demon Possession and the Warning against the Unforgivable Sin (3:22–30)

22And the teachers of the law who came down from Jerusalem said, "He is possessed by Beelzebub! By the prince of demons he is driving out demons."

---

[19]Some textual witnesses of medium and inferior quality add "and your sisters" (GNB). A fair case can be made for the originality of this reading because the omission can easily be explained as either accidental (skipping from the first instance of "your" to the second) or deliberate (because the sisters are not mentioned elsewhere in the passage). It is very difficult to explain the addition in one place only.

²³So Jesus called them and spoke to them in parables: "How can Satan drive out Satan? ²⁴If a kingdom is divided against itself, that kingdom cannot stand. ²⁵If a house is divided against itself, that house cannot stand. ²⁶And if Satan opposes himself and is divided, he cannot stand; his end has come. ²⁷In fact, no one can enter a strong man's house and carry off his possessions unless he first ties up the strong man. Then he can rob his house. ²⁸I tell you the truth, all the sins and blasphemies of men will be forgiven them. ²⁹But whoever blasphemes against the Holy Spirit will never be forgiven; he is guilty of an eternal sin."

³⁰He said this because they were saying, "He has an evil spirit."

3:22 Mark conveys the impression that Jesus' ministry had come to the attention of the "establishment" in Jerusalem. The verb "to come down" is regularly used in the Bible for journeying away from Jerusalem, which is situated in the hill country (cf. 10:32–33) rather than to mean *to come south* (Galilee is north of Jerusalem). The scribes acknowledged that Jesus performed unusual miracles and that he did so by supernatural power, but they claimed it was demonic power. They claimed that Jesus was demon possessed!

The spelling of the name of the prince of demons varies in the textual witnesses with "Beelzebub" (KJV, NKJV, NIV text, NEB) having the weaker attestation[20] and "Beelzebul" (RSV, NRSV, NASB, GNB, REB; "Beelzeboul," NIV note) the better. Beelzebul (or Baalzebul) was the name of a Canaanite deity and means *lord of the house/temple*. The form "Baal-Zebub," which appears in 2 Kgs 1:2ff., means *lord of flies* and is a deliberate alteration to show contempt. In Matt 12:24 and Luke 11:15 Beelzebul and the prince of demons (Satan) are certainly identified, and Mark probably does that also. There is no other evidence, however, that Satan was ever called Beelzebul.

3:23–27 Jesus replied by showing how foolish the accusation was. If he cast out demons by demonic power, Satan would be working against himself. Jesus illustrated his claim by three "parables":[21] the divided kingdom (v. 24), the divided house (v. 25), and the binding of the strong man by a stronger (v. 27). The "strong man" is Satan, and the stronger one is Jesus, who was in the process of tying up Satan and carrying off his possessions (those whom he controlled) by exorcising demons.

3:28 The plain and wonderful truth of v. 28 must not be overlooked because of the difficulty of v. 29. With but one exception—blasphemy against

---

[20] Textual criticism is not a strong point of the NIV. This is seen primarily in its insensitivity about the placement of textual notes, but occasionally the NIV translates a reading in the medieval, Byzantine text, where there is no justification for doing so.

[21] Although this is the first use of the word in Mark, its meaning will be commented on at 4:1–34. For the present it is enough to observe that parables take many different forms and that allegory (v. 27) cannot be excluded from parables. The use of the word here prepares for the parable discourse in chap. 4. Furthermore, it should be noted that an element in Mark's "theology" is that those outside of the kingdom are always addressed "in parables" (4:11–12,33–34; 7:17; 12:1).

the Holy Spirit—God will forgive all persons all sins![22] The importance of what Jesus said is underscored by Mark's first use of the word *amēn*, which along with the verb "to say" is translated "I tell you the truth" in the NIV and "I assure you" in the GNB. It is derived from a Hebrew word meaning *to be reliable*. It is used thirteen times in Mark and sixty-two times in the other Gospels,[23] always as Jesus' self-affirmation of what he said. Use as an introductory formula of self-affirmation was unknown among Jews, who used *amēn* as a *concluding* formula to affirm the truthfulness of what *another* person had said. Just because the introductory "amen" was not used by Judaism or the early church (no examples in Acts or the Epistles), it is highly likely that all statements accompanied by it were in fact spoken by Jesus himself.

The word "blasphemy," which is simply a transliteration of the Greek, refers to slandering human beings or, as here, being irreverent or defiant toward God.

3:29 The sudden injection of the Holy Spirit into the discussion is surprising. It must imply that Jesus worked by the power of the Holy Spirit rather than that of an evil spirit (v. 30) as the scribes charged. Instead of "he is guilty of an eternal sin," i.e., one with infinite consequences, the medieval text has "is subject to eternal condemnation" (NKJV, similar KJV).

3:30 Here Mark defined the sin that "will never be forgiven." It is ascribing to Satan and his demons the works of the Holy Spirit manifested in the ministry of Jesus. It is not a single act but a habitual action and attitude. The imperfect tense could be translated, "They kept on saying." In this instance at least the sin was committed by scholars and religious authorities, not laypersons. Apparently the sin is quite rare. In addition to the parallel passages in Matthew and Luke, the only other instance of a similar sin in the New Testament is the sin that leads to death in 1 John 5:16–17. That sin probably is refusal to identify the divine Christ with the human Jesus. Thus in both Mark and 1 John the unforgivable sin is the stubborn refusal to acknowledge that God is working/has worked in the man Jesus.

10. The Parable Discourse (4:1–34)

Mark frequently indicated that Jesus taught, but he gave comparatively little of the content of Jesus' teaching. Even when he did, it was usually in the form of short, detached sayings. Two major exceptions to this practice are the parable discourse of chap. 4 and the eschatological discourse of chap. 13.

---

[22] The passive voice is another example of the divine passive and suggests that God himself will do the forgiving. What the NIV translates "men" is literally "the sons of men," but the expression means *all human beings*.

[23] In John it is always doubled, "truly, truly." When this is taken into consideration, the total number of appearances is 100.

The English word "parable" simply transliterates the Greek word *parabolē*, which appears forty-eight times in the Synoptic Gospels and twice in Hebrews and means *that which is placed beside*, presumably for the purpose of comparison. The meaning of the Greek word is not significant, however, because the parables of Jesus are not related to Greek parables but to the *mashalim* of the Old Testament. The word *mashal* has a variety of meanings: *comparison, proverb, allegory, riddle, fable, oracle, ethical maxim, wisdom saying, byword, taunt, type, mystery, aphorism, simile or metaphor, similitude*, etc. Therefore one should not expect all of the parables of Jesus to represent the same oral or literary form, and that is certainly the case.

Following A. Jülicher, many contemporary scholars make a sharp distinction between parables and allegories. A parable, they say, has only one point of comparison so that the details are unimportant. In an allegory, however, all or most of the details represent something.

They claim further that Jesus never used allegory. Therefore when a parable in the Gospels has allegorical features or when the explanation of a parable is allegorical, they claim the parable or explanation could not have come from Jesus but was the invention of the primitive church.

Though long popular, Jülicher's reductionistic view has increasingly come under fire on a variety of fronts. First, the Hebrew word *mashal* can refer to an allegory: Ezek 17:2–10; 20:49; 24:3–5. Second, allegory was recognized as a legitimate literary form in Jesus' time. There is no a priori reason why Jesus could not have used allegory, i.e., a story with multiple comparisons as opposed to a story with only one. There are too many parables in the Gospels with allegorical features for none of them to be authentic. Third, recent literary criticism of the parables has challenged Jülicher's corollary that each parable can be reduced to a single, "universal truth" consistent with nineteenth-century liberalism. The rediscovery of metaphor has led to renewed openness to Jesus' use of allegory.[24]

It is now possible to define the word "parable" as it is used in the Gospels. In addition to referring occasionally to a proverb (Mark 3:23–26; Luke 4:23; 6:39 [cf. Matt 15:14–15]), a metaphor (Mark 7:14–17; Luke 5:36–38 [cf. Mark 2:21–22; Matt 9:16–17]), and a similitude (Matt 13:33; Mark 4:26–29 [cf. v. 34]; 4:30–32; 13:28–29 ["lesson," NIV]; Luke 15:3–7,8–10), the predominant use is to refer to a story from nature or human life to illustrate spiritual truth.[25] Whether there is one point of comparison or several must be determined from each parable. Common sense must play a large role in such

---

[24]P. R. Jones, *The Teaching of the Parables* (Nashville: Broadman, 1982), 14–18.

[25]C. H. Dodd's definition is classic: "The parable is a metaphor or simile drawn from nature or common life, arresting the hearer by its vividness or strangeness, and leaving the mind in sufficient doubt about its precise application to tease it into active thought" (*The Parables of the Kingdom* [New York: Scribner's, 1961], 5).

determination.[26] About thirty figures of speech and stories, many in more than one Gospel, are explicitly called parables. Of course many other parables are not referred to as such. There are at least seventeen of these and perhaps as many as forty-five.

According to the Synoptic Gospels, therefore, the parable was the most common and distinctive form of teaching employed by Jesus. He used parables not simply to illustrate spiritual truth but to provoke reflection and decision. His parables confronted his hearers with a challenge to submit themselves to the reign of God. In fact, the parables in Mark 4 tell what the kingdom of God is like (vv. 11,26,30). This fact must be kept in mind in interpreting them.

(1) The Parable of the Soils and Its Interpretation (4:1–9,13–20)

¹Again Jesus began to teach by the lake. The crowd that gathered around him was so large that he got into a boat and sat in it out on the lake, while all the people were along the shore at the water's edge. ²He taught them many things by parables, and in his teaching said: ³"Listen! A farmer went out to sow his seed. ⁴As he was scattering the seed, some fell along the path, and the birds came and ate it up. ⁵Some fell on rocky places, where it did not have much soil. It sprang up quickly, because the soil was shallow. ⁶But when the sun came up, the plants were scorched, and they withered because they had no root. ⁷Other seed fell among thorns, which grew up and choked the plants, so that they did not bear grain. ⁸Still other seed fell on good soil. It came up, grew and produced a crop, multiplying thirty, sixty, or even a hundred times."

⁹Then Jesus said, "He who has ears to hear, let him hear. . . . "

¹³Then Jesus said to them, "Don't you understand this parable? How then will you understand any parable? ¹⁴The farmer sows the word. ¹⁵Some people are like

---

[26]The contemporary rejection of *all* allegory is no doubt an overreaction to the ancient and medieval practice of *excessive* allegorization of the parables. The most notorious example is Augustine's treatment of the parable of the good Samaritan in his *Quaestiones Evangeliorum* 2.19. In addition to the obvious identification of the Samaritan with Jesus, the traveler is Adam; Jerusalem is heaven; Jericho is the moon, which symbolizes mortality; the robbers are the devil and his angels; the stripping of the man is depriving him of his immortality; the beating is persuading him to sin; leaving him half dead is the effects of sin; the priest is the Jewish priesthood; the Levite is the prophets; binding the wounds is restraint of sin; the oil is comfort and hope; the wine is encouragement to work for Christ; the donkey is the body of Christ; the inn is the church; the two coins are the two commandments to love; the innkeeper is the apostle Paul; and the return of the Samaritan is the resurrection of Christ! Such interpretation is preposterous, but a similar view was still held by R. C. Trench, *Notes on the Parables of Our Lord* (1841). The work which did more than any other to put a stop to such nonsense was A. Jülicher, *Die Gliechnisreden Jesu* (1888). Jülicher insisted that each parable had only one point of comparison and that it was a general moral truth. Contemporary scholarship has accepted the former but rejected the latter because people are not put to death for teaching simple moral truths. A most judicious treatment of the subject is R. H. Stein, *An Introduction to the Parables of Jesus* (Philadelphia: Westminster, 1981), and some of the above is indebted to his work. (Stein is the author of the commentary on Luke in the NAC.)

seed along the path, where the word is sown. As soon as they hear it, Satan comes and takes away the word that was sown in them. [16]Others, like seed sown on rocky places, hear the word and at once receive it with joy. [17]But since they have no root, they last only a short time. When trouble or persecution comes because of the word, they quickly fall away. [18]Still others, like seed sown among thorns, hear the word; [19]but the worries of this life, the deceitfulness of wealth and the desires for other things come in and choke the word, making it unfruitful. [20]Others, like seed sown on good soil, hear the word, accept it, and produce a crop—thirty, sixty or even a hundred times what was sown."

Mark 4:1–20 is the second example of the author's practice of inserting one account into another so that the two might interpret each other (cf. comments on 3:20–35). The statement about the purpose of the parables (4:10–12) explains why so many people are unreceptive to the gospel as is taught in the parable of the soils. Further explanation of purpose in vv. 21–25 makes this sandwich more complicated than the others. Specifically the two accounts explain why so many Jews rejected Jesus. The parable of the soils itself illustrates, first, God's lavish offer of salvation and, second, the mixed reception of that offer.

4:1   Unlike the other Markan parables, this one is not introduced with the formula "the kingdom of God is like." It doubtless describes, however, reactions to Jesus' preaching of the kingdom (cf. 1:15). It also differs from the others in that it alone is accompanied by an explanation. The references to the lake, the large crowd, and the boat reach back to 3:7–12. Here the boat serves not as a means of escape but as a pulpit.

4:2   Here and in vv. 10,13,33 Mark implied that he presented only a few of the many parables Jesus employed in his teaching.

4:3   The parable begins and ends (v. 9) with an admonition to listen thoughtfully, which shows that the meaning of parables is not always self-evident (cf. the comments on vv. 11–12). This admonitory feature, the place of the parable at the beginning of the discourse, its being the only one with an explanation, and its presence in all three of the Synoptic Gospels (Matt 13:1–9; Luke 8:4–8) and in the Coptic Gospel of Thomas 9 shows the importance it had in early church thought.

4:4–8   The parable is true to what is known about ancient Palestinian agriculture. Unlike the modern method, the seed was sown first and then plowed under. The sower held it in an apron with one hand and broadcast it with the other. It was inevitable that some would fall upon the hardened path through the field, some where the soil was too shallow, and some among thorns as well as on good ground. The stones and thistles that to this day infest Palestinian fields are legendary. Only one element in the parable is unusual, the superabundant harvest in v. 8. Because of the primitive agricultural methods, an average harvest in ancient Palestine was probably no more than seven or eight times the amount of seed sown, and a good harvest probably was about ten.

4:9 As indicated in the comments on v. 3, the command to hear suggests that some do not hear and understand parables. Verse 9 provides an appropriate transition to vv. 10–12. That Jesus spoke what is in v. 9 is not often questioned. The authenticity of v. 9 supports a dominical origin of vv. 10–12, which are often denied to Jesus.

What does the parable teach? Inasmuch as it is often claimed that the explanation in vv. 13–20 comes from the early church and not Jesus,[27] and since the parables are capable of more than one interpretation (cf. Matthew's and Luke's varied use of the parable of the lost sheep), it is important to try to interpret the parable without reference to that explanation. Many suggestions have been made: The abundance of the harvest despite the loss of some seed encourages Christians despite their failures; despite repeated failures the kingdom will come at last; contrary to appearances the kingdom has already come; the parable explains why the gospel was rejected by so many; the parable forces hearers to examine their reactions to the gospel; the parable assures preachers of success despite opposition, to name a few.

The key to the meaning seems to be in v. 8. The emphasis is not on the sowing because the seed is the same in each instance. Therefore the story should not be called the parable of the sower. More emphasis is placed on the different kinds of soil, and even without the explanation in vv. 13–20 one could conclude that the parable describes the different ways in which the gospel is received. Without the explanation, however, one could also conclude that the main point is the abundance of the harvest (note v. 8). The element of time is not present. The parable makes no distinction between the coming of the kingdom in Jesus' day, during any period of missionary endeavor, or at the end of the age. It has come, is coming, and will come. Despite opposition, setback, loss, and rejection, the reign of God is like a superabundant harvest. All kinds of applications may legitimately be made from this basic truth.

4:13–20 Most critical scholars deny that the explanation is from Jesus and attribute it to early Christians, who applied the parable to their own situation. Many objections have been given. One is that by the nature of the case, parables are so clear that Jesus would never have needed to explain them. If, however, the meaning of parables is always self-evident, why are modern scholars with all their critical tools often unable to agree on their meaning? Another is that the explanation allegorizes the parable whereas the parables of Jesus are simple comparisons. This claim has been dealt with in discussing the nature of parables. Furthermore the explanation does not identify the sower or deal in universal truths.

---

[27] It is interesting that few questions have been raised about Mark's accuracy in recounting the parable itself.

Another objection is that the vocabulary of the explanation is that of the Epistles rather than the Gospels and that Semitic features are absent. No doubt in the process of translation from Aramaic to Greek and application of the parable to a slightly different situation there has been some adaptation,[28] but this consideration fails to prove that Jesus offered no explanation or a radically different explanation from the one in vv. 13–20. Still another is that the explanation presupposes several decades of existence of the church and its missionary work and the repeated rejection of its message and that it explains that rejection. In reply, was not the message of Jesus largely rejected from the beginning, and would not his disciples need some explanation for that?

Yet one more objection is that the explanation ignores the eschatological emphasis of the parable and substitutes a psychological and temporal one. But this claim misses the applicability of the parable for any period between the life of Jesus and the consummation of God's kingdom. There is no decisive reason for denying that the substance of the explanation is from Jesus. There may have been adaptation and application between Jesus' pronouncement and Mark's writing, but not invention.

Verse 13 rebukes the disciples. Despite the statement in v. 11, they did not understand in the way they should have. In fact, this is the first *explicit* statement about their lack of understanding (see also 6:51–52; 7:18; 8:17,21; 9:32–33; cf. 4:40–41; 8:33). Verse 14 indicates that the seed is the word (cf. Jas 1:21, "Humbly accept the word planted in you, which can save you"), whereas vv. 15–16,18,20 compare the hearers to the seed. Such fluidity is possible in any kind of symbolic language. The message and its reception are simply two sides of the same coin. The problem is no greater if the explanation goes back to Jesus than if it comes from the early church. The birds of v. 4 are identified with Satan in v. 15. Just as Satan tempted Jesus (1:13), so he tempts those who hear the message, whether from Jesus himself or his heralds.

(2) The Purpose of Parables (4:10–12,21–25)

[10]**When he was alone, the Twelve and the others around him asked him about the parables. [11]He told them, "The secret of the kingdom of God has been given to you. But to those on the outside everything is said in parables [12]so that,**

"'they may be ever seeing but never perceiving,
    and ever hearing but never understanding;
  otherwise they might turn and be forgiven!' . . . "

[21]**He said to them, "Do you bring in a lamp to put it under a bowl or a bed? Instead, don't you put it on its stand? [22]For whatever is hidden is meant to be**

---

[28]For example, it has been pointed out that only in the explanation of this parable is the word "word" used absolutely in the Gospels to mean *the gospel*. Jesus himself may have actually used the word "gospel" or the expression "my words" in Aramaic, which was then translated by the Greek word *logos*. Translation is not an exact science and usually involves some adaptation.

disclosed, and whatever is concealed is meant to be brought out into the open. [23]If anyone has ears to hear, let him hear."

[24]"Consider carefully what you hear," he continued. "With the measure you use, it will be measured to you—and even more. [25]Whoever has will be given more; whoever does not have, even what he has will be taken from him."

Mark was as concerned about the purpose of parables as he was about providing a sampling of them. At two places in the discourse he dealt with the subject.

Verses 10–12 have been denied to Jesus and attributed to the early church as often as vv. 13–20. Many contemporary scholars are convinced that the *one* purpose of parables is to reveal truth, whereas v. 12 seems to indicate that the purpose is to conceal the truth. This conception of purpose is erroneous. Just as parables have many forms, they have many purposes. At this point Mark chose a saying of Jesus that indicates one of them, to veil the truth from those who are profane or indifferent, who could not profit from it, who would only distort it. Others, however, claim that Jesus spoke the words on another occasion and that they originally applied to his entire ministry and not just to his teaching in parables as Mark indicates. This is possible and perhaps even probable.

One factor favoring this view is that in vv. 1,35–36 Jesus was in a boat with a crowd on the shore, whereas in v. 10 he was with a small group of disciples and presumably in a house. That the saying has application to parables, however, should not be questioned. The "parable theory" of vv. 10–12 is simply another aspect of Mark's "messianic secret." The teaching as well as the identity of the Messiah could not be fully understood even by his followers, much less by outsiders, until after his death and resurrection. Throughout Mark's Gospel tension exists between Jesus as revealed and as hidden.

4:10 The expression "others around him" recalls those who were sitting around Jesus in 3:32,34; the expression "those on the outside" (4:11) recalls his mother and brothers, who according to 3:31–32 were outside the house. Although only one parable has been recorded up to this point, the question deals with parables—again suggesting that the account is not chronological or complete.

4:11 The word "secret" ("mystery," NASB) is found in the Gospels only here and in the parallels in Matt 13:11 and Luke 8:10. It appears, however, twenty-one times in Paul's letters and four in Revelation. Paul used it to mean a truth that was not known in the past, that cannot be known apart from divine revelation, and that has recently been revealed by God. This meaning best explains the present passage. The "secret" or better "revealed truth" is that the kingdom of God has drawn near in Jesus Christ. Note the term "kingdom of God" in vv. 26,30. God (implied by the passive voice) revealed the truth to some. Certainly the vast majority of the Jews of Jesus' day did not realize that.

To them everything about Jesus, including his parables, was a riddle. Indeed the word *parabolē* near the end of v. 11 probably means *riddles*. "Those on the outside," however, should not be limited to Jews. The expression includes all unbelievers.

4:12 Some have sought to avoid the conclusion that Jesus used parables to hide the truth by claiming that Mark or someone before him mistranslated Jesus' Aramaic word "so that" rather than "who." This is a possible explanation, but a better one focuses on the meaning of the quotation from Isa 6:9–10. God told the prophet to deliver his message even though it would be rejected. The seeing without perceiving, the hearing without understanding, and the failure to turn and be forgiven (Isaiah wrote "be healed") were the result, not the purpose, of his message. So it was also with the parables of Jesus. Therefore the Greek word *hina* (translated "so that" in the NIV) at the beginning of v. 12 ought to be translated "as a result." This is a well-established meaning. Jesus did not speak in parables for the purpose of withholding truth from anyone; but the result of his parables, the rest of his teaching, and even his miracles was that most did not understand and respond positively. He did speak in parables to provoke thought and invite commitment. Therefore parables are more than mere illustrations. They constitute spiritual tests that separate those who understand and believe from those who do not. Still another possibility is to translate *hina* "that is" (cf. its use in 9:12). This rendering and the translation "as a result" do not differ greatly.

Verses 21–25 contain five or six sayings of Jesus that technically are wisdom sayings dealing with lessons from everyday life but that are easily included under the broad term "parables." One is in each verse, and perhaps there are two in v. 24. Each may have previously circulated independently.[29] If so, Mark brought them together at the present place because of their relevancy to his understanding of the purpose of parables. Verses 10–12 emphasize how parables veil the truth from those who have no appreciation for it; vv. 21–25 emphasize how parables ultimately reveal the truth to those who consider them carefully and understand. The two passages balance each other. Emphasis on one of the ideas to the exclusion of the other will lead to error. Verses 23–25 express a related but different idea, that of the obligation to ponder the meaning of parables and all of Jesus' teachings. Only as one does this will additional understanding be given.

More is involved in vv. 21–25 than the understanding of parables. The idea of understanding Jesus is also present. During his ministry he was not understood even by his disciples. God's intention, however, was not for such

---

[29]Four of the five appear in Luke's account of the parable discourse (8:16–18) but only one of the five in Matthew's account (13:12). All five are found at other places in Matt (5:15; 10:26; 11:15; 7:2; 25:29), and four are found at other places in Luke (11:33; 12:2; 6:38; 19:26).

obscurity to continue indefinitely. After Jesus' death and resurrection his identity and mission became fully apparent.

4:21   The claim of the preceding paragraph can be seen in the Greek text, a literal translation of which is, "The lamp does not come." How can a lamp[30] "come"? Some have tried to explain Mark's term as a Semitism, but the best explanation is that the lamp represents either Jesus[31] as well as the parables with which he taught or the kingdom of God that drew near with his coming. Jesus and the kingdom did not come to be hidden but to be revealed to all. Such revelation, however, could not be made fully until after Jesus' death and resurrection.

4:22   The statement seems to contradict v. 21 by indicating that a lamp may be hidden temporarily. Jesus and the kingdom were in fact concealed temporarily. Jesus was fully revealed following his resurrection, but the kingdom will not be fully realized until the consummation. This verse informs the "messianic secret," indicating that Jesus intended a definite limit on it.

4:23–24   The command in v. 23 varies slightly from the one in v. 9. The substance of the injunction is repeated in v. 24a. Similar statements in Matt 7:2; Luke 6:38 refer to the final judgment. In v. 24b judgment is applied to understanding Jesus' parables, providing a good example of how the early church variously applied Jesus' teachings.

4:25   This verse is both a promise and a warning about understanding the parables. Whoever acquires some understanding and wants more will receive more. Proper understanding will lead to accepting Jesus and entering the kingdom and to more and more blessings from God. Those who have no interest in parables and the kingdom about which they teach will soon find themselves further from it than before they ever heard about it.

(3) The Parable of the Seed Growing Spontaneously (4:26–29)

26He also said, "This is what the kingdom of God is like. A man scatters seed on the ground. 27Night and day, whether he sleeps or gets up, the seed sprouts and grows, though he does not know how. 28All by itself the soil produces grain—first the stalk, then the head, then the full kernel in the head. 29As soon as the grain is ripe, he puts the sickle to it, because the harvest has come."

4:26   This parable is found exclusively in Mark. Though it shares several elements with the earlier parable of the soils—a man scattering seed, the seed, the harvest—the allegorical identifications operative in that parable should not be read into this parable. The parable of the seed growing by itself has its own

---

[30]Ancient lamps consisted of a bowl filled with olive oil and having a spout in which a wick was laid. The KJV translation "candle" is an anachronism because candles were not invented until the Middle Ages.

[31]The presence of the definite article before the word "lamp" supports this interpretation.

unique message to convey. Determining the precise focus of the parable is difficult. The sower plays a minimal role. Furthermore, the seed grows without his effort (or lack of effort) and in a way that is a mystery. The success of the Christian message similarly does not depend upon human effort or understanding—though Christians certainly need to scatter the seed—but upon divine power. It will succeed precisely because God is active. The kingdom cannot be precipitated by revolutionary activity or any other human effort unaided by God. A word of caution is necessary however. The idea of a gradual but inevitable coming of the kingdom of God is not taught by this parable or any other but is a later idea. The end emphasis and perhaps primary focus of the parable is the assurance of the harvest. The harvest almost certainly represents the judgment at the end of the age. Even so the concern is not the condemnation of the wicked (cf. Joel 3:13) but the manifestation of the righteous. Jesus by telling the story—and Mark by recording it—encouraged disciples who were experiencing rejection of their message and frustration at their lack of understanding of God's mysterious purposes that God's kingdom would surely come.

(4) The Parable of the Mustard Seed (4:30–32)

30Again he said, "What shall we say the kingdom of God is like, or what parable shall we use to describe it? 31It is like a mustard seed, which is the smallest seed you plant in the ground. 32Yet when planted, it grows and becomes the largest of all garden plants, with such big branches that the birds of the air can perch in its shade."

4:30–32 Undoubtedly emphasis falls on the contrast between the small beginning and the enormous consummation of the kingdom. The mustard seed was not the smallest seed in Palestine, but it was one of the smaller and was proverbial for smallness. (As usual the Bible does not give a technical or scientific description but a popular one. In doing so the Bible is guilty of no error whatsoever.) Although an herb, the mustard plant could grow to heights of ten to twelve feet and attain a thickness of three or four inches. The difference between the tiny seed and the huge herb that grows from it is an excellent illustration of the difference between the beginning and end of the manifestation of the kingdom of God. Mark and his readers/hearers were much nearer to the beginning than the end. Nor is the greatness of the kingdom readily apparent nineteen centuries later!

Some have questioned, however, whether the growth depicted by the parable is desirable. They have claimed that an abnormally large herb with its branches filled with birds (sometimes symbols of evil) represents an overgrown, apostate, institutional church. Such an interpretation is, however, completely at odds with the meaning of the parables of the soil and the seed and the meaning of the term "kingdom of God." Furthermore, growth is not the main emphasis; contrast between the beginning and the end is the main point of comparison. It is barely possible that the birds represent the inclusion of the Gentiles. In Dan 4:10–12 and Ezek 31:3–14 a tree symbolizes a foreign empire; and birds, those who enjoy its protection. In Ezek 17:22–24 the tree symbolizes restored Israel, and the birds symbolize those who enjoy its blessing.

(5) Conclusion (4:33–34)

33With many similar parables Jesus spoke the word to them, as much as they could understand. 34He did not say anything to them without using a parable. But when he was alone with his own disciples, he explained everything.

4:33–34   Verse 33 implies that Mark presented only a small selection of what Jesus taught. The same is true of the other Gospel writers so that no one of them or all of them together give a complete account of everything that Jesus did or taught (cf. John 20:30–31). Again Mark emphasized the necessity of understanding. A better translation of the last part of v. 33 may be "in a way they could understand." The first sentence in v. 34 applies only to a particular occasion, not to Jesus' entire ministry. It does, however, reflect Mark's view that everything Jesus taught was an enigma to those who were hostile or indifferent.

11. A Collection of Miracle Stories (4:35–5:43)

The four miracle stories in this section may have been brought together before Mark's time. His placement of them immediately after the parable discourse may indicate that Jesus' works vindicated his words. Specifically miracles are signs of the nearness of the kingdom of God, revealing the power of Jesus as the Son of God.

(1) The Stilling of the Storm (4:35–41)

35That day when evening came, he said to his disciples, "Let us go over to the other side." 36Leaving the crowd behind, they took him along, just as he was, in the boat. There were also other boats with him. 37A furious squall came up, and the waves broke over the boat, so that it was nearly swamped. 38Jesus was in the stern, sleeping on a cushion. The disciples woke him and said to him, "Teacher, don't you care if we drown?"

39He got up, rebuked the wind and said to the waves, "Quiet! Be still!" Then the wind died down and it was completely calm.

40He said to his disciples, "Why are you so afraid? Do you still have no faith?"

41They were terrified and asked each other, "Who is this? Even the wind and the waves obey him!"

Most of the miracles of Jesus were healings or exorcisms. Although the miracle in this section involves compassion for human need, as do the preceding, it is the first of two nature miracles in Mark.[32] Some deny the historicity of all miracles, but others accept the healings and deny the nature miracles. Nature miracles are, however, appropriate because they establish Jesus' authority over the inanimate part of creation just as the healings do over the animate part. Such miracles show that God is the Lord of nature as much as he is of individuals. A good case can be made for Mark having received the account from Peter or some other eyewitness from such incidental details as taking Jesus just as he was, the other boats that play no role in the remainder of the story, and Jesus' sleeping on the cushion.

4:35 Why Jesus wanted to go to the other, presumably eastern, side of the lake is not stated. Perhaps it was to escape the crowd, perhaps to expand his ministry.

4:36 The expression "just as he was" probably indicates that he did not go ashore after teaching from the boat (cf. 4:1).

4:37 The Lake of Galilee was—and still is—infamous for sudden squalls. Surrounded by mountains at most points, the lake swirls violently when a strong wind enters. The language may owe something to Jonah 1:4.

4:38 Not a few have compared the sleeping of Jesus and Jonah. It is, however, a mere coincidence and in no way implies that the story is modeled upon that of Jonah or a passage in Psalms, such as 89:9; 106:9; or 107:23–25. Jesus' sleeping does suggest confidence in God (cf. Ps 3:5; 4:8; Prov 3:24). Furthermore Jesus' sleeping is one of many indications in Mark of his humanity. The disciples' question strongly rebukes Jesus and is another example of Mark's candor, which Matt 8:25 and Luke 8:24 tone down. Note Moffatt's rendering: "Teacher, are we to drown, for all you care?" The verse contains the first of twelve times Jesus is addressed or described as "Teacher" (also 5:35; 9:17,38; 10:17,20,35; 12:14,19,32; 13:1; 14:14). The similar term "Rabbi" is used in 9:5 (10:51, "Rabboni" in Greek, but not the NIV); 11:21; 14:45. The verb "to teach" is used with reference to Jesus fifteen times (see the references in the comments on 1:21). Obviously Mark emphasized that Jesus was an authoritative teacher. Even so, it is doubtful that "Teacher" should be treated as a Christological title in the same way that "Son of God" or "Son of Man" are.

4:39 The words translated "rebuked" and "be still" were used in 1:25 with reference to an exorcism. This consideration may imply a demonic element in the storm. In fact the latter word (*pephimōso*) can be translated "be muzzled." If there is any allusion to Jonah, the story shows Jesus' superiority

---

[32]The other in 6:45–52 is also a sea miracle. Perhaps a third miracle ought to be classified as a nature miracle, the cursing of the fig tree in 11:12–14,20–25.

to him. Also the account pictures Jesus as doing what in the Old Testament only God could do (note especially Ps 107:29–30).

4:40 Jesus' response indicates that the disciples should have had faith rather than fear, and he rebuked them for their lack of faith (also in 9:19). Quite inadequate is the view that Jesus spoke of faith in his ability to work miracles. Some commentators have claimed that Jesus was advocating faith in God rather than in himself. No distinction should be made. Certainly Mark understood the meaning to be faith in the saving power of God as revealed in the action of Jesus. Mark likely intended to indicate that faith is more than intellectual assent, that it is trust in a Person. This kind of faith Jesus' original disciples should have had and all subsequent disciples should have.

4:41 The NIV may be right in translating "They were terrified" (similar NASB, GNB). The same Greek expression has that meaning in Jonah 1:10. In such case even after their deliverance the disciples still did not have faith. They still did not understand who Jesus really was. In Mark the mystery of who Jesus is continues until his death and resurrection and even beyond. The last part of the verse, however, seems to require the idea "they were filled with awe" (RSV; similar NRSV, NEB, REB). In this case the disciples' fear stemmed from a real understanding that somehow the divine had met them in this teacher. The use of a different word (*phobon*) from the one in v. 40 (*deilos*) may support this.

The entire story reassured the believers who had already experienced popular abuse and were facing the prospect of official persecution. Although Jesus may not always appear to be present or to care, he will deliver his people who are in various kinds of trouble. Therefore his disciples should never doubt.

(2) The Exorcising of the Demons from the Wild Man of Gerasa (5:1–20)

¹**They went across the lake to the region of the Gerasenes. ²When Jesus got out of the boat, a man with an evil spirit came from the tombs to meet him. ³This man lived in the tombs, and no one could bind him any more, not even with a chain. ⁴For he had often been chained hand and foot, but he tore the chains apart and broke the irons on his feet. No one was strong enough to subdue him. ⁵Night and day among the tombs and in the hills he would cry out and cut himself with stones.**

⁶**When he saw Jesus from a distance, he ran and fell on his knees in front of him. ⁷He shouted at the top of his voice, "What do you want with me, Jesus, Son of the Most High God? Swear to God that you won't torture me!" ⁸For Jesus had said to him, "Come out of this man, you evil spirit!"**

⁹**Then Jesus asked him, "What is your name?"**

"My name is Legion," he replied, "for we are many." ¹⁰And he begged Jesus again and again not to send them out of the area.

¹¹**A large herd of pigs was feeding on the nearby hillside.**

¹²The demons begged Jesus, "Send us among the pigs; allow us to go into them." ¹³He gave them permission, and the evil spirits came out and went into the pigs. The herd, about two thousand in number, rushed down the steep bank into the lake and were drowned.

¹⁴Those tending the pigs ran off and reported this in the town and countryside, and the people went out to see what had happened. ¹⁵When they came to Jesus, they saw the man who had been possessed by the legion of demons, sitting there, dressed and in his right mind; and they were afraid. ¹⁶Those who had seen it told the people what had happened to the demon-possessed man—and told about the pigs as well. ¹⁷Then the people began to plead with Jesus to leave their region.

¹⁸As Jesus was getting into the boat, the man who had been demon-possessed begged to go with him. ¹⁹Jesus did not let him, but said, "Go home to your family and tell them how much the Lord has done for you, and how he has had mercy on you." ²⁰So the man went away and began to tell in the Decapolis how much Jesus had done for him. And all the people were amazed.

This miracle or exorcism narrative reaffirms the power of Jesus over the demonic, as well as anticipates the Gentile mission. The account is the first that is set outside of Palestine (cf. 7:24–8:9).

5:1 New Testament students are immediately confronted with a textual problem involving the location of the miracle. The ancient Greek manuscripts, translations, and quotations of the New Testament vary among "Gerasenes," "Gadarenes," and "Gergesenes." The same variants appear in the parallels in Matt 8:28; Luke 8:26. "Gerasenes" is probably the original in Mark and Luke, "Gadarenes" in Matthew. The well-known city of Gerasa, however, was some thirty-three miles from Lake Galilee, and it is improbable that its territory extended to the lake. Nor could the herdsmen have traveled to the city and back in one day. Matthew and copyists of Mark probably recognized this and changed the reading to "Gadarenes." Gadara was six miles from the lake, and there is strong evidence that its territory extended to it. There are, however, no steep hills or caves along the southeast shore near Gadara, and distance is still a problem.

Origen, who died in A.D. 254 and who was one of the greatest biblical scholars in the ancient church, argued that both of the above are too difficult and suggested that "Gergesenes" was original. He associated the Gergesenes with the Old Testament Girgashites. That the former name is derived from the latter is unlikely, and no town by the name of Gergesa is known. The most likely solution is that Mark wrote "Gerasenes," intending to allude not to the famous city thirty-three miles from the lake but to a village on the eastern shore that existed until recently with the Arabic name Kersa. Kersa is possibly related to the Greek name Gerasa, and there are steep hills and cave-tombs about a mile to the south. If Gerasa is to be identified with Kersa, it was probably in the tetrarchy of Philip (Luke 3:1) but was only a mile or two north of the area known as the Decapolis (v. 20). Uncertainty must remain, however, except for the fact that Mark placed the miracle somewhere on the eastern shore in predominantly Gentile territory.[33]

5:2–5 The demoniac himself probably was a Gentile. "Evil spirit" is literally "unclean spirit." The man was unclean because of the demon, living in the tombs, and living in Gentile territory. The ancients believed that tombs were dwelling places for demons. The description emphasizes the destruction of his personality to the point of insanity by the demons and the ostracism and brutal treatment he had received from the people.

5:6 One cannot help noticing the contrast between the man's wildness in vv. 3–5 and his composure in the presence of Jesus. The composure, however, did not last.

5:7–8 Here the man seemed to speak for himself; elsewhere the demons spoke through him. Inasmuch as he was possessed, no distinction should be made. The demons employed the name and a title of Jesus in a vain attempt to render him ineffective. Just as knowing the name of a demon was thought to assist in its exorcism (cf. v. 9), likewise using the name of the exorcist was thought to hinder him (cf. 1:24; 3:11). The title "Most High God" is sometimes used in the Old Testament by a Gentile to refer to the God of Israel, and that seems to be the case here. Inasmuch as adjuration formulas were usually used by the exorcist, the one here by the possessed person and/or his demon parodies an attempt to gain the upper hand. The word "torture" probably alludes to eternal punishment following the last judgment. Verse 8 is awkward and may be Mark's addition to the story he received from the tradition.

5:9 Jesus turned the tables on the demon by demanding to know its name. A Roman legion consisted of four to six thousand men, but here the word merely refers to a large number ("mob," GNB). That the term alludes to the occupation of Palestine by Roman legions as a few have claimed is very doubtful. Whether the word is a proper name as in the NIV, an arrogant boast, or an attempt to avoid giving the actual name is uncertain. No such proper name is elsewhere attested. No significance should be attached to the fluctuation between the singular and plural; sometimes the demons are looked upon as a whole and sometimes as individuals.

5:10 This statement reflects the widespread association of demons with particular places. At this point the demons acknowledged their defeat but attempted to gain some concession, as also in v. 12.

5:11–13 The presence of the pigs further evidences that the event took place outside of Jewish Palestine. According to Lev 11:7 and Deut 14:8 swine were "unclean" and were not to be eaten. The demons thought they had won

---

[33] Another explanation is that the well-known Gerasa is meant and that the setting by the lake is redactional and due in part to the author's ignorance of Palestinian geography and in part to harmonization with the setting of chap. 4. There is, however, no body of water near Gerasa big enough to drown a herd of pigs.

a concession from Jesus, but the seeming concession led directly to their destruction because they presumably perished with the swine. No attempt should be made to equate the number of pigs with the number of demons. Nor should any attempt be made to rationalize the occurrence, such as claiming that the demoniac frightened the pigs by his paroxysm or that they were startled by the approach of strangers.

Some have seen an ethical and ecological problem in v. 13. This and the withering of the fig tree (11:12–14,20–21) are the only miracles of destruction attributed to Jesus in the canonical Gospels. Part of the problem is the difference in ancient and modern mentality. No first-century Jew would have had any concern for the pigs or the loss incurred by their Gentile owners. Furthermore, Jesus did not command the demons to inhabit them; he permitted them to do so. The destruction of the pigs also had a definite purpose, to dramatically symbolize the ability of Jesus to destroy the demonic in human beings. To say the least, the restoration of the demoniac and the destruction of the demons were more important than the pigs.

5:14–17 No doubt Mark's description of the man in v. 15 pictures conversion. The man's composure doubtless made a more positive impression on Jesus' disciples than on the local residents. Because of their superstition they were terrified by anyone who had such enormous power, and they begged Jesus to go away. Ironically they feared Jesus more than they did the demoniac and cared more for their pigs than for a fellow human being. As important as miracles are in Mark's account, he obviously did not use them to "prove" who Jesus was or to compel faith.

5:18–19 Quite different from the terror of the local people is the attitude of the cured demoniac toward Jesus. Even though Jesus did not grant the request, the clause "to go with him" (literally "that he might be with him," cf. 3:14) indicates the proper desire of every disciple. And v. 19 indicates the proper response of every convert: to tell what Jesus has done for him or her. Arguing over whether the word "Lord" refers to God or Jesus is meaningless. Jesus probably attributed the miracle to God, but those who told the story between the resurrection and the writing of the Gospels no doubt thought primarily in terms of Jesus.

5:20 Mark probably saw in the man the first missionary to the Gentiles and a preview of the Gentile mission that flourished during the quarter century before the writing of his Gospel. The "Decapolis" was a loosely connected group of ten Gentile cities that had been set free from Jewish domination by the Roman general Pompey when he occupied Palestine in 63 B.C.[34]

---

[34] According to Pliny the Elder, *Natural History* 5.18.74, they were Damascus, Philadelphia, Raphana, Scythopolis, Gadara, Hippos, Dios, Pella, Gerasa, and Kathana. Only Scythopolis, the Old Testament Beth-shan, was west of the Jordan. Note especially the references to Gerasa and Gadara, and cf. the comments on v. 1. Furthermore Hippos was only a few miles south of Kersa,

(3) The Raising of Jairus's Daughter (5:21–24a,35–43)

[21]When Jesus had again crossed over by boat to the other side of the lake, a large crowd gathered around him while he was by the lake. [22]Then one of the synagogue rulers, named Jairus, came there. Seeing Jesus, he fell at his feet [23]and pleaded earnestly with him, "My little daughter is dying. Please come and put your hands on her so that she will be healed and live." [24]So Jesus went with him. . . .

[35]While Jesus was still speaking, some men came from the house of Jairus, the synagogue ruler. "Your daughter is dead," they said. "Why bother the teacher any more?"

[36]Ignoring what they said, Jesus told the synagogue ruler, "Don't be afraid; just believe."

[37]He did not let anyone follow him except Peter, James and John the brother of James. [38]When they came to the home of the synagogue ruler, Jesus saw a commotion, with people crying and wailing loudly. [39]He went in and said to them, "Why all this commotion and wailing? The child is not dead but asleep." [40]But they laughed at him.

After he put them all out, he took the child's father and mother and the disciples who were with him, and went in where the child was. [41]He took her by the hand and said to her, "*Talitha koum!*" (which means, "Little girl, I say to you, get up!"). [42]Immediately the girl stood up and walked around (she was twelve years old). At this they were completely astonished. [43]He gave strict orders not to let anyone know about this, and told them to give her something to eat.

It is entirely possible that the healing of the woman with a hemorrhage (vv. 24b–34) took place as Jesus was on his way to raise Jairus's daughter; but because intercalation of one narrative into another is a well-established literary characteristic of Mark (see comments on 3:20 ff.), it is more likely that the two miracles took place at different times and that Mark brought them together because of their common themes and purposes.[35] Topical arrangement is a legitimate literary practice. There is nothing deceptive or unethical about it, nor is it incompatible with a high view of the inspiration of the Bible. It contributes to the appeal and effect of the story. Of course, some editing is necessary especially at the beginning and end of an account that is placed in another context; but the purpose of this is not to deceive but to produce a coherent narrative.

---

which might be significant if it (Kersa) is the Gerasa alluded to in v. 1. Later Ptolemy, *Geography* 5.14.22, added nine other names.

[35]Further evidence for this conclusion may be seen in the fact that the style of the Greek text of vv. 25–34 is different from that of vv. 20–24 and 35–43. Most of the Gospel is characterized by parataxis (the unliterary connection of independent clauses with the conjunction meaning *and*), but 5:25–34 is characterized by hypotaxis (the subordination of one clause to another by various grammatical devices). This implies that the two stories circulated independently prior to Mark's time.

Whereas 4:35–41 displays the power of Jesus over nature and 5:1–20 his power over demons, 5:21–43 emphasizes his power over sickness and death. The major theme in the two miracle stories in 5:21–43 is healing/salvation by faith. Both bring out the compassion of Jesus for those who had a lowly place in Jewish society: two females, one of whom was a child, the other an outcast due to her continuing state of ritual impurity. Jesus did not neglect the needs of a lowly woman to impress an influential religious official. Both incidents show that when human means have failed, God through Jesus can succeed. The juxtaposition of the faith of a humble woman and that of a religious dignitary reinforces the importance of faith. All must have it! Even the number "twelve" (v. 25, "bleeding for twelve years" and v. 42, "twelve years old") and touching (vv. 27–31,41) provide a link between the stories.

5:21 Elsewhere in Mark "the other side" refers to the eastern shore of Lake Galilee, but here it must refer to the western or northern side. Certainly both of the miracles presuppose a location in Jewish Palestine. Capernaum is a possible location. Quite unlike the Gerasenes (v. 17), the Jewish crowd evidently welcomed and followed Jesus (cf. also vv. 30–31).

5:22 Officials of Jewish synagogues included a ruler or president, who had the responsibility for conducting worship and instruction, and the attendant (Luke 4:20), who was in charge of the building and its contents. Both were laymen. Some synagogues had more than one person with the title of ruler (cf. Acts 13:15). A synagogue ruler was an important and highly respected person. This ruler's attitude toward Jesus contrasts sharply with that of some others (cf. Luke 13:14) and the scribes and Pharisees in general. Whether or not he had had previous contact with Jesus, he believed that Jesus could and would heal his daughter.

The words "named Jairus" are omitted by a few textual witnesses of medium quality that often have a longer text than other witnesses. They are also omitted by Matthew (9:18), who was presumably dependent on Mark's account.[36] Outside of the passion narrative, Mark rarely (only 10:46) gave the names of the characters in his story. On the other hand, the textual evidence in favor of the authenticity of the words is very strong; Luke (8:41), who was also dependent upon Mark, has them. A decision is difficult, but the evidence slightly favors the inclusion.

5:23 Healing by the imposition of hands is referred to again in 6:5; 7:32; 8:23,25 and was common in Jewish and pagan circles but not in the Hebrew Bible.[37] The verb translated "healed" elsewhere means *save*. It appears again in vv. 28 and 34. Certainly in v. 34 its meaning borders on salvation in the

---

[36]The Greek text of v. 35 reads, "They came from the [house] of the ruler of the synagogue." The word "Jairus" is supplied there for clarity by the NIV.

[37]It does occur in 2 Kgs 5:11 LXX.

theological sense. In all the miracles of Mark 5, physical healing is a parable of spiritual deliverance.

5:24a This editorial line provides the transition to the account of the healing of the woman with a hemorrhage. The first statement in v. 35 provides the transition back to the healing of Jairus's daughter.

5:35 One gets the impression the friends and/or servants of the ruler were not enthusiastic about his coming to Jesus. Here Mark indicated they rather sarcastically urged him not to bother, or bother with, Jesus any further.

5:36 The first verb can mean either "ignoring" (NIV, RSV), "paid no attention to" (GNB), or "overhearing" (NRSV, NEB, REB, NASB). The question arises whether Jesus rejected the report as false or whether he urged the ruler to believe despite his daughter's death. The matter is tied up with the meaning of the verb "to sleep" in v. 39. If it is a euphemism for death, Jesus was not telling the ruler to believe that his daughter had not died (v. 36). The best explanation is that Jesus overheard what the messengers said and accepted the reality of the child's death but that he refused to accept the finality of death. Though he did not tell the ruler how the crisis would end, Jesus urged him to believe that all would end well. In any event the necessity of faith is emphasized. Mark's account demonstrates the power of Jesus in hopeless situations.

5:37 Peter, James, and John constitute the so-called "inner circle" of the disciples (also at 9:2; 14:33; with the addition of Andrew at 13:3). Jesus' desire for privacy is connected with other miracles (7:33; 8:23).

5:38 The mourners may have been professionals, although some think there had not been time to procure them. The *Mishna* (completed about A.D. 220) quotes Rabbi Judah that for a burial "even the poorest in Israel should hire not less than two flutes and one wailing woman."[38] Of course, the ruler of the synagogue was not likely a poor man.

5:39 The verb "to sleep" could refer to literal sleep or, in this case, the deep sleep of a coma. In such case the child was not dead, and the miracle consisted of bringing her out of the coma—no small feat in itself! The verb is also used metaphorically to refer to death (e.g., John 11:11–14; 1 Cor 15:51; 1 Thess 4:13–15), and that is almost certainly the meaning here. The family and friends were unlikely to mistake a coma for death. Furthermore the verbs translated "get up" in v. 41 and "stood up" in v. 42 are often used with reference to the resurrection of Jesus and of Christians. Almost certainly Mark wanted his readers/hearers to see in the resurrection of the girl a preview of the resurrection of Christians.

5:40 The exclusion of the mourners has nothing to do with the "messianic secret." They were put out because of their unbelief, which contrasts with the

---

[38] *M. Ketub.* 4.4. H. Danby, trans., *The Mishnah* (London: Oxford University Press, 1933).

faith of the father (cf. v. 36).

5:41–42 Touching a corpse made Jesus ritually unclean, but this was of no consequence to him. Mark and the oral tradition before him valued and preserved the Aramaic words Jesus used on this momentous occasion. Four instances of this are in Mark (also 7:34; 14:36; 15:34), more than in any other Gospel and something that may indicate the primitiveness of Mark. Since the return from the Babylonian exile, Aramaic had been the language of the common people in Palestine. Jesus probably did most of his preaching and teaching in Aramaic. Therefore most if not all of his words in the Greek Gospels are a translation, and this fact is part of the reason the Gospels quote Jesus differently. Because Aramaic was not understood by Greek-speaking copyists of Mark's Gospel, the textual witnesses vary in their reading at this point. Mark interpreted the Aramaic by using a Greek word that elsewhere in the New Testament is used in connection with the resurrection of Jesus and Christians (as is also the word "live" in v. 23). The resurrection of the girl is therefore a preview of the resurrection of believers.

5:43 Because secrecy was impossible in this case, v. 43 sometimes has been cited as proof that the "messianic secret" is the invention of Mark and therefore without historical foundation. The statement need imply nothing more than that Jesus asked the parents not to reveal intimate details of the resurrection and to give him time to get away before it became evident the child had been brought back to life so there would be no acclaim in his presence. The final part of the verse serves two purposes: to show Jesus' concern for physical need and to show that the girl really was alive.

(4) The Healing of the Woman with a Hemorrhage (5:24b–34)

A large crowd followed and pressed around him. [25]And a woman was there who had been subject to bleeding for twelve years. [26]She had suffered a great deal under the care of many doctors and had spent all she had, yet instead of getting better she grew worse. [27]When she heard about Jesus, she came up behind him in the crowd and touched his cloak, [28]because she thought, "If I just touch his clothes, I will be healed." [29]Immediately her bleeding stopped and she felt in her body that she was freed from her suffering.

[30]At once Jesus realized that power had gone out from him. He turned around in the crowd and asked, "Who touched my clothes?"

[31]"You see the people crowding against you," his disciples answered, "and yet you can ask, 'Who touched me?' "

[32]But Jesus kept looking around to see who had done it. [33]Then the woman, knowing what had happened to her, came and fell at his feet and, trembling with fear, told him the whole truth. [34]He said to her, "Daughter, your faith has healed you. Go in peace and be freed from your suffering."

5:24b–25 Mark gave no description of the bleeding, but it was probably uterine. If so, it was not only debilitating but rendered the woman religiously unclean so that no pious Jew would have any contact with her (cf. Lev 15:25–30). She had lived as an outcast for 12 years. No doubt Mark recorded the incident to dramatize Jesus' rejection of the concept of ritual uncleanness and to affirm his acceptance of all persons no matter what their status in society.

5:26 The woman probably could not have lived much longer. Therefore Jesus rescued her from approaching death. Mark likely saw in her healing an anticipation of the resurrection of Jairus's daughter. The description of the medical profession was not intended to denigrate[39] but to show how the power of Jesus transcends human limitations.

5:27–28 The woman's determination to touch Jesus' clothing reflects the ancient idea that the power of a person extended to one's clothing (cf. 6:56; Acts 19:11–12) or one's shadow (Acts 5:15).

5:29 Mark's use of tenses is significant. The verbs translated "stopped" and "felt" are aorists, which tense usually reflects a completed action. The verb translated "was freed" (literally "healed," RSV, NRSV, NASB, GNB) is a perfect, which usually depicts the lasting effects of the action.

5:30 The miracle is extraordinary because it was performed without conscious effort on Jesus' part, although he immediately realized what had taken place. On the one hand, Mark may have seen in Jesus' awareness a sign of his deity; on the other, he candidly described the limitations of Jesus' humanity (also v. 32). Although some think Jesus knew all the while who had touched him and asked only to induce the woman to confess publicly her deed, more likely he needed to learn the person's identity. Self-limitation of the earthly Jesus is not incompatible with omniscience of the risen Christ. Mark, perhaps better than any other New Testament writer, realized that. Another purpose of Jesus' question may have been to begin to lead the person to a confession of faith.

5:31 The disciples' sarcastic reply is an example of Markan candor that is omitted by Matthew (cf. 9:20–22) and toned down in Luke (8:45).

5:32–33 The woman may have feared the consequences of defiling a holy man by touching him in her unclean state. She may have feared a rebuke for having delayed Jesus while he was on an important mission. Or she may have been overcome with awe and emotion as a result of all that had happened so quickly. Mark may have set forth her confession as an example of the confession all who have encountered Jesus should make.

5:34 Jesus explained to the woman that she had been healed not through physical touch or any kind of magic but by faith. Again Mark or those before him who transmitted the story chose the perfect tense of the Greek verb meaning *to save* (*sōzō*) to translate Jesus' Aramaic word. That Jesus affirmed not

---

[39] If Luke the physician wrote the Gospel bearing that name, it is nevertheless significant that he probably omitted the statement (cf. Luke 8:43, NIV, but note the variant reading).

only the woman's healing but her spiritual salvation as well is highly probable. He affirmed the permanence of both. He further pronounced the peace of God upon her. The biblical concept of peace does not refer to the absence of war and other kinds of trouble. To the contrary, it is something that can exist even in the midst of conflict. It is a status of wholeness and well-being because of a right relationship with God.

12. The Rejection at Nazareth (6:1–6a)

¹Jesus left there and went to his hometown, accompanied by his disciples. ²When the Sabbath came, he began to teach in the synagogue, and many who heard him were amazed.

"Where did this man get these things?" they asked. "What's this wisdom that has been given him, that he even does miracles! ³Isn't this the carpenter? Isn't this Mary's son and the brother of James, Joseph, Judas and Simon? Aren't his sisters here with us?" And they took offense at him.

⁴Jesus said to them, "Only in his hometown, among his relatives and in his own house is a prophet without honor." ⁵He could not do any miracles there, except lay his hands on a few sick people and heal them. ⁶And he was amazed at their lack of faith.

The misunderstanding and lack of sympathy of Jesus' relatives in 3:21,31 prepares for the present episode. The rejection of Jesus by the people of his hometown stands in stark contrast with his triumphs in the preceding miracle stories. Contrast the faith of the woman and Jairus with the unbelief of the residents of Nazareth. As always Mark was candid and realistic. As important as miracles were in attesting the nearness of the kingdom of God in Jesus, they did not convince all. Mark may have seen in the rejection at Nazareth by some villagers a preview of the rejection at Jerusalem by Jewish officialdom and to a large extent by the whole nation. This account anticipates the all-important passion. The passion itself, however, was a problem for the early church. If in fact Jesus was the Jewish Messiah, why was he rejected as such by his own people? Mark found at least part of the answer in a proverb Jesus quoted (v. 4).

Contrary to the claims of some radical critics that the story is an idealization created by the early church, various items assure its historicity. It is difficult to believe that the early church would have created a story about Jesus being treated so contemptuously by the people of his hometown. The same is true concerning the slur about Mary and James (v. 3), who by the time Mark wrote had become prominent people in the church. The statement in v. 5 about the inability of Jesus is also difficult. Whether Mark's source was Peter is much less certain.

6:1 The word Mark used (*patris*) can mean *hometown* or *homeland*. Here it is undoubtedly the former. There is no question that the reference is to Nazareth. In 1:9 Mark said Jesus went from Nazareth to the Jordan for his baptism. In 1:24; 10:47; and 16:6 he referred to his main character as "Jesus of Nazareth" and in 14:67 as "the Nazarene." Inasmuch as the word can also mean *homeland*, there may also be an allusion to the rejection of Jesus by the entire nation. The reference to the disciples shows that the visit was not a private, family visit but an "official" one of a teacher and his followers.

6:2 Jesus' invitation to speak in the synagogue indicates he had become well-known as a teacher. The word "many" does not imply that a minority was not "amazed" but that a large crowd was present. From what follows, the word "amazed" ("astonished," RSV, NASB; "astounded," NRSV) apparently is used in a negative sense; and most, if not all, of those present were offended by Jesus. The question about the source of Jesus' wisdom and power was prompted in part by the fact that he had not studied with a rabbi and therefore did not have proper credentials. This was Mark's last reference to Jesus' teaching in a synagogue. The synagogue had become a place of rejection (cf. 3:1–6). Later in the narrative the emphasis is placed on teaching in houses (7:17,24; 9:33; 10:10; cf. 6:10).

6:3 The people were also scandalized by Jesus' lowly origin. They found it difficult to believe he was any better than they or his family were. In their opinion he was nothing more than an ordinary craftsman. Their physical knowledge of Jesus prevented them from having a spiritual knowledge of him. Perhaps some of Mark's readers/hearers experienced the same difficulty as they tried to witness to their families and friends.

Deciding whether Mark wrote, "Is not this the carpenter, the son of Mary?" or, "Is not this the son of the carpenter and Mary?" is very difficult. The textual evidence heavily favors the former, which is the reading of the NIV as well as the RSV, NRSV, NASB, NEB, and GNB and the UBS Greek text. It is most unusual, however, to refer to a Jewish man as the son of his mother even if she was a widow.[40] Furthermore Origen (d. 254) insisted that Jesus is nowhere called a carpenter in the Gospels,[41] which implies that none of his manuscripts had the reading that later came to dominate. As a result some have concluded that Mark wrote "son of the carpenter and Mary" and that later scribes changed it to "the carpenter, the son of Mary" in order to add support to belief in the virgin birth.

The textual problem in Mark is not solved by the fact that Matt 13:55 has "son of the carpenter." Matthew may have followed his Markan source, or he may have altered Mark to prevent misunderstanding and offense. The best approach in this instance is to accept the reading that has overwhelming exter-

---

[40]The only biblical examples are Judg 11:1–2 in a bad sense and 1 Sam 26:6; 2 Sam 2:13,18, probably in a good sense. A possible but not very probable explanation for Mark's usage is that it reflects the fact that Joseph was dead.

[41]Origen, *Against Celsus* 6.34.36. Origen was replying to Celsus's accusation that Jesus was an insignificant carpenter.

nal evidence. The reference to Jesus as the son of Mary may reflect rumors that he was illegitimate and may have been a deliberate slur by the townspeople. If so, Mark accurately reported the statement even though it may have been offensive to some of his readers/hearers.[42] As for Origen, he may have forgotten about Mark 6:3, or his manuscripts may already have been assimilated to the Matthean parallel.

The word translated "carpenter" is *tektōn*, which can be observed in the last half of the English word "architect." It could refer to any kind of craftsman: mason, smith, shipbuilder, sculptor, and even physician. The word appears in the New Testament only here and in the parallel in Matt 13:55. It is not certain therefore that Joseph and Jesus were carpenters. That they were was the understanding of the early church.[43] Jews, in contrast to Greeks and Romans, had a high regard for manual labor—the derogatory allusion here notwithstanding. In fact, rabbis were expected to support themselves by a trade and teach without pay. Such was the practice of Paul.

The brothers of Jesus are named only here and in the parallel in Matt 13:55,[44] although they are referred to as a group in all four Gospels; Acts 1:14; and 1 Cor 9:5. James, however, is mentioned elsewhere in Acts 12:17; 15:13; 21:18; 1 Cor 15:7; Gal 1:19; 2:9,12; Jas 1:1 (?); Jude 1 (?). He later became the leader of the Jerusalem church. Judas may be the same person who is mentioned in Jude 1.[45] The sisters are mentioned only here; 3:32 variant reading; and Matt 13:56 (cf. the comments on 3:31–32 on the question of the exact relationship of Jesus and his "brothers" and "sisters").

The word translated "took offense" is *skandalizomai*, a member of the word group from which the English word "scandal" is derived. By the time Mark wrote, this word group was often used to describe the reaction of Jews to Jesus' death (Rom 9:33; 1 Cor 1:23; Gal 5:11). Mark's choice of the word is further evidence that he saw in the event a typical Jewish rejection of Jesus.

6:4 The proverb Jesus cited is found in various forms in Jewish and pagan literature and is a truism. Elsewhere in Mark others referred to Jesus as a prophet (6:15; 8:28). These references are of such nature and number that it is improbable Mark intended "prophet" to be a Christological title. The early church did not use the title because it was inadequate. The words "relatives" and "house" indicate that Jesus' family joined with their neighbors in rejecting his claims (cf. 3:20–21,31–35).

---

[42] In such case the statement is indirect evidence for the virgin birth, although not the kind the church would cherish.

[43] About A.D. 155 Justin, *Dialogue with Trypho* 88, states that Jesus made yokes and ploughs.

[44] Matthew substitutes Joseph for Joses, as does also the NIV in Mark 6:3, but this is a variant form of the same name.

[45] In Greek the names are the same. In English versions it has become the practice to transliterate the word as "Jude" rather than "Judas" in the title and first verse of Jude, probably to distinguish the person from Judas Iscariot.

6:5 This statement about Jesus' inability to do something is one of the most striking instances of Mark's boldness and candor. It is omitted by Luke 4:16–30 and toned down by Matt 13:58. The statement should not trouble contemporary Christians. God and his Son could do anything, but they have chosen to limit themselves in accordance to human response. Even in the present instance Jesus healed a few, perhaps some who did have faith or who were too sick to have an opinion about him. The statement clarifies that Jesus was not the kind of miracle worker whose primary purpose was to impress his viewers.

6:6a Again Mark described the very human reaction of Jesus. The word translated "amazed" in v. 6 (*thaumazō*), like the different Greek word in v. 2, describes a negative reaction of astonishment.

13. The Mission of the Twelve (6:6b–13,30)

Then Jesus went around teaching from village to village. [7]Calling the Twelve to him, he sent them out two by two and gave them authority over evil spirits.

[8]These were his instructions: "Take nothing for the journey except a staff—no bread, no bag, no money in your belts. [9]Wear sandals but not an extra tunic. [10]Whenever you enter a house, stay there until you leave that town. [11]And if any place will not welcome you or listen to you, shake the dust off your feet when you leave, as a testimony against them."

[12]They went out and preached that people should repent.

[13]They drove out many demons and anointed many sick people with oil and healed them. . . .

[30]The apostles gathered around Jesus and reported to him all they had done and taught.

Mark 6:6b–30 provides another example of the author's frequent practice of sandwiching accounts. The account of Herod's reaction to John and Jesus (6:14–29) is inserted into the account of the mission of the Twelve (6:6b–13,30). The mission of the Twelve may have been one way in which Herod came to know about Jesus. Herod's execution of John suggests the extent to which opposition to the Christian mission may extend. The martyrdom of John anticipated that of Jesus. Disciples of Jesus must be prepared for the supreme sacrifice. Furthermore, the two accounts contrast the indulgence and cruelty of a secular ruler with the dedication and sacrifice of the disciples.

Despite several features that obviously had validity only for one occasion,[46] Mark saw in the mission of the Twelve a charter for all subsequent Christian mission. The account emphasizes that all missionary work must be authorized and empowered by Jesus as an extension of his own mission.

---

[46]That Mark recorded items that were no longer relevant in his day is an indication that he faithfully passed on the tradition he received and did not invent the story as some have claimed.

Jesus sent out the Twelve to spread the gospel to more people than he alone could reach and to prepare the disciples for their later mission. No doubt Jesus sent his disciples on one or more preaching tours. The historicity of the account is supported even by one of the criteria of authenticity used by the "new quest" of the historical Jesus, namely that of multiple attestation. According to some analyses at least, an account of a mission of disciples is found not only in Mark but also in Q (the source presumably used in common by Matthew and Luke) and in the special material of both Matthew and Luke.

Here Mark showed the disciples in a good light. His positive treatments of the disciples must always be kept in mind while considering his negative ones.

6:6b The last sentence in v. 6 could go with the preceding, in which case it indicates what Jesus did as a result of his rejection at Nazareth. Or it could go with the following as the paragraphing in the NRSV, NIV, NEB, REB, and GNB indicates. In the latter case the statement provides the background for the disciples' mission. The RSV and NASB avoid the problem by printing the sentence as a separate paragraph.

6:7 The verb translated "sent out" is *apostellō,* which often is used for an official, authorized mission. It is cognate with the noun *apostolos,* which means *apostle* (v. 30), in which the idea of an official mission is even clearer. Going in pairs was a common Jewish practice. Compare Acts 13:1–3; 15:39–40. In the present instance it perhaps establishes the truthfulness of the message (cf. Deut 17:6). It may also tone down individualism and suggest the necessity of teamwork.

6:8–9 The prohibitions suggest the urgency of the mission and the necessity of trusting God for provisions. They make the disciples dependent upon God alone for all their necessities. The bag could have been a beggar's bag, in which case the disciples were not to beg as was common in both the Jewish and Greco-Roman worlds. Or it could have been a knapsack, in which case they were to take nothing with them. The word translated "tunic" usually refers to the inner garment, but here the second tunic may in fact be the outer garment that could double as a blanket. If so, the disciples were to depend upon their hosts for bedding and other necessities.

A problem arises when the conditions of Mark 6:8–9 are compared with those of Matt 10:9–10 and Luke 9:3. Both Matthew and Luke forbid taking a staff, and Matthew forbids taking sandals. Obviously the three accounts relate the same event. The more rigorous conditions of Matthew and Luke more likely reflect what Jesus actually said. Apparently Mark made some minor adaptations to make the conditions understandable to his Roman readers/hearers or perhaps to recall the Exodus (cf. Exod 12:11).[47]

---

[47] Another explanation is that different kinds of staffs and different kinds of sandals were in mind. Although two different Greek words meaning *sandals* are used, they are synonyms. Also the

6:10 The purpose of this injunction was to prevent the disciples from moving if later they found better accommodations. They were to be content with their situation.

Obviously the early church did not understand the provisions in vv. 8–10 to be binding upon later missionaries. There is no indication that Paul observed them, though he perhaps contended with persons who felt he had departed from apostolic practice by not relying on hospitality (2 Cor 11:7–12; 12:13). Whereas the provision of this verse implies an extended stay, *Didache* 11.5 (ca. A.D. 100) labels one who stays more than two days a false prophet. Nevertheless some basic mission principles have relevance for all times, such as simplicity of life-style and contentment with provisions. Many modern ministers in all their affluence have forgotten these things.

6:11 Jews returning to the Holy Land removed foreign dust from their shoes and clothing in order not to defile the land. What Jesus prescribed was a symbolic action in the tradition of the ancient prophets to indicate first a warning and then judgment if rejection of the message and messengers persisted. The action may also symbolize that a town which rejected the message of the disciples was not a part of the true Israel. Later missionaries took this injunction literally (Acts 13:51; 18:6). The last half of the verse in the KJV and NKJV ("it will be more tolerable for Sodom and Gomorrah") is a scribal assimilation to Matt 10:15 and has no claim to originality.

6:12 Here the promise of 1:17 begins to be fulfilled. The message of the disciples was similar to that of John the Baptist (1:4) and the same as a part of that of Jesus (1:15). It may be significant that Mark, unlike Matt 10:7 and Luke 9:2, did not indicate they proclaimed the nearness of the kingdom. That he reserved for Jesus. In his view the disciples could not understand and preach the full gospel until after the passion and resurrection.

6:13 The expulsion of demons is clearly distinguishable from ordinary healings. Oil (usually olive oil) was often used in biblical times as a medicine (cf. Luke 10:34), but here the anointing probably serves as a symbol of the presence, grace, and power of God. Anointing the sick is elsewhere prescribed only in Jas 5:14.

6:30 Mark did not indicate whether the mission was successful. Presumably it was. This verse does indicate that the disciples also taught. The word "apostles" probably is used in its nontechnical sense of missionaries, although Mark's readers/hearers may have thought of the office of apostle. Mark may have used "apostles" rather than "disciples" because the latter was used in the preceding verse with reference to the followers of John. (See also the comments on 3:14.)

---

word meaning *staff* is the same in the three accounts. Still another is that Matthew and Luke meant *extra* staffs and sandals. If so, why did they not say that? No explanation is fully satisfactory.

14. The Reaction of Herod to Jesus and John (6:14–29)

[14]King Herod heard about this, for Jesus' name had become well known. Some were saying, "John the Baptist has been raised from the dead, and that is why miraculous powers are at work in him."

[15]Others said, "He is Elijah."

And still others claimed, "He is a prophet, like one of the prophets of long ago."

[16]But when Herod heard this, he said, "John, the man I beheaded, has been raised from the dead!"

[17]For Herod himself had given orders to have John arrested, and he had him bound and put in prison. He did this because of Herodias, his brother Philip's wife, whom he had married. [18]For John had been saying to Herod, "It is not lawful for you to have your brother's wife." [19]So Herodias nursed a grudge against John and wanted to kill him. But she was not able to, [20]because Herod feared John and protected him, knowing him to be a righteous and holy man. When Herod heard John, he was greatly puzzled; yet he liked to listen to him.

[21]Finally the opportune time came. On his birthday Herod gave a banquet for his high officials and military commanders and the leading men of Galilee. [22]When the daughter of Herodias came in and danced, she pleased Herod and his dinner guests.

The king said to the girl, "Ask me for anything you want, and I'll give it to you." [23]And he promised her with an oath, "Whatever you ask I will give you, up to half my kingdom."

[24]She went out and said to her mother, "What shall I ask for?"

"The head of John the Baptist," she answered.

[25]At once the girl hurried in to the king with the request: "I want you to give me right now the head of John the Baptist on a platter."

[26]The king was greatly distressed, but because of his oaths and his dinner guests, he did not want to refuse her. [27]So he immediately sent an executioner with orders to bring John's head. The man went, beheaded John in the prison, [28]and brought back his head on a platter. He presented it to the girl, and she gave it to her mother. [29]On hearing of this, John's disciples came and took his body and laid it in a tomb.

This section consists of a lengthy account of the death of the Baptist (vv. 17–29) prefaced by a brief statement of Herod's fears about Jesus and popular opinions of Jesus (vv. 14–16). This and 1:4–8 are the only accounts in Mark that are not about Jesus. Mark devoted much more space to the death of John the Baptist than he did to his ministry (1:4–8) and more than any other Gospel. John's death was significant to Mark as a preview of the death of Jesus. John, like Jesus, was executed by a secular ruler. Herod, like Pilate, did not want to execute his prisoner but caved in to pressure from others. Herodias, like the chief priests, schemed to bring about the execution. John's disciples, like Joseph of Arimathea, tenderly buried the body of their leader.

The account is not extraneous but crucial. Other possible reasons for recording John's death include: (1) warning Mark's readers/hearers of the danger involved in proclaiming the word of God, (2) encouraging them by showing that no opposition can destroy the kingdom of God, and (3) suggesting that just as the mission of the Twelve followed the death of the Baptist—for certainly John was dead by this point in the Markan narrative—so also the mission of the church must follow the death of Jesus.

The Herod of this account was Herod Antipas, the tetrarch[48] of Galilee and Perea (the land to the east of the Jordan) from 4 B.C. to A.D. 39. He must be distinguished from Herod the Great, his father, who was the Roman client-king of all Palestine from 40–4 B.C. (Matt 2; Luke 1:5), and from Herod Agrippa I, who was client-king of part of Palestine from A.D. 37 and all of Palestine from A.D. 41–44 (cf. Acts 12).

6:14 Nothing in the Greek corresponds to "about this" in the NIV. Mark did not indicate what Herod heard. Accounts of the deeds of Jesus, the mission of the Twelve, or both are possible. Most textual witnesses read "he [i.e., Herod] was saying" rather than "some [literally "they"] were saying," but what follows were popular opinions of Jesus, requiring the plural (supported by the best manuscript of Mark plus a few other witnesses of medium value). According to one view Jesus was John raised from the dead. Neither the Gospels nor Josephus ascribes miracles to John, suggesting the word *dynameis* refers to supernatural power in general rather than miracles as such. Alternately, miraculous powers were believed to be at work precisely because John had returned from the dead. The association of John with Elijah perhaps suggests that he performed miracles (though cf. John 10:41).

6:15 According to a second view Jesus was Elijah. Mark later (9:11–13) implied that John and not Jesus was the Elijah of Mal 4:5. Still another view regarded Jesus as one of the Israelite prophets, although not necessarily *the* prophet of Deut 18:15,18–19. For Mark none of these views was satisfactory, but they were superior to those of Jesus' family and their friends (6:2–3). Nevertheless the time for the revelation of the true identity of Jesus had not come.

6:16 Herod believed Jesus was indeed John the Baptist, raised from the dead. The statement about the beheading of John introduces the account of his death.

6:17 Herodias was the daughter of Aristobulus, the son of Herod the Great, and the niece of Antipas. On a trip to Rome, Herod had fallen in love

---

[48]Literally "ruler of a fourth part." Actually he ruled by appointment of Rome more than a fourth of Palestine. The term designates the ruler of only a part of a land whatever the actual proportion. It is a less imposing title than "king." Mark referred to him as "king" in vv. 14,22 (in the Greek text but not the NIV), 25–27. Such a designation is not an error but merely reflects popular usage.

with her. In order to marry her he had divorced his first wife, the daughter of Aretas IV, the king of Nabatea to the east and south of Perea, and persuaded Herodias to divorce her husband. Mark said that this husband's name was Philip; Josephus identified her husband by the family name Herod.[49] Mark did not intend to say that Herodias was the wife of Philip the tetrarch (Luke 3:1), for Josephus indicated that this Philip was married to Salome, the daughter of Herodias.[50]

Virtually every son of Herod the Great had "Herod" as part of his name. The full name of the first husband of Herodias might have been Herod Philip, although this is not attested. Because this alleged person and Philip the tetrarch had different mothers, they could have had the same names. Josephus further indicated that Herod arrested John in fear that John's popularity might lead to a revolt.[51] Mark's reason does not contradict Josephus. Both could well have been true. Mark chose the one most germane to his purpose; Josephus, to his.

6:18 John's condemnation of the union was based on Lev 18:16; 20:21. Therefore Mark pictured the Baptist as affirming the law.

6:19 Some commentators have imagined a similarity between Herodias and Jezebel and between Herod and Ahab (1 Kgs 19:2; 21:4ff.). The only similarity is that Herodias and Jezebel plotted to kill someone while their husbands hesitated.

6:20–21 The KJV and NKJV follow the majority of medieval manuscripts in reading "he did many things" rather than "he was greatly puzzled." Herod is pictured as superstitiously fearing John because he knew that John's life was holy and his was wicked. As a result Herodias could not accomplish her purpose at first (v. 19) but had to wait for an opportune time (v. 21). Herod's hesitation anticipates that of Pilate (15:6–14).

6:22 The NIV and most English translations obscure a serious textual problem. Instead of "the daughter of Herodias herself" (the NIV does not translate the word meaning *herself*), a few very important Greek manuscripts have "his daughter Herodias." Most principles of textual criticism point to the originality of this reading, but it is intolerable. Mark scarcely thought that the girl was Herod's daughter or that her name was the same as her mother's. In vv. 24,28 the girl is referred to as Herodias's daughter, and Josephus said that her name was Salome,[52] though for Josephus, Salome was the former wife, not the daughter, of Herod Philip. Apparently one of the earliest copyists of

---

[49] Josephus, *Antiquities* 18.5.1,4.

[50] Josephus, *Antiquities* 18.5.4. The name "Philip" is omitted by one good and one poor manuscript of Mark, by some textual witnesses of medium value in Matt 14:3, and by Luke 3:19—no doubt because of the historical problem.

[51] Josephus, *Antiquities* 18.5.2.

[52] Josephus, *Antiquities* 18.5.4.

Mark accidentally substituted the masculine pronoun for the feminine one, which differs by only two letters. This mistake was corrected by most but not all later scribes. Critics have likewise denied the historicity of Mark's account because of the improbability of a princess performing a lewd dance in the presence of her step-father and his drunken guests. The depravity of the Herodian family, however, is well documented. The mother was determined to "get" John at all costs. Herod may have been too drunk to object. That she so much pleased the guests may have been due to the fact that she was a princess and not a common, professional dancer.

6:23 The banquet description has something in common with Esth 1, and Herod's vow recalls Esth 5:3,6; 7:2. Mark may have written the story by employing some terminology from Esther and even 1 Kings (cf. comments on v. 19), but this in no way suggests he invented the story.

6:24–28 Josephus stated that John was imprisoned and executed at Machaerus,[53] a fortress in southern Perea. Mark did not locate the banquet, but the most natural place would be Herod's capital, Tiberias, on the western shore of Lake Galilee, which was about eighty miles from Machaerus. Mark left the impression that the execution took place soon after the order, which of course could not be if the banquet was at Tiberias and the execution at Machaerus. There is, however, no serious problem. The banquet may have been at Machaerus rather than Tiberias, or Mark may have "telescoped" the account to save space.

The execution of John was not the only occasion when Herodias caused trouble for her husband. In A.D. 36 Aretas IV went to war with Herod to avenge the insult to his daughter by Herod's divorcing her. It was necessary for the governor of Syria to rescue Herod. Then in A.D. 39 Herodias, jealous that her brother Herod Agrippa I had been given part of Palestine and the title of king, persuaded her husband to ask for that title. Instead the emperor Gaius Caligula deposed and exiled him for supposedly plotting to secure independence.[54] To her credit Herodias followed him into exile. Nor was John's death the end of the Baptist movement. Paul and his assistants were confronted with disciples of John in the fifties (Acts 18:24–19:7).

6:29 The noble deed of John's disciples is a preview of that of Joseph of Arimathea (15:43–46). John was the forerunner of Jesus in death as well as ministry.

15. The Feeding of the Five Thousand (6:31–44)

31Then, because so many people were coming and going that they did not even have a chance to eat, he said to them, "Come with me by yourselves to a quiet place and get some rest."

---

[53] Josephus, *Antiquities* 18.5.2.
[54] Herod Agrippa I provided the evidence and received Antipas's territory as a result.

[32]So they went away by themselves in a boat to a solitary place. [33]But many who saw them leaving recognized them and ran on foot from all the towns and got there ahead of them. [34]When Jesus landed and saw a large crowd, he had compassion on them, because they were like sheep without a shepherd. So he began teaching them many things.

[35]By this time it was late in the day, so his disciples came to him. "This is a remote place," they said, "and it's already very late. [36]Send the people away so they can go to the surrounding countryside and villages and buy themselves something to eat."

[37]But he answered, "You give them something to eat."

They said to him, "That would take eight months of a man's wages! Are we to go and spend that much on bread and give it to them to eat?"

[38]"How many loaves do you have?" he asked. "Go and see."

When they found out, they said, "Five—and two fish."

[39]Then Jesus directed them to have all the people sit down in groups on the green grass. [40]So they sat down in groups of hundreds and fifties. [41]Taking the five loaves and the two fish and looking up to heaven, he gave thanks and broke the loaves. Then he gave them to his disciples to set before the people. He also divided the two fish among them all. [42]They all ate and were satisfied, [43]and the disciples picked up twelve basketfuls of broken pieces of bread and fish. [44]The number of the men who had eaten was five thousand.

The feeding of the five thousand is the only miracle of Jesus recorded by all four Gospels (also Matt 14:13–21; Luke 9:10–17; John 6:1–14). Furthermore, Mark 8:1–10 and Matt 15:32–39 record a feeding of four thousand. These six accounts of a feeding of a multitude show how important the early church considered them to be.[55] The miracle dramatically sets forth Jesus as a man of great compassion for human needs and as the supplier of such needs when ordinary resources are insufficient. It emphasizes the authority of Jesus in the natural world. Furthermore, all of the Evangelists may have seen the miracle as a preview of the institution of the Lord's Supper (see the comments on 6:41) and of the future messianic banquet when the kingdom is fully established.

Several elements in Mark's account of the feeding of the five thousand suggest its significance for him. The lengthy introduction (vv. 31–34) and the subsequent references (6:52; 8:17–21) to the failure of the disciples to understand the meaning do so. Mark specifically emphasized that the feeding took place in a deserted place (vv. 31–32,35, where the NIV translates the same Greek word "quiet," "solitary," and "remote," respectively).[56] As already observed in the comments on 1:4, in the Old Testament the desert was the place where God met, tested, and blessed his people. Specially important was

---

[55]Whether there was one feeding or two will be considered in connection with 8:1–10.

[56]The word *erēmos* is both a noun and an adjective and designates not so much a dry, barren place as an uninhabited one.

the experience of Israel in the wilderness following the Exodus. After the testing involved in that experience, "rest" was promised. Note how Mark introduced that idea (v. 31). Also the "sheep without a shepherd" (v. 34) recalls Moses' description of Israel in Num 27:17; and the "hundreds and fifties" of v. 40, the organization of Israel in Exod 18:21, not to mention the resemblance between the loaves and the manna. The literal rest in the desert and later in the promised land following the Exodus did not satisfy, and the prophets and psalmists began to look forward to a better rest in the messianic age.[57] This idea is developed most fully in Heb 3:7–4:13, but it is in the present passage in Mark also. Mark saw in Jesus' feeding of the five thousand an eschatological Moses giving perfect rest to and supplying all the needs of his people. The feeding anticipates the messianic banquet at the end of the age. The kingdom is at hand. The miracle as such is not as important for Mark as what it reveals about Jesus. Note that he did not record any amazement of the people.

The prophet Elisha performed a similar miracle according to 2 Kgs 4:42–44. In fact, Mark's wording owes something to this account and possibly 1 Kgs 17:9–16. Mark may also have seen in the event Jesus as the fulfillment of the law and the prophets.

6:31 The coming and going of so many people may suggest the success of the mission of the Twelve. Even in such a matter as withdrawal for rest, Jesus is pictured as concerned with human need.

6:32–33 Mark gave no indication of where they went. Luke 9:10, which makes no mention of a lonely place, indicates that it was Bethsaida (see comments on v. 45). For the crowd to have kept up with them, they must not have crossed the entire lake but only one of its corners.

6:34 Instead of being angry with the people for preventing the much needed rest, Jesus had "compassion" on them. The word is used in the New Testament only by or about Jesus (e.g., Matt 18:27; Luke 10:33; 15:20). It suggests something more than mere pity; it suggests actual help. Here the compassion is not just for physical need but for lostness. "Sheep without a shepherd" is an Old Testament picture of Israel without spiritual leadership (Num 27:17; 1 Kgs 22:17; Ezek 34:5). Jesus is pictured as the Good Shepherd who feeds the new Israel (cf. Ezek 34:23; Jer 23:4). First he "fed" the crowd with his teaching. Mark frequently emphasized that Jesus taught.

6:35–37 The mention of a "remote place" and "bread" suggests the giving of the manna in the desert (Exod 16) and the idea that Jesus will provide for the needs of his people. Again the disciples are pictured as not understanding. As usual the disrespectful answer in v. 37 is omitted by Matthew and Luke. The Greek text says "two hundred denarii worth of bread" (RSV,

---

[57] Isa 63:14 in context; Jer 31:2 in context; Ps 95:7–11.

NRSV). A denarius was a day's wage for an agricultural worker (cf. Matt 20:2). Therefore two hundred denarii was about "eight months of a man's wages" (NIV).

6:38 The two loaves were much smaller and flatter than modern loaves. The fish were no doubt dried and salted.

6:39 The "green grass" has often been thought to indicate that the miracle took place in the spring about Passover time—the only time when there is much grass in Palestine. If so, it must have been about a year before the Passover during which Jesus died. The grass may be part of the wilderness motif and may suggest the transformation of the desert into a garden, it may reflect the idea of Jesus as shepherd of God's people (Ps 23:2), or it may even suggest the messianic age.

6:40 The sitting down in groups may reflect the groupings of Exod 18:25 and may suggest the gathering and ordering of God's people in the last days.

6:41 The similarity of the terminology with that of the institution of the Lord's Supper in 14:22 is unmistakable: "taking . . . gave thanks . . . broke . . . gave." Yet these were part of common Jewish meals in which the husband/father gave thanks for the bread, broke it, and distributed it to the family members. There is no reference to wine. Fish and leftovers have no place in the Lord's Supper. Some, in trying to eliminate the miraculous, have claimed that only tiny portions were distributed as in a sacramental meal, but vv. 42–43 make this impossible.[58] Certainly neither the disciples nor the crowd saw any sacramental significance at the time. Only in reflecting on the event was the church to see a faint preview of the Eucharist.

6:42 Mark probably wanted his readers/hearers to think in terms of something more than physical satisfaction from all that Jesus gives.

6:43 The number "twelve" is that of the tribes of Israel. Mark probably saw in the twelve basketfuls of fragments Christ's superabundant provision for his own people Israel. Such abundance suggests the dawn of the messianic age. Compare 2 Kgs 4:42–44. Any allusion to Elisha here presents Jesus as one who is greater than he.

6:44 The word translated "men" means *males* and not *human beings*. Matt 14:21 makes this clear by adding "besides women and children."

---

[58]Other explanations include the claims that Jesus persuaded those who had provisions to share with those who did not and that the numbers were exaggerated in the course of oral transmission. With reference to the first, it is clear that the food came from the disciples and not the crowd. With reference to the second, even if the size of the crowd was exaggerated and the number of loaves and fish reduced, Jesus and the disciples could not have had enough to feed even fifty people. There is no question that Mark intended to describe a great miracle. The modern reader can of course reject the historicity of this particular miracle or all miracles. It may well be true, however, that only the disciples were aware of the miraculous multiplication. This may be why there was no amazement on the part of the crowd.

Considering that even the largest towns in the vicinity (e.g., Capernaum, Bethsaida, and Chorazin) probably were no more than one to three thousand in population, "five thousand" men plus women and children was a huge crowd. It shows how popular Jesus was. Popularity and commitment, however, have little in common.

16. The Walking on the Lake (6:45–52)

[45]Immediately Jesus made his disciples get into the boat and go on ahead of him to Bethsaida, while he dismissed the crowd. [46]After leaving them, he went up on a mountainside to pray.

[47]When evening came, the boat was in the middle of the lake, and he was alone on land. [48]He saw the disciples straining at the oars, because the wind was against them. About the fourth watch of the night he went out to them, walking on the lake. He was about to pass by them, [49]but when they saw him walking on the lake, they thought he was a ghost. They cried out, [50]because they all saw him and were terrified.

Immediately he spoke to them and said, "Take courage! It is I. Don't be afraid." [51]Then he climbed into the boat with them, and the wind died down. They were completely amazed, [52]for they had not understood about the loaves; their hearts were hardened.

In Matthew and John as well as Mark, the walking on the lake immediately follows the feeding of the five thousand. (Luke did not record the walking on the water.) This may indicate that the stories had been associated prior to the time of the writing of the Gospels and even that the events actually took place in succession. Whether these things are true, Mark so closely associated the two as to view them as complementary. The lake miracle also revealed that Jesus was the powerful Son of God. Instead of revealing him as the provider of the necessities for physical and spiritual life, it reveals him as the one who delivers his people from physical and spiritual danger (cf. the comments on vv. 48,50).

Some have claimed that the present narrative is simply a variant account of the same event that is recorded in 4:35–41, but the two have little in common except that a storm was stilled. Others have claimed that during the course of transmission miraculous details were added to a story of a crossing in a storm. Others have claimed that Jesus walked *beside*, not *on*, the lake (the Greek of v. 48 will bear that meaning). Still others have claimed that an account of a resurrection appearance was modified in the course of transmission until it took the form of the present story, but the close connection with the preceding miracle rules that out. Mark unquestionably described a miracle.

6:45–46 Why Jesus "made [or better "compelled"] his disciples to get into the boat" and depart Mark did not say. Probably it was to prevent them from getting involved in a messianic movement. For the same reason, he sent the crowd away. (John 6:14–15 explicitly states that the crowd recognized Jesus as the promised prophet and wanted to proclaim him as king.) He then prayed to strengthen himself against yielding to popular acclaim (cf. 1:35; 14:32–41).

The exact location of "Bethsaida" and whether it is identical with Bethsaida Julius, which was built by Philip the tetrarch, is uncertain. Josephus stated that Philip transformed a lakeside village in Gaulanitis just to the east of the Jordan River into a city,[59] but the Gospel accounts of the crossing of the lake and the statement that Philip was from Bethsaida in Galilee (John 12:21; cf. 1:44) seem to require a location on the western shore. Most geographers think the foundation of Philip was about two miles north of the fishing village but still on the east side of the Jordan. They point to traces of an aqueduct and Roman road connecting them. Neither site has been excavated, however. No solution is possible on the basis of present knowledge.

Strangely v. 53 states that "when they had crossed over, they landed at Gennesaret," not Bethsaida. An arrival at Bethsaida is recorded in 8:22, but that seems to be another occasion.

6:47   The site of the feeding is unknown, but it also was somewhere along the northern shore. Therefore if the expression "in the middle of the lake" is to be taken literally, the boat must have been blown well to the south by a strong north wind.

6:48   By stating that Jesus "saw the disciples" far out on the lake on a stormy night, Mark probably indicated a miracle. Here and in 13:35 Mark adopted the Roman reckoning of time. (The Jews thought in terms of three watches.) The Roman watches were from 6:00 to 9:00, from 9:00 to midnight, from midnight to 3:00, and from 3:00 to 6:00. Therefore Jesus appeared to the disciples sometime between 3:00 and 6:00 a.m. They apparently had been battling the elements all night.

Job 9:8 and 38:16 picture God as one who walks on water. That Jesus did so suggests that he performed divine functions. The preposition translated "on" in vv. 48–49 can also mean *beside*, but that cannot be the case here because "on the lake" is parallel to "on the land" in v. 47. Nor will a rationalistic explanation suffice, e.g., the water was very shallow. In such case the boat would have gotten stuck.

The statement that "he was about to pass by them" ("intended to," NASB, NRSV) is perplexing. The Greek reads literally, "He wanted to pass by them." It may reflect nothing more than the disciples' impression at the time, but more likely the verb "pass by" should be taken in the sense of "pass before" or "pass in view of" rather than "go beyond" (cf. Exod 33:19,22; 34:6; 1 Kgs 19:11). What Mark described was a theophany, or rather a Christophany. Jesus

---

[59] Josephus, *Antiquities* 18.2.1; *War* 2.9.1.

revealed himself to the disciples, but their unbelief and terror prevented their comprehension.

6:49–50a The identification of Jesus as a ghost (*phantasma*), the crying out, the terror, and the amazement (v. 51) are further indications of the disciples' unbelief and misunderstanding (see v. 52).

6:50b "It is I" may be nothing more than a statement of identification, but more likely it alludes to the revelation formula of Exod 3:14 (cf. Isa 43:25; 48:12; 51:12; in fact, 51:9–16 provides interesting background for the miracle).

6:51 This verse suggests a third miracle took place. Some think Mark combined two originally independent miracle stories. In any event Mark probably recorded another instance (cf. 4:39) of a stilling of a storm to reassure his church that Jesus could give them peace in their troubles.

6:52 Mark's point was that if the disciples had seen in the miracle of the loaves and fish an indication of the identity of Jesus rather than a mere miracle of multiplication of food, they would have recognized him when he came to them on the water for the purpose of revealing himself. This verse contains one of the harshest statements about the disciples' lack of understanding. Even so they were still followers of Jesus and not enemies. This is Markan irony at its boldest.

17. The Healings at Gennesaret (6:53–56)

53When they had crossed over, they landed at Gennesaret and anchored there. 54As soon as they got out of the boat, people recognized Jesus. 55They ran throughout that whole region and carried the sick on mats to wherever they heard he was. 56And wherever he went—into villages, towns or countryside—they placed the sick in the marketplaces. They begged him to let them touch even the edge of his cloak, and all who touched him were healed.

The passage is a Markan summary of Jesus' activity during the period before he departed from Galilee (cf. the summaries in 1:32–34; 3:7–12).

6:53 Gennesaret, also called Gennesar,[60] is a fertile plain about one mile wide and three miles long at the northwest corner of Lake Galilee. There may have been a village by the same name, but there is no evidence for that. Why the boat came to Gennesaret rather than Bethsaida is not explained, but Mark's location of the landing has led some to conjecture the existence of another Bethsaida on the northwestern shore.

6:54 Mark deliberately contrasted the recognition of the crowds and the failure of the disciples to recognize Jesus.

---

[60] According to a variant reading with fair support; 1 Macc 11:67, KJV; and Josephus, *Antiquities* 13.5.7; 18.2.1; *War* 3.10.7.

6:55–56 Some have tried to see magic in the touching of Jesus' garments, but the statement needs to be read in light of 5:25–34, where faith was the cause of the healing of the woman who touched Jesus' garments. The "edge of his cloak" probably was the tassel that pious Jews wore in accordance with Num 15:38–41 and Deut 22:12. The word translated "healed" is again the one often translated "saved." Mark probably saw in physical healing a sign of spiritual healing.

18. Disputes over Scribal Tradition (7:1–23)

Mark brought together the three accounts in this section because of their common theme: Jesus' rejection of the scribal/oral interpretation of the law. Specifically the first and third accounts deal with ritual defilement. The adjective "unclean" appears in vv. 2,5, and the cognate verb "make unclean" or "defile" (RSV, NRSV, NASB, NEB, REB) appears in vv. 15,18,20,23. The second account concerns a scribal device for circumventing a legitimate requirement of the Mosaic/written law. Mark previously had shown how Jesus rejected the scribal prohibition of association with outcasts (2:15–17), requirement of fasting (2:18–22), and restrictions on the observance of the Sabbath (2:23–3:6).

Although the major concern of the section is that Jesus rejected the oral interpretation of the written law, something more appears in the third account (vv. 14–23). Jesus seems to have rejected one aspect of the Mosaic law, that of ritual cleanness. The early church struggled with what should be its attitude toward the Mosaic law in general and food laws in particular, and this was a reason for Mark's treatment of the subject.

Mark probably intended this section on scribal tradition as a transition and as an introduction to Jesus' ministry to Gentiles beyond the traditional boundaries of Palestine (7:24–8:10). With the stranglehold of Jewish tradition broken, the gospel could go out to all people; and Christianity could become a universal religion.

Mark recorded these accounts because they were relevant to his church. He and the Gentile Christians in Rome were likely still in dialogue with Jews and Jewish Christians. They needed an authoritative word of Jesus about the matters that divided them from Jews and Jewish Christians.

(1) Concerning Unwashed Hands (7:1–8)

[1]The Pharisees and some of the teachers of the law who had come from Jerusalem gathered around Jesus and [2]saw some of his disciples eating food with hands that were "unclean," that is, unwashed. [3](The Pharisees and all the Jews do not eat unless they give their hands a ceremonial washing, holding to the tradition of the elders. [4]When they come from the marketplace they do not eat unless they

wash. And they observe many other traditions, such as the washing of cups, pitchers and kettles.)

⁵So the Pharisees and teachers of the law asked Jesus, "Why don't your disciples live according to the tradition of the elders instead of eating their food with 'unclean' hands?"

⁶He replied, "Isaiah was right when he prophesied about you hypocrites; as it is written:

> " 'These people honor me with their lips,
>   but their hearts are far from me.
> ⁷They worship me in vain;
>   their teachings are but rules taught by men.'

⁸You have let go of the commands of God and are holding on to the traditions of men."

This and the following account are what some scholars call pronouncement stories. The pronouncements of Jesus in vv. 6–8,13 are the most important parts of these passages. A reason for recording the incident was to justify Christian nonobservance of Jewish rites.

7:1 On the identity and the relationship of the "Pharisees and . . . the teachers of the law" ("scribes," RSV, NRSV, NASB, REB; "doctors of the law," NEB) see the comments on 1:22 and 2:16. Both of these groups were centered in Jerusalem, and several times Mark pictured them as going to Galilee to investigate Jesus (also 3:22).

7:2 The scribes and Pharisees were not concerned with hygiene but with ritual purity. Mark clarified that by explaining the word "unclean" for his Gentile readers who were not familiar with Jewish practices. In classical Greek the word translated "unclean" meant *public* as opposed to *private*, and that meaning is found in the LXX (the Septuagint, the Greek translation of the Hebrew Old Testament). In 1 Macc 1:47,62, however, it means *ritually unclean*, and that is certainly the meaning here. In the Old Testament ritual washings were imposed primarily upon the priests (e.g., Exod 30:17–21; 40:12), but apparently by the first Christian century the scribes and Pharisees had begun to practice them and to attempt to impose them on all Jews (cf. v. 3).

7:3 Verses 3–4 are a parenthesis providing some examples of ritual cleansing. The phrase "all the Jews" is no doubt a hyperbole, but the expression does show that the practice was widespread. The NIV and most English versions obscure a serious textual, translational, and interpretational problem in this verse.

As for the textual problem, by far the best attested reading is a word meaning *with a fist*. A very literal translation would be, "The Pharisees and all the Jews do not eat unless they wash their hands with a fist." Because of the difficulty of this reading, some witnesses substitute a word meaning *often* or *diligently.* One witness substitutes "in a moment," another substitutes "first," and some omit the word altogether. The NIV either does not translate the word or represents it by the word "ceremonial." The RSV says in a note that it does not translate it because of the uncertain meaning. The NRSV has "thoroughly"; the NASB, "carefully." The GNB has "proper way." The note in the NEB and REB implies they adopt the Greek text which omits the word. If, however, one accepts the best attested Greek text, the meaning could be *up to the fist* or even "up to the elbow" (Moffatt) or the rubbing of a closed fist in the palm of the other hand, or pouring water over a clinched fist, or the use of a handful of water. The *Mishna* tractate *Yadaim* (meaning *Hands*) deals with ritual washings but does not enlighten the present passage. The interpreter must confess his or her inability to determine the matter. Some factors, however, point to minor defilement, which requires a superficial washing as opposed to major defilement, which requires total immersion (cf. v. 4).

The "tradition of the elders" is simply the oral, scribal interpretation of the written, Mosaic law. This tradition was later (ca. A.D. 220) collected and reduced to writing in the *Mishna*. The "elders" were scribes, Pharisees, leaders of synagogues, and revered persons in general.

7:4 The textual witnesses are divided between a word meaning *to immerse* and one meaning *to sprinkle.* The reader cannot tell which of these is behind the NIV's "wash." The two earliest and best Greek manuscripts of Mark have "sprinkle," but this reading probably represents a deliberate change in order to reserve the original word for Christian baptism. Furthermore, nothing in the Greek corresponds to "when they come," and therefore the expression "from the marketplace" may refer to things brought from the marketplace rather than the persons who come from the marketplace ("nor do they eat anything that comes from the market unless they wash it first," GNB; similar in NRSV). The middle voice of the Greek verb ("wash themselves") favors the interpretation of the NIV and most English versions, though an intensive interpretation ("they themselves wash") is possible.

7:5 The narrative that began in vv. 1–2 is resumed in v. 5. Although the complaint ostensibly was about the disciples, its true object was Jesus. The question as such is never answered, but all that follows is an indirect answer.

7:6–7 The quotation is from Isa 29:13 LXX, which differs slightly from the Hebrew text. The point attributed to Jesus is best made in the Greek rather than the Hebrew version of Isaiah, but it is not absent from the Hebrew text. The basic point of both versions of Isaiah is that external observance is no substitute for inward piety. A more serious problem is whether Jesus the Palestinian Jew would have known and used the Septuagint. Quite frankly the LXX wording of the quotation may be due to Mark rather than Jesus. Jesus no doubt quoted the verse in Aramaic; Mark had to use some translation. As a result of the discovery of the Dead Sea Scrolls, however, it is now known that several different Hebrew texts circulated in first-century Palestine. Jesus may have used the one that earlier had been used as the basis of the LXX rather than the LXX itself. The word "hypocrites" in v. 6 originally referred to an actor who wore different masks during a play. Here it refers not to those who deliberately play a part but to those whose lives are inconsistent with their profession.

7:8 The "commands of God" are those in the written law, i.e., the Old Testament. Because the word "commands" is singular in the Greek text, some think the reference is to the great command to love God with all one's being (Deut 6:4–5). The "traditions of men" are the scribal interpretations that had been imposed on the law (cf. vv. 3,5). It is often difficult to distinguish a particular tradition or interpretation from the real meaning of Scripture.

Contemporary Christians may do the same kind of thing that Jesus accused the scribes and Pharisees of doing. Conscientious persons may be tempted to overemphasize the letter and ignore the spirit of Scripture.

(2) Concerning the Corban Vow (7:9–13)

⁹And he said to them: "You have a fine way of setting aside the commands of God in order to observe your own traditions! ¹⁰For Moses said, 'Honor your father and your mother,' and, 'Anyone who curses his father or mother must be put to death.' ¹¹But you say that if a man says to his father or mother: 'Whatever help you might otherwise have received from me is Corban' (that is, a gift devoted to God), ¹²then you no longer let him do anything for his father or mother. ¹³Thus you nullify the word of God by your tradition that you have handed down. And you do many things like that."

Jesus accused the scribes of overthrowing a law of primary importance (the law to honor parents by caring for them in their old age) in order to observe one of secondary importance (the law of performing vows). Such a thing often results from extreme legalism.

7:9 Although the difference in meaning is not great, the textual evidence is evenly divided between a word meaning "observe" (NIV) or "keep" (RSV, NRSV, NASB) or "maintain" (NEB, REB) and one meaning "set up" (NIV margin) or "establish" (NEB margin, REB margin). The GNB apparently translates the latter with "uphold."

7:10 The quotations are from the LXX of Exod 20:12 (cf. Deut 5:16) and Exod 21:17 (cf. Lev 20:9), respectively. The word in the Hebrew text clearly means *to curse*, but the one in the LXX and Mark is more general and means *to speak evil of* (cf. RSV, NRSV, NASB). The translation in the NIV, NEB, REB, and GNB, though not wrong, represents an attempt at harmonization.

7:11–12 "Corban" is the English transliteration of the Greek transliteration of a Hebrew word meaning *a gift dedicated to God*, i.e., *an offering*.

The Hebrew word appears about eighty times in Leviticus, Numbers, and Ezekiel only. Mark defined the word in a parenthetical statement for his

Greek-speaking readers/hearers who were unfamiliar with both the Hebrew language and Jewish customs. His definition, however, does not bring out that the offering involved a vow to dedicate it irrevocably to God. As a result the offering was placed under a ban so that it could not be used for any other purpose, as is implied by v. 12. Under no circumstances would the scribes of Jesus' day permit a person to annul such a vow. By A.D. 220, however, when the *Mishna* was completed, provision was made for annulment.[61]

The exact circumstances of the vow are unclear. The vow may have been made in a fit of anger with the primary purpose of refusing to help the parents, or the primary purpose may have been to dedicate one's possessions to God's temple. Apparently the person was not required to surrender possession. One could continue to use and enjoy the property until death, at which time the remainder would presumably go to the temple.

7:13   Again (cf. v. 9) Mark quoted Jesus as accusing those who were supposedly so devoted to observing the law of violating it. Note the progression from "let go" (v. 8) to "setting aside" (v. 9) to "nullify" (v. 13). Furthermore, the rigidity of the Corban vow was not an isolated instance of scribal manipulation of the law but only one of many instances.

(3) Concerning Kosher Food (7:14–23)

[14]Again Jesus called the crowd to him and said, "Listen to me, everyone, and understand this. [15]Nothing outside a man can make him 'unclean' by going into him. Rather, it is what comes out of a man that makes him 'unclean.' "

[17]After he had left the crowd and entered the house, his disciples asked him about this parable. [18]"Are you so dull?" he asked. "Don't you see that nothing that enters a man from the outside can make him 'unclean'? [19]For it doesn't go into his heart but into his stomach, and then out of his body." (In saying this, Jesus declared all foods "clean.")

[20]He went on: "What comes out of a man is what makes him 'unclean.' [21]For from within, out of men's hearts, come evil thoughts, sexual immorality, theft, murder, adultery, [22]greed, malice, deceit, lewdness, envy, slander, arrogance and folly. [23]All these evils come from inside and make a man 'unclean.' "

7:14   The main passages that treat Jewish food laws are Lev 11 and Deut 14:1–21. The early church had difficulty deciding what to do with these laws and other questions about food (Acts 10:1–11:18; 15:1–29; Rom 14; 1 Cor 8:1–11:1; Gal 2:11–14; Col 2:20–23). Mark found in the material available to him some teaching of Jesus about the matter. It is not as clear as the modern reader might think, or it would have settled the question, which obviously it did not. Although the statement in v. 15 is called a parable (*parabolē*) in v. 17, a better translation in context is "riddle."

---

[61]*M. Ned.* 9.1.

7:15 The basic affirmation in v. 15 is elaborated in vv. 17–23. The authenticity of the statement is guaranteed by its form (antithetic parallelism, which is a characteristic of Semitic speech), its difference from Jewish teaching and even some teaching in the early church (the criterion of dissimilarity), and its obscurity (if the early church had invented the saying, it would have been clearer).

[7:16] "If anyone has ears to hear, let him hear" is not found in the earliest and best manuscripts of Mark and is properly omitted by the NIV, RSV, NRSV, NEB, REB, and GNB.[62] The statement is probably a scribal addition from 4:9,23 under the influence of 7:14.

7:17 Several times Mark pictured Jesus as instructing his disciples in a house (also 9:28,33; 10:10) so that the house becomes a symbol of revelation. Mark and his readers/hearers doubtless thought of their own house churches. Perhaps the significance of "house" can be seen by contrasting it with the synagogue, which Mark earlier identified as a place of rejection.

7:18–19 Again Mark described the disciples as without understanding despite their privileged position. Then he explained the statement in v. 15. Verse 19 clarifies that what enters a person from the outside is food. Neither the eating of an unclean animal nor the eating of approved food with unwashed hands can defile a person. Food merely goes first into the stomach and then into the latrine (so the Greek text; cf. "into the drain," NEB, REB and "into the sewer," NRSV, which, however, are anachronisms).[63]

The "heart" in the Bible is a symbol of the rational, intellectual, decision-making element in human beings and not the emotional, affectionate element. The parenthetical statement at the end of v. 19 is Mark's understanding of the ultimate significance of Jesus' teaching, not what Jesus said at the time. There is, however, nothing in the Greek text corresponding to the NIV's insertion "In saying this, Jesus declared." It says simply but very awkwardly "cleansing all foods," and it is barely possible that the reference is not to the intention of Jesus' teaching but to food ultimately being disposed of in a latrine, namely, that all foods are equal in the end.

7:20–22 Just as vv. 18–19 explain the first half of the claim in v. 15, vv. 20–23 explain the last half. Verses 21–22 explain what Jesus had in mind when referring to what comes out of a person making that person unclean. Evil that comes out of a person's heart, mind, or will makes the person unclean. In the Greek text the first seven items (those in v. 21 and the first three in v. 22) are plural, implying they are repeated acts; and the last six are singular, implying they are attitudes or vices. In English translation it is difficult to maintain

---

[62] The NASB prints the verse in brackets and in the introduction states, "Brackets in the text are around words probably not in the original writings."

[63] One Greek manuscript of medium quality has "into the bowel."

the distinction between the plural and singular, although the NASB and NEB do. Except for the parallel in Matt 15:19, this is the only list of vices in the Synoptics, but similar lists are in a variety of Hellenistic literature, including pagan, Jewish, and Christian sources (Rom 1:29–31; Gal 5:19–21; Col 3:5,8–9; 1 Tim 1:9–10; 2 Tim 3:2–4; 1 Pet 4:3). In fact, some have argued that the vocabulary of the list is that of Paul and the early church rather than Jesus and that Jesus could not have given the list. The list may well be a summary rather than a verbatim report of what Jesus said, but doubtless Jesus set forth a list of similar vices.

The GNB understands the "evil thoughts" or "evil ideas" as designs and attitudes that produce the following vices rather than one of the vices. "Sexual immorality" or "fornication" (RSV, NRSV, NASB, NEB, REB) is a general term for any kind of sexual relationship outside of marriage, whereas sexual relationships between two persons at least one of whom is married to someone else is "adultery." "Greed" is translated "coveting" in the RSV and NASB and "avarice" in the NRSV. The reference could be to coveting a woman and thus to lust. "Malice" is translated "wickedness" in the RSV, NRSV, and NASB and "all sorts of evil things" in the GNB. "Deceit" is translated "fraud" in the NEB and REB. "Lewdness" is "licentiousness" in the RSV and NRSV, "sensuality" in the NASB, and "indecency" in the NEB, REB, and GNB. "Envy" is "jealousy" in the GNB (a very literal translation of the Greek text is "evil eye"). All the translations cited here have "slander" because all the other vices involve human relationships. When the object is God, however, the word means *blasphemy* as in 3:28. "Arrogance" is "pride" in the RSV, NRSV, NASB, and GNB. And "folly" is "foolishness" in the NASB. The reference is to a person who has no moral judgment.

7:23 Jesus' main point is that uncleanness is moral rather than ritual. In fact, throughout the section the NIV puts the words "clean" and "unclean" in quotation marks to clarify that this is not a matter of sanitation. The first-century Jewish concept of clean and unclean is foreign to most persons reared in contemporary Western culture. Observant Moslems and Jews continue to abstain from "unclean" foods.

19. The Exorcising of a Demon from the Daughter of a Syrophoenician Woman (7:24–30)

[24]Jesus left that place and went to the vicinity of Tyre. He entered a house and did not want anyone to know it; yet he could not keep his presence secret. [25]In fact, as soon as she heard about him, a woman whose little daughter was possessed by an evil spirit came and fell at his feet. [26]The woman was a Greek, born in Syrian Phoenicia. She begged Jesus to drive the demon out of her daughter.

[27]"First let the children eat all they want," he told her, "for it is not right to take the children's bread and toss it to their dogs."

²⁸"Yes, Lord," she replied, "but even the dogs under the table eat the children's crumbs."
²⁹Then he told her, "For such a reply, you may go; the demon has left your daughter."
³⁰She went home and found her child lying on the bed, and the demon gone.

Whether Jesus went into Phoenicia immediately after the preceding event(s) is unimportant,[64] but Mark's placing the account immediately after 7:1–23 is most significant. If the proper inference from the teaching of Jesus in 7:1–23 is that all foods are clean (v. 19), the lesson to be learned from 7:24–30 is that all people are clean! For Mark the excursion of Jesus into "unclean" Gentile territory exemplified his disregard for the concept of ritual defilement. He saw in the ministry to the woman a preview of the Gentile mission and in the response of the woman a preview of the acceptance of the gospel by the Gentiles.[65] Mark's Gentile readers/hearers no doubt found in the account reassurance that they were part of the true people of God.

In connection with these considerations, the emphasis is not on the exorcism but on the teaching of Jesus. The account is more of a pronouncement story than a miracle story in form. Furthermore, the woman's faith stands in contrast with the unbelief of the scribes and Pharisees, and her understanding contrasts with the disciples' dullness.

7:24 The reference in "that place" is unclear: the house of 7:17 or Gennesaret in 6:53 or some other if Mark was not chronological in his arrangement. "Tyre" was located on the Phoenician coast about thirty-five miles northwest of Lake Galilee. Most manuscripts, including the best ones, add "and Sidon" (KJV, NKJV); but this probably is a scribal assimilation to the parallel in Matt 15:21, where the words are authentic, and perhaps also to Mark 3:8 and even 7:31. Mark did not indicate how far Jesus went into the territory of Tyre, whether he entered that or any other city, or the purpose of his journey. No intimation is given that he journeyed to escape from Herod Antipas. His desire for privacy rules out a preaching mission. The purpose could have been to rest or to instruct the disciples or to plan his future course of action in view of his rejection by many of his own people. The impossibility of remaining unrecognized may have been due to his previous contact with people from Tyre and Sidon (3:8).

7:25 Prostration was an indication of both grief and reverence. A ruler of a synagogue also fell at the feet of Jesus (5:22). The implication of two such

---

[64] See the comments on v. 24.

[65] It is significant that Mark does not picture Jesus as a cosmopolitan preacher to all nations, although by doing so he could have provided incontrovertible justification for the Gentile mission that was in progress in his day but that was still opposed by some Jewish Christians. He has faithfully passed on the tradition he received, even though the account only *intimates* the mission to and the positive response of the Gentiles.

different persons doing so is that all should bow before Jesus as Lord (cf. Phil 2:10).

7:26 The woman was not likely a "Greek" by birth or nationality. She may have been thoroughly Hellenized, i.e., a Greek with reference to language and culture. Probably the word also denotes that she was a Gentile as opposed to a Jew. Mark wrote "Syrian Phoenicia" or Syrophoenicia (RSV, NASB; similar NRSV) in order to distinguish the place from Libyan or Carthagenian Phoenicia in North Africa. Phoenicia—modern Lebanon—was part of the geographical area and the Roman province of Syria. It is interesting to compare the present account with Elijah's provision of food for a Syrophoenician woman and her son at Zarephath between Tyre and Sidon and his resurrection of the son (1 Kgs 17:8–24).

7:27 Jews often used the word "dogs" to refer to Gentiles. Even though it seems out of character for him to have done so, Jesus almost certainly used it in the same way.[66] The obvious meaning is that Jews took precedence over Gentiles during the ministry of Jesus. Even Paul later adhered to a similar principle (Rom 1:16). The harshness is softened somewhat by the use of the diminutive form that could be translated "puppies" and could refer to house pets rather than the scavengers of the streets. The phrase probably is best understood as an "acted parable." Yet, the seeming harshness could have served to test the woman's faith. Incidentally, on this occasion Jesus may have spoken in Greek rather than Aramaic. There is every reason to believe that he knew some Greek.

7:28 The woman did not deny the precedence of Israel, but she suggested that this did not exclude the Gentiles. Only here in Mark's Gospel is Jesus addressed as "Lord," although he is quoted as referring to himself as such in 2:28; 5:19 (?); 11:3. Significantly, a Gentile used this title.[67]

7:29–30 To say the least, Jesus commended the woman for her humility. Although her faith is not explicitly mentioned, it is certainly implicit. This is the only instance in Mark of an exorcism or a healing from a distance, although similar cases are found in Matt 8:5–13; Luke 7:1–10; John 4:43–53. All of these likely involve healings of Gentiles.

20. The Healing of the Deaf Man with a Speech Impediment (7:31–37)

31Then Jesus left the vicinity of Tyre and went through Sidon, down to the Sea of Galilee and into the region of the Decapolis. 32There some people brought to

---

[66]The fact that the statement is unexpected is an argument for its authenticity. It is unlikely that the early church would have invented and attributed to Jesus a saying that could reflect adversely upon him.

[67]It is true that the word could be translated "Sir" (NEB, REB, GNB). It is obvious, however, that the woman recognized the presence of divine power in Jesus. The idea of reverence is therefore more appropriate than mere respect.

him a man who was deaf and could hardly talk, and they begged him to place his hand on the man.

³³After he took him aside, away from the crowd, Jesus put his fingers into the man's ears. Then he spit and touched the man's tongue. ³⁴He looked up to heaven and with a deep sigh said to him, *"Ephphatha!"* (which means, "Be opened!"). ³⁵At this, the man's ears were opened, his tongue was loosened and he began to speak plainly.

³⁶Jesus commanded them not to tell anyone. But the more he did so, the more they kept talking about it. ³⁷People were overwhelmed with amazement. "He has done everything well," they said. "He even makes the deaf hear and the mute speak."

Because the emphasis is on the healing itself, this is a true miracle story. The account, found only in Mark, obviously exemplifies Jesus' power to heal. Not so obvious is the intimation that Jesus is the fulfillment of Isaiah's description of the messianic age (see the comments on v. 37). This healing has much in common with that of the blind man in 8:22–26.

7:31 Mark pictured Jesus continuing north from Tyre (cf. 7:24) to Sidon and then southeast to Lake Galilee and the region of the Decapolis (see comments on 5:20), which was a strange route to take. It is similar to going from New York City to Chicago via Boston! As a result some have cited this verse as another example of the author's ignorance of Palestinian and Syrian geography, with the implication that he could not have been a native of Palestine and, therefore, not John Mark of Jerusalem. Of course a native of Jerusalem may not have been well versed on the geography of Galilee and beyond, though one who traveled on missions with Paul, Barnabas, and perhaps Peter would doubtless know something of geography outside Palestine. Even so the route is not impossible, and it is unnecessary to charge the author—whoever he was—with an error.

If Jesus' excursion into Phoenicia was to escape the crowds (cf. v. 24) and to have time with his disciples, he may well have chosen a circuitous rather than a direct route. The expression "through Sidon" is shorthand for "through the region of Sidon" and does not necessarily indicate that Jesus entered the city itself.[68] Sidon's territory probably extended at least twenty miles to the east of the city itself. It was important for Mark to show that Jesus spent some time in Gentile territory—also the Decapolis—in order to provide some justification for the Gentile mission in his own day. Mark remained faithful to the tradition, however, and did not invent a preaching mission outside of Palestine.

7:32 Whether the man "could hardly talk" (NIV) or was mute, i.e., unable to utter any sound, is difficult to decide. The word in the Greek text

---

[68]The variant reading "and Sidon" probably results from an attempt to lessen the geographical difficulty.

(*mogilalon*) properly means *speaking with difficulty*. It is not found elsewhere in the New Testament and appears in the LXX only in Isa 35:6, where, however, it translates a Hebrew word meaning *mute*. The statement "began to speak plainly" in v. 35 also suggests the meaning in v. 32 should be "hardly talk," but the adjective in v. 37 properly means *unable to speak at all*. Verse 37, however, refers to Jesus' healing ministry as a whole and not just the healing in the preceding verses. Probably the NIV is correct in its interpretation. Whether the man was a Jew or a Gentile is not stated. If the miracle took place in the Decapolis, the latter is more likely.

7:33–35 Again Mark suggested that Jesus wanted to get away from the crowd in order to avoid its acclaim (see further the comments on 8:22–26). Touching a person, using saliva, uttering deep groans, and using foreign words were common in ancient healing stories; but this in no way suggests that Mark invented the details to conform to the usual practice. Inasmuch as Jesus could not speak to the man, touching him was an important way of expressing concern. Looking up to heaven indicates that Jesus prayed for divine help before performing the cure (cf. 6:41). Scholars are uncertain whether "*Ephphatha*" is Hebrew or Aramaic—probably the latter. If it refers to the healing itself, it must be the opening of the ears to hear (cf. v. 35) rather than the loosening of the tongue to speak; but it may be directed to the whole person.

7:36 The injunction to silence is somewhat surprising since the miracle could not be concealed, as the last part of the verse clearly indicates. Ironically the Gospel that most emphasizes the "messianic secret" also indicates it could not be kept even in Jesus' lifetime. Nevertheless Jesus did not want to be known as a Hellenistic miracle worker, and Mark reiterated that Jesus' true identity could not be understood until after the passion and resurrection.

7:37 "He has done everything well" recalls Gen 1:31, and "He even makes the deaf hear and the mute speak" recalls Isa 35:5–6. Isaiah 35 describes the messianic age poetically. Mark's allusion to the passage implies that the age had drawn near in the ministry of Jesus.

21. The Feeding of the Four Thousand (8:1–10)

¹During those days another large crowd gathered. Since they had nothing to eat, Jesus called his disciples to him and said, ²"I have compassion for these people; they have already been with me three days and have nothing to eat. ³If I send them home hungry, they will collapse on the way, because some of them have come a long distance."

⁴His disciples answered, "But where in this remote place can anyone get enough bread to feed them?"

⁵"How many loaves do you have?" Jesus asked.

"Seven," they replied.

⁶He told the crowd to sit down on the ground. When he had taken the seven loaves and given thanks, he broke them and gave them to his disciples to set

before the people, and they did so. ⁷They had a few small fish as well; he gave thanks for them also and told the disciples to distribute them. ⁸The people ate and were satisfied. Afterward the disciples picked up seven basketfuls of broken pieces that were left over. ⁹About four thousand men were present. And having sent them away, ¹⁰he got into the boat with his disciples and went to the region of Dalmanutha.

Before commenting on this section, something needs to be said about the parallels between 6:31–7:37 and 8:1–30. They can be observed in the following:

6:31–44	Feeding a multitude	8:1–9
6:45–56	Crossing the lake	8:10
7:1–23	Dispute with the Pharisees	8:11–13
7:24–30	Discussion about bread	8:14–21
7:31–36	Healing	8:22–26
7:37	Confession of faith	8:27–30

Mark's probable motive for arranging his material in this manner was to show how the dullness of the disciples required that Jesus repeat his teaching and miracles before they could understand.

The episode recorded in 8:1–10 has often been identified as a doublet, i.e., a variant account of the same event as the one described in 6:31–44 (the feeding of the five thousand). Form critics point to the two accounts as examples of how details were modified in the course of oral transmission. It has been argued that if there were only one account of a feeding, one might think the details are indicative of an eyewitness. Inasmuch as there are two different accounts of the same event, the details are nothing more than an example of the storyteller's art.

Were there two feedings, or was there only one? Matthew followed Mark in describing two (14:13–21; 15:32–39), whereas Luke and John recorded only one (9:10–17; 6:1–14, respectively). One might think that Mark and Matthew were in a better position than modern interpreters to know whether there was one or two. Doubtless they understood and recorded two feedings (note especially Mark 8:19–20). Jesus' feeding more than one multitude is not improbable. The details are different and significant.

On the other hand, the statements of the disciples in Mark 8:4 and Matt 15:33 are difficult to understand if there had been an earlier miraculous feeding. This consideration and not the similarities of the accounts is the real reason many commentators believe there was only one feeding. But is the statement really so difficult? If some months had passed since the first feeding, and if since that time there had been several occasions when Jesus did not feed crowds, the disciples would have had no reason to think that he would do so on the occasion here described. The statement in v. 4 may not indicate they had forgotten the first feeding or that they had no idea Jesus *could* feed the crowd but that they did not know what he would do. It could even be thought to reflect an unwillingness to be presumptuous. However, v. 4 more likely exemplifies the incredible dullness of the disciples, which is not out of line with the way Mark described them elsewhere. Inasmuch as Mark's Gospel is not strictly chronological, a slight possibility is that the feeding of the four thousand took place before the feeding of the five thousand, although that would only transfer the problem to 6:37 and perhaps create a problem with 8:19–20.

A decision on the matter is difficult. Perhaps certainty or even confidence in a position is impossible. Both proponents of a doublet and traditional interpreters ought to recognize the possibility that the other might be right. That multiple attestation supports the historicity of a miraculous feeding of at least one large crowd is often overlooked. One must also allow for the possibility that there were still other feedings that are not recorded in any Gospel.

Given that Jesus did feed two multitudes—the position of this commentary—why did Mark record both when space was at a premium? The answer must be the different symbolic significance of the two. For Mark the feeding of the five thousand seems to symbolize Jesus' provision for the Jews; the feeding of the four thousand, his provision for the Gentiles.

8:1 Although Mark did not specifically locate the feeding of the four thousand, "during those days" seems to place it during Jesus' tour of Phoenicia and the Decapolis (7:24,31). The most likely location is somewhere in the Decapolis, which was inhabited by a Jewish minority and a Gentile majority.

8:2 Whatever other motives Mark had, he certainly exemplified Jesus' compassion. In fact, Jesus seems to have had more concern for physical need in this feeding than the previous one. There is no reference to teaching in this account as there is in the other.

8:3 The expression translated "a long distance" and cognates are used in the LXX to describe the Gentile lands to which Israel had been exiled (e.g., Isa 43:6; 49:12; 60:4,9; Jer 26:27 LXX only; 30:10; 38:10 LXX only; 46:27 Hebrew only; cf. Josh 9:6; Acts 2:39; 22:21; Eph 2:11–12). The early church sometimes referred these passages to the calling of the Gentiles. Mark, therefore, may have wanted his readers/hearers to see an allusion to the Gentiles.

8:4 The difficulties this verse presents have already been discussed in the introduction to the section. The "remote place" was more likely in the region east of Lake Galilee than in Galilee itself. Again the dullness of the disciples comes to the front. The juxtaposition of "remote place" and "bread" (cf. 6:35ff.) again recalls the giving of the manna in the desert (Exod 16), which implies for Christians that God will also supply their physical needs.

8:5 Here there are seven loaves and a "few" fish (v. 7) instead of the five and two in 6:38. Also the diminutive form of the word "fish" is used. Some think the seven loaves reflect the Noachian commandments of Gen 9:4–6 and therefore provision for the Gentiles, whereas five symbolizes the five books of the law and provision for the Jews. Certainty about such matters is impossible.

8:6 There is no reference to groups of hundreds and fifties as in 6:40. The statement "When he had taken the . . . loaves and had given thanks, he broke them" corresponds closely with the account of the institution of the Lord's Supper in 1 Cor 11:24. As with the earlier feeding narrative, Mark and other early Christians may have seen a preview of the Lord's Supper; but the absence of the cup and the introduction of the fish (v. 7) preclude any significant Eucharistic connection. The recognition that the two feedings and the Lord's Supper point to the same deep truths, i.e., Christ's gracious provision for his people's needs and the festive consummation of God's kingdom, accounts for what connections there are.

8:7 Although Mark used a different verb in v. 7 from the one in v. 6, the NIV is correct to translate both with "give thanks." Jesus did not bless the loaves and fish (RSV, NRSV, NASB, NEB, REB) but gave thanks to God for them (NIV, GNB). The two Greek verbs probably are different translations of the same Aramaic verb. Perhaps the account is to exemplify thanksgiving. Probably because of their continued unbelief (v. 4), the disciples played a less prominent role in this feeding than the previous one.

8:8 The word here meaning *basket* (*spyris*) is different from the one (*kophinos*) in 6:43. It refers to a large basket (cf. Acts 9:25) made of wicker or rope for carrying provisions. Therefore the seven basketfuls here may have contained more than the twelve. The number "twelve" in the previous account obviously is relevant to Israel; the number "seven" here may symbolize fullness and completion and therefore the Gentiles.

8:9 Again women and children are not included in the enumeration (cf. 6:44). Inasmuch as there were so many more Gentiles than Jews, a question arises about how the larger number could symbolize Jews and the smaller one Gentiles. Perhaps the answer is that the larger number or the placement of the accounts symbolize the precedence of the Jews. According to one interpretation the four thousand men symbolize the four corners of the earth from which the Gentiles came.

8:10 The location of "Dalmanutha" is unknown. Matthew 15:39 has "Magadan," but its location is also unknown. "Magdala" (among others) is a variant reading with fair attestation in both passages. It is barely possible that Magdala, Dalmanutha, and Magadan are different names for the same place. Magdala, on the western shore of the lake, was certainly in the right place for a landing following a crossing from the eastern side. However, at present Mark and Matthew cannot be completely or satisfactorily reconciled at this point.

22. A Demand for a Sign (8:11–13)

[11]The Pharisees came and began to question Jesus. To test him, they asked him for a sign from heaven. [12]He sighed deeply and said, "Why does this generation ask for a miraculous sign? I tell you the truth, no sign will be given to it." [13]Then he left them, got back into the boat and crossed to the other side.

This paragraph probably is a pronouncement story with the pronouncement in v. 12. The account has much in common with the controversy in 3:22–30. No reference to time or place is made, but the presence of the Pharisees suggests Galilee rather than the Decapolis.

8:11 Considering how many miracles Jesus had already performed, it is surprising at first that the Pharisees would ask for another. The modern reader needs to realize that miracles were quite common in ancient times—whether in reality or in people's imagination—and the fact that a person performed miracles did not by itself make him an exceptional person. What the Pharisees wanted was not another healing or exorcism or feeding or subjugation of nature but a "sign from heaven," i.e., an apocalyptic manifestation that would prove beyond all doubt that Jesus had God's approval. The word "heaven" is a Jewish substitute for the divine name. The Pharisees wanted God to vindicate Jesus before they would accept him. Mark did not elsewhere use the word "sign" to mean *a miracle*.[69] Jesus' refusal to provide a sign is quite in keeping with his initial call to "believe the good news" (1:15). An irrefutable sign would compel faith. Commitment to Jesus must be voluntary.

The word here translated "test" is translated "tempted" in 1:13. Mark perhaps suggested that the Pharisees were in league with Satan in trying to tempt Jesus.

8:12 The first part of the verse provides another example of Mark's willingness to describe candidly Jesus' emotions. The word may refer to anger (cf. 1:41 variant reading) or to spiritual intensity. The parallel in Matt 16:1–4 does not contain the statement. The expression "this generation" echoes the "warped and crooked generation" of Deut 32:5 (cf. Gen 7:1; Deut 32:20; Ps 95:10). The NIV is not incorrect in interpreting the last part of the verse to mean "no sign will be given to it." The Greek involves an elliptical sentence with only a protasis ("if a sign shall be given to this generation"). The apodosis that must be supplied is probably "may I die" or "may I be cursed." The result then is an emphatic denial of the request for a sign. Perhaps Jesus deliberately made an incomplete statement in order to let his hearers decide for

---

[69]Although its use of the word "miracle" is confusing, the GNB has the right idea: "They asked him to perform a miracle to show that God approved of him." Mark used the word elsewhere only in 13:4,22, where it also refers to something that demonstrates divine approval. (This commentator does not believe that Mark wrote 16:9–20, where the word does have the meaning of *miracle* in vv. 17,20. See the comments following 16:1–8.)

themselves whether a sign should be given. That Jesus probably spoke in Aramaic and what Mark reported is a translation further complicate the matter.

8:13 Almost certainly Mark saw in Jesus' departure an indication of his displeasure toward the Pharisees and possibly a rejection of Judaism as the divinely approved religion (cf. 11:12–21; also 11:22 if the temple mount is in view). The best textual witnesses omit the words "the boat" and state simply that Jesus embarked. Of course, the word "embarked" implies a boat, and translations such as the NIV that are based on a critical text are justified in supplying the words.

23. The Failure to Bring Bread and a Warning against Leaven (8:14–21)

¹⁴The disciples had forgotten to bring bread, except for one loaf they had with them in the boat. ¹⁵"Be careful," Jesus warned them. "Watch out for the yeast of the Pharisees and that of Herod."

¹⁶They discussed this with one another and said, "It is because we have no bread."

¹⁷Aware of their discussion, Jesus asked them: "Why are you talking about having no bread? Do you still not see or understand? Are your hearts hardened? ¹⁸Do you have eyes but fail to see, and ears but fail to hear? And don't you remember? ¹⁹When I broke the five loaves for the five thousand, how many basketfuls of pieces did you pick up?"

"Twelve," they replied.

²⁰"And when I broke the seven loaves for the four thousand, how many basketfuls of pieces did you pick up?"

They answered, "Seven."

²¹He said to them, "Do you still not understand?"

Many have claimed that this section presents the same kind of problem as 8:1–10, namely, how the disciples could be so obtuse if they had previously witnessed a miraculous feeding—actually two such feedings. The situation is somewhat different from that in 8:1–10, however. It was by no means easy to understand what Jesus meant by the "yeast of the Pharisees and that of Herod." It is not incredible that in grasping for the meaning the disciples would think that Jesus was rebuking them for failing to bring bread. The disciples had no reason to believe that just because he had fed the crowds he would feed them. The only instance of a miraculous feeding of the disciples is in John 21:4–14. Nevertheless the account contributes further to Mark's theme of the dullness of the disciples. In fact, it constitutes the climax of that theme because in the following division the disciples began to perceive who Jesus is. The disciples' unbelief provides a link with the previous section (8:11–13), which emphasizes the unbelief of the Pharisees; and the reference to bread provides a link with the one before that (8:1–10).

8:14 A minor problem is the reference to "one loaf" here and "no bread" in v. 16. In context the latter probably means *not enough bread* or *none to speak of*. It is quite uncertain whether Mark saw in the "one loaf" an allusion to Jesus. In any event the disciples should have realized that if they had Jesus, they had enough.

8:15 This pronouncement of Jesus is commonly held to be an independent saying Mark inserted into the account because of the connection between yeast and bread. A variant saying is found in a different context in Luke 12:1. The warning seems to break the connection between v. 14 and v. 16 and does not figure in the remainder of the story. There is some question, however, whether v. 16 follows naturally after v. 14, especially if one adopts the variant readings in v. 16, which are apparently translated by the NIV. Furthermore, Mark did not make a habit of inserting sayings into accounts.

What then is the "yeast ["leaven," RSV, NASB, NEB, REB] of the Pharisees and that of Herod"? With the exception of Matt 13:33 (cf. Luke 13:20–21), yeast or leaven in the New Testament symbolizes evil (1 Cor 5:6–8; Gal 5:9; cf. Exod 12:15,19f.; 13:7; Lev 2:11; 6:17; Deut 16:4; but also cf. Lev 23:17). In the rabbinic literature of the several centuries following the New Testament, it stands for the evil disposition in people. The parallel in Matt 16:12 identifies the yeast of the Pharisees as their teaching, whereas Luke 12:1, which reflects a different setting, identifies it as their hypocrisy. In Mark the yeast likely reflects their unbelief and demand for a sign. As for the yeast of Herod,[70] it could be adultery, murder, and political ambition. One would expect the yeast of the Pharisees and the yeast of Herod to have been the same thing. Therefore the yeast of Herod probably was also unbelief connected with miracles. He did not demand a miraculous sign, but he did misinterpret the miracles of Jesus as an indication that John had been raised. Jesus' purpose in mentioning the matter was to indicate that the disciples were dangerously close to unbelief. Alternately, Mark's reference is general: "Beware of the influence of the Pharisees and Herod." The warning to the disciples concerned not only the evil influence of Herod (with which they were aware) but also the evil that characterized the Pharisees.

8:16 What Jesus intended to be taken metaphorically the disciples took literally. The text translated by the NIV probably means that the disciples could not understand why Jesus was concerned about yeast when they had little or no bread. This reading requires v. 15 in order to make sense. The text translated by the NASB, which omits the participle translated "said" in the NIV and changes the following verb from first to the third person plural, probably means that the disciples argued among themselves as to who was responsible for the failure to bring bread. The evidence is evenly balanced, and a decision is difficult.

---

[70] A variant reading with fair to good attestation is "the Herodians."

8:17–18 In vv. 17–21 Jesus rebuked the disciples' preoccupation with material things by asking a series of questions. The third (the last in v. 17) and fourth (the first in v. 18) recall the rebuke of ancient Israel in Isa 6:9–10 (cf. Ps 95:8; Isa 63:17; Jer 5:21; Ezek 12:2), which already has been applied to the Israel of Jesus' day in 4:12. The unbelief of the disciples was bordering on that of Jesus' enemies! Furthermore, in the Old Testament remembering was a major element in Israel's religious experience. The disciples, like Israel, had failed to remember.

8:19–20 To say the least, these verses confirm Mark's understanding that there were two feedings. Even the different words meaning *basket* are maintained. Just as the word "yeast" has a symbolic meaning, so do the feedings. By performing these miracles, Jesus did more than feed hungry people and more than suggest spiritual provision first for the Jews and then for the Gentiles. He intended to show the disciples that he was the Christ. They failed to understand this great truth at that time.

8:21 The word "still" suggests that there was hope for the disciples, that they would yet understand. The question is for the readers/hearers of the gospel as well as the disciples. All need to realize that Jesus is the Christ.

———————————— *SECTION OUTLINE* ————————————

III. THE GOOD NEWS ABOUT JESUS' TEACHING ON DISCIPLESHIP
(8:22–10:52)
   1. Introduction: The Healing of the Blind Man at Bethsaida (8:22–26)
   2. The Confession of Peter at Caesarea Philippi (8:27–30)
   3. The First Passion and Resurrection Prediction (8:31–33)
   4. The Cost of Discipleship (8:34–9:1)
   5. The Transfiguration (9:2–10)
   6. The Question about Elijah (9:11–13)
   7. The Exorcising of a Demon from a Deaf and Mute Boy (9:14–29)
   8. The Second Passion and Resurrection Prediction (9:30–32)
   9. The Discussion about Greatness (9:33–37)
   10. The Question about the Independent Exorcist (9:38–41)
   11. A Warning against Offenses (9:42–50)
   12. The Journey to Jerusalem (10:1–45)
       (1) The Teaching about Divorce (10:1–12)
       (2) The Blessing of the Children (10:13–16)
       (3) The Inquiry of the Rich Man and Jesus' Teaching about Wealth
           and Rewards (10:17–31)
       (4) The Third Passion and Resurrection Prediction (10:32–34)
       (5) The Ambition of James and John (10:35–45)
   13. Conclusion: The Healing of Blind Bartimaeus at Jericho (10:46–52)

———— **III. THE GOOD NEWS ABOUT JESUS' TEACHING** ————
ON DISCIPLESHIP (8:22–10:52)

In the first division most of Jesus' ministry focused on the crowds. In the second Mark traced Jesus' ministry to the disciples. The first division deals with many different subjects. The second concentrates on the identity and fate of Jesus and the implications of these for discipleship. In the first division only the demons recognized the true identity of Jesus; in the second the disciples started to understand, although their comprehension was still inadequate.

The second major division is the most carefully constructed and stands out the most clearly of the three. This is seen first in its introduction and con-clusion with giving-of-sight stories (8:22–26; 10:46–52, respectively). These are the only miracles of healing blind persons in Mark's Gospel, and they are in the last half of the Gospel, where relatively few miracles of any kind are recorded. The first division ends with Mark's emphasis on the disciples' spiritual blindness (8:17–21). Near the beginning of the second, the disciples began to move toward an understanding of who Jesus is (8:27–30). Indeed, the enlightenment of the disciples is a major theme in the second division. Therefore the two miracles of restoration of physical sight function by suggesting the need of the disciples for spiritual insight and the ability of Jesus to cure their "blindness." Mark no doubt wanted his readers/hearers to identify with the disciples and acknowledge their need for spiritual perception.

Another way in which the careful construction of the second division is seen is in the recurring pattern within its main body, i.e., 8:27–10:45.

Geographical reference	8:27	9:30	10:32
Passion/resurrection prediction	8:31	9:31	10:33–34
Misunderstanding	8:32–33	9:32–34	10:35–41
Correction	8:34–9:1	9:35–37	10:42–45

The passion predictions play a major role. They show what kind of Messiah (cf. 8:29) Jesus really is. He is a suffering and dying Messiah. The predictions prepare for the third major division, the passion narrative. In addition to the three passion predictions, a brief reference is made in 9:9 to Jesus' death and resurrection.

1. Introduction: The Healing of the Blind Man at Bethsaida (8:22–26)

[22]**They came to Bethsaida, and some people brought a blind man and begged Jesus to touch him. **[23]**He took the blind man by the hand and led him outside the village. When he had spit on the man's eyes and put his hands on him, Jesus asked, "Do you see anything?"**

[24]**He looked up and said, "I see people; they look like trees walking around."**

[25]**Once more Jesus put his hands on the man's eyes. Then his eyes were opened, his sight was restored, and he saw everything clearly. **[26]**Jesus sent him home, saying, "Don't go into the village."**

Commentators differ on whether to treat this miracle story as the conclusion or the beginning of a major division. The main reason for treating it as the conclusion of the first division is to make Peter's confession in 8:27–30 the beginning of a new division. Certainly the confession marks a turning point in the narrative. If, however, 8:22–26 functions as the introduction to a new division, 8:27–30 can still be the turning point. The reason for making 8:22–26 the introduction to the division has been given, but one additional comment is desirable. A miracle in which physical sight is restored in two stages is an appropriate setting for an account of the progression of spiritual insight in two stages (8:27–30). There are two levels of meaning: outward vision and inner perception, though it must be noted that Peter's perception remained fuzzy at this stage. Jesus' rebuke of Peter (8:33) shows that Peter, like the first blind man, had spiritual sight but failed to see the true contours of Jesus' messiahship. The healing serves to introduce the whole central section on discipleship, which is the account of progression in spiritual insight.

The present section, which is found only in Mark, has many verbal parallels with the healing of the deaf and mute man in 7:31–37, which is also peculiar to Mark. This in no way suggests that the two are variant accounts of the same miracle as a few have claimed, only that Mark used some of the same "standardized" language to describe the two.

Perhaps Mark recorded the story to show that the messianic age as prophesied by Isaiah (e.g., 29:18; 35:5) was present in Jesus. Very important is the symbolism of the two-stage healing. The disciples, like the blind man, had been "touched" by Jesus and had received a preliminary blessing. Their spiritual insight, however, was far from complete. It was not much better than that of the Pharisees. They needed a "second touch" for complete understanding.

8:22 For the location of Bethsaida, see the comments on 6:45. The reference to it as a village in v. 23 would seem to distinguish the small fishing village from the nearby city and capital of Philip the tetrarch.

8:23 The withdrawal from the city was probably to avoid the gaze and clamor of the crowd. For a similar action see 5:40; 7:33. For the use of spittle see again 7:33. Only here does Jesus ask a question of one whom he healed. The questions related to the healings in 5:31 and 10:51 are of a different kind altogether.

8:24 The NIV does a good job of making sense out of a difficult and awkward Greek construction. The man's reply may indicate that he was not born blind and had some concept of what he ought to see. Another possible explanation is the man had bumped into trees in his blindness; now he dimly began to see something like tree trunks walking around. The statement implies that the cure was not complete.

8:25 This is the only example in the Gospels of a healing in two stages. An incomplete cure and a two-stage healing may have been thought by some to be discrediting to Jesus. This consideration may be why Matthew and Luke omitted the story. In any event the early church would not have invented it. Its historicity is beyond question. Equally important is the symbolism of the two-stage healing. The disciples, like the blind man, had been "touched" by Jesus and had received a preliminary blessing. Their spiritual insight, however, was far from complete. They too needed a second touch.

8:26 Jesus' gift of spiritual and physical sight to the blind enables Mark's readers both to see who Jesus is (Isa 35:5) and to know what Jesus can provide for them. This verse appears to be another, although veiled, example of the "messianic secret." In fact, many textual witnesses add a statement about not speaking to anyone.

2. The Confession of Peter at Caesarea Philippi (8:27–30)

[27]Jesus and his disciples went on to the villages around Caesarea Philippi. On the way he asked them, "Who do people say I am?"
[28]They replied, "Some say John the Baptist; others say Elijah; and still others, one of the prophets."
[29]"But what about you?" he asked. "Who do you say I am?"
Peter answered, "You are the Christ."
[30]Jesus warned them not to tell anyone about him.

Radical form critics label this account as a legend. The term is unfortunate because it implies that the account is not historical. Its historicity is guaranteed, however, by the fact that Jesus did not fully accept the confession and in v. 33 called the prince of the apostles Satan. More appropriate therefore is the term used by moderate and evangelical form critics: a story about Jesus. Even the word "story" is offensive to some because they think it raises questions about the historicity of the account. The word itself, however, is neutral. Historicity must be decided on other grounds.

8:27 Caesarea Philippi constituted a rebuilding and enlargement of the ancient city of Paneas by Philip the tetrarch. Paneas was the site of a grotto dedicated to the god Pan. When Herod the Great acquired Iturea, he built a temple in Paneas and dedicated it to the emperor Augustus. When Herod died and Philip succeeded him as the Roman client-king, he renamed the city for the emperor and for himself. The qualification "of Philip" was a necessity in order to distinguish the city, which was about twenty-five miles north of Lake Galilee, from the Caesarea on the Mediterranean Sea, which was built by Herod the Great and also named for Augustus. The city enjoyed a most beautiful setting at the foot of Mt. Hermon and beside some gushing springs that constitute one of the sources of the Jordan River.

The Greek expression "on the way" appears seven times in this division (also 9:33,34; 10:17,32,46,52) and only twice elsewhere (8:3; 11:8). It characterizes the division and perhaps even sets forth a theme of the division. Some describe the entire division as a journey to Jerusalem, but that journey does not begin until 10:1. The entire division is, however, a journey to discipleship.

In rabbinic circles the students usually asked the questions, and the teacher provided the answers. That Jesus here asked the question is just one of many indications that he was not a typical rabbi. "People" (REB, NRSV) is a better translation than "men" because the Greek word properly means *human being*.

8:28 These "popular" opinions of Jesus are quite similar to those of 6:14–15. Mark cited them only to show their inadequacy.

8:29 In the Greek text the word translated "you" is emphatic because it is the first word in the clause. The NIV evidently tries to bring that out by inserting "But what about you?" Peter functioned as the spokesman for the group so that the confession was as much theirs as it was his. The term "Christ" has not appeared since 1:1. "Christ" is the Greek equivalent of the Hebrew "Messiah." It is translated "Messiah" here by the NRSV, NEB, REB, and GNB.

The account provides another instance of Mark's use of irony. On the one hand, Peter's confession went beyond that of the crowds. Jesus was the promised Messiah/Christ. On the other hand, the sequel shows that Peter and the other disciples did not understand what kind of Messiah Jesus was. No doubt Peter had a typical Jewish understanding of a military conqueror who would free the Jews from foreign domination. There is no evidence that any Jew in pre-Christian times thought in terms of a suffering Messiah. The confession, although correct, was also inadequate.[1] For this reason Mark did not indicate that Jesus either accepted or rejected it (cf. Matt 16:17–19). The confession resembles the first, incomplete phase of the previous healing.

8:30 Understanding why Jesus would command silence about a healing or exorcism is relatively easy, but why he would attempt to prevent further confession of his identity is relatively difficult. The answer has to do both with the popular misconception of the nature and role of the Messiah and with the insufficiency of identifying Jesus only as the Messiah. The verb translated "warned" ordinarily means *to rebuke* (previously in 1:25; 3:12; 4:39 and in vv. 32–33 following, although the first two are obscured in the NIV). The association of this term with demons and Satan (1:25; 3:12; 8:33) suggests that the popular conception of messiahship is not only inadequate but erroneous.

3. The First Passion and Resurrection Prediction (8:31–33)

[31]He then began to teach them that the Son of Man must suffer many things and be rejected by the elders, chief priests and teachers of the law, and that he must be killed and after three days rise again. [32]He spoke plainly about this, and Peter took him aside and began to rebuke him.

[33]But when Jesus turned and looked at his disciples, he rebuked Peter. "Get behind me, Satan!" he said. "You do not have in mind the things of God, but the things of men."

This is the first of three predictions of Jesus' death and resurrection in the middle division of Mark (also 9:31; 10:33–34).[2] They indicate that Jesus foresaw his death and resurrection. The first, following as it does immediately after the confession of Jesus as the Messiah/Christ, also shows what kind of Messiah Jesus is.

---

[1]Following the word "Christ," a few textual witnesses, including one very good one, add "the son of God" or "the Son of the living God"; but this is clearly an assimilation to Matt 16:15, where the words are authentic (cf. also Luke 9:20).

[2]They usually are called passion predictions, but they also predict Jesus' resurrection.

8:31 This verse explains why the disciples were not yet ready to proclaim Jesus as the Christ. He had to die first. Only here did Mark suggest a reason for the "messianic secret." The expression "began to teach" suggests that the teaching was new. The term "Son of Man" was used previously only in 2:10,28 with reference to Jesus' ministry in Galilee. In the last half of the Gospel, it is used more frequently with reference to Jesus' suffering and death (here; 9:9,12,31; 10:33,45; 14:21,41) and his glorious return (8:38; 13:26; 14:62). A comparison of Mark 8:29,31 clearly shows that Jesus preferred the term "Son of Man" to "Messiah/Christ."

The verb translated "must" (*dei*) suggests divine necessity, probably as it is indicated in the Scriptures. The most obvious Scripture is Isa 52:13–53:12, which also avoids the title "Messiah." The word "elders" refers to the Jewish leaders in general. The New Testament is not the only work to use the plural "chief priests." In Josephus it includes the chief priest, former chief priests, and members of the aristocratic families who had important positions in the priestly hierarchy. As before, "teachers of the law" is the NIV's paraphrase of the term that traditionally has been translated "scribes."

Here and in 9:31 Mark has "after three days." In 10:34 Mark has "three days later." In each instance Matthew and Luke substitute "on the third day" (Matt 16:21; 17:23; 20:19; Luke 9:22; 18:33) perhaps because this is a more natural way of stating the matter in Greek, perhaps to prevent any idea of a contradiction since Jesus was not in the grave for three full days. As a matter of fact, "after three days" and "on the third day" mean the same thing (cf. Gen 42:17–18). The expression "after three days" reflects the Jewish practice of inclusive reckoning in which any part of a day or year is treated as a whole day or year.

8:32 The plain speaking about Jesus' death contrasts sharply with the command to silence about his person. Mark never suggested that Jesus tried to hide the necessity of his suffering and death. Peter, however, possessed as he was by a nationalistic concept of the Messiah, contradicted Jesus. Mark used the same word as in v. 30 and the same word he used elsewhere to refer to rebuking demons.

8:33 Jesus in turn rebuked (same word as in v. 32) Peter. The severity of the rebuke was because Peter was trying to dissuade Jesus from going to the cross, which Mark properly looked upon as an absolute necessity. Some have thought the expression "get behind me" refers to following after Jesus as a disciple, but the reference to Satan makes it likely that Jesus meant to get out of sight, to stop tempting. Jesus' rebuke of Peter's protest continues to challenge disciples both to accept the scandal of a suffering Messiah and to accept its implications for discipleship.

4. The Cost of Discipleship (8:34–9:1)

[34]Then he called the crowd to him along with his disciples and said: "If anyone would come after me, he must deny himself and take up his cross and follow me. [35]For whoever wants to save his life will lose it, but whoever loses his life for me and for the gospel will save it. [36]What good is it for a man to gain the whole world, yet forfeit his soul? [37]Or what can a man give in exchange for his soul? [38]If anyone is ashamed of me and my words in this adulterous and sinful generation, the Son of Man will be ashamed of him when he comes in his Father's glory with the holy angels."

[1]And he said to them, "I tell you the truth, some who are standing here will not taste death before they see the kingdom of God come with power."

It is widely agreed that the present section consists of a collection of the sayings of Jesus, which originally circulated independently and which Mark brought together because they deal with the sacrificial aspect of discipleship. Discipleship involves suffering. The presentation of such sayings is appropriate at this point immediately following the first passion prediction. If the Messiah must suffer, so must his followers.

8:34 The reference to "the crowd" is admittedly surprising. Its significance seems to be that the teaching is not just for the Twelve but for all who would follow Jesus. To "come after" and "follow" Jesus is to be his disciple. To deny oneself is not to do without something or even many things. It is not asceticism, not self-rejection or self-hatred, nor is it even the disowning of particular sins. It is to renounce the self as the dominant element in life. It is to replace the self with God-in-Christ as the object of affections. It is to place the divine will before self-will.

In the first Christian century an admonition to take up a cross could only have been an admonition to martyrdom. It reflected the practice of compelling a condemned person to carry the horizontal piece of the cross on which he was going to die. Evidently Jesus was too weak to carry his (15:21) or at least to do so all the way (cf. John 19:17), but he died nonetheless. That is what Jesus called on his followers to be willing to do. Many of his early followers did in fact die by crucifixion and in other ways. When martyrdom ceased to be common, cross bearing properly became a symbol of following Jesus in sacrificial service. The concept should never be cheapened by applying it to enduring some irritation or even a major burden. It is closely related to self-denial, involving a willingness to give up everything dear in life and even life itself for the sake of Jesus. It is a willingness to suffer for Jesus and for others. Such a concept of discipleship is so radical that many contemporary Christians in the West have difficulty relating to it.

8:35–37 The word translated "life" (*psychē*) in v. 35 is sometimes translated "soul," as in vv. 36–37 of the NIV. Generally, when people read or hear the word "soul," they think in Greek terms of an independent element in human nature that is separate from the physical body. This is not a biblical concept. The biblical emphasis in the word is on the wholeness and oneness of the person or self. Therefore "life" is the best translation, and it ought also to be used in vv. 36–37, as in the RSV, NRSV, GNB, and REB.[3] Of course, more is involved than mere physical life, and that probably is why some translations revert to "soul" in vv. 36–37.

8:38 In the first century being ashamed of Jesus and his words had particular reference to denying him in time of persecution. The idea can be applied to other situations. The background of the expression "adulterous . . . generation" is the Old Testament, where unfaithfulness to God is sometimes described as adultery (e.g., Jer 3:6–9; 13:27; and Hosea, where Gomer is a picture of unfaithful Israel).

Mark indicated that Jesus predicted not only his death and resurrection but also his return. Some interpreters, however, claim that Jesus here made a distinction between himself and the coming Son of Man. In view of the fact that the term "Son of Man" is often a substitute for the pronoun "I," this claim is most unlikely.

9:1 Unlike the previous sentence, the authenticity of this one is not often questioned. The use of the word *amēn* (translated "truth" in the NIV and "truly" in the RSV, NRSV, NASB, REB) characterizes the teaching of Jesus. The unique usage is a major factor in affirming authenticity, as is the obvious difficulty of the saying. If authenticity is not a consideration, interpretation is. In 8:34 Mark emphasized that Jesus "called the crowd to him along with the disciples." Does the "some who are standing here" (9:1) mean *some of the crowd* or *some of the disciples?* It is clear enough that "taste death" is simply a Semitism meaning *die* (GNB), but what did Jesus mean by "see the kingdom of God come with power"? Inasmuch as Matthew and Luke as well as Mark immediately followed the statement with an account of the transfiguration, the most likely view is that he understood the reference to be to that event. Furthermore, the transfiguration is a preview of the return of the Lord, which is referred to in v. 38 immediately preceding.

One problem with this understanding is that the statement about some who were present not tasting death before the coming of the kingdom in power seems to imply that some would do so. None of the disciples died during the six days between the announcement of v. 1 and the transfiguration (v. 2). The statement, however, does not necessarily imply that. All it certainly indicates is that some but not all would witness the event. More serious is the charge that the kingdom of God did not *come in power* at the transfiguration (the verb form, a perfect participle, suggests the meaning *come and stay*). This difficulty perhaps prompted Luke to omit the phrase "come in power" (cf. Luke 9:27).

---

[3]The NEB has "self" in vv. 36–37, and this too is a good translation.

J. Calvin took the difficult phrase to mean "the revelation of the heavenly glory which Christ began with the resurrection and then more fully offered when he sent the Holy Spirit and worked marvelous deeds of power."[4] M. Luther and K. Barth championed similar interpretations.[5] That God's kingdom came in power in Jesus' resurrection from the dead is a common New Testament idea (cf. Rom 1:4; 1 Cor 6:14; 2 Cor 13:4; Phil 3:10). Only Judas did not live to witness the resurrection and Pentecost, and therefore this interpretation creates a possible problem with the word "some," though of course it does not if "some" refers to the crowds (8:34).

A third interpretation is that the kingdom had already come in power through the healing and teaching ministry of Jesus (cf. the use of the term "authority" in 1:22,27; 2:10; 3:15; 6:7; etc.). There is, however, a difference between the nearness of the kingdom in 1:15 and the powerful manifestation of it here. Furthermore, why would not all the disciples have been able to observe the kingdom if it had already come with power? One possibility is the disciples' inability to see, which we have noted is a recurring Markan theme. Another possibility is that the reference points to the coming of the Spirit at Pentecost.

A fourth view is that Jesus meant the world mission of the church. This, however, was a gradual manifestation and not a sudden event as the statement implies.

A fifth view finds the fulfillment in the destruction of Jerusalem in A.D. 70. By then, however, tradition suggests that most of the disciples had died, and again there is a problem with the word "some." Furthermore, the destruction of Jerusalem was primarily an event in the history of Judaism, not Christianity, although it had some implications for Christianity. Though the coming of God was often for judgment in the Old Testament (Isa 13:5–16; 30:27–33; 64:1–2; Jer 51:25–26; Mal 3:1–2,5), this usage would be unusual for the New Testament, which generally associates the coming of the kingdom of God in power with salvation.[6]

A sixth view argues from the Markan context (8:38; cf. 13:26) that the kingdom of God comes in power at the Parousia. The improbability of these other views is another reason for identifying the event with the transfiguration

---

[4]J. Calvin, *Commentarius in Harmoniam evangelicam,* Corpus Reformatum 73:483, cited by G. R. Beasley-Murray, *Jesus and the Kingdom of God* (Grand Rapids: Eerdmans, 1986), 188.

[5]M. Luther, "Annotationes in aliquot capita Matt." *Weimar Ausgabe* 38:648ff.; K. Barth, *Church Dogmatics* 3/2, ed. G. Bromiley and T. F. Torrance, trans. H. Knight (Edinburgh: T & T Clark, 1969), 499.

[6]Beasley-Murray, *Jesus and the Kingdom,* 6, observes: "The Lord comes for the punishment of the wicked and the deliverance of his people. A survey of the references in the Old Testament to the coming of God would show that a preponderance of the passages feature the former motif, which reflects the early associations of the language of theophany with battle and of the coming of God with the 'wars of the Lord.'"

(see further the comments on the "Date" in the introduction). Despite interpretive difficulties, this saying was a word of encouragement to the powerless
ones in Mark's community who struggled to remain loyal to Jesus despite har-
rassment and the prospect of real persecution (cf. the warning in 8:38): some
will indeed live to see God exercise his reign.

5. The Transfiguration (9:2–10)

²**After six days Jesus took Peter, James and John with him and led them up a
high mountain, where they were all alone. There he was transfigured before them.
³His clothes became dazzling white, whiter than anyone in the world could bleach
them. ⁴And there appeared before them Elijah and Moses, who were talking with
Jesus.**

**⁵Peter said to Jesus, "Rabbi, it is good for us to be here. Let us put up three
shelters—one for you, one for Moses and one for Elijah." ⁶(He did not know what
to say, they were so frightened.)**

**⁷Then a cloud appeared and enveloped them, and a voice came from the cloud:
"This is my Son, whom I love. Listen to him!"**

**⁸Suddenly, when they looked around, they no longer saw anyone with them
except Jesus.**

**⁹As they were coming down the mountain, Jesus gave them orders not to tell
anyone what they had seen until the Son of Man had risen from the dead. ¹⁰They
kept the matter to themselves, discussing what "rising from the dead" meant.**

Questions often have been raised about the historicity of the account. A
number of indications, however, suggest that the event really took place. First,
this is the only description in Mark of a transcendent Christ, although Mark
elsewhere certainly affirmed the deity of Jesus. That Mark elsewhere
described Jesus in human terms strongly suggests this exception commended
itself to him because of its historicity and importance in the tradition. Second,
the exact chronological reference in v. 2, something that is quite unusual in
Mark, suggests a historical reminiscence. Third, the reference to Jesus as
"Rabbi" in v. 5 uses a term that was not used in the early church if one may
judge from its absence in Acts and the Epistles.

In a slightly different vein, some have claimed that the story is a misplaced
account of a resurrection appearance. It differs from such accounts in several
particulars. Resurrection stories usually begin with Jesus being absent and
then appearing. In the account of the transfiguration he was present from the
beginning. Resurrection stories sometimes begin with Jesus present but
unrecognized and progress to recognition (Luke 24:15–31; John 20:11–18;
21:4–7). In contrast, Mark's narrative begins with the recognizable and
moves to the unexpected transformation. In resurrection appearances Jesus
usually spoke to those around him during his appearance, but in this one he
said nothing until the transfiguration was complete and he and the disciples

were coming down the mountain. The prominence of Moses and Elijah in the transfiguration is also significant because elsewhere they were not associated with the resurrection.

A reasonable conclusion, therefore, is that the transfiguration actually happened, that it was an objective experience and not just a vision, and that it was reported to the early church by the participants. If in fact Peter was a source of information for Mark, the account is an eyewitness report.

The story functions in Mark to show that Jesus is more than what he appeared to be, that he is in fact the Son of God in the most advanced sense of that term. He had to suffer, but suffering was not his ultimate destiny. His ultimate destiny was to be glorified. The transfiguration is a preview of the full establishment of the kingdom of God at the glorious return of Jesus prophesied in 8:38. (Note 2 Pet 1:16–18, where the transfiguration is also associated with the coming of Christ.) The transfiguration serves as a preview of the full establishment of the kingdom of God at Jesus' return. The experience, occurring as it did soon after the first passion prediction, no doubt reassured the original disciples. It does the same for the readers of the Gospel, both ancient and modern.

9:2 Outside of the passion narrative the "six days" is the most precise chronological indicator in the Gospel and should be taken at face value. It may indicate that Jesus was still in the vicinity of Caesarea Philippi (8:27), although six days was more than enough time to return to Galilee. "Peter, James and John" are singled out for special favor as also in 5:37 and 14:33 and, with the addition of Andrew, in 13:3. As a result these three are sometimes referred to as the inner circle of the disciples.

The traditional location of the "high mountain" is Mt. Tabor in lower Galilee. It is convenient for pilgrims and is very beautiful and appealing. Though it is only 1,929 feet above sea level, the Old Testament compares this so-called "high mountain" with both Mt. Hermon (Ps 89:12) and Mt. Carmel (Jer 46:18). Its comparatively small summit probably was occupied by a fortress in Jesus' day. Most contemporary scholars, however, think Mt. Hermon, about twelve miles north of Caesarea Philippi, is a much more likely identification for this "high mountain." It attains a maximum elevation of 9,232 feet above sea level and, with its many spurs, covers a large area. The exact site, however, is unknown and unimportant. What is significant is that a high mountain in the Bible was often the place of revelation.

The word translated "transfigured" is found elsewhere in the New Testament in Rom 12:2 and 2 Cor 3:18 (and the parallel in Matt 17:2). In Romans and 2 Corinthians it refers to moral transformation, in Mark and Matthew to physical transformation. The cognate noun, which does not appear in the New Testament, is the source of the English word "metamorphosis," which is used to describe such things as the change of organic matter into rock, a tadpole into a frog, and a caterpillar into a butterfly. In whatever context the Greek or English derivative appears, the reference is to a radical change, to a complete transformation. Jesus' appearance was temporarily changed from that of an ordinary human being to a divine being in all of his glory.

9:3 The Greek text actually says "intensely white, as no fuller ["launderer," NASB; "bleacher," NEB and REB] on earth could bleach them" (RSV). Only Mark recorded this statement, i.e., what is in the last part of the verse. The brightness recalls the shekinah glory of God in the Old Testament.[7]

9:4 Moses and Elijah are usually thought to be representatives of the law and the prophets, respectively. This identification probably is correct, although in Deut 18:15, which is echoed in the statement "Listen to him" in v. 7, Moses is a prototype of the eschatological prophet of whom Jesus is the antitype. Their appearance to Jesus suggests that the law and the prophets bear witness to him and that he is the fulfillment of the ancient Scriptures. Both Moses and Elijah are associated with high mountains, Moses with Mt. Sinai (e.g., Exod 19) and Elijah with Mt. Horeb (1 Kgs 19). Both men underwent transformations, Moses when his face shown with reflected glory (Exod 34:29–35) and Elijah when he was taken up to heaven in a chariot of fire (2 Kgs 2:11).

Contrary to Matt 17:3 and Luke 9:30, Elijah is mentioned before Moses in v. 4 (but not v. 5). The reason no doubt is that the following narrative (vv. 11–13) deals with Elijah. Mark did not indicate the topic of conversation. Luke 9:31 indicates that it was Jesus' "exodus," i.e., his coming death.

9:5 For Jesus to be addressed as "Rabbi" on such a solemn occasion is quite unexpected. Matthew 17:4 changes the term to "Lord" and Luke 9:33 to "Master" to suggest greater reverence. Mark's use of a less flattering term probably indicates that he preserved the very word Peter used. Peter's use of the term probably indicates that he did not yet fully understand who Jesus was. "Rabbi" means *my great one* or *my esteemed teacher*. Mark used it again in 11:21 and 14:45.[8]

Peter's lack of understanding is seen further in his desire to erect three "shelters" ("booths," RSV; "tabernacles," NASB; "tents," GNB). He may have gotten the idea from the use of booths in the wilderness and at the Feast of Tabernacles (cf. Lev 23:39–43; Hos 12:9; Zech 14:16–19). The transfiguration may have taken place in the early fall about the time of that feast. To have erected shelters as Peter wished would have put Jesus on the same level as

---

[7]The word "Shekinah" is found in the targums and rabbinic writings, but not in the Old Testament itself. Nevertheless it is a convenient term for describing the radiance, the glory, and the presence of God as manifested, for example, in the cloud that hovered above the tabernacle and went before Israel during the journeys through the desert.

[8]The NIV notwithstanding, the word in 10:51 is the related word "Rabboni" (NASB).

Moses and Elijah. It would have prolonged or even made permanent the situation. To do so, however, would have detoured Jesus from the cross. Although the transfiguration gave a preview of Jesus' future glory, in actual fact the cross had to precede glory. Mark wanted to emphasize that suffering was also a necessity in the case of Jesus' disciples.

Indeed, the association of the Feast of Tabernacles with the messianic age may have been a reason Peter wanted to build the shelters. He thought the end had come. The kingdom did in fact draw near with the appearance of Jesus, but it was not fully established at that time.

9:6 The statement probably is Mark's own comment rather than something he received in the tradition. It possibly reflects a statement by Peter to Mark, "I was so afraid that I did not know what to say."

9:7 The cloud just like the bright, white clothes (v. 3) suggests the shekinah glory and calls to mind the tent of meeting. In the Old Testament clouds are symbols of God's presence, protection, and authority (Exod 13:21; 16:10; 19:9,16; 24:15–16; 33:9). In the New Testament clouds are associated with the return of Christ (13:26; 14:62; Acts 1:9–11; 1 Thess 4:17), of which the transfiguration is a preview. Interpreters are divided whether the cloud here reveals or conceals. There is no reason it could not do both.[9]

The expression "whom I love" recalls Isaac, the beloved son of Abraham (Gen 22:2); and it also repeats in essence the divine declaration at the baptism (1:11). The command "Listen to him" alludes to the prophet like Moses to whom the Israelites were to listen (Deut 18:15–19). Likely the command here refers especially to Jesus' teaching about his death.

9:8 The account ends abruptly. Mark evidently emphasized that the transfiguration was but an interlude, that Jesus had to get on his way to Jerusalem to die.

9:9–10 It quickly becomes apparent that the disciples did not understand the significance of the transfiguration. For this very reason Jesus demanded silence. Verse 9 is the last injunction to silence in Mark, it is the only one that gives a reason for the command, and it places a time limit on the "secret." Therefore this verse is the key to understanding all the commands of silence. Until Jesus had died and had been raised, his true identity and significance could not be known. He could not be proclaimed until then. Just as people pondered whether John was the Christ (cf. Luke 3:15), so, according to Mark, Jesus intended that during his lifetime they should ponder whether he was the Christ. The "messianic secret" was not the invention of Mark but the intention of Jesus.

---

[9]The voice is the voice of God, not the *bath qol,* which means "the daughter of the voice," i.e., an echo of the divine voice. With the rise of the belief that prophecy had ceased, the scribes taught that only a whisper or echo of the word of God could still be heard. Early Christians believed, however, that true prophecy resumed with John, Jesus, and the apostles.

It is possible to interpret the verb translated "kept" in the NIV to mean *obeyed* and to connect the phrase "to themselves" with "discussing" so that the result is "They obeyed his order, but among themselves they started discussing the matter" (GNB). Furthermore, the NASB, NEB, and REB translate the first verb "seized upon" rather than "kept" or "obeyed." Whatever the exact meaning of the Greek construction, the two interpretations are similar in resultant meaning.

6. The Question about Elijah (9:11–13)

¹¹And they asked him, "Why do the teachers of the law say that Elijah must come first?"
¹²Jesus replied, "To be sure, Elijah does come first, and restores all things. Why then is it written that the Son of Man must suffer much and be rejected? ¹³But I tell you, Elijah has come, and they have done to him everything they wished, just as it is written about him."

The disciples' question was prompted by the appearance of Elijah on the mount and their continuing uncertainty about the identity of Jesus. Many Jews of the time believed that Elijah would precede the Messiah, though perhaps the expectation was for Elijah to appear before the general resurrection. Jesus' disciples may even have wondered how he could be the Messiah in the absence of any return by Elijah. Jesus and his followers had to show that an Elijah-like person had appeared in John the Baptist. Justin Martyr, *Dialogue with Trypho* 49 (ca. A.D. 135), encountered this very objection. No doubt Mark and his readers/hearers had also. In addition to answering the objection, Mark may have recorded the account to show again that the rejection and execution of the forerunner was a prophecy of the rejection and death of Jesus himself.

9:11 The phrasing of the question is a subtle indication that for many first-century Jews the scribal tradition took precedence over the written law. Not only did the scribes ("teachers of the law," NIV) teach that Elijah had to precede the Messiah, but Mal 3:1 and 4:4–6 do as well. We should note that Malachi did not mention the Messiah per se; Malachi expected Elijah to come before the Day of the Lord's judgment (Mal 4:5).

9:12 For once Jesus affirmed the truthfulness of the scribal teaching, in this instance because it was also the teaching of Scripture. The primary passage about the suffering of the Son of Man that Jesus had in mind must have been Isa 52:13–53:12. Psalm 22 is another possibility. Significantly, Jesus shifted the emphasis. Elijah is not the central or crucial issue but the suffering of the Son of Man. John/Elijah was important as Christ's forerunner in suffering and death. Only the cross makes Elijah's role clear.

9:13 If finding passages that predict the suffering of Jesus is difficult, finding ones that predict the suffering of John/Elijah is even more difficult.

Evidently the allusion to which Jesus was referring was 1 Kgs 19:2,10, where Jezebel threatened the prophet. There is a striking parallel between the death of John at the instigation of a wicked woman who manipulated a weak king and the persecution of Elijah by another such woman who manipulated another king. Mark and his contemporaries probably saw in John's death a prophecy of the death of Jesus. Revelation 11 records a later Christian tradition that another Elijah-like person is to be killed because of his testimony about Jesus. See also the comments on 1:1–8.

7. The Exorcising of a Demon from a Deaf and Mute Boy (9:14–29)

[14]When they came to the other disciples, they saw a large crowd around them and the teachers of the law arguing with them. [15]As soon as all the people saw Jesus, they were overwhelmed with wonder and ran to greet him.

[16]"What are you arguing with them about?" he asked.

[17]A man in the crowd answered, "Teacher, I brought you my son, who is possessed by a spirit that has robbed him of speech. [18]Whenever it seizes him, it throws him to the ground. He foams at the mouth, gnashes his teeth and becomes rigid. I asked your disciples to drive out the spirit, but they could not."

[19]"O unbelieving generation," Jesus replied, "how long shall I stay with you? How long shall I put up with you? Bring the boy to me."

[20]So they brought him. When the spirit saw Jesus, it immediately threw the boy into a convulsion. He fell to the ground and rolled around, foaming at the mouth.

[21]Jesus asked the boy's father, "How long has he been like this?"

"From childhood," he answered. [22]"It has often thrown him into fire or water to kill him. But if you can do anything, take pity on us and help us."

[23]" 'If you can'?" said Jesus. "Everything is possible for him who believes."

[24]Immediately the boy's father exclaimed, "I do believe; help me overcome my unbelief!"

[25]When Jesus saw that a crowd was running to the scene, he rebuked the evil spirit. "You deaf and mute spirit," he said, "I command you, come out of him and never enter him again."

[26]The spirit shrieked, convulsed him violently and came out. The boy looked so much like a corpse that many said, "He's dead." [27]But Jesus took him by the hand and lifted him to his feet, and he stood up.

[28]After Jesus had gone indoors, his disciples asked him privately, "Why couldn't we drive it out?"

[29]He replied, "This kind can come out only by prayer."

This is the last exorcism in Mark, but it is not simply another miracle story with the primary purpose of demonstrating the power of Jesus. Just as the miracles that introduce (8:22–26) and conclude (10:46–52) the second major division have a theological purpose, so does this one. Actually there are several purposes. One is to give another example of the inability of the disciples.

This time it is not inability to understand but inability to act. Another purpose is to stress the necessity and give insight into the nature of faith in discipleship. Another is to instruct the church about its ministry after the departure of Jesus. (In this connection note v. 19.) Yet another is to prefigure Jesus' death and resurrection.

The wealth of detail may indicate a personal recollection, possibly that of Peter. Some technical scholars, however, think that the existing account has come from the combination of two originally independent miracle stories. The reasons given include the two references to a crowd (vv. 14,25), the different descriptions of the problem (vv. 17,25 on the one hand and vv. 18,20,22,26 on the other), and the shift of emphasis from the disciples to the father. The theory is not impossible, but it is improbable. None of the elements in the story is irreconcilable with the others, and confusion is a major element in the event itself.

Some have tried to find an analogy between what Moses found when he came down from the mountain (Exod 32) and what Jesus found. The scribes are thought to take the place of the rebellious Israelites. However, the situations are quite different. Moses found gross immorality; Jesus found unbelief, inability to heal, and controversy.

Preachers have often contrasted the glories of the mountain and the agonies of the valley. Such an application is appropriate. Mark no doubt indicated not only what was the ministry of Jesus but also what should be that of the disciples. As wonderful and important as mountaintop experiences can be, the disciple's primary occupation is in the valley of service.

9:14   The textual witnesses vary between the plural "they came" and "they saw" and the singular "he came" and "he saw" (KJV, NKJV), but the context and perhaps Mark's style favor the former. If in fact the transfiguration took place on Mt. Hermon (see the comments on 9:2), the presence of the "teachers of the law" is surprising, but not impossible. They may have pursued Jesus in order to gather evidence against him. Of course, the transfiguration may not have taken place on Mt. Hermon, and Mark may have employed topical rather than chronological arrangement.

9:15   Some have claimed that the crowd's astonishment was due to Jesus' face shining like that of Moses (Exod 34:29–35). This is not impossible, but none of the Evangelists makes any such claim; and it is best not to read into the text what is not there. The astonishment probably was due to the unexpected arrival of Jesus. Mark may have wanted his readers to contrast the "wonder" of the crowd with the disciples' slow recognition.

9:16   It is difficult to determine whether the antecedent of "you" is the teachers of the law or the disciples. If it is the teachers of the law, the word "them" would refer to the disciples; if it is the disciples, the word "them" would refer to the teachers of the law. Clearly there had been a dispute between the two groups. It is also difficult to see the relation between the disciples' inability to heal and the scribes' accusations. Perhaps the scribes took advantage of the situation and reproached the disciples for their impotence. In any event the former disappear from the story after v. 16.

9:17–18 In v. 17 the child's malady is described as both demon possession and inability to speak. In v. 25 deafness is also included. In vv. 18,20,22, however, the symptoms are those of epilepsy. There is no reason the same person could not have been the victim of all these. The meaning of the second verb in v. 18 (*rhēssō*) is uncertain. Most translations understand it to mean *throw down*, but it could also mean *tear apart* (cf. KJV). Likewise the verb translated "becomes rigid" (*xērainomai*) in the NIV and most other contemporary translations can also mean *to dehydrate* or *exhaust*.

9:19 In 8:12,38 the word "generation" is applied to unbelievers who oppose Jesus, but here it probably refers to the disciples. Jesus soon would be gone and then his disciples would take his place and do what he had been doing. This they had failed to do during a temporary absence. Having previously been able to exorcise demons (6:13), the disciples assumed they could do so whenever they wished. They failed, however, because of their lack of faith. Spiritual power is not something which once possessed will always be available. It must be maintained and renewed. Disciples then and now must constantly learn and relearn this lesson.

9:20–22a Most of Mark's detail is omitted by Matt 17:14–21 and Luke 9:37–43a, in part because it is repetitious and in part simply to save space for other accounts. The repetition heightens the greatness of the cure.

9:22b The inability of the disciples to cast out the demon appears to have shaken the faith of the father. In v. 24 the father confessed his unbelief.

9:23 The Greek text is awkward and created problems for ancient copyists. A very literal translation would be, "The 'if you can.' " Some scribes omitted the article "the," and others added "believe." The article, however, merely serves to introduce a quotation. The construction could be paraphrased, "With reference to your statement, 'If you can.' " Up to this point the emphasis has been on the lack of faith of the would-be healers (i.e., the disciples), but here it begins to shift to the father who brought the child to be healed. (Evidently the boy was not capable of exercising faith.) There is little or no problem with this shift. All need faith: those who would heal or perform any other ministry and those who would be healed or have someone else healed or in some other way be blessed.

9:24 This time the NIV translates the key Markan word "immediately" (*euthys*). Mark wanted to emphasize that faith should be exercised at once. Although there is tension, no contradiction exists between an affirmation of faith and a confession of unbelief. Both are the frequent experience of disciples of all times.

9:25 As on other occasions, Jesus avoided unnecessary publicity and acted before the crowd grew larger or got out of hand. Mark alone emphasized the permanence of the cure.

9:26–27 Whether the boy actually died, Mark's description suggests the idea of resurrection. The second and third verbs in v. 27 are often used in connection with resurrection. The account has much in common with the raising of Jairus's daughter (5:41–42). Therefore the exorcism constitutes a preview of Jesus' own death and resurrection and the resurrection of believers.

9:28 This is the second of four times where Mark indicated that Jesus withdrew to a house in order to instruct the disciples privately (also 7:17; 9:33; 10:10; cf. 4:10; 7:24).

9:29 Up to this point the account has emphasized the necessity of faith. Here the idea of prayer is injected. The two are closely related. Prayer, especially a whole life of prayer, is the avenue to faith. All except the two earliest and generally regarded best Greek manuscripts, two early versions, and one early Christian writer add "and fasting" (KJV, NKJV), no doubt because of the prevalence of fasting in the early and medieval church (a similar addition is in Acts 10:30; 1 Cor 7:5). The idea is completely out of place, however, in a passage that stresses the necessity of dependence on God instead of human resources of any kind.

8. The Second Passion and Resurrection Prediction (9:30–32)

30They left that place and passed through Galilee. Jesus did not want anyone to know where they were, 31because he was teaching his disciples. He said to them, "The Son of Man is going to be betrayed into the hands of men. They will kill him, and after three days he will rise." 32But they did not understand what he meant and were afraid to ask him about it.

Some have argued that the three passion and resurrection predictions are merely different versions of a single saying of Jesus. There is no reason, however, Jesus would not have predicted his death and resurrection more than once.

9:30 "That place" is either the "house" (literal translation) of v. 28 or the region of Caesarea Philippi of 8:27 and/or the mountain of the transfiguration of 9:2. The reason for secrecy was not to escape from Herod (6:14) or the teachers of the law (9:14) but to escape from the crowds and to have time to instruct the disciples, especially about the passion (v. 31). According to Mark, Jesus' public ministry in Galilee was over. The trip through Galilee was the first leg of the journey to Jerusalem and to the cross.

9:31 What is distinctive in the second passion prediction is the use of the word that literally means *to give over* or *hand over* (*paradidōmi*). Here the NIV offers the translation "betrayed." The Greek Old Testament used it with reference to the fate of the prophets (e.g., Jer 26:24 [LXX 33:24]), and it became an important term in the Jewish theology of martyrdom. Mark used it to indicate what happened to John (1:14, "was put in prison"), what Judas did to Jesus (3:19; 14:10–11,18,21,42,44), what happened to Jesus (here; 10:33; 14:41; 15:1,10,15), and what will happen to Jesus' disciples (13:9,11–12). Certainly the word can mean *betrayed by a man*, and Judas could be the implied subject as the NIV translation suggests. In Rom 1:24,26,28 it refers to how God handed over the wicked to their fate and in 4:25 and 8:32 to how God delivered Jesus to die for humanity's sin. In Gal 2:20 and Eph 5:2,25 it refers to how Jesus gave himself for people's sin. Inasmuch as the word was often used by early Christians for what God and/or Jesus did to save the world, it is not farfetched to see that meaning here. If the reference were only to what Judas did, the words "into the hands of men" would be superfluous. The play on the words "Son of Man" and "men" should be noted.

9:32 Again Mark emphasized the dullness of the disciples. He did not shy away from this emphasis. There is, however, some evidence that the disciples were gaining insight. Probably they feared further questioning about what Jesus said due to the apprehension of facing a complete revelation of the suffering that lay ahead. Or they may have feared being rebuked like Peter. Nevertheless, as the following passage indicates, their minds were wrongly occupied with the question about who among them was the most important.

9. The Discussion about Greatness (9:33–37)

³³**They came to Capernaum. When he was in the house, he asked them, "What were you arguing about on the road?"** ³⁴**But they kept quiet because on the way they had argued about who was the greatest.**
³⁵**Sitting down, Jesus called the Twelve and said, "If anyone wants to be first, he must be the very last, and the servant of all."**
³⁶**He took a little child and had him stand among them. Taking him in his arms, he said to them,** ³⁷**"Whoever welcomes one of these little children in my name welcomes me; and whoever welcomes me does not welcome me but the one who sent me."**

Many agree that vv. 33–50 consist of a collection of Jesus' sayings of various occasions on the general subject of discipleship. One reason is that they are found in other orders and contexts in Matthew and Luke. Another is that they are related to one another by catchwords. Notice the repetition of the expressions "in my name" and "in your name" in vv. 37–39,41. Notice the reference to children in vv. 36–37,42. See also the repetition of the expression "causes . . . to sin" in vv. 42–43,45,47; the repetition of the word "Gehenna" ("hell," NIV) in vv. 43,45,47; the repetition of "enter life/kingdom of God" in vv. 43,45,47; the repetition of the word "fire" in vv. 43,48,49; and the various allusions to salt in vv. 49–50. Arrangement by catchwords was sometimes used in ancient times to facilitate memorization. The serious student of the Gospels must recognize the presence of topical as well as chronological arrangement. It is possible, but not probable, that everything in vv. 33–50 followed in order after the events of 9:1–32.

The discussion about greatness may have resulted from the selection of the three to witness the transfiguration (v. 2). Its inappropriateness is highlighted by placing it immediately after the second passion prediction. Mark intended the words and actions of Jesus in this section to be a commentary on the implications of his death for discipleship. The one who follows Jesus in the way of the cross must live a life of sacrifice and service.

There can be no question about the authenticity of various sayings in vv. 33–50, which represent a dramatic reversal of human values in all ages.

9:33 The house was probably that of Peter and Andrew (1:29). Again the house is the place of private instruction of the disciples. The instruction in the house presumably continues as far as v. 50 (cf. 10:1).

9:34 Some commentators have labeled the account artificial because of the improbability of grown men arguing about who was the greatest. The Essenes at Qumran, however, were concerned about their individual rank within the community. Pride and ambition are temptations in every age. Mark correctly analyzed that the disciples' attitude was at the heart of the problem.

9:35 Sitting was the usual posture of a Jewish teacher (cf. Matt 5:1; Luke 5:3; John 8:2). Some have found a contradiction in Jesus' calling the Twelve when they were already with him, but this was Mark's way of saying that Jesus called them to attention. Jesus' point was that in the kingdom ordinary human values are reversed. The paradox of the gospel is that the way of service—the way of Jesus himself—is the way to true greatness.

9:36–37 In much the same way as the ancient prophets, Jesus taught not only by his words but also by symbolic actions. His use of the child is an acted parable, a dramatized illustration. The meaning of the symbolic action cannot be grasped without recognition of the lowly place occupied by children in ancient society and a realization that the same Aramaic word means both *child* and *servant*. A child in the Bible is both a symbol of innocence and of helplessness and vulnerability. In 10:13–16 and in Matt 18:3–4 disciples are exhorted to become humble like a child, but here and in Matt 18:5 and Luke 9:48 the child represents any helpless person but especially a humble fellow believer whom the true disciple is to receive. To "welcome" or "receive" (RSV, NASB, NEB, REB) means *to be concerned about, to care for, to show kindness to.* To do so in the name of Jesus means to do as he would do, to do so for his sake, to do so as a Christian. To accept the outcasts and oppressed is a way of accepting both God and Jesus. Greatness in the kingdom consists not of position but of ministry.

10. The Question about the Independent Exorcist (9:38–41)

38"Teacher," said John, "we saw a man driving out demons in your name and we told him to stop, because he was not one of us."
39"Do not stop him," Jesus said. "No one who does a miracle in my name can in the next moment say anything bad about me, 40for whoever is not against us is for us. 41I tell you the truth, anyone who gives you a cup of water in my name because you belong to Christ will certainly not lose his reward.

In this brief pronouncement story all but the first verse is a pronouncement of Jesus on the subjects of acceptance and hospitality. It may have been preserved and recorded here because of its relevance to the treatment of those engaged in the Gentile mission, which is alluded to several times in Mark. Mark wanted his readers/hearers to be open toward other Christian groups just as Jesus had been.

That the early church would have invented a story about Jesus' tolerance is hard to believe because early Christians were not always tolerant (cf. Luke 9:54; 2 Cor 2:6–8; and especially the unwillingness of many Jewish Christians to accept fully Gentile Christians as seen frequently in Acts). Jesus' openness here, however, is similar to his attitude toward Gentiles and Samaritans as recorded in Matt 8:5–13; Luke 7:2–10; 9:52–56; 10:29–37; John 4. Comparing the account with Joshua's attempt to restrain Eldad and Medad from prophesying in Num 11:26–29 is interesting, but there is no reason to think that the Old Testament story has influenced the New Testament one.

9:38 Only here in Mark is any action or saying of the disciple John recorded. His intolerance here is compatible with that in Luke 9:54–55. Driving out a demon in Jesus' name involved invoking that name in doing so. Acts 19:13–14 indicates that Jewish exorcists sometimes used the name of Jesus in their work. There the practice was condemned, probably because they had no sympathy with Jesus or his followers and employed the name only as a magical incantation. Here it was approved, probably because the exorcist was a believer. The objection of John, who evidently was speaking on behalf of all the disciples, was only that the man was not part of their little group and had not been authorized by Jesus to use his name. From what follows, the objection evidently was not valid.

9:39–40 Jesus'—and Mark's—point was that all who with any degree of sincerity do something for or on behalf of Jesus (note "in my name") were to be recognized as allies, if not fellow disciples. The lesson for the church today is that tolerance, acceptance, and recognition should be extended to other denominations and to persons of other theological persuasions. Sadly, few individual Christians and Christian groups throughout the history of the church have followed this teaching of Jesus. Exclusiveness rather than inclusiveness has been the rule. The saying in v. 40 seems to contradict the one in

Matt 12:30 (cf. Luke 11:23). In the latter case, however, the allusion is to those who unquestionably opposed Jesus. Here it is to one who was in basic sympathy with Jesus and his work.

9:41   The "cup of water" may be taken literally because water was precious in a semiarid climate, or it may be viewed as symbolic of any kind of hospitality. The word "you" refers to any disciple of Jesus who is engaged in any kind of ministry or who is in any kind of need. The word "my" is not in the best attested Greek text, but the NIV may be interpreting that text rather than translating an inferior one. Even more interpretative is the RSV "because you bear the name of Christ." The Greek expression is an idiom meaning *on the basis of* or *on the ground that* or simply *because*. One could leave out the word "name" and translate "because you belong to Christ" (NIV). The word "Christ" (without any article in Greek) is used as a proper name, as is common in the Pauline Letters but rare in the Gospels and Acts. This verse and 10:21,30 are the only references to reward in Mark. He did not look upon it as a major motive for discipleship.

11. A Warning against Offenses (9:42–50)

42"And if anyone causes one of these little ones who believe in me to sin, it would be better for him to be thrown into the sea with a large millstone tied around his neck. 43If your hand causes you to sin, cut it off. It is better for you to enter life maimed than with two hands to go into hell, where the fire never goes out. 45And if your foot causes you to sin, cut it off. It is better for you to enter life crippled than to have two feet and be thrown into hell. 47And if your eye causes you to sin, pluck it out. It is better for you to enter the kingdom of God with one eye than to have two eyes and be thrown into hell, 48where

> **" 'their worm does not die,**
> **and the fire is not quenched.'**

49Everyone will be salted with fire.

50"Salt is good, but if it loses its saltiness, how can you make it salty again? Have salt in yourselves, and be at peace with each other."

Some commentators begin this section with v. 41, others with v. 43. But at least vv. 42–48 deal with the subject of offenses, whereas v. 41 does not. Some make vv. 49–50 a separate section, but there is also a warning element in it; multiplying sections unnecessarily is not desirable.

9:42   The "little ones" of this verse represent the same persons as the "child" in vv. 36–37: immature, weak, and perhaps new believers. To cause these (whom society views as insignificant) to sin or stumble will bring serious judgment. The judgment is pictured as a large millstone tied around the neck. The "large millstone" was one turned by a donkey (so the Greek construction) rather than a hand mill used by a woman.

9:43–48   Whereas v. 42 deals with causing someone else to sin, vv. 43–48 are concerned with permitting oneself to sin. These verses contain metaphors that must not be taken literally, as did the church father Origen (d. A.D. 254).[10] Neither must they be ignored. Jesus used the most startling metaphors possible to show that the possession of spiritual life is worth the most costly sacrifice. Whatever endangers spiritual life must be totally removed even as a surgeon amputates a limb that endangers the life of the rest of the body. Romans 8:13 and Col 3:5 provide a good commentary on the teaching of Jesus here. The "life" of vv. 43,45 is obviously the same as the "kingdom of God" of v. 47 and the "eternal life" of 10:17,30.

The word translated "hell" in vv. 43,45,47 is *gehenna*. The Greek word is a transliteration of two Hebrew words meaning *valley of Hinnom*. The reference is to the deep valley on the south and west side of Jerusalem. In pre-Israelite times it was the site of child sacrifice to Molech. Some Israelites, in times of spiritual decline, seem to have adopted the practice also (Jer 7:31; 19:6; 32:35; cf. 2 Kgs 16:3). In an attempt to stop the practice, Josiah desecrated the site (2 Kgs 23:10). During intertestamental times it became the garbage and sewage dump of Jerusalem and a symbol of the place of punishment (1 Enoch 27:2; 4 Ezra 7:36) because worms and fires were always consuming the refuse (v. 48). Although the KJV translates both alike, one should always distinguish between *gehenna* and *hades*. The latter is the place of the dead or simply the grave.

The quotation in 9:48 is from Isa 66:24 LXX, which was important in the development of the symbolism of *gehenna*. The worm and the fire are symbols of destruction. Verses 44 and 46 are not found in the earliest and best textual witnesses and are a scribal repetition based on v. 48, where the statement is unquestionably authentic.

9:49   The verse is found only in Mark. Matthew and Luke probably omitted it because of its difficulty. First, there is a textual problem. The earliest and best witnesses have the reading translated by the NIV (also RSV, NRSV, NASB, NEB, REB, GNB). A small group of witnesses belonging to the Western type of text has "every sacrifice will be salted with salt," which alludes to Lev 2:13, which in turn some scribe evidently thought was the key to the meaning of the reading above. The majority of medieval manuscripts combine the two earlier readings (KJV, NKJV).

Second, there is an interpretive problem: what does it mean to be salted with fire, and who will have such an experience? The key to the meaning is to recognize that the word "fire" has a different reference from what it has in

---

[10] When Origen was not able to suppress completely his lust, he mutilated himself (Eusebius, *Church History* 6.8, however, associated the act with the saying in Matt 19:12).

vv. 43 and 48. In the latter it is obviously a symbol of punishment. In v. 49, however, both salt and fire symbolize purification. The reference is probably to the purifying effect of persecution (cf. 1 Pet 1:7; 4:12). The only connection between vv. 48 and 49 is the catchword "fire." The two verses must be interpreted independently. Here is a rare case where consideration of the context hinders rather than helps the interpretation. The word "everyone" refers to Jesus' disciples—not just the Twelve but the larger group that included those among Mark's readers who had already experienced abuse and would soon face martyrdom.[11] Disciples must be like the ancient sacrifices that were powdered with salt and consumed by fire.

9:50 Here the allusion is to salt used in domestic life. "Salt is good" in that it is a necessity for life and a preservative. Christians are likewise a source of spiritual life for the world. They restrain evil and thus preserve the moral order. Christians, however, can and sometimes do cease to function as the "salt" of the world, and it is against this that Jesus warned. Pure salt cannot lose it saltiness. What was used as salt in ancient times, however, and especially what was gathered from the Dead Sea in Palestine, contained many impurities. If the true salt were removed, what remained might still look like salt but could not perform the life-giving and life-saving function of salt. A person may have the external appearance of a disciple, but not the internal properties.

"Have salt in yourselves" has been variously interpreted to refer to being willing to be sacrificed, common sense (cf. Col 4:6), loving neighbors, wisdom, fellowship and friendship, and being at peace. Probably the idea is simply to give life and preservation to the world.

This miscellaneous collection of the sayings of Jesus on discipleship began with a dispute (vv. 33–34), and it concludes with an admonition to be at peace with one another. Peace (reconciliation) is disrupted by ambition to be great in a worldly fashion; it is promoted by the servant attitude.

12. The Journey to Jerusalem (10:1–45)

Some describe the entire second section (8:22–10:52) as a journey to Jerusalem. Others begin it in 8:27 or 8:31. It is true that Mark indicated that Jesus left Galilee when he departed for Caesarea Philippi (8:27) and that he did not again minister publicly in Galilee (cf. 9:30), but still it is difficult to include a northward journey to Caesarea Philippi and perhaps beyond in a southward journey to Jerusalem. The latter clearly begins, however, in 10:1.

---

[11] According to those who date the book after A.D. 64–65, they had already experienced martyrdom.

The material in chap. 10 has something in common with the "tables of household duties" in Eph 5:21–6:9; Col 3:18–4:1; 1 Pet 2:18–3:7 because it treats married persons (vv. 1–12), children (vv. 13–16), rich people (vv. 17–27), and church leaders (vv. 28–31,35–45). Some would even include the treatment of "little ones" in 9:33–42. To say the least, chap. 10 is not a typical "table of household duties." Jesus' affirmation of the goodness of marriage (10:1–12) is not a guideline for order within marriage. The difficulty the rich experience in entering the kingdom (10:23–27) is a poor analogy to the responsibilities of masters and slaves; the servant spirit demanded of church leaders does not parallel lists of qualifications for specific offices. This section of Mark is not so much concerned with order as with discipleship. Mark shows that discipleship expresses itself within relationships.

(1) The Teaching about Divorce (10:1–12)

¹Jesus then left that place and went into the region of Judea and across the Jordan. Again crowds of people came to him, and as was his custom, he taught them.
²Some Pharisees came and tested him by asking, "Is it lawful for a man to divorce his wife?"
³"What did Moses command you?" he replied.
⁴They said, "Moses permitted a man to write a certificate of divorce and send her away."
⁵"It was because your hearts were hard that Moses wrote you this law," Jesus replied. ⁶"But at the beginning of creation God 'made them male and female.'
⁷'For this reason a man will leave his father and mother and be united to his wife,
⁸and the two will become one flesh.' So they are no longer two, but one. ⁹Therefore what God has joined together, let man not separate."
¹⁰When they were in the house again, the disciples asked Jesus about this. ¹¹He answered, "Anyone who divorces his wife and marries another woman commits adultery against her. ¹²And if she divorces her husband and marries another man, she commits adultery."

The question about divorce was one of interest in the time of Jesus because of the recent divorces of Herod Antipas and Herodias in order to marry each other (cf. 6:17–18) and because of the debates between the rabbinical schools of Hillel and Shammai. There is no evidence that any Jewish teacher prior to Jesus denied the legitimacy of divorce. The issue was what constituted justifiable grounds for divorce, and that depended in large part on the interpretation of the vague expression in Deut 24:1, which is quite properly translated in the GNB "something about her that he doesn't like." The conservative school of Shammai held that it referred to adultery. (This is apparently also the understanding of the NIV, RSV, NASB, NEB, REB, which have "something indecent" or "something shameful" or a similar translation.) The liberal school of Hillel, however, claimed that a man could divorce his wife for anything that displeased him, even burning a meal.[12]

The question of divorce was important to Mark's readers/hearers because divorce was easy and frequent in Rome and because it was tempting for Christians in the city to be caught up in the conventions of their society. The same is true of Christians today.

The account is a pronouncement story. Most important are the pronouncements of Jesus in vv. 5–9,11–12. There is no question about the authenticity of such pronouncements, which are utterly different from the teaching of both Judaism and paganism.

10:1 The expression "that place" must refer to Galilee and/or Capernaum, the last places mentioned (9:30,33). Where Jesus went is complicated by a textual problem. The best attested text is that translated by the NIV, "the region of Judea and across the Jordan" (the same Greek text lies behind the other translations cited in this commentary except for the KJV and NKJV). On first reading at least this translation seems to suggest that Jesus went first to Judea (via Samaria?) and then to Perea (the territory on the east side of the Jordan River). One gets the impression from the account as a whole, however, that Mark intended to describe a continuous journey to Jerusalem and the cross. It is unlikely he intended to say that Jesus approached Jerusalem and then detoured to Perea.

A variant reading with fair to good attestation omits the word "and" so that the reference is to "Judea beyond the Jordan." This reading is almost certainly a secondary assimilation to Matt 19:1. The third reading is that of the majority of medieval manuscripts, "to the region of Judea by the other side of the Jordan" (NKJV, similarly KJV). It successfully solves the problem but for just that reason is also suspect. Scribes tended to eliminate difficulties, not create them. The best procedure is to accept the best attested text and to take the position that Mark made no attempt to list the places in the order Jesus went through them. He did a similar thing in 11:1, where he mentioned Jerusalem before Bethphage and Bethany, although the real order was Bethany, Bethphage, and Jerusalem. Claiming that Mark had little knowledge of Palestinian geography is unnecessary. Jesus probably did go down the east side of the Jordan and then cross into Judea, as the medieval text suggests. Here and in what follows, Mark indicated that after leaving Galilee, Jesus resumed public ministry.

10:2 Some witnesses of medium value omit "some Pharisees came" and read simply "they tested him by asking." The word "tested" indicates that the question was hostile and had Jesus' entrapment as its object. The fact that the

---

[12] "The School of Shammai say: A man may not divorce his wife unless he has found unchastity in her. . . . And the School of Hillel say: [He may divorce her] even if she spoiled a dish for him. . . . R. Akiba says: Even if he found another fairer than she." *M. Git.* 9.10, trans. Danby.

question was asked in Perea, part of the territory of Herod Antipas, may be significant. Perhaps the Pharisees hoped Jesus would offend Herod, even as John had done, and that he would meet the same fate at the hands of Herod as John did. If not that, he would surely alienate one or both of the rabbinical schools—one if he opted for either strict or lax rules for divorce, both if he disallowed all divorce.

10:3–4 Instead of a direct answer, Jesus asked a counterquestion: "What did Moses command you?" The allusion in v. 4 is to Deut 24:1. Prior to Moses' time, a man apparently could divorce his wife by a mere word. Although it did not constitute God's ultimate intention for marriage, Deut 24:1 offered some protection for the helpless wife. A husband had to go to the trouble of getting a bill of divorce drawn up and witnessed and formally presenting it to her.

10:5 First, Jesus indicated that provision for divorce was due to human rebellion against the divine ideal ("because your hearts were hard"). The provision was an attempt to limit the effects of human sinfulness. Distinguishing between God's ultimate intention for the human race, more particularly his own people, and his temporary accommodation to human inability or unwillingness to accept his high standards is important. Moses did not command or encourage divorce. He merely permitted it.

10:6 Second, Jesus moved the discussion to a higher plane by going beyond interpreting Moses' legislation to God's original intention for marriage as seen in the creation. The quotation is from Gen 1:27. The entire verse reads: "God created man in his own image, in the image of God he created him; male and female he created them." Just as God is inseparably one being, so he intended for a male and a female in marriage to become one being who would not be divided.

10:7–8 The second quotation is from Gen 2:24. The key terms are "united," "one flesh," and "one." The words "and be united to his wife" are omitted from the two earliest Greek manuscripts and a few other good quality textual witnesses (and from the NASB). The textual problem is whether the words were added by copyists to conform Mark to Gen 2:24 and/or Matt 19:5 or whether they were accidentally omitted when an early scribe skipped from the second "and" in v. 7 to "and" at the beginning of v. 8. It is impossible to say with confidence.

The divine ideal as seen in creation is the permanent union of a man and a woman in marriage and no divorce whatsoever.

10:9 The "man" of this verse is a husband and not a judicial authority. In first-century Jewish and pagan society, divorce was not effected by courts but by individuals.

10:10 For instruction of the disciples in a house, see the comments on 7:17.

10:11 The word "her" refers to the first wife, the one who was divorced. The teaching of Jesus was quite contrary to that of Judaism. According to Jewish law, a wife could commit adultery against her husband by having relations with another man; and a man, whether or not married, could commit adultery against another man by having relations with that man's wife. But a husband could not commit adultery against his own wife by being unfaithful to her. By insisting that a husband could commit adultery against his own wife, Jesus greatly elevated the status of wives and women in general.

10:12 This verse is found only in Mark. In ancient Jewish society a wife did not have the right to divorce her husband.[13] The claim has often been made that Jesus did not speak the words in v. 12 but that they reflect the situation of the early Gentile church. In Roman society men and women had equal rights of divorce. A student of the Gospels must allow for the possibility that the Evangelists adapted the words of Jesus to make them relevant to their situation. This in no way denies that Jesus actually spoke the words. Roman law and Jewish law functioned side by side in first-century Palestine, and within limits a person could be governed by either. If a Jewish woman demanded a divorce, she could get one on the basis of Roman law, although this might cut her off from Jewish society. Furthermore, it is not impossible that Jesus foresaw the extension of his teachings beyond the bounds of Palestine.

The interpretation of v. 12 is complicated somewhat by a textual problem. One variant reading with fair support substitutes a verb meaning *to separate* for the one meaning *to divorce*. The reference could be to a wife separating from her husband without formally divorcing him, as the Herodias of 6:17–28 seems to have done. This reading, however, is probably a scribal attempt to alleviate the difficulty of the original text.

The effect of Jesus' teaching is to condemn all divorce as contrary to God's will and to set forth the highest standards of marriage for his disciples. Christians of all eras have often fallen short of the ideal just as ancient Jews did, and there is no reason to think the same provision for human imperfection that existed in Moses' day does not still exist today. God can forgive divorce as well as other sins. Divorce may sometimes be the lesser of two evils, but it is never pleasing to God or good in itself. It should not be looked upon by conscientious Christians as the preferred option.

(2) The Blessing of the Children (10:13–16)

13People were bringing little children to Jesus to have him touch them, but the disciples rebuked them. 14When Jesus saw this, he was indignant. He said to them,

---

[13]Josephus, *Antiquities* 15.7.10: "Salome had a quarrel with Costobar and sent him a document that dissolved their marriage, although this was not according to Jewish law. With us it is lawful for a husband to do this, but a divorced woman by herself may not marry unless her first husband permits it."

"Let the little children come to me, and do not hinder them, for the kingdom of God belongs to such as these. [15]I tell you the truth, anyone who will not receive the kingdom of God like a little child will never enter it." [16]And he took the children in his arms, put his hands on them and blessed them.

This beautiful and moving story about Jesus' love for children has been a favorite throughout the centuries. The main concern of the account, however, is not children as such but the kind of people who may enter the kingdom of God. There is also commendation of coming to Jesus and bringing others as well. Those who come may be assured of acceptance.

This is a pronouncement story, and its authenticity is guaranteed by the fact that the teaching and action of Jesus were different from that of most elements of his society. In fact, the story cannot be appreciated without a realization of the lowly place children occupied in ancient society, more so in pagan than Jewish. Regardless of when in Jesus' ministry the event occurred, Mark appropriately placed this account immediately after the preceding section because children and marriage naturally are associated.

The account should be compared with 9:36–37. There, however, the child represents any helpless person, but especially a humble fellow disciple, who is to be received by other disciples. Here the children represent characteristics disciples should possess.

10:13 The word translated "children" could refer to any age between infancy and twelve (cf. its use in 5:39,42 to refer to a twelve-year-old girl). Verse 16, however, suggests that these children were small. Although touching is used elsewhere in Mark in connection with healing, the intent of those who brought the children to Jesus was for a "holy man" to bless them.

Why the disciples rebuked those who brought the children is not stated, but they probably thought Jesus was too busy or too important to be bothered by such insignificant persons. In any event Mark set forth another example of the lack of perception of the disciples. The second instance of "them" could, from a strictly grammatical standpoint, refer to the children; and in order to avoid that understanding, the mass of medieval manuscripts substituted "those who brought *them*" (NKJV, similarly KJV).

10:14 Both Matt 19:14 and Luke 18:16 omit the statement that Jesus was indignant, no doubt to avoid any thought of Jesus being guilty of a sinful passion. This is sometimes said to be the only example in the Gospels of Jesus being angry, but see 3:5 and the comments on 1:41 and compare the accounts of the cleansing of the temple. The variant reading in 1:41, however, employs a different Greek verb from the one here; and the cleansing accounts do not explicitly state that Jesus was angry.

The word translated "hinder" is used in Acts 8:36; 10:47; 11:17 (also Matt 3:14) in connection with baptism, and as a result some commentators have claimed that Jesus meant that children were not to be hindered from being baptized. Such a view is eisegesis (reading an idea *into* the text) rather than exegesis (drawing out the meaning of the text). It is true, however, that the second-century and later church used the passage to justify the practice of infant baptism.

The word "children" in vv. 13–14,16 refers to literal children who were being brought to Jesus; but to whom do the words "such as these" in v. 14 and "like a little child" in v. 15 refer, to literal children or to adults who possess childlike characteristics? Without going into the question of the extent to which children can be part of the kingdom of God, the expressions certainly include older people who in their relationship to God possess childlike characteristics. What are these characteristics? Such things as innocence, humility, lack of self-consciousness, receptivity, and trustfulness have been suggested. Not all children share these characteristics, however. The main point of comparison probably is the insignificance, weakness, helplessness, and dependency shared by children in ancient society and those who enter the kingdom at any time. The ultimate focus of the passage is not only on the attitude with which one comes to Jesus but on *coming to Jesus*, the object of one's faith.

10:15   Some have suggested that this verse breaks the train of thought between vv. 14 and 16 and is a saying of Jesus from another occasion that Mark inserted here. The possibility of this must be admitted. A similar saying is found in a different context in Matt 18:3. But the content of v. 15 is altogether appropriate to its present context.

The one Greek word *amēn*, which the NIV translates "I tell you the truth," emphasizes the importance of the pronouncement. Note that the kingdom is both to be received and entered—two ideas that stand side by side throughout the Bible. The blessings of the kingdom are to be received as a gift, yet we enter the kingdom through responsive faith and obedience. Furthermore, the kingdom and Jesus, in whom it drew near, are virtually synonymous. The expression "like a child" could refer to the way in which one receives a child, but the context favors the idea of the way in which a child receives what is offered to him or her: totally dependent on the person giving it.

10:16   Here Jesus is pictured as supporting his teaching with his actions, visually demonstrating that the blessings of the kingdom are available to those who will come to Jesus. By taking the children in his arms, he did more than he was asked to do.

(3) *The Inquiry of the Rich Man and Jesus' Teaching about Wealth and Rewards (10:17–31)*

17As Jesus started on his way, a man ran up to him and fell on his knees before him. "Good teacher," he asked, "what must I do to inherit eternal life?"
18"Why do you call me good?" Jesus answered. "No one is good—except God alone. 19You know the commandments: 'Do not murder, do not commit adultery,

do not steal, do not give false testimony, do not defraud, honor your father and mother.' "

²⁰"Teacher," he declared, "all these I have kept since I was a boy."

²¹Jesus looked at him and loved him. "One thing you lack," he said. "Go, sell everything you have and give to the poor, and you will have treasure in heaven. Then come, follow me."

²²At this the man's face fell. He went away sad, because he had great wealth.

²³Jesus looked around and said to his disciples, "How hard it is for the rich to enter the kingdom of God!"

²⁴The disciples were amazed at his words. But Jesus said again, "Children, how hard it is to enter the kingdom of God! ²⁵It is easier for a camel to go through the eye of a needle than for a rich man to enter the kingdom of God."

²⁶The disciples were even more amazed, and said to each other, "Who then can be saved?"

²⁷Jesus looked at them and said, "With man this is impossible, but not with God; all things are possible with God."

²⁸Peter said to him, "We have left everything to follow you!"

²⁹"I tell you the truth," Jesus replied, "no one who has left home or brothers or sisters or mother or father or children or fields for me and the gospel ³⁰will fail to receive a hundred times as much in this present age (homes, brothers, sisters, mothers, children and fields—and with them, persecutions) and in the age to come, eternal life. ³¹But many who are first will be last, and the last first."

Whether vv. 17–31 should be treated as a unit or broken up into two (vv. 17–27,28–31) or three (vv. 17–22,23–27,28–31) sections is debated. Verses 23–27 follow so naturally after vv. 17–22 that Mark may have received them as a unit that deals with the same event in Jesus' life. Verses 28–31 are not so closely bound to the preceding, may have taken place at another time, may have circulated independently, and may have been inserted by Mark because of their relevance to the subject of possessions.

Verses 17–22 contain what is usually referred to as the story of the rich young ruler. The term, however, is a composite. Although all three accounts indicate that the man was rich (Mark in v. 22), only Matt 19:20 stated that he was young; and only Luke 18:18, that he was a ruler. It is a pronouncement story with the pronouncement in v. 21. What is in vv. 23–25,27,29–31 supplements and explains the pronouncement in v. 21.

The entire section emphasizes that riches make being a disciple difficult but the rewards of discipleship are worth more than material possessions. Jesus did not teach that wealth is evil. He did not teach that poverty is better than riches. He did not teach that only the poor can be saved. He did teach that discipleship is costly and that wealth often is a hindrance to repentance and acceptance of the gospel.

Verses 23–27 contain the two aspects of the kingdom mentioned above: it is to be entered through responsive faith and obedience and received as a gift.

The rich man is an example of one who tried to enter it by doing something. He stands in stark contrast with the children who had nothing and who could do nothing.

10:17   Mark began the section by reminding his readers/hearers that Jesus was on his way to Jerusalem and the cross. Commentators are divided as to whether the man's running up to Jesus, falling on his knees, and calling Jesus "good"—all of which were quite unusual—indicate flattery or respect. In view of Jesus' reaction the latter seems more probable. The question is also unusual because most Jews would have no doubts about what to do: observe the law. Probably the man had heard about Jesus' teaching that mere obedience to the law was not enough. It was natural for a man who may have inherited some of his wealth to ask about *inheriting* eternal life. Although common in John's Gospel, the term "eternal life" is found only here and in v. 30 in Mark (and elsewhere in the Synoptics only in Matt 19:29; 25:46; Luke 10:25; 18:18,30). The emphasis is on the quality rather than the quantity of the life.

10:18   In Jewish thought God was preeminently good (1 Chr 16:34; 2 Chr 5:13; Ezra 3:11; Ps 118:1; 145:9, etc.), so much so that it was unusual to apply the term to anyone else. That was the main reason for Jesus' question and statement. The statement does not reflect a consciousness of sinfulness on the part of Jesus. It is not a disclaimer of goodness or deity. Such ideas are totally irrelevant. It simply points to God as the supreme example of goodness and the source of all good things, including the commandments in v. 19 and the commands in v. 21. Throughout his life Jesus was concerned to exalt and glorify God. Luke 18:19 lets Mark's statement stand, but Matt 19:17 restates it so as to minimize the possibility of misunderstanding or offense. Certainly the church would never have invented the Markan statement. It is unquestionably a genuine saying of Jesus.

10:19   Jesus further directed the man's thoughts to God by calling his attention to the second table of the Ten Commandments of Exod 20:12–16 and Deut 5:16–20. According to the best attested text, the Commandments are listed in an unusual order: six, seven, eight, nine, and five. The command "do not defraud" between the references to the Ninth and Fifth Commandments is substituted for the Tenth Commandment, "You shall not covet."[14] Fraud is a concrete example of covetousness and a special temptation of the rich. Jesus probably limited his reference to the second table of the law, the one dealing with relationships of human beings to each other, because obedience to it pro-

---

[14]The majority of medieval manuscripts and some others reverse the sixth and seventh although this takes them out of their biblical order (so KJV, NKJV). A few witnesses of medium value substitute "immorality" for "murder." One excellent witness omits "do not defraud" to conform to the Old Testament sources and the Matthean and Lukan parallels. Interestingly no copyists attempted to put the Fifth Commandment back in its proper place.

vides evidence of obedience to the first table, the one dealing with the relationships of human beings to God.

10:20   How to evaluate the claim made in this verse is difficult. On the one hand, Jesus did not explicitly deny in v. 21 that the man had kept the letter of the Commandments; on the other, he asked him to do something to demonstrate that he was willing to observe the spirit of the last six Commandments. Alternately, Jesus called the man to a greater obedience than that embodied in the Ten Commandments (cf. Matt 19:21, "If you want to be *perfect*"; also Matt 5:20–48). According to v. 22 he was not willing to do what Jesus asked of him. The rich man apparently did not understand what was involved in keeping the Commandments. Alternately, the "one thing" this man lacked was not understanding of the requirements of the law but radical trust in God, who alone is good, that would allow him to abandon all his property and follow Jesus. The word "boy" probably refers to the time since his thirteenth birthday when he became a *bar mitzvah*, a *son of the commandment*, one who took upon himself the obligation to obey the law.

10:21   The word "loved" in the present context refers to something more than embrace, attraction, or affection. It refers to genuine love based on need and not merit or response. The one thing the man lacked was devotion to God, as demonstrated by compassion for the needy. Had this man truly trusted in the goodness of God (v. 18), he would have welcomed Jesus' command as God's best for him. The command "sell everything . . . and give to the poor" should not be universalized and applied literally to every professing Christian. It pertains to the need of a particular person. It should not be ignored either. Other persons may have to give up other things in order to follow Jesus: a vocation, a style of life, a sinful passion, or a relationship. The call is not to poverty but to discipleship, which takes many forms. Discipleship, however, is costly. It involves sacrifice. It involves obedience. It involves following the example of Jesus. It also involves reward, something that is elaborated in vv. 29–31. The words "take up the cross" (KJV, NKJV) are found mainly in the medieval Greek text and are an assimilation to 8:34, where there are no variations in the text.

10:22   The words "great wealth" probably refer to estates. This is the only example in Mark of someone being called to discipleship but refusing. Not only did the man go away sad, but many of those who have read the account over the years have also been saddened. In fact, this verse has been described as the saddest in the Bible.

10:23   The event became the occasion for a brief discourse. Jesus' statement must be contrasted with the Jewish attitude toward riches. The dominant Jewish view was that riches were an indication of divine favor and a reward for piety (Job 1:10; 42:10; Ps 128:1–2; Isa 3:10). Although provision was made for the protection and assistance of the poor (Deut 15:7–11;

Prov 22:22–23), rarely was poverty associated with piety. The Psalms
sometimes picture the poor as the righteous who rely on God for aid (Pss
37:14,16; 69:32–33; 86:1–2). The Psalms frequently portray God as the
special help of the poor. Especially during the Maccabean period (142–63
B.C.), the rich became associated with the priestly aristocracy ready to compromise with foreign oppressors; the poor, with those who remained faithful
to God (cf. *T. Jud.* 25:4; *Pss. Sol.* 10:6). The Qumran community apparently used "the poor" as a self-designation (1 QM 11:9,13; 13:14; 1QH
5:13–22, in which "the poor" parallels those eager for righteousness;
1QpHab 12:3,6,10; 4QpPs 2:9–10; 3:10).

The teaching of Jesus was nonetheless revolutionary in its time and remains
scandalous even today. However, Jesus did not condemn riches as evil in
themselves. They are a temptation, a hindrance, a diversion. They provide
false security that makes radical trust in God difficult.

10:24 In view of the prevailing Jewish attitude toward riches, the disciples' amazement is not surprising. Whereas v. 23 describes the difficulty of the
rich in entering the kingdom, this verse, according to the best attested Greek
text, affirms the difficulty of *all* in so doing.[15]

10:25 A few witnesses of medium quality reverse the order of vv. 24 and
25 and make minor changes in v. 25. Verse 25, however, appropriately follows v. 24 as a concrete example of the uncompromising statement in that
verse. All attempts to ease the harsh meaning of v. 25 must be resisted, e.g.,
the substitution of the Greek word meaning *rope* for the one meaning *camel*
(there is only one letter difference in Greek) or the idea that the reference is to
a small gate in Jerusalem called "Eye of the Needle" through which a camel
could go only with great difficulty.

The mere existence of the word meaning *rope* is unattested until at least the
fifth Christian century and perhaps until medieval times. Furthermore, to put
a rope through the eye of a needle would be almost as difficult as to put a
camel through it. No early evidence exists that there was a small gate called
"Eye of the Needle." The claim first appears in the ninth Christian century,
long after the destruction of the Jerusalem of Jesus' day. The contrast between
the largest Palestinian animal and one of the smallest openings is clearly
intended to indicate the impossibility of a rich person—or anyone else
(v. 24)—entering the kingdom by doing something for himself or herself.

10:26 For once the NIV, NRSV, NEB, and GNB do not follow the earliest and usually best manuscripts, which have "to him" (RSV, NASB). The latter probably is a grammatical improvement upon the former reading "to each

---

[15] The words "those who trust in riches" (KJV, NKJV) are attested not only by the late textual
witnesses but also by some early and good ones. Nevertheless they are clearly an attempt to soften
the impact of the statement. The two earliest manuscripts plus a few others have the shorter text
translated by the NIV.

other" by the Alexandrian text-type, which is sometimes guilty of such a thing. It should be noted that being saved, the kingdom of God (vv. 23–25), and eternal life (v. 17) all refer to the same thing, a right relationship with God.

10:27   This verse probably is the key to understanding the entire passage. Inheriting eternal life, entering the kingdom, and being saved are impossible for any human being, but not for God, who is good and desires the salvation of all. Therefore all must depend entirely upon God. Such absolute trust in God makes possible a life of faithful discipleship (v. 28).

10:28   Again Peter appears in the narrative as the spokesman for all the disciples. One may question, however, the accuracy of his use of the word "everything." It is probably an exaggeration. In leaving occupation and family, however, observe that Peter, James, and John did leave far more than many modern-day disciples (1:18,20).

10:29   From warning, Jesus turned to promise. The medieval text adds the word "wife" after "mother" (KJV, NKJV), doubtless in an attempt to apply Peter's example to celibate priests and monks.

10:30   Though v. 29 mentions leaving father to follow Christ, fathers are noticeably absent in the enumeration of relationships in v. 30. This absence suggests that God is the one "Father" of disciples. Some commentators have questioned whether Jesus included the word "persecutions" as part of the "reward" of discipleship, and they have suggested that it is the addition of the early church in light of its experiences. Jesus, however, could have foreseen the persecution of his followers. He himself was persecuted, and it was reasonable to expect that his disciples would be also. Significantly, both Matthew and Luke omit this reference to persecution. If this had been added by the early church, it most likely would have found its way into all three accounts. Persecution is a specially Markan emphasis.

10:31   The different contexts of this saying in Matt 20:16 and Luke 13:30 suggest it was probably a "floating" saying. It is, however, the kind of statement Jesus could have made more than once. Mark likely placed it here to provide an appropriate warning about being preoccupied with rewards and also to summarize and nicely conclude vv. 17–30.

(4) The Third Passion and Resurrection Prediction (10:32–34)

[32]They were on their way up to Jerusalem, with Jesus leading the way, and the disciples were astonished, while those who followed were afraid. Again he took the Twelve aside and told them what was going to happen to him. [33]"We are going up to Jerusalem," he said, "and the Son of Man will be betrayed to the chief priests and teachers of the law. They will condemn him to death and will hand him over to the Gentiles, [34]who will mock him and spit on him, flog him and kill him. Three days later he will rise."

The third passion prediction is more detailed than the first two individually or combined—so much so that many have concluded that it is a "prediction after the event" written after Jesus' death and then ascribed to him by the early church. The most significant difference in this prediction and the previous ones is the distinction between condemnation by the Jewish authorities and execution by the Gentiles. If Jesus had supernatural insight, there is no problem with a detailed prediction that concurs with what actually happened. Although an objective interpreter should not deny all possibility of coloring of the report of the prediction by the fulfilled event, the fact that the events in v. 34 are not in the same order or wording as those in 15:15–20 weighs against the claim. Indeed, specific reference to crucifixion might be expected after the fact. The passion predictions, however, speak generally of Jesus' death. If one must have a source for v. 34, Ps 22:6–8 and Isa 50:6 are likely. There is no reason why Jesus could not have seen his fate reflected in these Scriptures.

10:32 Again Mark reminded his readers/hearers that Jesus was on the road, but for the first time he specifically mentioned Jerusalem as the destination. The expression "going up to Jerusalem" could be taken literally because the road climbs about 3,300 feet in the twenty miles from Jericho to Jerusalem, but almost certainly it is used in the common way as a technical term for going to the Holy City on a pilgrimage or for some other important purpose. In Mark, Jerusalem is a symbol of opposition to Jesus (e.g., 3:22; 7:1).

Rabbis usually walked ahead of their disciples, but Mark had something more than that in mind by his statement "with Jesus leading the way." He pictured Jesus as resolutely pressing toward his goal, as deliberately going to his death. This steadfast determination on the part of Jesus produced the astonishment and fear. Commentators are much divided as to whether Mark intended to depict one or two groups, i.e., the disciples alone or the disciples and some other pilgrims who were in the same party. The matter troubled ancient copyists as well, some of which omitted "while those who followed were afraid" so as to have only one group, the disciples.[16] The grammar of the passage probably favors concluding that two groups were in Mark's mind despite the unusual nature of the Greek construction. Unusual constructions are characteristic of Mark's Greek. Note how Mark again pictured Jesus as giving the disciples private instruction.

10:33–34 The elements not in either of the previous passion predictions are the handing over to the Gentiles and the mocking, spitting, and flogging—and perhaps also the explicit reference to the sentence of death.

---

[16]It has been conjectured that Mark wrote "he [Jesus] was amazed" rather than "they [the disciples, as the NIV properly interprets] were amazed"; but in addition to the lack of manuscript evidence, this is contrary to Mark's picture of Jesus as resolutely going to the cross.

(5) The Ambition of James and John (10:35–45)

[35]Then James and John, the sons of Zebedee, came to him. "Teacher," they said, "we want you to do for us whatever we ask."

[36]"What do you want me to do for you?" he asked.

[37]They replied, "Let one of us sit at your right and the other at your left in your glory."

[38]"You don't know what you are asking," Jesus said. "Can you drink the cup I drink or be baptized with the baptism I am baptized with?"

[39]"We can," they answered.

Jesus said to them, "You will drink the cup I drink and be baptized with the baptism I am baptized with, [40]but to sit at my right or left is not for me to grant. These places belong to those for whom they have been prepared."

[41]When the ten heard about this, they became indignant with James and John. [42]Jesus called them together and said, "You know that those who are regarded as rulers of the Gentiles lord it over them, and their high officials exercise authority over them. [43]Not so with you. Instead, whoever wants to become great among you must be your servant, [44]and whoever wants to be first must be slave of all. [45]For even the Son of Man did not come to be served, but to serve, and to give his life as a ransom for many."

A passion prediction is again followed by an account of incomprehension on the part of the disciples. No doubt Mark's own readers/hearers had difficulty in understanding the full significance of the passion and needed to realize that Jesus' first disciples had a similar difficulty. Mark's repeated references to the incomprehension of the original disciples are his way of helping his readers/hearers understand the truth. This section specifically develops the significance of Jesus' death for discipleship by providing exhortation to humility, servanthood, and perhaps even martyrdom.

Although the source of the sayings in vv. 39,45 has been questioned, the historicity of the account as a whole is beyond question. The early church would never have invented a story that is so discrediting to two of the most prominent apostles and indeed to all twelve.

10:35 James and John have been mentioned previously and favorably in 1:19,29; 3:17; 5:37; 9:2. In Matt 20:20 the mother of James and John made the request. Matthew adapted this story for his audience as did Luke (22:24–27), who has the event in another context. Luke also "spares" the apostles by omitting any reference to a request and beginning the account with "a dispute arose among them."

10:36 One manuscript of medium value omits "What do you want me" so that Jesus answers "I will do it for you." Several other variants try to smooth out the difficult Greek construction. There is no question, however, about the original text or its meaning.

10:37 In Jewish thought the right hand of the king was the place of greatest prominence; and the left hand, second in prominence (1 Kgs 2:19;

Ps 110:1, etc.). James and John apparently expected Jesus to establish his kingdom and enter into his glory when he reached Jerusalem. They wanted a prominent place in the messianic, earthly kingdom. Though they recognized Jesus as the Messiah, they completely misunderstood the nature of the kingdom Jesus came to establish.[17] Though Mark's readers/hearers had recognized Jesus as a suffering Messiah, some of them probably misunderstood the implications for their discipleship and needed to be corrected.

10:38 Despite the audacity of James and John, Jesus did not rebuke them directly but indicated they did not realize the implications of their request. In the kingdom the way to glory is sacrifice, service, and suffering. In the kingdom exaltation involves lowliness.

In the Old Testament a cup is sometimes a symbol of joy and salvation (Pss 16:5; 23:5; 116:13), but more often it is a symbol of the wrath of God (Pss 11:6 [NIV "lot"]; 75:8; Isa 51:17,22; Jer 25:15–17,27–28; 49:12; 51:7, etc.). The latter is certainly the case here. In the Old Testament the word "baptize" is not used, but there are several references to being engulfed by trouble (Job 22:11; Pss 11:6; 18:16; 42:7; 69:1–2,15; 124:4–5; Isa 43:2). Here the word does not refer literally to Christian baptism but metaphorically to being immersed in calamity.

As for Jesus the metaphors "cup" and "baptism" signify his coming death. As for the disciples they could refer to martyrdom but do not necessarily do so. They could refer to any kind of suffering for their religious faith. If the common symbolism of the cup is allowed, and if the word "ransom" in v. 45 is taken into consideration, Jesus endured the wrath of God in the place of sinners when he died on the cross. Obviously martyrdom and other forms of suffering of disciples do not serve the same redemptive purpose. Jesus did no more than ask if they were willing to suffer and die as he would do. He did not deal with the significance of their suffering.

10:39 The unhesitating answer of the two probably indicates that they still did not understand what was involved in being a disciple. In view of their expectation of a glorious kingdom (v. 37), it is surprising that they would so readily have agreed to suffer. Mark indicated that Jesus ironically predicted they would indeed share his "cup" and "baptism." A few modern scholars, however, have argued that the prediction comes not from Jesus but from the early church, that it is another "prophecy after the event."

This theory arises first from failure to realize that vv. 38–39 do not necessarily refer to the disciples' martyrdom. Just as the disciples' death would not have the same significance as that of Jesus, so their "cup" and "baptism"

---

[17] The fact that Jesus had no intention of establishing a temporal kingdom during his earthly ministry does not rule out the possibility that he will do so in the future. That question will have to be decided on the basis of other passages of Scripture.

would not necessarily take the same form as his. Second, the theory accepts an early martyrdom of John despite the slender evidence for it. According to Acts 12:2 James was indeed martyred at the hands of Herod Agrippa I, probably in A.D. 44, and this alone is sufficient fulfillment of the prophecy. The New Testament does not record the death of John. The later epitomizer of the Chronicle of Philip of Side (ca. A.D. 450) claimed that Papias (ca. A.D. 130) indicated John and James were killed by the Jews. George the Sinner (ca. A.D. 840), who may have been dependent on Philip, said the same thing and claimed their deaths were a fulfillment of Mark 10:39. A Syriac martyrology of the early fifth century and a Carthagenian martyrology of the early sixth century celebrate the deaths of both James and John on December 27.[18] Philip, however, so far as can be judged from the surviving fragments of his works and the comments of ancient historians about him, was unreliable. There is the further question as to whether the epitomizer accurately represented him. Irenaeus (ca. A.D. 180) and Eusebius (ca. A.D. 325) had read Papias, and they mentioned no such statement. The much earlier and more widespread tradition is that John the apostle lived to a very old age and died a natural death in Ephesus in Asia Minor. His death, however, came after suffering exile and torture during the time of the emperor Domitian (ca. A.D. 95). The last item is also sufficient fulfillment of the prophecy. There is no good reason to conclude therefore that the early church formulated a "prophecy" to explain the deaths of both James and John.

10:40   It is unclear whether Jesus meant that God alone could give places of honor or whether he meant that he himself could do so only to those for whom the places had been prepared. The use of the so-called divine passive probably favors the former. One good manuscript and several other textual witnesses of medium quality actually add "by my Father" after "prepared." This view should present no problem even to an interpreter with a very high Christology because of the obvious self-imposed limitations of Jesus during his earthly life.

10:41   The reaction of the ten is no more commendable than the arrogance of the two. Probably they were angry because they wanted the positions for themselves!

10:42   Jesus used the entire incident to teach the necessity of humility and service, especially for Christian leaders. Mark's diction is not the best, and his word, which usually means *to seem* or *to appear* has been variously translated: "regarded as rulers" (NIV), "recognized as rulers" (NASB, similarly NRSV, NEB and REB), "considered rulers" (GNB), "supposed to rule" (RSV), and

---

[18] Cited by V. Taylor, *The Gospel According to St. Mark*, 2nd ed. (London: Macmillan, 1966), 442. Actually the Carthagenian martyrology mentions John the Baptist, but this is probably a mistake for John the apostle.

even "aspire to rule" (some commentators). In any case the authoritarian ways of ancient rulers, even the most petty of them, is well known. Today the description of authoritarian ways could well be extended beyond governmental officials to some business and church leaders.

The last part of the verse as well as vv. 43–44 and v. 45 provide good examples of synonymous parallelism that characterizes Hebrew poetry. Such form makes it probable that the statements go back to Jesus rather than to the later Gentile church.

10:43–44 By aspiring to places of greatness, the disciples were in danger of becoming like Gentile rulers. Here Jesus emphatically stated that his disciples must not be like Gentile rulers but like "servants" (*diakonoi*), originally those who waited on tables,[19] and like a "slave" (*doulos,* one totally owned by another and possessing no rights except those given by his or her master). A servant type of ministry, of which Jesus himself is the best example, is set forth.

10:45 Whether Jesus actually spoke the words in this verse or whether they had their origin in the early church and were then attributed to him is much debated by the scholarly interpreters of Mark. First, some point out that the word "ransom" appears nowhere else in the teaching of Jesus (only in the parallel in Matt 20:28) and reflects a later Pauline interpretation of Jesus' death. Actually the word appears nowhere else in the New Testament, which is strange if Paul is the source of the idea.[20] The word is common in the LXX and sets forth a well-established Old Testament idea. Therefore there is no reason Jesus could not have used it, or at least the Aramaic equivalent.

Second, some claim "ransom" is out of harmony with the idea of service. Death as a ransom is, however, simply the greatest example of service. The unusual association of ideas in fact supports Jesus rather than the early church as the source of the connection. The ideas stand together in Isa 53:11–12, which may have been in Jesus' mind.

Third, and similar to the preceding, some have suggested that Luke 22:27, which mentions service, but not ransom, is the original form of the statement. In reply, by no means is it certain or even probable that Luke 22:27 and Mark 10:45 (cf. Matt 20:28) represent the same saying of Jesus.

Fourth, some argue that the expression "did not come" reflects a time after Jesus' life. It need not suggest, however, that his entire life was in the past, only that his coming into the world, only that a substantial part of his ministry was. Furthermore, the vocabulary ("Son of Man," "to give . . . life," and "many") and the structure (the use of parallelism) are Jewish and not Greco-

---

[19] In other contexts the word refers to a church officer. Its nontechnical meaning, however, has considerable significance for the kind of persons deacons should be.

[20] The word is *lytron.* The compound form *antilytron* appears in 1 Tim 2:6.

Roman and more likely go back to Jesus than the Gentile church. Implicit in this statement is a bold challenge reminiscent of other sayings of Jesus: those who readily accept Jesus' ransom ought also accept his example of service.

The word translated "to be served" and "to serve" (*diakoneō*) is the verbal form of the noun in v. 43. The noun and the verb originally referred to menial service such as waiting on tables. Jesus did not identify the kind of service he performed but affirmed that his life was characterized by a servant attitude and by actually performing many kinds of service and ministry. By so affirming he set himself before the disciples as an example to follow—something that often has been forgotten by his followers.

The word translated "ransom" was often used in secular Greek to refer to purchasing the freedom of a slave or a prisoner of war. The emphasis was on the price that was paid. It is used in this way in the LXX (Lev 25:51–52). In the LXX it is also used for the half-shekel tax each male paid to the sanctuary for his own redemption (Exod 30:12), the money paid to spare the life of one whose ox had gored another to death (Exod 21:30), the price paid for the redemption of the firstborn (Num 18:15), and the payment used to redeem mortgaged property (Lev 25:26).

Although the word used in Mark 10:45 is never used in the LXX to translate the Hebrew word meaning *guilt offering*, the meaning of the latter probably has influenced that of the former. See Lev 5:14–6:7; 7:1–7; Num 5:5–8; and especially Isa 53:10. Again the possibility that Jesus understood his approaching death in terms of Isa 53 must be recognized. He viewed his death as a vicarious sacrifice for sin. In fact, the word translated "for" properly means *in the place of* and not merely *on behalf of*. Jesus spoke in Aramaic, however, which may not have made the distinction. To say the least, Mark presented Jesus' death as a substitutionary offering for the sins of others. The substitutionary idea comes out again in 14:24 and possibly in 14:27. No attempt should be made to limit how many are those for whom Jesus died. The word in context does not mean *many but not all*. Rather it is a Semitism that means *all who are many*. In the similar statement in 1 Tim 2:6 the word "all" is actually used.

The lengthy comments on v. 45 indicate its importance. Some even think that it is the key verse and that it suggests an outline of the book: chaps. 1–10: the service of the Son of Man; chaps. 11–16: the ransom of the Son of Man. There is, however, a problem of what to do with 10:46–52 and 16:1–8.

13. Conclusion: The Healing of Blind Bartimaeus at Jericho (10:46–52)

⁴⁶Then they came to Jericho. As Jesus and his disciples, together with a large crowd, were leaving the city, a blind man, Bartimaeus (that is, the Son of Timaeus), was sitting by the roadside begging. ⁴⁷When he heard that it was Jesus of Nazareth, he began to shout, "Jesus, Son of David, have mercy on me!"

48Many rebuked him and told him to be quiet, but he shouted all the more, "Son of David, have mercy on me!"

49Jesus stopped and said, "Call him."

So they called to the blind man, "Cheer up! On your feet! He's calling you." **50**Throwing his cloak aside, he jumped to his feet and came to Jesus.

51"What do you want me to do for you?" Jesus asked him.

The blind man said, "Rabbi, I want to see."

52"Go," said Jesus, "your faith has healed you." Immediately he received his sight and followed Jesus along the road.

Just as the healing of the blind man at Bethsaida (8:22–26) introduces the second major division, so the healing of blind Bartimaeus at Jericho concludes it. Note how both contain exact geographical references—something that is unusual in Mark. Bracketing the division as they do, the two accounts suggest that a major purpose of the division is to show how Jesus gave not only physical sight but spiritual insight to his disciples. In this division the disciples began to realize who Jesus was and what was involved in following him as disciples.

This is the last healing miracle in Mark; and if one does not consider the cursing of the fig tree in 11:12–14,20–22, it is the last and therefore climactic miracle performed by Jesus. It provides an example of one who understood who Jesus was, responded immediately to his call despite discouragement from others, believed in him, and followed him as a disciple. It remains an example for others to follow. The story is connected with the preceding pericope by the identity of the question Jesus asked James and John (v. 36) and Bartimaeus (v. 51). The replies, however, are quite different. James and John wanted positions of prominence; the blind man wanted to see (cf. 10:51). The story is also connected with the following section, as a comparison of 10:47–48 and 11:10 will show.

10:46   Jericho is five miles west of the Jordan, six miles north of the Dead Sea, and fifteen air miles and twenty-one road miles northeast of Jerusalem. It was considered to be a Judean city. Therefore Jesus had crossed back over the Jordan and was nearing the completion of his journey to Jerusalem. The Jericho of New Testament times was about two miles south of the one of the Old Testament period and before. The former had been built by Herod the Great (37–4 B.C.) as a winter palace. It is not likely that Jesus or the crowd was permitted to enter the palace. The public part of the city was presumably nearby, perhaps a little to the east where the modern city is.

Luke 18:35 locates the healing at the entrance to Jericho, no doubt to give prominence to the story about Zacchaeus. Matthew 20:30 indicates that there were two blind men. Exact accuracy of detail simply was not the purpose of the Gospel writers, and a recognition of this fact in no way compromises the integrity of their accounts.

The Aramaic word *bar* means *son of;* and "Bartimaeus," as the NIV explains, means "Son of Timaeus." Mark's Greek, however, is difficult and involves redundancy. It does not, by some estimates, reflect Mark's style, though one might argue that Mark did tend to explain Aramaic phrases (5:41; 7:34; 14:36; cf. 7:11; 15:34).

Some therefore think "Son of Timaeus" originated as a marginal gloss that later was accidentally taken into the text, though no manuscript evidence favors such an omission. Only Mark gave the name of the person who was healed, and this is the only place where he did so.[21] This may indicate that the name was remembered because Bartimaeus became a Christian and was known by the early Palestinian churches.

10:47–48 Although Matthew did so nine times, this is the only place in Mark where Jesus is explicitly called "Son of David" (but cf. 11:10, where it is implied). Obviously the title does not play a large part in Mark's Christology. It is going too far, however, to say that Mark rejected it because "Rabboni" (NASB) is substituted in v. 51, the exact expression is not used in 11:10, and the use of the term is questioned in 12:35–37. Mark's little use was probably due to the inadequacy of the term. To the Gentile Christians for whom Mark wrote, Jesus was more than the Son of David. Significantly Luke, who also wrote for Gentile Christians, used it only twice. This messianic term indicates that Jesus is not only a descendant of David but the one who is to inherit and fulfill the promises made to David in 2 Sam 7:12–16; 1 Chr 17:11–14; and Ps 89:29–37. See also Isa 11:1,10; Jer 23:5–6; 30:9; Ezek 34:23–24; Hos 3:5.

Previously Jesus was pictured as commanding silence, but here the crowd did so. The crowd's rebuke probably was because Bartimaeus was creating a disturbance, not because he used the term "Son of David." Mark emphasized the man's persistence despite opposition perhaps because he wanted to encourage the same persistent faith in his own readers/hearers.

10:49 The account is not a typical miracle story. Although New Testament form critics do not have such a category, it is really a "call" story. The expression "Cheer up" is used elsewhere in the New Testament six times, all on the lips of Jesus. Although Jesus did not speak the words in the present instance, the effect is the same. Cheer is associated with something Jesus does or says.

10:50 The cloak or outer garment may also have served as a pallet; and by recording such a trivial thing, Mark may have wanted to symbolize the casting off of illness and other disability. Alternately, Bartimaeus's action recalls Jesus' instructions for disciples on mission (6:9). Certainly he wanted to emphasize immediate and ideal response.

---

[21] In 5:22 the name of the father of a child who was healed is given.

10:51 The Greek text reads *Rabbo(u)ni*, which transliterates an Aramaic word that is simply a strengthened form of *Rabbi*. It appears elsewhere in the New Testament only in John 20:16 and means *my lord, my master,* or *my teacher*. The NIV, in an attempt to simplify and clarify, substitutes the more familiar "Rabbi." This choice of address is perhaps significant, for this major section focused on Jesus' teaching on discipleship (8:22–10:52). Equally significant is the request "I want to see." Only Jesus, the Master Teacher, can give the needed insight. The healing of the blind is associated with the messianic age in Isa 29:18; 32:3; and 35:5.

10:52 Again (cf. 2:5; 5:34; 9:23–24; even 6:5–6) Mark emphasized the importance—even the necessity—of faith. This is highlighted by the absence of a description of the healing. The word translated "healed" (*sōzō*) can also mean *saved*, and Mark probably intended a double meaning. The man was healed physically and saved spiritually. The latter is implied by the fact that he began to follow Jesus. The statement certainly means that Bartimaeus joined with the other pilgrims in accompanying Jesus on the road to Jerusalem—as the NIV indicates—but again it is likely that Mark intended a double reference. "Following Jesus on the way" is a technical term for discipleship. That Bartimaeus's name was remembered and recorded probably means that he did become a disciple. The contrast between his sitting beside the road (v. 46) and his following Jesus on the road (v. 51) serves as a graphic picture of conversion.

Even though this concluding section has not been included in the preceding section entitled "The Journey to Jerusalem," the journey continues at least through 10:52 and in fact until 11:11.

―――――――――――― *SECTION OUTLINE* ――――――――――

IV. THE GOOD NEWS ABOUT JESUS' DEATH (11:1–15:47)
1. The Entry into Jerusalem (11:1–11)
2. The Cursing of the Fig Tree (11:12–14,20–25)
3. The Expulsion of the Merchants from the Temple (11:15–19)
4. Controversies in the Temple (11:27–12:40)
   (1) About Jesus' Authority (11:27–33)
   (2) About the Rejection of Israel: The Parable of the Wicked Tenant Farmers (12:1–12)
   (3) About the Payment of Taxes (12:13–17)
   (4) About Marriage at the Resurrection (12:18–27)
   (5) About the Greatest Commandment (12:28–34)
   (6) About the Identity of David's Son (12:35–37)
   (7) About the Evils of Scribism (12:38–40)
5. The Widow's Gift (12:41–44)
6. The Eschatological Discourse (13:1–37)
   (1) The Destruction of the Temple (13:1–4)
   (2) False Signs of the End of the Age (13:5–13)
   (3) True Signs of the End of the Age (13:14–23)
   (4) The Return of the Son of Man and the Gathering of His Elect (13:24–27)
   (5) The Certainty of the Fact but Uncertainty about the Time of the Return (13:28–37)
7. The Plot to Kill Jesus (14:1–2,10–11)
8. The Anointing at Bethany (14:3–9)
9. The Institution of the Lord's Supper (14:12–26)
10. The Prediction of Desertion and Denial (14:27–31)
11. The Agony in Gethsemane (14:32–42)
12. The Arrest (14:43–52)
13. The Jewish Trial (14:53,55–65)
14. The Denial of Peter (14:54,66–72)
15. The Roman Trial (15:1–15)
16. The Mockery of the Soldiers (15:16–20)
17. The Crucifixion (15:21–41)
18. The Burial (15:42–47)

―― **IV. THE GOOD NEWS ABOUT JESUS' DEATH (11:1–15:47)** ――

Mark's Gospel has sometimes been described as a passion narrative with a lengthy introduction. Such a description is, of course, an exaggeration. Mark had other purposes for his Gospel, but the passion was of overriding importance. Approximately 38 percent of the Gospel is devoted to the week of the passion (chaps. 11–16) and 20 percent to the day of Jesus' death (chaps. 14–15). Everything in chaps. 11–16 takes place in or very near Jerusalem. In Mark's thinking, Galilee was the place of the revelation of Jesus as the Son of Man and Son of God, but Jerusalem was the place of opposition to and condemnation of Jesus. Much of the account relates to controversies with the authorities (11:27–12:40). They conspired to kill Jesus (11:18; 14:1–2); he condemned the temple as a "den of robbers" (11:17) and predicted its destruction (13:2).

Unlike the previous part of the Gospel, the passion narrative is characterized by specific time references. At its beginning the events are set forth as having taken place on three distinct days: 11:1–11,12–19,20ff. No indication is given in 11:27–13:37 of where the third day ended. The next indication of time is in 14:1, which states that when the Passover was "two days away" the authorities conspired further against Jesus. The following day preparation was made for the Passover meal (14:12), and it was eaten that evening (14:17). The crucifixion took place the next morning (15:1,25) and the death and burial that afternoon (15:33,42). The day of the crucifixion was the day of preparation for the Sabbath (15:42), i.e., Friday. The resurrection took place on the day after the Sabbath (16:1), i.e., Sunday.

Apparently Mark placed the entry into Jerusalem on Sunday, the cursing of the fig tree and the clearing of the temple on Monday, the observation of the withered fig tree on Tuesday, the final conspiracy against Jesus and the anointing in Bethany on Wednesday (but see the comments on 14:1), the preparation for the Passover on Thursday, the Passover meal and arrest on Thursday evening, the trials and crucifixion and burial on Friday, and the resurrection on Sunday. The time of the disputes in the temple and the eschatological discourse is uncertain, perhaps Tuesday, perhaps Wednesday.

Though Mark seems to indicate that all of these events took place in one week, some uncertainty regarding the exact chronology exists. The statement "Every day I was with you, teaching in the temple courts, and you did not arrest me" in 14:49 may imply that Jesus had been in Jerusalem more than a week. The waving of branches and shouting "Hosanna" (11:8–10) are more appropriate in connection with the Feast of Tabernacles in the fall and Dedication in the winter than Passover in the spring (but see the comments on 11:9–10). Matthew 23:37 (cf. Luke 13:34) suggests either an extended period in Jerusalem or several previous visits. The fact that Jesus had friends in the city (14:3 and possibly 11:2–3; 14:13–15; 15:43) may imply that he had not come to the city for the first time. John's Gospel describes several visits to Jerusalem. (See also the comments on 11:13,15.) The serious student of the Gospels must allow the possibility of topical as opposed to chronological arrangement. Therefore the duration of the events in chaps. 11–13 cannot be determined with much confidence. They may have taken place in one week; they may have taken place over several months.

Although it is not apparent in the outline employed in this commentary, Mark's passion narrative could be divided into two parts: events preceding Jesus' death (chaps. 11–13) and Jesus' last hours with his disciples, his arrest, trial, and crucifixion (chaps. 14–15). For the most part chaps. 11–13 contain individual accounts that probably circulated independently in oral form prior to the writing of Mark's Gospel, but chaps. 14–15 tell a continuous story in chronological order. Most of what is in chaps. 14–15 must have circulated as a unit from the beginning. This consideration does not rule out the probability that Mark and others before him adapted some items, added some, and deleted others according to the needs of those to whom they told the story.

Chapters 14–15 are the climax of the Gospel. Everything else leads up to them. They answer two crucial questions: Why did Jesus have to die? How did he die? Mark answered the first question by indicating that Jesus' death was an absolute necessity, part of the divine plan, the will of God. He no doubt did this to answer the objections of opponents that the shameful death of Jesus showed he was an imposter. Members of his own community may have wondered why God did not rescue Jesus. Mark answered the second question by showing that Jesus died with dignity and integrity. His account is characterized by reserve.

1. The Entry into Jerusalem (11:1–11)

[1]As they approached Jerusalem and came to Bethphage and Bethany at the Mount of Olives, Jesus sent two of his disciples, [2]saying to them, "Go to the village ahead of you, and just as you enter it, you will find a colt tied there, which no one has ever ridden. Untie it and bring it here. [3]If anyone asks you, 'Why are you doing this?' tell him, 'The Lord needs it and will send it back here shortly.'"

[4]They went and found a colt outside in the street, tied at a doorway. As they untied it, [5]some people standing there asked, "What are you doing, untying that colt?" [6]They answered as Jesus had told them to, and the people let them go. [7]When they brought the colt to Jesus and threw their cloaks over it, he sat on it. [8]Many people spread their cloaks on the road, while others spread branches they had cut in the fields. [9]Those who went ahead and those who followed shouted,

"Hosanna!"

"Blessed is he who comes in the name of the Lord!"

[10]"Blessed is the coming kingdom of our father David!"

"Hosanna in the highest!"

[11]Jesus entered Jerusalem and went to the temple. He looked around at everything, but since it was already late, he went out to Bethany with the Twelve.

Mark's account can hardly be called "the triumphal entry," as could Matt 21:1–9; Luke 19:28–40; John 12:12–19. The first and most obvious reason is that Mark had no crowds to come out to meet Jesus. The acclamation seems to have been by those who had accompanied Jesus from Jericho to Jerusalem. For another, nothing of great significance happened. When Jesus entered the city, those who had accompanied and acclaimed him seem to have dispersed; and he merely entered the temple and looked around. For still another, the messianic character of the account, although present, is quite muted in comparison with the other Gospels. The "messianic secret" still appears to have been influencing the account.

Although Mark did not quote Zech 9:9 as does Matt 21:5, he likely had it in mind, and it influenced his account. Even without that passage the messianic nature of the entry is still seen in the references to the Mount of Olives in v. 1 (Zech 14:4), the colt that previously had not been ridden in vv. 2–7 (Zech 9:9; cf. Num 19:2; Deut 21:3; 1 Sam 6:7), and the kingdom of David in v. 10 (2 Sam 7). Whether Jesus intended to present himself as the Messiah remains a question. He probably did but in such a way as to indicate that he was a serving and suffering Messiah rather than a conquering one. The first point was made by riding rather than walking into the city, as pilgrims ordinarily did. The second was made by riding upon a donkey rather than a horse. What Jesus did should probably be looked upon as a symbolic action after the fashion of the Old Testament prophets.[1]

11:1 The "Mount of Olives" is across the Kidron Valley and directly to the east of Jerusalem. Its summit and western slopes afford a marvelous view of the city (cf. 13:3). "Bethany" was on its southeast slope out of sight of and about two miles from Jerusalem. The exact location of "Bethphage" is uncertain, but it probably was nearer to Jerusalem than Bethany. The order of mention therefore is strange and has been used as another indication that the author was not a native of Palestine. The matter troubled ancient copyists, some of whom omitted "Bethphage." Some modern scholars have conjectured that "Bethany" did not appear in Mark's original (it does not in Matt 21:1) and that it was taken from vv. 11–12 and added to an early copy. More likely Jerusalem is mentioned first as the goal of the journey, and the order of Bethphage and Bethany is determined by their relationship to Jerusalem.

11:2 Whether the village was Bethany or Bethphage (or even some other) is uncertain, but most think it was Bethphage because it was nearer to Jerusalem. The word "colt" could refer to the young of many different animals, but in view of Matt 21:2 most agree that it was a young donkey. Matthew, incidentally, mentioned both a donkey and her colt. The passages just cited indicate that an animal that previously had not been used was thought to be appropriate for sacred use. Skeptics have questioned how the two unnamed

---

[1] A more certain example of a symbolic action is the following account of the cursing of the fig tree. See the comments there.

disciples could have known the donkey had not been ridden previously.[2]

11:3–6 Many questions have been raised about the meaning and reference of the word the NIV translates "Lord" in v. 3. Should it be translated "Lord," or "master" (i.e., the owner), or even "God"? The last is most unlikely. If the second, was Jesus its owner; or was its owner with Jesus at the time? If Jesus were not the owner, and if the owner were not with Jesus, had Jesus made prior arrangements for its use?[3] Nowhere else in Mark did Jesus refer to himself as "Lord" (though cf. 2:28; 5:19; 12:36; 13:35), but that does not mean he could not have done so in the present instance. Although there is still a trace of the "messianic secret" in the account, since 8:29 that secret has been in the process of being revealed (note especially 10:46–52). Whatever Aramaic word Jesus actually used, Mark probably used the Greek word *kyrios* to indicate further the true identity of Jesus. If so, it should be translated "Lord" and understood to refer to Jesus. Mark likely saw in the event an example of the supernatural knowledge and power of Jesus—the latter in influencing the bystanders to permit the disciples to take the colt (v. 6).

11:7–8 A comparison with what was done for Jehu according to 2 Kgs 9:13 suggests that spreading garments under a person was a recognition of royal dignity. The word Mark used does not indicate the kind of branches. Only John 12:13 mentions palm branches.

11:9–10 The quotation is from Ps 118:25–26. Psalm 118 is one of the "Hallel" (praise) psalms (104–106; 111–118; 135; 146–150). The second group, of which Ps 118 is the conclusion, was called the "Egyptian Hallel" because it praised God for the deliverance from Egypt. The psalms comprising it were sung at the Feast of Passover as well as at Pentecost, Tabernacles, and Dedication. This consideration increases the possibility that the entry took place soon before the Passover. "Hosanna" literally means *save us, we pray* and was originally a plea for help;[4] but it later also became a shout of praise, as it is here. The statement "Blessed is he who comes in the name of the Lord" was originally directed to pilgrims as they approached the temple, but Mark no doubt wanted his readers/hearers to apply it to Jesus and to see him as the coming Messiah. Some evidence exists that the expression "he who comes" is a messianic title (cf. Gen 49:10). In v. 10 Jesus is not explicitly designated as the coming Davidic king. The kingdom and not the

---

[2]Perhaps we should also point out that some commentators have seen the colt's being tied as an allusion to Gen 49:11. Genesis 49:8–12 is the account of Jacob's prophecy about his son Judah. Mark, however, never connected Jesus with Judah as does Matt 1:2; Luke 3:33; Heb 7:14; Rev 5:5; and therefore any allusion on Mark's part is doubtful.

[3]Note the implication of several of these possibilities for the length of time Jesus had been in Jerusalem (see discussion above).

[4]Note its use in 2 Sam 14:4; 2 Kgs 6:26; Pss 20:9; 118:25 (the last being the passage quoted here).

king is acclaimed. The implication that Jesus will establish the kingdom is, however, quite apparent.

11:11   Note that Jesus entered not just the city but the temple as well.[5] This was probably in preparation for its clearing the following day. If Jesus and his companions had walked in one day the twenty-one miles from Jericho—most of it uphill—one can understand why it was late, why the crowd dispersed, and why Jesus took no further action.

2. The Cursing of the Fig Tree (11:12–14,20–25)

[12]The next day as they were leaving Bethany, Jesus was hungry. [13]Seeing in the distance a fig tree in leaf, he went to find out if it had any fruit. When he reached it, he found nothing but leaves, because it was not the season for figs. [14]Then he said to the tree, "May no one ever eat fruit from you again." And his disciples heard him say it. . . .

[20]In the morning, as they went along, they saw the fig tree withered from the roots. [21]Peter remembered and said to Jesus, "Rabbi, look! The fig tree you cursed has withered!"

[22]"Have faith in God," Jesus answered. [23]"I tell you the truth, if anyone says to this mountain, 'Go, throw yourself into the sea,' and does not doubt in his heart but believes that what he says will happen, it will be done for him. [24]Therefore I tell you, whatever you ask for in prayer, believe that you have received it, and it will be yours. [25]And when you stand praying, if you hold anything against anyone, forgive him, so that your Father in heaven may forgive you your sins."

Again Mark employed the device of bracketing/intercalation. (See the comments on 3:20–21, 31–35.) The cursing of the fig tree and the expulsion of the merchants from the temple (11:15–19) are prophetic actions that symbolize the same thing, the coming judgment on unfaithful Israel by the destruction of Jerusalem and its temple. Israel, like the fig tree, appeared to be thriving; but the appearances were deceiving because Israel and the fig tree were bearing no fruit. The magnificence of the temple masked the corruption and false security associated with it. Just as the fig tree was cursed and withered, so Israel was about to be condemned and decline in importance. Just as the merchants were expelled from the temple, so the religious establishment that authorized the merchants was about to be expelled from its favored place.

Both the cursing and the expulsion are acted or dramatized parables in the tradition of the Old Testament prophets. Compare Isaiah's walking around naked and barefoot to symbolize the "stripping" of Egypt (20:1–6), Jeremiah's retrieving a rotten waistband to symbolize the humiliation of Judah (13:1–11), Jeremiah's breaking of an earthen jar to symbolize the "breaking" of Judah (19:1–3,10–11), and Jeremiah's wearing a yoke around his neck to

---

[5]The word translated "temple" refers to the entire temple complex and not just the sacred building in the center.

symbolize enslavement to the king of Babylon (27:1–15; 28:10–17; see also 2 Chr 18:10 and Ezek 4–5).

The fig tree symbolizes faithless Israel. It is so used in the Old Testament: Jer 8:13; 29:17; Hos 9:10,16–17; Joel 1:6–7; Mic 7:1. The fig tree is an object of judgment in Isa 34:4 and Hos 2:12.

Few accounts in the Gospels are more difficult than the cursing of the fig tree. This is probably the reason Luke omitted it altogether and Matthew reshaped it (21:18–22) without some of the difficulties of Mark. The incident seems out of character with all else that is known about Jesus. The only other miracle of destruction is that of the pigs (5:11–13). Nowhere else did Jesus curse anything (though the "woes" of Matt 23:13–32; Luke 6:24–26 are real equivalents, especially given the power of Jesus' words).

Some have seen in the act a fit of anger. Furthermore, it seems utterly irrational to expect figs when they are out of season. Various attempts have been made to explain the event. One is that it actually took place at another time when figs were in season and that Mark did not realize this and created much of the difficulty by inserting the erroneous statement at the end of v. 13. Such a view is not possible for those who affirm the veracity of Holy Scripture. The possibility that Jesus came to Jerusalem as early as the previous fall has already been examined, but this explanation solves only a small part of the difficulty and creates others as well.

Several other explanations have been offered. One is that during the course of transmission what was originally a parable (cf. Luke 13:6–9) was somehow transformed into a miracle story. In addition to calling in question the historicity of the story, this explanation cannot account for such details as Peter remembering (v. 21). Another is that the early church later tried to explain the unusual death of a fig tree near Bethany by supposing that Jesus had cursed it, but this also leaves the story without historical basis and fails to explain how the early church could have invented a story with so many difficulties involved in it. Still another is that the comment in v. 13b originated as a scribal gloss, but there is no manuscript evidence for its omission.

By far the best explanation is that the act was deliberately staged by Jesus as a symbolic act. Nothing in the account suggests that Jesus lost his temper or good judgment. He did something most out of the ordinary to get attention and enforce his point. He may well have been hungry, but that was quite incidental. Just as some of the details of a spoken parable are inconsequential, so are some of those of this acted parable.

The account of the cursing of the fig tree consists of vv. 12–14 and 20–21 only. Verses 22–25 contain some miscellaneous sayings of Jesus on faith and prayer, which are found in other contexts in Matthew and Luke and which likely were spoken on various occasions. In the inner portion of this "literary sandwich," the temple was judged for not being "a house of prayer for all nations" (11:17). Mark probably included the sayings in vv. 22–25 to encourage the disciples to pray for God to keep them faithful to their mission. The sayings also indicate that the disciples were not to let the destruction of Jerusalem and its temple upset their faith and that they were to believe that God would continue to work out his purpose through his new people. Instead of finding any satisfaction in the judgment upon Israel, they were to learn from Israel's experiences and take heed lest a similar thing happen to them.

11:12 Inasmuch as the first meal of the day was not eaten until midmorning, Jesus was understandably hungry. The disciples were also, and Jesus used the situation for a dramatic display.

11:13 Leaves are found on Palestinian fig trees except for the three winter months, and ripe figs are present from June until November. Therefore the event must have taken place during March, April, or May. Of course the Passover usually came in April. According to some, small green figs, which in an emergency could be eaten but ordinarily were not, appear in March even before the leaves; but it is doubtful that anything should be made of this. Mark's parenthetical statement "it was not the season for figs" alerts the reader/hearer to look for symbolic meaning (such parenthetical statements are another element of Markan style; cf. 1:16; 5:42; 7:3–4; 13:14). The statement may be an allusion to Mic 7:1 and/or Jer 8:13. If so, it could mean that at the time Jesus spoke Israel was not producing the fruit God expected. Israel, like the fig tree, was barren when Jesus came to it. This understanding would ease some of the difficulty.

11:14 Jesus' statement in the first part of the verse indicates that Israel would not again be the primary instrument of accomplishing God's purpose. The statement that the disciples heard him means that they grasped the truth. Although Mark did not record it, they must have been horrified. Mark felt a need to present the encouraging statements of vv. 22–25 because later disciples were also perplexed about the fate of Israel.

11:20–21 The language recalls Hos 9:16 LXX. The reference to Peter in v. 21 may indicate he was the source or at least a source of the account.

11:22 At this point Mark shifted the emphasis from the negative to the positive and from Israel and the temple to Jesus. Some good textual witnesses read "If you have faith," which makes the verb an indicative rather than an imperative (the two have the same form in Greek) and therefore makes v. 22 the "if" clause of the sentence that continues into v. 23. Mark did not elsewhere precede "I tell you the truth" with an "if" clause, and the variant appears to be an assimilation to Luke 17:6. Mark evidently was saying, "Despite the cursing of the fig tree (i.e., Israel), continue to trust in God" because faith and prayer and not the temple are now the way to God.

11:23 The faith Mark seems to have had in mind is not that which is needed to work spectacular miracles but to accomplish the Christian mission.

A mountain is sometimes a symbol of difficulty. The fall of Jerusalem was a difficulty for the church as well as the synagogue. The early church encountered many other difficulties in carrying out its commission (e.g., persecution). Verse 23 involves a hyperbole quite as much as 10:25. Jesus was speaking generally, but there may be some allusion to the Mount of Olives (11:1) and the Dead Sea. On a clear day the latter can be seen from the summit of the former. Alternately, the allusion may be to the temple mount, in which case faith in God makes the temple system obsolete (cf. John 4:19–24).

11:24 The statement is not to be universalized and applied without exception, but neither is it to be localized and confined to the original disciples or ignored as having no practical value. Faith *is* an indispensable element in answer to prayer.

11:25 Standing probably was the most common Jewish posture for prayer, but both standing and kneeling are well attested in the Old and New Testaments. Mark seems to have understood that forgiveness of others is another prerequisite for answer to prayer. Some think the verse indicates that Mark and his readers knew the Lord's Prayer, but no confident decision seems possible. What is certain is that effective prayer must be offered in faith with a spirit of forgiveness.

[11:26] Verse 26 (see the NIV note) is found in the large number of medieval manuscripts, in some earlier ones of good and fair quality, in the KJV, and in NKJV. If original, it could have been accidentally omitted as a result of a copyist skipping from the words "your sins" at the end of v. 25 to the same words at the end of v. 26, but more likely it was added under the influence of Matt 6:15.

3. The Expulsion of the Merchants from the Temple (11:15–19)

15On reaching Jerusalem, Jesus entered the temple area and began driving out those who were buying and selling there. He overturned the tables of the money changers and the benches of those selling doves, 16and would not allow anyone to carry merchandise through the temple courts. 17And as he taught them, he said, "Is it not written:

> **" 'My house will be called
> a house of prayer for all nations'?
> But you have made it 'a den of robbers.' "**

18The chief priests and the teachers of the law heard this and began looking for a way to kill him, for they feared him, because the whole crowd was amazed at his teaching.

19When evening came, they went out of the city.

Here begins the antitemple theme that appears also in 13:2; 14:58; 15:38. The usual designation, "the cleansing of the temple," leaves a wrong impression. Jesus' purpose was not to reform the temple but to abolish it. This is symbolized by the expulsion of the merchants, who in turn represent the priestly establishment and beyond that the whole nation. Israel was symbolically expelled from the temple, and it was symbolically abandoned by Jesus. This is the third consecutive prophetic, symbolic action recorded by Mark (see the comments on the preceding sections). The church soon came to be recognized as the new temple (cf. 1 Cor 3:16–17), and Mark may have wanted to suggest this.

The account is found in all four Gospels (also Matt 21:12–13; Luke 19:45–48; John 2:13–17). The three Synoptic Gospels place it during Passion Week; John, at the beginning of Jesus' ministry. It is barely possible that Jesus took action in the temple both at the beginning and the end of his ministry, but most are convinced that the Synoptic chronology is correct. The expulsion was such a direct challenge to the authority of the high priestly officials that they were forced to take decisive action against Jesus. John placed the account near the beginning of his Gospel for a theological reason.

Many scholars are skeptical of the historicity of the account. They claim that Jesus could not have cleared the temple without intervention by both the Jewish temple police and the Roman army, which kept watch from the fortress Antonia at the northwest corner of the temple compound. They claim that Jesus could have done no more than drive away a few of the merchants and that the account of this was later blown up into a full-scale expulsion. The claim overlooks v. 18. Public apprehension of Jesus was not safe because of his popularity with the crowds.

Furthermore, Jesus seems not to have been alone in objecting to the use of the temple as a market. The assumption that the practice was a long-standing one and widely accepted appears to be erroneous. For a long time markets had been set up on the Mount of Olives opposite the temple, but their introduction into the temple area itself seems to have been as recently as A.D. 30, the probable year of the crucifixion.[6]

Although the Jews despised Herod, they gloried in the temple he built for them. It was virtually synonymous with Judaism itself. Although the notion proved to be false, it was believed there could be no Judaism without it. Therefore for Jesus to expel Jews from the temple was looked upon as expelling them from the presence and favor of God. Herod's temple was the third Jewish temple. The temple of Solomon was destroyed by the Babylonians in 586 B.C. A much less imposing building was completed under Zerubbabel in 515 B.C. This temple was often damaged but never destroyed until it was "reverently" replaced by the client-king Herod the Great. Herod's temple was

---

[6]This conclusion is based on no one source but on inferences from various passages in the *Mishna* and the *Talmuds*. See V. Eppstein, "The Historicity of the Gospel Account of the Cleansing of the Temple," *ZNW* 55 (1964): 42–58, especially 55.

begun in 20–19 B.C. The inner shrine was completed in eighteen months; and the main building, in ten years. The outer courts were not finally completed until A.D. 64, just six years before the destruction of the entire complex by the Romans while suppressing the Jewish revolt of A.D. 66–70. This temple was a huge and magnificent complex. The outer courts were about 1,000 feet by 1,600 feet, encompassed about thirty-five acres, and were surrounded by beautiful colonnades or covered porches (cf. John 10:23; Acts 3:11; 5:12). The main building was about 350 feet by 575 feet by 150 feet.

11:15 Whereas Matt 21:12 and Luke 19:45 appear to indicate that Jesus intervened in the temple the same day he entered the city, Mark clearly indicates that it was the following day when he did so (see v. 12). Again the best explanation is that the Gospel writers were not concerned to produce an exact chronology.

The scene is the outer courts, the so-called court of the Gentiles, the only area into which Gentiles could go. The money changers were those who exchanged Roman money for the Tyrian shekel, which was required for the annual temple tax imposed upon all Jewish males (Exod 30:11–16). The Tyrian shekel was the nearest available equivalent to the Old Testament shekel. According to the *Mishna*, the tax was due on the first of Nisan (two weeks before the Passover); and the exchange tables were set up in the temple during the five days prior to the due date.[7] Doves were the prescribed offering for the poor who could not afford an animal (Lev 12:6; 14:22; 15:14,29; cf. Luke 2:22–24).

11:16 The *Mishna* later prohibited carrying vessels through the temple: "He may not enter into the Temple Mount with his staff or his sandal or his wallet, or with the dust upon his feet, nor may he make of it a short by-path; still less may he spit there."[8]

11:17 The quotation in the middle part of the verse is from Isa 56:7, and the allusion in the last part is to Jer 7:11. Jeremiah continued in vv. 12–15 to say that God was going to do to the temple of Solomon what he did to the shrine at Shiloh—utterly destroy it. By quoting from Jeremiah, Jesus suggested that God would do the same to the temple of Herod that existed in his day.

Interestingly, only Mark included the words "for all nations" in his quotation. This may be significant. Isaiah predicted that the Gentiles would have a place among the people of God and in the temple of God. In Herod's temple, however, they were always excluded from the inner shrine (cf. Acts 21:27–

---

[7]*Šeqal.* 1.1–3. This may constitute additional evidence that Jesus was in Jerusalem for more than a week before his death. The *Mishna*, however, was not put together until two centuries after Jesus' time; and there is always the problem of how accurately it describes the situation prior to the destruction of Jerusalem in A.D. 70.

[8]*M. Ber.* 9.5, trans. Danby.

32). With the conversion of the court of the Gentiles into a bazaar with all its noise and commotion and stench, they were deprived of the only place in the temple where they could worship. By clearing out the traders Jesus literally *and symbolically* provided a place for Gentiles in the temple of God, although as indicated reforming the temple was not his primary purpose.

The expression "den of robbers" does not refer so much to a place of dishonest dealings as a place of refuge for unjust persons. The Jews had come to look upon the temple as a place of security regardless of what they did. Participating in the ritual was thought to assure acceptance with God. Furthermore, many Jews thought they alone were acceptable to God. Against all this Jesus most emphatically protested.[9]

11:18 The chief priests and teachers regarded Jesus as a threat to their very way of life. They, therefore, began looking for ways to kill him. The crowds were infatuated with Jesus' teaching. The word "teaching" probably refers both to Jesus' teaching in general and to his "teaching" by the symbolic act of expelling the merchants from the temple.

11:19 Jesus may have left the city at night because it was unsafe to remain there or because there were no accommodations available during the crowded Passover season or because he wanted to be with friends at Bethany (cf. 11:11; 14:3).

4. Controversies in the Temple (11:27–12:40)

This section contains accounts of seven controversies between Jesus and the religious authorities. For an earlier series of five controversies see 2:1–3:6. The stories here are set forth by Mark to show how Jesus refuted the errors of the Jewish leaders and how they rejected him. The stories were useful to Mark's readers in their continuing disputes with the synagogue.

(1) About Jesus' Authority (11:27–33)

²⁷They arrived again in Jerusalem, and while Jesus was walking in the temple courts, the chief priests, the teachers of the law and the elders came to him. ²⁸"By what authority are you doing these things?" they asked. "And who gave you authority to do this?"

²⁹Jesus replied, "I will ask you one question. Answer me, and I will tell you by what authority I am doing these things. ³⁰John's baptism—was it from heaven, or from men? Tell me!"

³¹They discussed it among themselves and said, "If we say, 'From heaven,' he will ask, 'Then why didn't you believe him?' ³²But if we say, 'From men'...." (They feared the people, for everyone held that John really was a prophet.)

---

[9]The temple was the last refuge of the rebels in A.D. 70 when the Romans destroyed the city. Interestingly Josephus used the same word to describe them as the NIV translates "robbers." Either "bandits" or "outlaws" might be a better translation.

33So they answered Jesus, "We don't know."
Jesus said, "Neither will I tell you by what authority I am doing these things."

This brief account affirms the divine authority of Jesus and shows that it is superior to the authority of Jewish officialdom. This pronouncement story lacks an explicit pronouncement. The implied pronouncement is nevertheless quite clear.

11:27 Some have questioned whether Jesus could have walked around in the temple after clearing it. The encounter could have taken place at an earlier time and could have been placed here by Mark for topical reasons. But even on the assumption that it did take place the day following the clearing, Jesus' popularity may have prevented the authorities from taking immediate action against him (cf. v. 18).

"The chief priests, the teachers of the law and the elders" comprised the Sanhedrin, the Jewish executive, legislative, and judicial council. It consisted of seventy members plus its presiding officer, the high priest. The reference here, however, is not to the entire Sanhedrin but to a delegation sent from it. The reference is not necessarily to Caiaphas, the chief priest at the time, or to Annas and other former chief priests but to officials in the priestly hierarchy, to the Sadducees in general.

11:28 The purpose of the question was to force Jesus to admit that he had no authority to teach and act the way he did. The Sanhedrin claimed it was the authority in religious matters. "Authority" (*exousia*) is an important term in Mark (1:22,27; 2:10; 3:15; 6:7; 13:34 in addition to four times in the present passage). "These things" (twice in the Greek text, "this" in the second instance in the NIV to avoid redundancy) probably refer to the clearing of the temple, the public entry into Jerusalem, and Jesus' teaching in the temple.

11:29 The use of counterquestions was common in rabbinic discussions (cf. 10:2–3), but the one of Jesus here is unusual in that he made his answer depend on the answer of his opponents. Jesus' use of a counterquestion was not an evasion but a means of establishing the source of his own authority and all authority in the spiritual realm.

11:30 The expression "John's baptism" embraces John's preaching of repentance as a prerequisite of forgiveness and his proclamation of a "coming one" (cf. 1:1–8) as well as the act of baptism itself. In fact, what Jesus said here suggests the reason Mark began his Gospel the way he did. The clear implication of the question is that John's ministry was divinely authorized. If John's message had God's approval, then Jesus and his message also had to have divine authority because of John's inspired attestation. "Heaven" is a reverential substitute for "God."

11:31–33a The religious officials immediately recognized their dilemma. They did not believe that John was a prophet from God, but they dared not say so publicly because of the high esteem in which John was held. Nor in the present situation could they admit that John's baptism was from heaven because Jesus would castigate them for not repenting and being baptized as a sign of their repentance. The only way out, even though it was not a good one, was to confess inability to decide. What they did not realize was that such inability disqualified them from being religious authorities.

11:33b   The nature of Jesus' pronouncement may still reflect the "messianic secret" that dominated the earlier parts of the Gospel. Although Jesus refused to tell, he did not refuse to claim. The claim of divine authority is as clear as if it had been stated explicitly.

(2) About the Rejection of Israel: The Parable of the Wicked Tenant Farmers (12:1–12)

¹**He then began to speak to them in parables: "A man planted a vineyard. He put a wall around it, dug a pit for the winepress and built a watchtower. Then he rented the vineyard to some farmers and went away on a journey. ²At harvest time he sent a servant to the tenants to collect from them some of the fruit of the vineyard. ³But they seized him, beat him and sent him away empty-handed. ⁴Then he sent another servant to them; they struck this man on the head and treated him shamefully. ⁵He sent still another, and that one they killed. He sent many others; some of them they beat, others they killed.**

⁶**"He had one left to send, a son, whom he loved. He sent him last of all, saying, 'They will respect my son.'**

⁷**"But the tenants said to one another, 'This is the heir. Come, let's kill him, and the inheritance will be ours.' ⁸So they took him and killed him, and threw him out of the vineyard.**

⁹**"What then will the owner of the vineyard do? He will come and kill those tenants and give the vineyard to others. ¹⁰Haven't you read this scripture:**

> **" 'The stone the builders rejected**
> **has become the capstone;**
> ¹¹**the Lord has done this,**
> **and it is marvelous in our eyes'?"**

¹²**Then they looked for a way to arrest him because they knew he had spoken the parable against them. But they were afraid of the crowd; so they left him and went away.**

The origin of this item has often been denied to Jesus and assigned to the early church because it is an allegory rather than a parable. It implies that Jesus knew in advance about his death (vv. 7–8) and about the destruction of Jerusalem forty years before the event (v. 9b), and it implies that Jesus made messianic claims (vv. 10–11). Some have argued several of the actions in the story are improbable, such as the repeated sending of slaves in vv. 2–5, the sending of the son in v. 6, and the idea that the tenants could acquire ownership of the vineyard by killing the son in v. 7. The allusion in v. 1 and the quotation in vv. 10–11, both of which are from the LXX rather than the Hebrew text, are also held to reflect the work of the early church.

None of these claims can be substantiated. Whether any significant distinction exists between parable and allegory and whether Jesus could have used allegory have already been discussed in the introductory comments to 4:1–34. Whether Jesus could have predicted his death has been discussed in connection with 10:32–34. Also the phrase "Killed him, and threw him out of the vineyard" (v. 8) is not a very accurate *prediction after the event*, whereas it is a satisfactory statement if a true prediction.

As for the prediction of the fall of Jerusalem, v. 9b is a vague statement and does not appear to have been written after the event. Even apart from any attribution of supernatural knowledge to Jesus, an insightful person in A.D. 30 could have foreseen the eventual result of Jewish opposition to Roman rule. Also Mark probably was written before A.D. 70, and therefore a problem remains even if the statement originated in the early church rather than with Jesus.

The denial that Jesus made messianic claims is said to be supported by the commands of silence (e.g., 1:44; 5:43; 7:36; 9:9–10). Such commands, however, do not imply Jesus denied that he was the Messiah, only that he did not want the fact to be proclaimed publicly. Also the objection fails to take note of the time when the claim—vague as it is—was made, i.e., just before Jesus' death when there was no longer any reason for secrecy. The alleged improbable actions are not to be taken literally but simply as part of the story. They are just as much a problem if the early church invented the story. Finally, the question of whether Jesus could have known a Hebrew text similar to that used by the LXX has been considered in the comments on 7:6–7.

Still another reason for believing that the parable goes back to Jesus is that its details are true to Palestinian life in the third decade of the first century. First, the description of the vineyard in v. 1c is entirely accurate (see the comments on v. 1). Second, absentee landlords of huge estates and landless tenant farmers were quite common in Galilee in Jesus' day. The tenants usually were required to turn over between one-fourth and one-half of the produce to the owner's agents. As a result they were barely able to survive—a situation that produced much discontent. If the parable was invented by the early church, it must have been by the earliest Palestinian church and not the Gentile church outside of Palestine. A perusal of Acts and the epistles, however, shows that the early church was not in the habit of inventing parables. There are none in these books.[10]

---

[10]Paul often used metaphor and possibly allegory (Gal 4:21–31). Both would be comparable to the Hebrew *mashal*.

Yet another reason for doubting that the parable had its origin after the time of Jesus is the absence of any explicit reference to vindication of the slain Son, i.e., to the resurrection of Jesus, although vv. 10–11 contain an implicit vindication.

The story primarily justifies the church's replacement of Israel as God's favored people. It also functions in the book as preparation for the passion narrative.

12:1 The expression "in parables" means *in a parabolic manner* and does not imply more than one, although Matt 21:33–22:14 records two parables at this point.

The allusion is to Isa 5:1–7, where the vineyard clearly is Israel, and the owner is God. The same identifications are to be made in the parable here. No attempt should be made, however, to identify the wall, the pit, or the tower as the law, the altar, and the temple, respectively, as did the medieval church in its excessive allegorical interpretations. They simply are part of the apparatus of the story. They do accurately describe a first-century Palestinian vineyard. The wall ("hedge," RSV, NKJV; but not "fence," NRSV, GNB) was to keep animals rather than people out. The "pit for the winepress" was actually a trough into which the juice ran after having been crushed from the grapes. The tower was to provide an elevated observation point and shelter for those who kept watch against animals and thieves.

In Isaiah the problem is a fruitless vineyard, i.e., a nation that failed to produce the fruits of righteousness. In the present parable the emphasis is on the wickedness (greed, dishonesty, violence, murder) of the tenants, who seem to represent the leaders of the nation. Unfortunately such things actually characterized the Sadducees, the priestly aristocracy.

12:2–5 The servants represent the prophets of Israel. In fact, they often were referred to as God's servants in the Old Testament (Jer 7:25; Ezek 38:17; Dan 9:6,10; Amos 3:7; Zech 1:6). The rejection, abuse, and even killing of the prophets was so common as to be proverbial. All of the translations cited in this commentary agree that in v. 4 Mark meant that the prophet was struck on the head, but everywhere else the word he used means *to summarize, to recapitulate.* The matter troubled medieval scribes who added "by throwing stones" (cf. KJV, NKJV). Evidently Mark gave the word a new meaning. As a result some think there is an allusion to John the Baptist, who was decapitated. It is doubtful, however, that any particular person was intended. This is another detail added for the sake of making a good story.

12:6 The "son, whom he loved" is of course Jesus (see 1:11; 9:7). Whether the original hearers of the parable realized this is unlikely, but the original readers/hearers of Mark's Gospel certainly did. The Greek could be translated simply, "He still had one beloved son." Commentators and lexicographers differ, however, on whether in context the word means "beloved"

(RSV, NASB, REB; cf. NEB) or "only" (NEB, REB margin). The NIV (as well as the GNB) attempts to convey both ideas. Etymologically the word is related to the word "love," but in Gen 22:2,12,16 LXX it means *only*, in the sense that Isaac was certainly the only child of the promise.

12:7 A piece of land could be acquired by its occupants if no living person claimed ownership. The tenants must have assumed that the son had come because the father was dead, which assumption was false. Remember, however, that a parable is a story and not an account of something that actually took place.

12:8 The ultimate insult was to leave a corpse unburied. That was not the fate of Jesus, and again the early church does not appear to have invented the parable on the basis of what had happened previously. Jesus, rather, suffered outside the city (cf. Heb 13:12).

12:9 The origin of this verse has been denied to Jesus because elsewhere he did not answer his own questions. He may not have done so in the present instance, as Matt 21:41 indicates. Mark simply was not concerned to identify who gave the answer. The "others" to whom the vineyard was given were, of course, the Gentile church. The church is the inheritor of the position formerly held by Israel, the recipient of many of the promises originally made to Israel. It is the new Israel, the true Israel. By recording the statement of Jesus, Mark may have wanted to make that point.

12:10–11 Here the metaphor changes from a vineyard to a building. The quotation is from Ps 118:22–23, a passage quoted two other times in the New Testament in addition to the parallels in Matt 21:42 and Luke 20:17 (Acts 4:11; 1 Pet 2:7). The Jews understood the stone to be their own nation, which was rejected by other nations but which would be restored by the Lord. The early Christians understood it to be Jesus Christ (note especially Eph 2:20). Other "stone" passages are Rom 9:33 and 1 Pet 2:8, which quote Isa 8:14, and 1 Pet 2:6, which quotes Isa 28:16. As the NIV note indicates, the Greek word Mark used can mean either *the capstone of an arch* or *the cornerstone of a wall*.

12:12 The statement is similar to 11:18–19, and the word "they" must refer to "the chief priests and teachers of the law." The parable is directed not so much against the nation as a whole as against its leaders. Inasmuch as 11:18–19 ends the second day in Jerusalem, 12:12 may end the third day. See the introductory comments to the third division.

The parable has a long-range application to church leaders who cease to be servants and stewards and seek to be owners and lords.

(3) About the Payment of Taxes (12:13–17)

13Later they sent some of the Pharisees and Herodians to Jesus to catch him in his words. 14They came to him and said, "Teacher, we know you are a man of

integrity. You aren't swayed by men, because you pay no attention to who they are; but you teach the way of God in accordance with the truth. Is it right to pay taxes to Caesar or not? ¹⁵Should we pay or shouldn't we?"

But Jesus knew their hypocrisy. "Why are you trying to trap me?" he asked. "Bring me a denarius and let me look at it." ¹⁶They brought the coin, and he asked them, "Whose portrait is this? And whose inscription?"

"Caesar's," they replied.

¹⁷Then Jesus said to them, "Give to Caesar what is Caesar's and to God what is God's."

And they were amazed at him.

This section is one of the best examples of a pronouncement story in the Gospels. All that precedes merely prepares for the authoritative word in v. 17.

12:13 The pronoun "they" must refer again to the "chief priests and the teachers of the law" (11:18). For the identity of the "Herodians" and their relationship to the "Pharisees," see the comments on 3:6. The word translated "catch" ("entrap," RSV; "trap," NRSV, NEB, REB, NASB, GNB) often was used to refer to catching an animal in a snare or hooking a fish. The use of the word implies deceit and treachery.

12:14 The insincerity of the questioners is seen further in the flattery they employed. All the things they said were true, but their motive was wrong. They were willing to concede some virtues to Jesus in order to get him to relax his guard and to ruin him at another point.

The Greek word translated "taxes" (it is singular in Greek) is *kēnsos* and is a transliteration of the Latin word *census*. The reference is to the census, poll, or head tax that was imposed on all residents of Judea, Idumea, and Samaria in A.D. 6. At that time Archelaus (cf. Matt 2:22), the Jewish client-king (actually his modest title was "ethnarch") of that part of Palestine, was deposed by Rome. It was annexed as an imperial province, and a legate was appointed by the emperor to govern it.[11] The tax amounted to only a "denarius" a year (v. 15), i.e., a day's wage of an agricultural laborer. It was opposed at its inception by Judas the Galilean (cf. Acts 5:37), who led an abortive revolt,[12] and it was still deeply resented in Jesus' time. The tax was hated not because of its amount but because it was a symbol of foreign domination and because it had to be paid with a coin that bore an image of the emperor and an offensive inscription (see the comments on v. 16). The "Caesar" or emperor at the time was Tiberius (A.D. 14–37).

12:15 The questions in vv. 14–15 posed a serious dilemma for Jesus. If he advised payment, he would lose what popularity he still had with the people.

---

[11] The tax was not imposed on Galilee and Perea and on northeast Palestine, which continued to be client kingdoms under the rule of Herod Antipas and Philip, respectively. They were permitted to collect their own taxes.

[12] Josephus, *Antiquities* 18.1.6; *War* 2.8.1.

If he advised against payment, he would surely be arrested by the Roman authorities. The word translated "trap" (*peirazō*) is different from the one in v. 13 (*agreuō*) and means *to test* (cf. RSV, NRSV, NASB, NKJV), *to try*, and (in other contexts) *to tempt* (KJV). The value of a "denarius" was indicated in the comments on the previous verse.

12:16 It may be significant that Jesus did not possess the coin but that his inquisitors did. The fact that they did showed they implicitly recognized the authority of the emperor and therefore were hypocrites in asking the question. The Herodians (as well as the Sadducees who are mentioned in v. 18) had no reservations at all about paying the tax. The Pharisees did not want to pay it, but they grudgingly did so. Only the Zealots actively opposed payment. The "portrait" (*eikōn*) or "image" (KJV, NKJV) or "likeness" (RSV, NASB) or "head" (NRSV, NEB, REB) or "face" (GNB) was objectionable to most Jews because it was looked upon as an idol. The inscriptions were equally offensive. On a typical coin of the time one side read, "Tiberius Caesar, son of the divine Augustus" (or "son of god"), the other "high priest." Even at this early date the emperor made a modest claim to divinity—modest in comparison with later claims.

12:17 The coin that was minted by the emperor and had his image stamped on it was considered to be his personal property even while it was in circulation. Therefore it was proper for Jews and (later) Christians to return it to him. By so saying, Jesus acknowledged that God's people have an obligation to the state, although he did not define that obligation. In fact, the word translated "give" means *to pay what is owed*. It was important for Mark's Roman readers/hearers to know this pronouncement of their Lord so they could defend themselves with it against charges of disloyalty to the state. Jesus refused to identify himself with the revolutionaries.

By far the greater obligation, however, is to God. The use of the word "portrait" or "image" or "likeness" in v. 16 recalls Gen 1:26–27. Coins have the image of a ruler, and they may be returned to him. Human beings are made in the image of God; they and all they have belong to him.

This famous statement by Jesus does not provide a full account of the Christian's obligation to the state. It does not justify the medieval concept of two empires, the ecclesiastical and secular, each supreme in its own sphere. It does not justify the modern dichotomy between politics and religion. It simply affirms that obedience to a secular power does not necessarily conflict with obligation to God. The lesser obligation may be included in the greater. Other passages on the subject are Rom 13:1–7; 1 Tim 2:1–3; Titus 3:1–2; 1 Pet 2:13–17.

(4) About Marriage at the Resurrection (12:18–27)

18Then the Sadducees, who say there is no resurrection, came to him with a question. 19"Teacher," they said, "Moses wrote for us that if a man's brother dies

and leaves a wife but no children, the man must marry the widow and have children for his brother. [20]Now there were seven brothers. The first one married and died without leaving any children. [21]The second one married the widow, but he also died, leaving no child. It was the same with the third. [22]In fact, none of the seven left any children. Last of all, the woman died too. [23]At the resurrection whose wife will she be, since the seven were married to her?"

[24]Jesus replied, "Are you not in error because you do not know the Scriptures or the power of God? [25]When the dead rise, they will neither marry nor be given in marriage; they will be like the angels in heaven. [26]Now about the dead rising— have you not read in the book of Moses, in the account of the bush, how God said to him, 'I am the God of Abraham, the God of Isaac, and the God of Jacob'? [27]He is not the God of the dead, but of the living. You are badly mistaken!"

The main assertions of this pronouncement story are in vv. 25 and 27. The account certainly has Palestinian roots and was not the invention of the Gentile church. This is seen in the rabbinic form of argument of both the Sadducees and Jesus and the allusion to the Jewish law of levirate marriage.

In recording the account, Mark set forth evidence for the Christian belief in resurrection, a belief often assailed by Greco-Roman critics who conceived of the body as something evil and worthy only of perishing. Mark also gave some indication of the spiritual nature of the resurrection. No doubt some Christians in his day were still influenced by the crude, materialistic concept of some Pharisees. Mark's emphasis on the spiritual nature of the resurrection places him at one with Paul (1 Cor 15:35–50).

12:18 The Sadducees are mentioned explicitly only here in Mark's Gospel. Comparatively little is known about them, and there is uncertainty about several items. None of their own literature has survived, and all references to them are in the writings of their enemies (the New Testament, Josephus, rabbinic literature). The name is thought to be derived from that of Zadok, a high priest in David's time (2 Sam 20:25).

The Sadducees seem to have emerged as an identifiable party during late Maccabean or early Hasmonean times, i.e., the second century B.C. They were wealthy aristocrats and were probably among the absentee estate owners alluded to in 12:1. Politically they were very liberal and were quite willing to cooperate with the authorities of the Roman occupation in order to preserve their favored position. In fact, they were more of a political than a religious party, despite the following considerations. Theologically they were quite conservative. They usually were associated with the temple, the high priesthood itself, and the high priestly officialdom, although only one high priest was explicitly identified as a Sadducee.[13] It is uncertain whether they accepted only the Pentateuch as Scripture, as was claimed by later Christian writers, or whether they merely ascribed more authority to it than the Prophets and the

---

[13] Josephus, *Antiquities* 20.9.1.

Writings. What is certain is that they rejected the oral tradition of the scribes ("teachers of the law," NIV) and Pharisees. Very important for the present passage is their denial of resurrection of the body.[14] According to Acts 23:8 they also denied the existence of angels and other spirits, but this claim has been questioned because references to angels are in the Pentateuch (e.g., Gen 19:1; Deut 33:2). The Sadducees perished in the debacle of A.D. 70.

12:19 The allusion is to the law of levirate[15] marriage, as recorded in Deut 25:5–10. Actually the practice preceded the time of Moses, as can be seen in Gen 38, especially v. 8. Ruth 3–4 exemplifies the application of this law. The law provided that if a man died without a male heir, his brother was to marry his wife and impregnate her so that his brother's name might be preserved and his property kept within the tribe and family.

12:20–22 No doubt the Sadducees had used this preposterous story many times in their debates with the Pharisees. They falsely presumed that Jesus held the same materialistic doctrine of resurrection as did many Pharisees. This doctrine held that defects in the physical body and various earthly relationships would be carried over into future life.

12:23 The usual Pharisaic answer may have been that the first would be the woman's husband following the resurrection because the others were merely producing children for their brother. Jesus lifted the discussion to a higher plane.

As implied in the NIV margin, the mass of medieval Greek manuscripts plus a few other textual witnesses of medium quality add "when men rise from the dead" (cf. KJV, NKJV) after the word "resurrection." Although this reading has poor external attestation, it may be original because it is Semitic in character and in accord with Mark's style. It is hard to conceive of a Gentile scribe with any skill in Greek glossing "at the resurrection" with "when men rise from the dead." Indeed, Matthew omitted it, evidently without variation in the manuscripts of his Gospel.

12:24 The use of counterquestions is typical of the practice of the rabbis in general and Jesus in particular. Note well the two errors Jesus pointed out: not knowing the content and/or proper interpretation of their own Scriptures and not having personally experienced the power of God in their lives. Christian readers need to realize that such deficiencies are not limited to Sadducees or other Jews.

---

[14] In addition to the parallels in Matt 22:23 and Luke 20:27, this denial is attested in Acts 23:8 and in Josephus, *Antiquities* 18.1.4 and *War* 2.8.14. Their denial of resurrection probably was because the few references to it in the Hebrew Scriptures are in the later books (Job 19:25–26; Ps 73:23–24; Isa 26:19; Dan 12:2). The attitude of the Sadducees is reflected in such passages as Pss 88:5; 115:17; Isa 38:18.

[15] From the Latin *levir, brother-in-law*.

12:25 Twice before, Jesus revalued family relationships (3:31–35; 10:29–30). Here Jesus taught that resurrection life will be different from earthly life. People will not marry and have children but in some sense will be like angels, either sexless or concerned only with serving and worshiping God. Some persons have feared that a future life without their spouses will not be happy. As a result some have argued that Jesus meant only that there will be no further marriages in heaven. Probably the best understanding is that no Christian will be deprived of any meaningful relationship with believing family members and friends. Not the grief of loss but the surpassing joy of new and equally meaningful relationships marks life in God's family, whether now in the church or in the future.

12:26–27 The inexact way in which Exod 3:6 is cited is understandable since ancient Bibles had no chapters and verses as do modern ones.[16] The Greek reads literally "at the bush," but the meaning is *at the passage about the burning bush*. For another example of citation by reference to key words in a narrative, see Rom 11:2 and compare the comments on 2:26.

The crux of the argument is the use of the present tense in Exod 3:6. Abraham, Isaac, and Jacob had been dead for centuries at the time God spoke to Moses. Yet God told Moses that he was still their God at the time he spoke— thus implying that, from the perspective of the resurrection, they were still alive. In making the statement Jesus made no distinction between life after death and resurrection, which elsewhere is a future event.

Jesus' line of reasoning has not commended itself to many modern interpreters, but it was quite acceptable in his own day. The matter must be judged in part on that basis. The reasoning, however, is not as superficial as some have thought. One of the most important reasons for a Christian's assurance of future life and resurrection is the nature of his or her relationship to God. The fact that the phrase "the God of Abraham, the God of Isaac, and the God of Jacob" carried with it the idea of the covenant faithfulness of God emphasizes the central truth of Jesus' words for Mark's original readers and for believers today: God is faithful, and we can rely on his promises.

(5) About the Greatest Commandment (12:28:34)

28One of the teachers of the law came and heard them debating. Noticing that Jesus had given them a good answer, he asked him, "Of all the commandments, which is the most important?"

---

[16]The chapter divisions were made in the thirteenth century, probably by S. Langton the Archbishop of Canterbury, possibly by Cardinal Hugh of St. Cher. The New Testament verse divisions were made in 1551 by R. Estienne, who is also known by his Latin surname Stephanus. The Old Testament verse divisions are medieval or even earlier.

[29] "The most important one," answered Jesus, "is this: 'Hear, O Israel, the Lord our God, the Lord is one. [30]Love the Lord your God with all your heart and with all your soul and with all your mind and with all your strength.' [31]The second is this: 'Love your neighbor as yourself.' There is no commandment greater than these."

[32] "Well said, teacher," the man replied. "You are right in saying that God is one and there is no other but him. [33]To love him with all your heart, with all your understanding and with all your strength, and to love your neighbor as yourself is more important than all burnt offerings and sacrifices."

[34]When Jesus saw that he had answered wisely, he said to him, "You are not far from the kingdom of God." And from then on no one dared ask him any more questions.

This pronouncement story contains two authoritative sayings, one in vv. 29–31 and one in v. 34. The former is by far the more important. This story differs somewhat from the preceding one in that it does not involve a controversy. Indeed, the friendly attitude of the scribe, which is different from all other exchanges between Jesus and these teachers of the law, supports the authenticity of Mark's account.

12:28 The question reflects the fact that the scribes had identified 613 separate commandments, 365 of which were negative and 248 of which were positive. They divided them further into "heavy" and "light," i.e., more important and less important. An example of a similar question but a different answer is found in the reply of Hillel (ca. 40 B.C.–A.D. 10) to a Gentile who asked him to summarize the law while he stood on one leg: "What is hateful to you, do not to your neighbour: that is the whole Torah, while the rest is the commentary thereof." [17]

12:29–30 The quotation is from Deut 6:4–5, the first part of the famous *Shema*. In the second century the confession of faith that consisted of Deut 6:4–9; 11:13–21; Num 15:37–41 was recited twice daily by pious Jews. Matthew and Luke do not have the prefatory sentence, "Hear, O Israel, the Lord our God, the Lord is one"; but it is crucial because the obligation to love God is based on his oneness. Because he is one, love for him must be undivided. The inclusion was important for Mark's church in their debates with Jews in order to affirm that they also were monotheists, not polytheists as the Jews sometimes accused them of being. "With all your mind" is added to the statement in Deuteronomy. The piling up of the terms "heart," "soul," and "mind" is just a way of saying "with your whole being" and is not intended to designate the component parts of human nature.

The New Testament contains comparatively few references to loving God. In addition to the present passage and its parallels in Matt 22:37 and Luke 10:27, there are: Luke 11:42; John 5:42; 14:31; Rom 8:28; 1 Cor 2:9; 8:3;

---

[17]*B. Šabb.* 31a. I. Epstein, ed., *Babylonian Talmud* (London: Soncino Press, 1935–52).

Jas 1:12; 2:5; 1 John 2:5,15; 4:20; 5:2–3; Jude 21; Rev 2:4. John 14:15,24; 21:15–17; 1 Cor 16:22; Eph 6:24; 1 Pet 1:8 refer to loving Christ. If any significance can be attributed to this phenomenon, it is that the New Testament writers were preoccupied with the amazing love of God for sinful human beings.

12:31   The second quotation is from Lev 19:18. In the first part of that verse the neighbor is defined as "one of your people," i.e., a fellow Israelite. Leviticus 19:33–34 extends the love command to resident aliens. It is not likely that many first-century Jews extended it any further. Therefore one of the most significant elements in the teaching of Jesus was to redefine the neighbor as everybody, including the hated Samaritans and Gentiles (cf. Luke 10:30–37, which follows immediately his account of the discussion about the greatest commandment).

One of Jesus' other great teaching contributions was to bring together and virtually merge the commands to love God and to love fellow human beings. Some deny that Jesus was the first to relate the two. The *Testaments of the Twelve Patriarchs* (second cent. B.C.) seem to do so.[18] Philo of Alexandria, a contemporary of Jesus who probably died about A.D. 50, seems to have also.[19] Even if a few others before or during the time of Jesus saw the interrelationship of the commands to love God and love others, no one else put such great emphasis on the combination and made it essential. Jesus showed that it was impossible to really love God without loving neighbors. Love for God is expressed by loving others.

The statement "as yourself" does not justify the self-love advocated by modern psychology as necessary for a healthy self-image. It merely acknowledges that human beings do love themselves—far too much in fact—and that God deserves as much—actually far more.

12:32   The material in vv. 32–34 is peculiar to Mark. Verse 32 is the only place in the Gospels where a scribe is described as being favorably disposed toward Jesus, and v. 34 is the only place where Jesus commends a scribe. Not all scribes and Pharisees were bad. Indeed, at their best they represented the finest element in Judaism.

---

[18]T. Issachar 5:2, "Love the Lord and your neighbor"; 7:6, "The Lord I loved with all my strength; likewise, I loved every human being as I love my children"; T. Dan 5:3, "Throughout all your life love the Lord, and one another with a true heart," J. H. Charlesworth, ed., *The Old Testament Pseudepigrapha*, 2 vols. (Garden City, NY: Doubleday, 1983–85).

[19]*Special Laws* 2.15 (63): "Among the vast number of particular truths and principles there studied, there stand out practically [sic] high above the others two main heads: one of duty to God as shewn by piety and holiness, one of duty to men as shewn by humanity and justice," F. H. Colson et al., eds., *Philo*, 12 vols. Loeb Classical Library (Cambridge, MA: Harvard University Press, 1929–62). To say the least, this is not an exact parallel to Jesus' combination of the two commands to love.

12:33 The elevation of an ethical quality over sacrificial worship stands in the tradition of 1 Sam 15:22; Hos 6:6; and perhaps also Isa 1:11–17. The word translated "burnt offerings" refers to those offerings totally consumed on the altar. The word translated "sacrifices" refers to offerings in general, only a small portion of which was burned, and the remainder was given to the priest or returned to the worshiper to eat as a sacred meal. The two terms summarize and represent the entire sacrificial system.

12:34 There is not much difference in loving God and trusting him. In addition to acknowledging the necessity of loving God and humanity, the man evidently committed himself to do just that. He was receptive to Jesus as a person as well as to his teaching. No wonder Jesus indicated that the man was not far from entering the kingdom, from letting God reign in his life. By saying that he was not far, Jesus encouraged him to go the remainder of the way by wholeheartedly following Jesus. Whether he did so cannot be known, but every reader of Mark hopes so.

(6) About the Identity of David's Son (12:35–37)

35While Jesus was teaching in the temple courts, he asked, "How is it that the teachers of the law say that the Christ is the son of David? 36David himself, speaking by the Holy Spirit, declared:

> **" 'The Lord said to my Lord:**
> **"Sit at my right hand**
> **until I put your enemies**
> **under your feet." '**

37David himself calls him 'Lord.' How then can he be his son?"
The large crowd listened to him with delight.

Jesus' purpose probably was to expose the inadequacy of the scribes' interpretation in general but especially their concept of the Messiah. Certainly Mark's purpose in recording the incident was to give insight into the true nature of the Messiah.

The authenticity of the account has sometimes been questioned, but even on rational grounds it is made probable by the typically allusive nature of Jesus' teaching and by the improbability that the early church would have invented an account that *could be* interpreted to contradict a well-established belief, that of the Davidic descent of the Messiah.

The question arises, What did Jesus and/or Mark mean? Some have claimed the passage denies that the Messiah was to be of Davidic descent. The idea of a Davidic origin of the Messiah, or at least an ideal king, is so firmly established in the Old Testament, however, that such a denial either on the part of Jesus or Mark is most unlikely. The most important Old Testament passages that speak to the Davidic origin of the Messiah are: 2 Sam 7:11–16; 22:51; Pss 18:50; 89; Isa 9:6–7; 11:1–9; 16:5; Jer 23:5–6; 30:8–9;

33:15,17,22; Ezek 34:23–24; 37:24; Hos 3:5; Amos 9:11.[20] In the New Testament the title "Son of David" appears outside of Mark in Matt 1:1; 9:27; 12:23; 15:22; 20:30–31; 21:9,15; Luke 18:38–39; 20:41. The concept is present in Luke 2:4; Rom 1:3; 2 Tim 2:8. The first certain Christian denial of Davidic descent is the so-called *Epistle of Barnabas* 12:10–11 (ca. A.D. 130), and that denial was forged in the heat of controversies with Jews. For Jesus to have denied the Davidic descent of the Messiah would have subjected him to attack, but there is no trace of such an attack in any Gospel. For Mark to have denied Davidic descent would have contradicted his earlier "acceptance" of the term (10:47–48, which, if it can be accepted at face value, indicates that Jesus accepted it as well). The best conclusion therefore is Jesus and Mark intended to correct an inadequate Jewish concept of the Messiah.

12:35 After having been asked several questions in the preceding sections, Jesus asked the question. Of whom it was asked is not stated (Matt 22:41 says that it was the Pharisees). The word translated "son" (*huios*) might well be translated in context as "descendant" (GNB) because the reference is not to a son of David and one of his wives but to an ideal king of the Davidic line.

12:36 Jesus first affirmed the Davidic authorship of Ps 110, something that usually is denied by modern scholarship. Until recently the psalm was often assigned to Maccabean times with the second word, "Lord," referring to Simon (142–135 B.C.), the first of the Hasmonean priest-kings (although he did not actually use the title "king") during the period of independence between the Maccabean Revolt and Roman subjugation in 63 B.C. Discovery of a psalter with this psalm at Qumran has made that view unlikely. Even so Davidic authorship is not proved. Jesus also affirmed the inspiration of the psalm in particular and—probably—the Scriptures (what Christians call the Old Testament) in general. Such affirmation is found elsewhere in the Gospels only in the parallel in Matt 22:43. A similar claim can be found in Acts 1:16; 4:25; 28:25; Heb 3:7; 9:8; 10:15; cf. 2 Tim 3:16.

The quotation is of Ps 110:1.[21] In the Hebrew the first word meaning "Lord" is *Yahweh*, which always refers to God; but the second is *Adonai*, which sometimes refers to God and sometimes not—as in the psalm where it originally referred to a king, whoever and whenever he was. One might paraphrase, "God said to my superior." In Greek, however, the same word (*kyrios*, lord) is used in both places.

---

[20] Intertestamental literature also contains references to a Davidic messiah (e.g., *Pss Sol* 17:23; cf. 18:6–8), and the Qumran library (1QS 9:11; 1QSa 2:14,20; CD 20:1).

[21] Ps 110 is the psalm most frequently quoted and alluded to in the New Testament. See also Matt 22:44; 26:64; Mark 14:62; [16:19]; Luke 20:42–43; 22:69; Acts 2:34–35; Rom 2:5; 8:34; 11:29; 1 Cor 15:25; Eph 1:20; Col 3:1; Heb 1:3,13; 5:6,10; 6:20; 7:3,11,15,17,21; 8:1; 10:12–13; 12:2.

12:37 The point is that in ancient Israelite society fathers did not refer to their sons or even more distant descendants as "lords." Just the opposite was true. Inasmuch as David spoke of a descendant as his lord, he must have been referring to someone who was more than a physical descendant.

Apparently Jesus was not denying that he was David's descendant or the Messiah. In a veiled way typical of the "messianic secret" that pervades Mark's Gospel, he corrected the common Jewish notion that the Messiah was to be a warrior-king like David. The issue in the passage is not whether Jesus is the Son of David but what it means for him to be the Son of David. Jesus' riddle captures the *mystery* of the incarnation in a way unusual for Mark. Mark acknowledged that Jesus is the Messiah and Son of David, but he also recognized that these terms were inadequate. As David's *Lord*, Jesus cannot be limited to Davidic categories. Jesus is more than Son of David; he is Son of Man, i.e., the representative of all humanity and not just the Jews, who had to suffer and then be exalted at God's right hand. Still more important he is Son of God! The crowd was delighted no doubt because Jesus put the scribes to shame. It is uncertain, however, whether the sentence should be associated with the preceding (RSV, NRSV) or the following section (NEB, REB, GNB). By making it a separate paragraph, the NIV allows either.

The passage should force the modern church to reconsider the way in which Jesus is king and the way in which God puts enemies under his feet. The Jesus of Mark is a servant and minister (10:45), not a militant and triumphant king. This concept of Jesus himself and of the Christian ministry needs to be recovered.

(7) About the Evils of Scribism (12:38–40)

[38]As he taught, Jesus said, "Watch out for the teachers of the law. They like to walk around in flowing robes and be greeted in the marketplaces, [39]and have the most important seats in the synagogues and the places of honor at banquets. [40]They devour widows' houses and for a show make lengthy prayers. Such men will be punished most severely."

This passage recalls the warning in 8:15. There is no indication of time or place, and the incident could have happened earlier. Mark appropriately placed it here as a summary or a conclusion to the section that began at 11:27. A much more lengthy denunciation of the scribes and Pharisees appears in Matt 23. Luke's parallel in 20:45–47 is quite similar to Mark, but other denunciations are scattered throughout that Gospel.

In the previous section the scribes' teaching was questioned; here their practice was condemned. It must be emphatically said, however, that not all scribes and perhaps not even most scribes were guilty of the things indicated (cf. 12:28–34). The frequently heard charge that Mark and the other Gospel writers were anti-Jewish is abated when one realizes that this passage, for example, functions not only as a condemnation of a Jewish practice but also as a warning against a Christian one. Certainly the church has produced a multitude of leaders who have been characterized by pride and greed as were some of the Jewish teachers. The present passage, as well as others in Mark, distinguishes between the Jewish leaders and the Jewish people. Therefore this is not a blanket condemnation of Jews or Judaism.

12:38 The term "flowing robes" evidently refers to the *tallith*, a shawl worn during formal prayer and other religious acts in the synagogues. Some scribes may have worn these in public to attract attention. The greetings in the marketplaces were not ordinary greetings but expressions of deference to a religious authority.

12:39 The "most important seats in the synagogues" were on the bench facing the congregation and in front of the chest that contained the biblical scrolls. The "places of honor at banquets" were on the right and left of the host or at least at his table.

12:40 Exactly what was involved in devouring widows' houses is uncertain. The scribes were forbidden to receive payment for their teaching.[22] They either had to support themselves with secular employment (cf. Paul's practice) or had to be dependent upon gifts (again, cf. Paul). Such a situation easily led to undue expectation of gifts. Some may have ingratiated themselves to widows in hopes of being willed their houses, or they may have found technicalities in the law whereby they could lay claim to the houses of defenseless persons, such as widows. They may have "expected" generous sums from credulous widows for praying for them (note the reference to prayer). The reference might not be to personal gain but to exactions for the benefit of religious institutions.

Again, such abuses were not confined to Judaism but have been common in the Christian ministry throughout the history of the church.

5. The Widow's Gift (12:41–44)

41Jesus sat down opposite the place where the offerings were put and watched the crowd putting their money into the temple treasury. Many rich people threw in large amounts. **42**But a poor widow came and put in two very small copper coins, worth only a fraction of a penny.

43Calling his disciples to him, Jesus said, "I tell you the truth, this poor widow has put more into the treasury than all the others. **44**They all gave out of their wealth; but she, out of her poverty, put in everything—all she had to live on."

This pronouncement story is linked to the preceding by the common word "widow" in vv. 40,42, the common location in the temple, and the contrast

---

[22]*M. Abot.* 1.13; *m. Bek.* 4.6; *b. Ned.* 37a; 62a.

between the greed of the scribes and the generosity of the widow. The last of these is another example of Mark's contrast between the leaders who rejected Jesus and the common people who accepted him.

Most commentators praise the beauty of the story and acknowledge that it is in accord with all that is known about Jesus' character. Some, however, doubt its historicity because of the improbability that Jesus could know how much the woman gave, that it was all her livelihood, that she was a widow, and because similar stories exist in Jewish and pagan literature. As for Jesus' inability to know, certainly he was subject to most of the limitations of all human beings, but this consideration does not rule out the possibility that on certain occasions he was given unusual insight. The real question is not whether he had some supernatural knowledge but whether he was in fact Son of God as Mark claimed. A keenly observant person, which Jesus certainly was to have spoken the parables he did, could with a large amount of confidence have determined the particulars.

12:41   The "treasury" appears to have been located in the court of women and appears to have consisted of thirteen trumpet-shaped receptacles for both the temple tax and money given voluntarily for various purposes.[23]

12:42   The "two very small copper coins" were two *lepta* (so the Greek text). The *lepton* was the smallest coin in circulation in Palestine and was worth 1/64 of a *denarius*, a day's wages for a common laborer. It was not in circulation in the western part of the Roman Empire, where Mark apparently wrote. Therefore he explained that two *lepta* had the same value as a *kodrantēs*, the Greek transliteration of the Latin *quadrans*, which was a coin familiar to his readers/hearers. (The statement "which is a *quadrans*" is obscured by the NIV's "worth only a fraction of a penny." A similar obfuscation appears in most translations because most modern readers have no knowledge of ancient coins or their values.)

12:43–44   Jesus indicated that the thing of most importance is not how much is given but the extent to which the gift is a sacrificial one. Or to put it another way, the most significant thing is not how much is given but how much is left for one's personal use after the gift. A major element of Jesus' teaching is that attitude is more important than action. The widow's total giving demonstrates an attitude of absolute trust in God.

Quite different is the interpretation that claims the widow was guilty of imprudence and that Jesus could not have commended her. Rather he condemned a system that permitted widows to be destitute and perhaps even made them destitute by pressuring them to give all they had. The same kind

---

[23] "There were thirteen Shofar-chests in the Temple, whereon was inscribed: 'New Shekel dues,' 'Old Shekel dues,' 'Bird-offerings,' 'Young birds for the Whole offering,' 'Wood,' 'Frankincense,' 'Gold for the Mercy-seat,' and, on six of them, 'Freewill-offerings'" (*m. Šeqal.* 6.5, trans. Danby).

of extravagance, however, is commended in 14:6. There was so much poverty in ancient Palestine that the authorities could do little about it. The commendation of the widow does not imply that every disciple should give away everything.

The expression "calling his disciples to him" indicates that the teaching was intended for them and for all subsequent disciples. They too were to be generous in the extreme but without any ostentatiousness. In various ways they were to give their all as the widow did. But there is an additional lesson in the account. The sacrificial gift of the widow points to the sacrificial gift of Jesus. She gave her entire livelihood; he gave his very life. As Paul put it, "You know the grace of our Lord Jesus Christ, that though he was rich, yet for your sakes he became poor, so that you through his poverty might become rich" (2 Cor 8:9). Therefore the account functions as a transition to the passion narrative in chaps. 14–15. With this beautiful story Mark ended his account of Jesus' public ministry.

6. The Eschatological Discourse (13:1–37)

Mark 13 is variously called the eschatological discourse (because it deals with the end of the age), the prophetic discourse (because it prophesies the future), the Olivet discourse (because it was given on the Mount of Olives, v. 3), and the Little Apocalypse (because some claim Mark used a brief apocalyptic writing as a source). It is the longest and one of only two extended discourses in the Gospel, the other being 4:1–34.[24] For this reason and because of its placement at the end of Jesus' ministry and immediately before the passion narrative, its importance in Mark's story is obvious.

The discourse combines two literary forms, apocalyptic and testamental. The clearest biblical examples of apocalyptic literature are Daniel in the Old Testament and Revelation in the New Testament. In fact, Daniel is alluded to in vv. 14,19,26. The word "apocalyptic" itself means *revealed*, and apocalyptic literature claims to reveal the future of the world, especially things pertaining to the end of the present world and the establishment of a new world. That concern certainly is present in Mark 13. In apocalyptic literature the future usually is revealed in visions and by means of grotesque symbols. These elements are missing in Mark, so that chap. 13 is not a typical apocalypse. Another distinction of Mark 13 from most apocalyptic literature is the presence of a large amount of exhortation and ethical material. Therefore it has more immediacy and practical value than most apocalyptic literature.

---

[24] Also 7:6–23 and 9:33–50 appear to be discourses, but they do not deal with a single subject.

Some of these differences are due to the fusion of apocalyptic with the genres of last will and testament and/or farewell discourse, which are seen for example in Gen 49; the *Testaments of the Twelve Patriarchs*; Matt 28:16–20; Luke 24:36–49; John 14–17; Acts 1:6–11; 20:17–38; 2 Timothy. The major concerns in Mark's account of Jesus' last words to his disciples are to watch for his return and not to be deceived by upsetting events or persons in the meantime. Not even the destruction of Jerusalem and its temple was to dismay the disciples. The temple was no longer to be the focus of Christian hope.

The scholarly world has exercised itself in attempting to determine which parts of the discourse go back to Jesus himself, to an earlier Jewish or Christian apocalypse, and to Mark or other early interpreters. A popular theory has been that Mark or someone before him adapted a brief apocalyptic flier, which was written possibly when Pilate tried to bring the idolatrous standards of his army into Jerusalem soon after A.D. 26[25] or probably when Caligula tried to set up his statue in the Jerusalem temple in A.D. 40.[26] There has been little agreement, however, as to what portions of chap. 13 go back to this "Little Apocalypse"; and the theory is not as popular today as it once was. The unusual combination of exhortation and revelation also weighs against the theory. In fact, the criterion of dissimilarity supports the authenticity of the discourse. If the ancient prophets prophesied the fall of Jerusalem and its temple,[27] which took place in 586 B.C., and if others foretold the destruction of the temple, which took place in A.D. 70,[28] there is no reason why Jesus, if nothing more than a discerning person, could not have done so.

This claim that the substance of the discourse goes back to Jesus himself should not be extended to claim that it is a verbatim report or free from any adaptation and application on Mark's part or spoken on one occasion. That portions of it are found in other contexts in Matthew and Luke suggests Mark included some comments Jesus spoke on other occasions.

The location of the discourse in Mark's Gospel is significant. It is presented as the last and one of the more important elements in Jesus' teaching. It immediately precedes the passion account and has various points of contact with it. The implication is that in order to understand who he really is, the disciples must look beyond Jesus' death to his glorious return. The Son of Man had to suffer and die, but after that he would be vindicated and glorified. A similar idea is found in the transfiguration account (9:2–10). Inasmuch as he said so little about the resurrection of Jesus, Mark seems to have made Jesus' return the more important ground for Christian confidence.

---

[25] Josephus, *Antiquities* 18.3.1; *War* 2.9.2–3.
[26] Josephus, *Antiquities* 18.8.2–9; *War* 2.10.1–5; Philo, *Embassy to Gaius;* Tacitus, *History* 5.9.
[27] Jer 7:14; 9:11; 26:6,18; Mic 3:12.
[28] Josephus, *War* 6.5.3; *y. Yoma* 43c; *b. Yoma* 39b.

The disciples were to look beyond their present suffering to their eschatological salvation (v. 13), including their reunion with Jesus (v. 27). Suffering, if disciples are to follow their Lord, is the way to glory. Appearances are deceiving. God is still in control of history, and the righteous will ultimately triumph. Assurance of the return and vindication of their Lord were both very important to Mark's readers as they faced the prospect of persecution at the hands of Nero.

A word of clarification is necessary about the purpose of the discourse. Certainly the primary purpose was to provide assurance about the return and by implication the true identity of Jesus. But the repeated warnings against being deceived suggest that Mark was also concerned to dampen uncontrolled enthusiasm and speculation about the future. The purpose of the discourse was not to give details about the future but to provide assurance of Christ's return and thereby to promote faithfulness in the present. In its application to the contemporary church, the discourse warns against both fanaticism and skepticism and against both preoccupation with the future only or with the present only. The discourse encourages balance and perspective.

(1) The Destruction of the Temple (13:1–4)

[1]As he was leaving the temple, one of his disciples said to him, "Look, Teacher! What massive stones! What magnificent buildings!"

[2]"Do you see all these great buildings?" replied Jesus. "Not one stone here will be left on another; every one will be thrown down."

[3]As Jesus was sitting on the Mount of Olives opposite the temple, Peter, James, John and Andrew asked him privately, [4]"Tell us, when will these things happen? And what will be the sign that they are all about to be fulfilled?"

13:1 Mark may have intended his statement about Jesus "leaving the temple" to suggest a rejection of it. Certainly it was obsolete for the Gentile Christians to whom he wrote. It was more than obsolete; it was dangerous because the continuation of its sacrificial system undermined the finality of Jesus' sacrifice. The disciples' amazement is understandable. The temple of Jesus' time is described in Josephus, *Antiquities* 15.11 and *War* 5.5.1–6, and in the tractate *Middot* of the *Mishna*. According to Josephus, some of the stones were thirty-seven feet long by twelve feet high by eighteen feet deep![29] Small portions of the southeast corner of the wall and of the western wall of the temple still remain in place, and the large stones there, although not quite as large as what Josephus said,[30] contrast significantly with the much smaller

---

[29]Josephus, *Antiquities* 15.11.3.

[30]Larger stones may have been used more in the construction of the main building than the walls.

stones used in the medieval rebuilding of the walls. See also the introductory comments to 11:15–19 for a further description of the temple.

13:2 This prophecy was fulfilled in A.D. 70 when the Romans utterly destroyed the temple and the whole city while putting down the Jewish rebellion that began in A.D. 66. Only a faulty hermeneutic would question the fulfillment because, as previously indicated, a few of the huge stones were left in place and can be viewed today. That the early church invented this pronouncement, as has been claimed, is unlikely because the temple was destroyed by fire,[31] of which there is no mention here. Only after the fire had gutted it were the remaining walls pulled down.[32]

13:3 The setting of the discourse was the Mount of Olives, which was across the Kidron Valley (cf. John 18:1) and to the east of the temple area. This was appropriate because it was higher than the city, and therefore afforded a marvelous view of the temple, and because of its association with the Day of the Lord (Zech 14:4), which the early church reinterpreted to refer to the return of Christ. It also had a place in contemporary Jewish messianic expectation.[33] The four disciples were those of 1:16–20 and therefore the ones who had been with Jesus the longest.

13:4 The authenticity of the second question at least has been questioned because it seems to conflict with 8:11–13. If, however, there were any contradiction, surely Mark would have eliminated it. No doubt Jesus rejected the Pharisees' demand for a sign and granted the disciples' request because of the difference of motive. The Pharisees desired a present sign as proof that God had authorized Jesus for his mission; the disciples accepted Jesus' authority and desired a future sign to indicate the beginning of the events Jesus foretold. Mark frequently pictured Jesus providing the disciples information in private that he did not divulge publicly.

Although two questions were asked, they are parallel and refer to the same event. The first question obviously refers to the destruction of the temple (v. 2), and the second must also. The addition of the word "all" in the second question, however, opens the possibility the disciples sensed that something more than the destruction of the temple was involved in Jesus' pronouncement. They no doubt looked upon the destruction of the institution that they (erroneously) associated with the essence of Judaism as one of a series of events constituting the end of the world.

The preceding statement suggests an important consideration in order to interpret properly the discourse. The disciples' question dealt primarily with the end of the temple. Jesus' answer went far beyond that to the end of the

---

[31] Josephus, *War* 6.4.5.
[32] Josephus, *War* 7.1.1.
[33] Cf. Josephus, *War* 2.13.5; *Antiquities* 20.8.6.

world and his own return—which things he distinguished from the fall of Jerusalem. In v. 32 the question about time is minimized.

Recognition of the dual application of Jesus' answer will go a long way toward solving the difficulties of the discourse and arriving at a sound interpretation. His answer applied first to events in the near future, especially the destruction of Jerusalem and its temple in A.D. 70, and second to the end of the world and his own return.

(2) False Signs of the End of the Age (13:5–13)

⁵Jesus said to them: "Watch out that no one deceives you. ⁶Many will come in my name, claiming, 'I am he,' and will deceive many. ⁷When you hear of wars and rumors of wars, do not be alarmed. Such things must happen, but the end is still to come. ⁸Nation will rise against nation, and kingdom against kingdom. There will be earthquakes in various places, and famines. These are the beginning of birth pains.

⁹"You must be on your guard. You will be handed over to the local councils and flogged in the synagogues. On account of me you will stand before governors and kings as witnesses to them. ¹⁰And the gospel must first be preached to all nations. ¹¹Whenever you are arrested and brought to trial, do not worry beforehand about what to say. Just say whatever is given you at the time, for it is not you speaking, but the Holy Spirit.

¹²"Brother will betray brother to death, and a father his child. Children will rebel against their parents and have them put to death. ¹³All men will hate you because of me, but he who stands firm to the end will be saved.

The discourse proper begins at this point and continues to the end of the chapter.

13:5   The command to "watch out" (*blepete*) runs throughout the discourse (also in v. 9, "Be on your guard"; v. 23, "Be on your guard"; v. 33, "Be on guard! Be alert!"; and v. 37, "Watch!"—a different Greek word is used in v. 37 [*grēgoreite*]). Jesus evidently thought his disciples were in danger of being deceived, and Mark evidently thought the danger still persisted in his day. The modern interpreter is justified in going another step and saying that the threat still exists. Mark evidently needed to cool eschatological enthusiasm in his church.

13:6   In vv. 6–13 four things are set forth that some claimed were signs of the nearness of the destruction of Jerusalem and/or the end of the world: false messiahs (v. 6), wars (vv. 7–8a), natural disasters (v. 8b), and persecution (vv. 9,11–13). Jesus insisted that they are not. The expression "in my name" could indicate that some persons would claim to be the Messiah or that they would claim to represent him. Some object that so far as is known no one between A.D. 30–70 explicitly claimed to be the Messiah. This may be true, but there certainly were messianic figures, such as the Egyptian in Acts 21:38

(and Josephus, *Antiquities* 20.8.6; *War* 2.13.5) and the Theudas in Josephus (*Antiquities* 20.5.1). Furthermore, Jesus' answer is not limited to the period ending with the destruction of the temple in A.D. 70. About A.D. 132 Simon bar Kosiba evidently claimed to be the Messiah and led another revolt against Rome. His followers called him bar Kochba ("son of the star," see Num 24:17).

What the NIV translates "I am he" could be translated "I am" and could be an allusion to the divine name of Exod 3:13–14.

13:7–8 The immediate reference in v. 7 is to the war with Rome, which resulted from the Jewish rebellion in A.D. 66 and lasted until the fall of Jerusalem in A.D. 70 and beyond that to the fall of the fortress Masada in A.D. 73 or 74. As momentous as its consequences were, Jesus indicated that it would not be a sign of the end of the world or his return. Verse 8 indicates that it was just one of many wars during the present age. The statement "Such things must happen" in v. 7 indicates divine necessity. Although every Christian should strive to prevent war, it is a part of sinful human existence and not a "sign of the times."

The middle part of v. 8 mentions another phenomenon that is not an indicator of the consummation: natural disasters, such as earthquakes and famines. Such disasters have been so numerous that it is unnecessary to give specific examples.

The last part of v. 8 alludes to the "birth pains" or woes that precede the establishment of the messianic kingdom. The idea goes back to such passages as Isa 13:8; 26:17–18; 66:8; Jer 4:31; 6:24; 13:21; 22:23; 49:22; 50:43; Hos 13:13; Mic 4:9–10.

13:9 Verses 9,11–12 are held together by *paradidōmi*, a word the NIV translates "handed over" in v. 9, "brought to trial" in v. 11, and "betray" in v. 12. Such use of catchwords was common in ancient writing. The word is the same one that is used ten times in chaps. 14–15 with reference to Jesus' betrayal by Judas and deliverance to Pilate, and its use in chap. 13 suggests a correspondence between the fate of the disciples and their Lord.

The NIV properly interprets the word *synedria* to refer to local councils rather than the great Sanhedrin in Jerusalem. Josephus and the *Mishna* attest that such councils operated.[34] The flogging consisted of the traditional forty lashes less one. Deuteronomy 25:1–3 mercifully limited the number to forty, but the scribes reduced the number to thirty-nine, probably to avoid violating the commandment as a result of miscounting.[35] Paul indicated that he had endured the punishment five times prior to the writing of 2 Cor 11:24. He and other Jewish Christians were looked upon as heretics or even apostates.

---

[34] Josephus, *Antiquities* 4.8.14 and *m. Sanh.* 1.6, respectively.
[35] *M. Mak.* 3.10.

The "governors" would include such persons as Sergius Paulus (Acts 13:7), Gallio (Acts 18:12), Felix (Acts 24), and Festus (Acts 25–26). The kings would include Jewish client-kings such as Herod Agrippa I (Acts 12) and Herod Agrippa II (Acts 25–26) and perhaps even the emperor himself (Acts 25:11–12; 27:24). The last words of the verse could be translated either "witnesses to them" as in the NIV or "witnesses against them."

13:10 The authenticity of this verse has been denied because it breaks the natural connection between vv. 9 and 11 and because of the improbability that Jesus could have foreseen the Gentile mission. The first claim contains some truth, but a better explanation is that Jesus made the statement on another occasion and that Mark inserted it here in order to elaborate upon the preceding sentence. As for the second, the Old Testament prophets predicted the conversion of the Gentiles (e.g., Ps 96; Isa 42:6; 49:6,12; 52:10; 60:6); and if for no other reason than that, Jesus could have done so as well. The statement in no way reflects the later dispute about whether Gentiles could be admitted to the church without circumcision. Jesus was receptive toward all persons. There simply is no valid reason he could not have made the statement. As in v. 7 the word "must" again implies divine necessity.

The statement could be looked upon as a legitimate sign of the end, but there would still be uncertainty about the extent to which the gospel must be preached to all nations. Had the condition been met by the time Paul was martyred in the early or midsixties? Has it been met today? Was the return of Christ really imminent during the first decade or two of the church's existence before there was a world mission? Is it today? No certain answers can be given to these questions, and interpreters of differing views should respect other opinions. In any event the statement looks beyond the end of Mark's account. In various ways Mark conditions his readers/hearers to continue the gospel in their lives and ministries. The application of this principle becomes important at the end of Mark.

13:11 In vv. 11–13 Mark returned to the subject of persecution. On the one hand, his readers/hearers needed to know that it was not a sign of the end of the age; on the other, they needed to know how to conduct themselves in it. They were to continue to give testimony despite persecution (v. 9), to depend on the Spirit to help them know what to say (v. 11), and to stand firm to the end (v. 13). Verse 11 is primarily a prohibition against anxiety, not against preparation. Verse 11 is also one of the few references to the Holy Spirit in Mark (also 1:8,10,12; 3:29; 12:36).

13:12 Micah 7:6 makes a similar prophecy. Therefore one need not conclude that this is another "prophecy after the fact," that Jesus could not have spoken the words, that they were written by the early church after family betrayals had already taken place.

13:13 Tacitus said that Christians were "hated for their abominations."[36] The expression "to the end" probably does not refer to the end of the age or to the end of life but to total endurance, to endurance without wavering. The word translated "be saved" could mean *be delivered from persecution*, but the reference probably is to spiritual salvation, final salvation, eschatological salvation.

(3) True Signs of the End of the Age (13:14–23)

[14]"When you see 'the abomination that causes desolation' standing where it does not belong—let the reader understand—then let those who are in Judea flee to the mountains. [15]Let no one on the roof of his house go down or enter the house to take anything out. [16]Let no one in the field go back to get his cloak. [17]How dreadful it will be in those days for pregnant women and nursing mothers! [18]Pray that this will not take place in winter, [19]because those will be days of distress unequaled from the beginning, when God created the world, until now—and never to be equaled again. [20]If the Lord had not cut short those days, no one would survive. But for the sake of the elect, whom he has chosen, he has shortened them. [21]At that time if anyone says to you, 'Look, here is the Christ!' or, 'Look, there he is!' do not believe it. [22]For false Christs and false prophets will appear and perform signs and miracles to deceive the elect—if that were possible. [23]So be on your guard; I have told you everything ahead of time.

This passage undoubtedly looks ahead to the siege of Jerusalem in A.D. 70. (Note especially vv. 14b–16 and see the comments on them.) Certainly the parallel in Luke 21:20 refers to that: "When you see Jerusalem being surrounded by armies, you will know that its desolation is near." The only question is whether there is a double reference, whether the paragraph also looks ahead to another "abomination that causes desolation" (v. 14) and to another period of "distress" (vv. 19,24) at the end of the age long after the fall of Jerusalem in A.D. 70.

If the former interpretation is correct, the siege of Jerusalem in A.D. 70 was just another false sign of the end of the world, and vv. 14–23 ought to be included in the previous section. There is much to be said for this position. No doubt many Jews and Jewish Christians thought that the fall of Jerusalem and the destruction of the temple would be the end of the world. It was not, and one can see why Jesus warned his disciples not to think that it was and admonished them not to lament the fate of the city but to get on with their mission to the Gentiles.

The statements in vv. 19–20, however, appear to deal with a far greater distress than Jerusalem experienced in A.D. 70. There is no reason to think that it was the worst distress there ever had been or ever would be. Verses 19–20

---

[36]Tacitus, *Annals* 15.44. Cf. Justin, *Apology* 1.4; Tertullian, *Apology* 2; Pliny, *Letters* 10.96.

refer to a climactic distress at the end of the age, which leads to the end of the world. Furthermore vv. 24–27 indicate that the return of the Son of Man will take place soon after the distress described in vv. 14–23. Jesus did not return after the fall of Jerusalem and dissolution of the Jewish nation in A.D. 70. In fact, he still has not returned over nineteen hundred years later. One should conclude that here, as elsewhere in the discourse, there is a double reference to things in the near future and things in the far future. The destruction of Jerusalem in A.D. 70 was not a sign of the end of the world; the period of great distress in the future is.

13:14 The expression "abomination that causes desolation" ("desolating sacrilege," RSV, NRSV; "abomination of desolation," NASB, NEB, REB; "Awful Horror," GNB) goes back to Dan 9:27; 11:31; 12:11; 1 Macc 1:54. The word "abomination" indicates that which is repulsive to God and his people. The word "desolation" suggests that as a result of its profanation the temple is abandoned by the true people of God. In Daniel and 1 Maccabees the words refer to the statue of Zeus Olympus and the pagan altar Antiochus IV Epiphanes of Seleucid Syria erected in the Jerusalem temple in 167 B.C. Originally the expression referred not to the destruction of the temple but to its desecration by a foreign persecutor. The desecration by Antiochus became the prototype of future desecrations of the temple: by the Roman general Pompey in 63 B.C. when he conquered the city and entered the holy of holies,[37] by the governor Pilate when he brought idolatrous standards into the city about A.D. 26–27,[38] by the emperor Caligula when he unsuccessfully tried to erect his statue in the temple in A.D. 40,[39] and by the Zealots when they got control of the temple during the Jewish rebellion in A.D. 66–70.[40]

As used by Jesus and Mark, the term evidently refers in the first instance to the profanation of the temple by the Romans when they were in the process of destroying it in A.D. 70. Titus, for example, entered the holy of holies and removed various items and took them to Rome to adorn his victory procession.[41] In the second instance the term appears to refer to a future sacrilege by some profane and oppressive person, possibly the man of lawlessness of 2 Thess 2:1–12.

The word "abomination" is neuter, but the participle "standing," contrary to proper grammar, is masculine. See the NIV marginal note, and observe the NEB and REB: "When you see 'the abomination of desolation' usurping a place which is not his." This consideration may indicate that the future

---

[37] Josephus, *Antiquities* 14.4.4.

[38] Josephus, *Antiquities* 18.3.1; *War* 2.9.2.

[39] Josephus, *Antiquities* 18.8.2–9; *War* 2.10.1–5; Philo, *Embassy to Gaius;* Tacitus, *History* 5.9.

[40] Josephus, *War* 4.3.6–10; 4.4.4.

[41] Josephus, *War* 6.4.7; 7.5.5; the Arch of Titus in Rome.

abomination is a person rather than an object or event.

The statement "let the reader understand" probably is that of Mark rather than Jesus and probably refers to the prophecy of Daniel rather than the statement of Jesus. As a matter of fact, it is an allusion to Dan 9:23,25. Mark was pointing out the esoteric nature of the teaching, which he often set forth.

Jerusalem itself, and even Judea, is in mountains. Some have claimed that the words are not those of Jesus but of the author of the Gospel, who knew little about Palestinian geography. The mountains to which the disciples were to flee, however, were simply uninhabited places where they could find refuge.

The church historian Eusebius (ca. A.D. 325) said that the Jerusalem church was warned to flee from the doomed city by an "oracle"—perhaps a Christian prophet, perhaps this very passage—and that it did so and took refuge in the city of Pella on the east side of the Jordan across from Galilee.[42]

13:15 The picture is that of a flat-roofed Palestinian house with an outside staircase. Such roofs were used for relaxation and cooling off during summer evenings.

13:16 The "cloak" was the outer garment that was used as a coat during a cold day and as a blanket during the night. Except on the coldest days it was removed during work.

The idea in vv. 14b–16 is that the danger is so great that there is no time for any delay. Life itself is at stake.

13:17 Hasty flight without provisions is difficult for anyone. For "pregnant women and nursing mothers" it is doubly so because of their weakness and inability to hurry.

13:18 The word can mean either *winter* or *storm*. In winter the swollen wadis, which were dry creek beds in the summer, were difficult to cross; and no food could be gleaned from the countryside.

13:19–20 The statement alludes to Dan 12:1. The RSV, NASB, and NKJV read "tribulation" rather than "distress." The KJV has "affliction," and the GNB has "trouble." The reference apparently is to what is sometimes called "the Great Tribulation," the one at the end of the age (cf. the comments on these verses in the introduction to this section). Another reason for thinking that the prediction goes beyond the fall of Jerusalem in A.D. 70 is that following the flight of the church, few of the "elect" were still in the city.

13:21–22 Some have argued that these verses are merely a doublet of vv. 5–6, i.e., different accounts of the same saying of Jesus. The differences in wording are significant, however, as are also the points being made. In vv. 5–6 the warning is against being deceived into thinking that the Christ had returned. In vv. 21–22 the warning is against delaying one's escape because someone claims to be the Messiah who can protect against the impending

---

[42] Eusebius, *Church History* 3.5.3.

danger. At the end of v. 21 one could also translate, "Do not believe him." In v. 22 Mark probably intended a contrast between false christs, who eagerly performed spectacular miracles, and the true Christ, who was reluctant to do so and who maintained an air of secrecy. The final statement seems to indicate that in crucial situations it is not possible to deceive the elect.

13:23 The word translated "everything" is plural in Greek and is the same as is used twice in v. 4. To a very limited extent vv. 14–23 answer the question in v. 4. No definite time is given. The destruction of Jerusalem is no indicator that the end of the world is near. The final tribulation that exceeds anything previously known is a true indicator. The Revelation to John evidently describes this tribulation.

(4) The Return of the Son of Man and the Gathering of His Elect (13:24–27)

²⁴" But in those days, following that distress,
   " 'the sun will be darkened,
      and the moon will not give its light;
²⁵the stars will fall from the sky,
      and the heavenly bodies will be shaken.'
²⁶" At that time men will see the Son of Man coming in clouds with great power and glory. ²⁷And he will send his angels and gather his elect from the four winds, from the ends of the earth to the ends of the heavens.

At this point the dual reference of the discourse becomes undeniable—at least for all readers since A.D. 70. The disciples who first heard what Jesus said and even some of the original readers/hearers of the Gospel may have thought the fall of Jerusalem would constitute the end of the world, but that has not proved to be true. The modern reader may conclude that Jesus and/or Mark were mistaken (this conclusion is not possible for those who affirm the total truthfulness of Scripture), but no objective interpreter can deny they intended to describe an event that as yet has not taken place and one that transcends history.

Virtually the entire section consists of allusions to various Old Testament texts. One must conclude that the return of the Lord fulfills many of the promises originally given to Israel. What Mark described amounts to the consummation of the kingdom of God. Whereas throughout most of the Gospel Christ and his kingdom have been veiled, here they are fully revealed. Mark prepared his readers/hearers for the passion account by showing them the ultimate triumph of Jesus.

13:24–25 The word "but" contrasts what follows with what precedes and suggests that the return of the Son of Man is an altogether different event from the fall of Jerusalem and other sufferings of the present age. "In those days" is an Old Testament expression (e.g., Jer 3:16,18; Joel 3:1; Zech 8:23). Mark used the Greek equivalent several times (also 1:9, "At that time"; 8:1, "During those days"; 13:17,19,20), which is more of an indicator of the certainty of

God's will than a particular time. Here it simply refers to a time after the "distress" or "tribulation" or "trouble" of vv. 2–23, but no one can determine how long the period of trouble lasts.

Verses 24b–25 are not a direct quotation, as the NIV implies by its use of quotation marks, but an allusion to such passages as Isa 13:10: Ezek 32:7–8; Joel 2:10,31; 3:15. The four statements are parallel, as the poetic arrangement in the NIV indicates. The various items are not to be taken literally but as symbolic of an event of cosmic significance. Certainly the darkening of the sun at Jesus' crucifixion (15:33) does not constitute fulfillment of v. 24b, although it too is a symbol of divine wrath.

13:26 "At that time" (*tote*, "then," RSV, NRSV, NASB, NEB, REB, GNB) also refers to a time after the distresses of the present age. The statement "men will see" in the NIV, in the Greek text is literally "they will see" (RSV, NRSV, NASB, NEB, REB). It presumably means that all persons and not just disciples will observe the return.

The affirmation is a clear allusion to, if not a quotation of, Dan 7:13. In fact, this is the only passage that specifically associates the Son of Man in Mark with the one in Daniel, but Daniel likely is the source of all of the references to this person. It is significant that the term "Son of Man" is used here. The same one who humbly ministered on earth (10:45), the same one who suffered and died (8:31), will return with "great power and glory." In the Old Testament "glory" is a characteristic of God (e.g., Exod 16:7,10; 24:16–17). Jesus' glorious return is further indication of his deity.

13:27 Nothing is said about judgment, either punishment or rewards. Nothing is said about resurrection or reigning. The only purpose of the coming mentioned is the gathering of the scattered elect. The "elect" are those who are chosen and blessed by God. The word itself gives no indication of why God chose them. The idea of gathering the scattered people of God goes back to the Old Testament, where it is a function of God himself (e.g., Deut 30:3–4; Ps 147:2; Isa 11:12; 43:6; Jer 32:37; Ezek 11:17; 34:13; 36:24). The expression "four winds" appears five times in the Old Testament (e.g., Zech 2:6). The Old Testament several times uses the expressions "end(s) of the earth" (e.g., Deut 13:7; 30:4; Jer 12:12) and "end of the heavens" (Deut 4:32; 30:4 LXX; Ps 19:6) but does not combine them as here. The idea is that Jesus will regather his people from wherever they have been scattered. This was a comforting word for Mark's readers/hearers who were about to be—and according to some datings of Mark's Gospel had been—scattered.

(5) The Certainty of the Fact but Uncertainty about the Time of the Return (13:28–37)

28"Now learn this lesson from the fig tree: As soon as its twigs get tender and its leaves come out, you know that summer is near. **29**Even so, when you see these things happening, you know that it is near, right at the door. [30]I tell you the truth, this generation will certainly not pass away until all these things have happened. [31]Heaven and earth will pass away, but my words will never pass away.

[32]"No one knows about that day or hour, not even the angels in heaven, nor the Son, but only the Father. [33]Be on guard! Be alert! You do not know when that time will come. [34]It's like a man going away: He leaves his house and puts his servants in charge, each with his assigned task, and tells the one at the door to keep watch.

[35]"Therefore keep watch because you do not know when the owner of the house will come back—whether in the evening, or at midnight, or when the rooster crows, or at dawn. [36]If he comes suddenly, do not let him find you sleeping. [37]What I say to you, I say to everyone: 'Watch!' "

The discourse ends with a collection of sayings and parables that deal with the uncertainty of the time of the end and the resulting necessity of readiness. More specifically the section contains the parable of the fig tree (vv. 28–29), two sentences about what is and is not transitory (vv. 30–31), two sentences about the uncertainty of the time of the end and the necessity of vigilance (vv. 32–33), the parable of the doorkeeper (vv. 34–36), and a final command to watch (v. 37). Some of the sayings may have been spoken by Jesus on other occasions and placed here by Mark because of their appropriateness. The arrangement appears to be according to catchwords: "these things happening" (v. 29) and "all these things have happened" (v. 30); "pass away" (vv. 30–31); "be on guard" (v. 33); "keep watch" (vv. 34–35); "watch" (v. 37); "at the door" (v. 29); and "the one at the door" (v. 34). Compare the comments on 9:33–50.

13:28–29 The parable compares the coming of the Son of Man to the coming of summer. Just as the leafing out of fig trees indicates the nearness of summer in Palestine, so the things spoken by Jesus indicate the nearness of his return. Jesus used a fig tree in his illustration because, whereas in Palestine most trees are evergreens, the fig tree loses its leaves in winter.

Some uncertainty exists about the reference of the words "these things" and "all these things" (v. 30). The nearest antecedents are the coming of the Son of Man and the gathering of the elect in vv. 26–27, but it is not likely that either Jesus or Mark would have said that when people see the coming of the Son of Man they could know that he is near. (The Greek expression could be translated either "it is near" or "he is near," RSV, NASB.) The events of vv. 24–27 constitute the end, not things that must precede the end.

Furthermore, the various items in vv. 24–27 together constitute one climactic event that takes place at one point of time rather than a series of events spread over a long period of time. Therefore "these things" and "all these things" must refer to the events of vv. 5–23 and especially those of vv. 14–23, i.e., the sufferings associated with the fall of Jerusalem. Note how the expression "when you see" appears in both vv. 14 and 29.

13:30–31 This interpretation is confirmed by the term "this generation." Especially those who have tried to limit "all these things" to the return of Christ (see the comments on vv. 28–29) have tended to identify "this generation" with the Christian era, but elsewhere in Mark (8:12,38; 9:19)[43] the term refers to the contemporaries of Jesus. That is certainly the most natural interpretation here. Jesus meant that some of the people of his generation, and more particularly some of his disciples, would not die until the things of vv. 5–23 had happened, including the very significant destruction of Jerusalem and its temple. To a limited extent v. 30 answers the first question in v. 4.

"Heaven and earth" is a way of depicting the entire universe. Jesus affirmed that the physical universe will eventually perish. His word, however, is of a different order and will never perish. Jesus' word includes all that he taught and is not limited to the eschatological discourse. Such a fantastic claim is another indication that for Mark the Son of Man was also the Son of God.

13:32–33 On the surface the statement affirms that no one except God knows the exact time of the coming of Christ. The expression "that day," however, recalls the Old Testament concept of the Day of the Lord (e.g., Amos 5:18–20; Zeph 1:7,14–16), the day of judgment of both Israel and the nations that marks the end of the present evil age and the beginning of the coming age of righteousness. In referring to the Day of the Lord, the Old Testament uses the very expression "that day" (e.g., Amos 8:3,9,13). Inasmuch as the New Testament elsewhere reinterprets the Day of the Lord to be the return of Christ (e.g., 1 Thess 5:2; 2 Thess 2:2; 2 Pet 3:10; cf. 1 Cor 5:5; Phil 1:6,10; 2:16), Mark here likely intended the term specifically to denote the parousia and not just the end of the world in general.

Scholarly opinion is divided about the authenticity of the words "nor the Son." Most find it inconceivable that the early church would have invented a saying that ascribed ignorance to Jesus, and we would certainly place ourselves among those. A few think the early church did place the words on the lips of Jesus in order to absolve him from error when it became apparent that the return was not going to take place within the first Christian generation. If the church felt a need to absolve Jesus from predicting an early return, however, it would have found a way to do it without attributing ignorance to him. The difficulty of the statement can be seen in the fact that many manuscripts of Matt 24:36 and a few of Mark omit the statement and that Luke omits the verse altogether.[44] There is little question that Jesus actually spoke the words.

---

[43] It is certainly true, however, that 8:38 could be applied to the entire Christian era.

[44] It is also possible that Matthew himself omitted the statement, as he often did in the case of difficult statements in Mark, and that later scribes added it in order to harmonize Matthew with Mark. Inasmuch as Matthew was more highly regarded and more frequently used than Mark in the medieval church, however, Mark usually was harmonized to Matthew rather than vice versa.

One need not be embarrassed about them. Ignorance of certain things was simply a part of Jesus' humanity, a part of his becoming a real human being.

The generally regarded best Greek manuscript of Mark plus one of medium quality and some versional manuscripts omit the words "and pray" with the NIV and most other translations cited in this commentary. Despite the strong attestation for inclusion (KJV, NKJV), it is difficult to see why the words would have been omitted if original. Probably they were added under the influence of 14:38.

"Be alert" probably is a better translation than "watch" (KJV, NKJV, RSV) because the way in which disciples are to be ready for the return of the Lord is not to watch for it or for signs of it but to be busy with their assigned tasks (v. 34). Because disciples "do not know when the time will come," they must always be prepared. Ignorance of the date is no excuse for unpreparedness.

13:34–36 The miniparable is in v. 34, and the comments on it are in vv. 35–36. No doubt Mark's readers/hearers identified Jesus as the head of the house who had gone away and themselves as the servants. Mark wanted each member of his community to realize that he or she had an "assigned task" and the obligation to "watch" (the Greek word in vv. 34,35,37 is different from the one translated "watch" in the KJV and "be alert" in the NIV in v. 33). The parable is true to life because although in ancient Palestine people did not ordinarily travel at night, they might do so if returning from a late banquet or from abroad.

As in 6:48, Mark again used the Roman way of reckoning four watches rather than the Jewish way of three watches (cf. Luke 12:38). The opposite of being on guard, being alert, and watching is sleeping. It is a symbol of spiritual lethargy.

13:37 That Mark ended his account of the discourse with another command to watch is no accident. The discourse began with the idea, and it also appears in vv. 5,9,23,33–35 (several different Greek words are used to convey the same basic idea). Mark's concerns throughout were to warn against deception, i.e., the claims that the Christ had already returned or that the end was about to take place, and to promote devotion to Christian duty. And, not accidentally, he quoted Jesus as saying that the command applies to all disciples and not just the four of v. 3 or the twelve original disciples. The discourse is not just for a past day or a future day but for all Christians of all times.

7. The Plot to Kill Jesus (14:1–2,10–11)

¹Now the Passover and the Feast of Unleavened Bread were only two days away, and the chief priests and the teachers of the law were looking for some sly way to arrest Jesus and kill him. ²"But not during the Feast," they said, "or the people may riot." . . .

¹⁰**Then Judas Iscariot, one of the Twelve, went to the chief priests to betray Jesus to them. ¹¹They were delighted to hear this and promised to give him money. So he watched for an opportunity to hand him over.**

Again Mark resorted to intercalation/bracketing (cf. comments on 3:20ff.), this time to contrast forcefully the hatred of Jesus' enemies and the love of the woman who anointed him. Mark previously mentioned plots against Jesus in 3:6; 11:18; 12:12. Here he described the final and successful one.

14:1 The Passover was a meal eaten on the evening of 15 Nisan (March/April and also called *Abib*), and it celebrated the "passing over" of the Israelites when the firstborn of the Egyptians were slain immediately prior to the exodus from Egypt (Exod 12:1–14,42–49; Num 9:1–14; Deut 16:1–8). The date was the first full moon following the vernal equinox. The lamb that was to be eaten was slain on the afternoon of 14 Nisan, i.e., the afternoon before it was eaten in the evening. (Jewish days began at sundown, not midnight.) The lamb could be slain only in the Jerusalem temple and eaten only within the city. No work was permitted on the afternoon of the 14th and throughout the 15th. The Passover was one of the three "pilgrim festivals" all Jewish males were supposed to attend, although universal attendance was not possible in the first century.

The Feast of Unleavened Bread began at the same time as the Passover, but it lasted for seven days through 21 Nisan (Exod 12:15–20; 23:15; 34:18; Deut 16:3–4). It celebrated both the barley harvest and the time when the Israelites ate unleavened bread while leaving Egypt. Actually leaven had to be removed from homes by noon of 14 Nisan, and it would appear that the 14th was sometimes referred to as the first day of unleavened bread (see the comments on v. 12) and that in some sense the feast lasted eight days. No work was permitted on the first and last days, and a religious assembly took place on the first and seventh days. In popular thinking the two feasts had been merged (cf. Luke 22:1).

The Greek text could be translated literally "after two days," but the statement is ambiguous. If Mark used Roman reckoning, he probably meant *two days later;* but if he used inclusive Jewish reckoning, he probably meant *on the next day.* The question is not when the meal took place—almost certainly it was on a Thursday evening—but when the plot was made—whether on Tuesday or Wednesday. Inasmuch as "after three days" in 8:31; 9:31; 10:34 most likely means *on the third day*, i.e., two days later according to modern reckoning, the reference is probably to Wednesday. In any event the precise chronological reference was Mark's way of indicating the importance of the event (cf. 9:2).

The last part of the verse does not describe a formal meeting of the Sanhedrin but a consultation of some of its leaders. The use of the imperfect tense indicates a repeated action over a period of time and, therefore, the determination of the leaders to destroy Jesus.

14:2 Mark made a distinction between the people who were often favorable to Jesus and the leaders who were usually hostile. The statement in this verse is problematic because according to the subsequent account Jesus was arrested during the feast. One possibility is that the plans were changed, perhaps due to the offer of Judas (vv. 10–11). Another is that Mark wanted to show that the timing of Jesus' enemies was overturned by God. Still another is that Jesus was arrested the night before the official Passover (see the comments on 14:12). Still another is that the idea is not "during the Feast" but "in the presence of the crowd which had come to the feast." The concern of the officials about a riot is understandable because during the pilgrim feasts the inhabitants of Jerusalem doubled, tripled, quadrupled, or more; and emotions ran high.

14:10–11 Even the most radical interpreters agree that the account of Judas's betrayal is historical. It is inconceivable that the early church would have invented such a discrediting story.

Judas was mentioned previously only in 3:19 on the list of the Twelve, and the probable meaning of the word "Iscariot" was explained in the comments on that verse. The Greek text has the article "the" before the word "one." This may be nothing more than the anaphoric use of the article to refer to the previously mentioned Judas, or the idea may be to emphasize that Judas was the only one of the Twelve to betray Jesus.

In comparison with the other Gospels, Mark's account is very restrained. He said nothing about Judas's motive. Matthew 26:15 suggests that it was money and indicates that the amount was thirty silver coins, something else about which Mark was silent. Luke 22:3 and John 13:2,27 indicate that he was demon possessed. There has been much speculation about the motive. Was Judas disappointed about Jesus' refusal to be a political Messiah? Was he attempting to force Jesus to take decisive action against his enemies? Was he a spy all along? No confident answer can be given.

There has also been speculation about just what Judas betrayed. Was it the fact that Jesus claimed to be the Messiah? On the one hand, Mark did not indicate that Jesus made many messianic claims; on the other, the leaders probably had already concluded that Jesus was a false messiah. Was it that Jesus advocated rebellion against Rome? If so, Judas's action was not so much a betrayal as a false accusation. Was it the place where Jesus stayed at night (cf. John 18:2)? If Jesus stayed at the same place each night, it seems the authorities would have already known it; if Jesus stayed at different places, Judas could not have been certain where. Was Judas's role merely to identify Jesus in the darkness (cf. vv. 44–45)? It is unlikely that the soldiers would have needed such help. What we do know is that the efforts of the religious authorities had been renewed and intensified. They, however, had to move with caution so as not to create a riot. They looked for the right time and right way to accomplish their plans. Judas became the vehicle through which Jesus would be handed over (*paradidōmi*) to them.

8. The Anointing at Bethany (14:3–9)

[3]While he was in Bethany, reclining at the table in the home of a man known as Simon the Leper, a woman came with an alabaster jar of very expensive perfume, made of pure nard. She broke the jar and poured the perfume on his head.

[4]Some of those present were saying indignantly to one another, "Why this waste of perfume? [5]It could have been sold for more than a year's wages and the money given to the poor." And they rebuked her harshly.

[6]"Leave her alone," said Jesus. "Why are you bothering her? She has done a beautiful thing to me. [7]The poor you will always have with you, and you can help them any time you want. But you will not always have me. [8]She did what she could. She poured perfume on my body beforehand to prepare for my burial. [9]I tell you the truth, wherever the gospel is preached throughout the world, what she has done will also be told, in memory of her."

Each of the Gospels has an anointing story (also Matt 26:6–13; Luke 7:36–50; John 12:1–8). Despite differences in detail,[45] it is reasonably certain that the ones in Matthew, Mark, and John reflect the same event. It is much less certain that the one in Luke does, not merely because he placed it much earlier in Jesus' ministry but because of his description of the woman as a prostitute. The Markan account takes the form of a pronouncement story.

14:3 Mark previously implied that Jesus spent his nights at Bethany (11:11–12; see comments on 11:1 for the location of Bethany). "Reclining" rather than "sat" (KJV, NKJV) is the correct translation because the Jews reclined rather than sat at formal meals. "Simon the Leper" is not otherwise known. He possibly was a leper whom Jesus had healed.[46]

The presence of the unnamed woman was most unusual; Jewish women did not ordinarily attend banquets with men except in the capacity of servants. The "alabaster jar" was a flask with a long neck and no handles, and it was sealed

---

[45]Matthew and Mark locate the anointing two days before the Passover; John, six. Matthew and Mark locate it in the home of Simon the Leper; John locates it in the home of Mary, Martha, and Lazarus; Luke, in a Pharisee's home. In Matthew and Mark Jesus' head is anointed; in John (as well as Luke), his feet. A comparison of these accounts shows how difficult it is to harmonize the Gospels. One can only conclude that the Gospel writers were not concerned in every instance to reproduce the exact details. In the present instance the least one can do is to allow for the possibility that the anointing took place at some time other than one or two days before the Passover.

[46]It is also possible that Jesus defied custom and had close contact with lepers, but it is unlikely that others would do so at a banquet.

to preserve the ointment. The fact that the woman broke the flask implies that she poured all of its contents on Jesus. "Nard" was an aromatic oil extracted from a root found primarily in India—thus its costliness. The word translated "pure" may be related to a word meaning *faithful* or *genuine*, as the NIV seems to indicate. It could also be derived from a Greek word meaning *liquid* or an Aramaic one meaning *pistachio nut*. The oil of this nut was used as a base for perfumes.

Whether the woman anointed Jesus in gratitude for some favor (e.g., a healing) or whether she recognized him as the Messiah, Mark did not say; but he likely expected his readers/hearers to see messianic significance in the action. In the Old Testament kings (e.g., 1 Sam 10:1; 16:12–13; 1 Kgs 1:38–39; 2 Kgs 9:1–6), priests (e.g., Exod 28:41), and prophets (1 Kgs 19:16) were anointed. The very word Messiah/Christ means *the anointed one*. It is also true of course that sometimes anointing had no political or religious significance (cf. Ps 23:5).

14:4 The "some" were evidently the disciples because vv. 6–9 appear to be addressed to them, and here Mark provided another example of their lack of understanding. In fact, some textual witnesses of medium value explicitly state that it was the disciples, as does also Matt 26:8 (John 12:4, however, says that it was Judas). The objection was not to the act as such but to its extravagance.

14:5 As the NIV footnote indicates, the Greek text has "three hundred denarii." A denarius was a day's wage for a common laborer; therefore the NIV is correct in its approximation "a year's wages." Concern for the poor is understandable because making a gift to them at Passover time was a custom.[47]

14:6 The word translated "beautiful" (*kalos*) can mean just that or *morally or ethically good*. The woman's action was both of these.

14:7 The idea here is not unlike that of 2:19–20, where Jesus said that one does not fast while the bridegroom is still present. Jesus was not condoning poverty. Indeed, the statement may be an allusion to Deut 15:11, which commands generosity to the poor. Other passages show Jesus' concern for them (Matt 6:2–4; 19:21; cf. Mark 10:21; Luke 16:19–31; 21:1–4; John 13:29). The point is simply that the disciples would have many opportunities to help the poor but no more to minister directly to Jesus.

14:8 The Greek text has "She did what she had." That could be rendered as in the NIV or "She gave what she had" or "She gave all that she had."

Whether the woman intended to anoint Jesus' body prior to his death and burial is uncertain. The last part of the verse sets forth Jesus' interpretation and application of what she did. It also suggests the importance of the passion to

---

[47] *M. Pesah.* 10.1; John 13:29.

Mark's understanding of messiahship: Jesus was anointed as king in connection with his death and burial.

14:9 This prophecy of Jesus was fulfilled when Mark and Matthew (26:13) recorded the statement and their Gospels began to be read widely. The story was told orally before that time. The authenticity of the statement has been denied, however, because of the allusion to the later world mission. If, however, Jesus preached a new message that constituted good news, why could he not have believed that it would continue to be preached after his death? The use of the word *amēn* ("I tell you the truth"), which was characteristic of Jesus' teaching, but not that of the early church, favors authenticity. The absence of the woman's name does as well. If Jesus spoke the words, he envisioned a period of time between his death and return during which the gospel would be preached. Some early Christians failed to realize this and looked for an early return.

9. The Institution of the Lord's Supper (14:12–26)

¹²On the first day of the Feast of Unleavened Bread, when it was customary to sacrifice the Passover lamb, Jesus' disciples asked him, "Where do you want us to go and make preparations for you to eat the Passover?"

¹³So he sent two of his disciples, telling them, "Go into the city, and a man carrying a jar of water will meet you. Follow him. ¹⁴Say to the owner of the house he enters, 'The Teacher asks: Where is my guest room, where I may eat the Passover with my disciples?' ¹⁵He will show you a large upper room, furnished and ready. Make preparations for us there."

¹⁶The disciples left, went into the city and found things just as Jesus had told them. So they prepared the Passover.

¹⁷When evening came, Jesus arrived with the Twelve. ¹⁸While they were reclining at the table eating, he said, "I tell you the truth, one of you will betray me—one who is eating with me."

¹⁹They were saddened, and one by one they said to him, "Surely not I?"

²⁰"It is one of the Twelve," he replied, "one who dips bread into the bowl with me. ²¹The Son of Man will go just as it is written about him. But woe to that man who betrays the Son of Man! It would be better for him if he had not been born."

²²While they were eating, Jesus took bread, gave thanks and broke it, and gave it to his disciples, saying, "Take it; this is my body."

²³Then he took the cup, gave thanks and offered it to them, and they all drank from it.

²⁴"This is my blood of the covenant, which is poured out for many," he said to them. ²⁵"I tell you the truth, I will not drink again of the fruit of the vine until that day when I drink it anew in the kingdom of God."

²⁶When they had sung a hymn, they went out to the Mount of Olives.

This section could be further subdivided: preparation for the Passover meal (vv. 12–16), prediction of betrayal (vv. 17–21), and the eating of the Passover meal and institution of the Lord's Supper (vv. 22–26).[48] The first of these is strikingly similar in structure and language to 11:1–6 (preparation for the entry to Jerusalem). This does not indicate that they are different accounts of the same event but that they were composed by the same person. Mark had a habit of repeating himself. He was not the best stylist in the New Testament.

In this section Mark identified Jesus as the fulfillment of what was foreshadowed by the Passover, i.e., freedom from whatever oppresses, and he showed how the Lord's Supper took the place of the Passover meal. Mark also showed that Jesus was not surprised or overcome by his betrayal and death but that he foresaw everything and acted in accordance with prophecy and the will of God.

Accounts of the institution of the Lord's Supper are also found in Matt 26:26–29; Luke 22:15–20; 1 Cor 11:23–25. John described the last supper, but not the institution of the Lord's Supper. Much effort has been expended to determine which is the most primitive but with no clear result. Paul's account was the first to be written (ca. A.D. 56). All four accounts have much in common, but among them Matthew and Mark have the most in common. Some radical critics have tried to trace the origin of the Christian rite to cult meals in various Hellenistic religions and especially the so-called mystery religions; but the vocabulary, style, and the various items in the account are typically Jewish. The least one can claim is that the account goes back to the earliest Palestinian church, but it is only a step from there to Jesus himself.

14:12 Properly "the first day of the Feast of Unleavened Bread" was 15 Nisan (Lev 23:6; Num 28:17), but the Passover lambs were killed on the afternoon of 14 Nisan. Some other evidence, however, suggests that 14 Nisan was sometimes loosely referred to as the first day of the Feast of Unleavened Bread.[49] In any event vv. 12,14,16 clearly describe the last supper as a Passover meal. Matthew and Luke did the same (note especially Luke 22:15). Nevertheless, there is a serious question whether the last supper was in fact a Passover meal.

In addition to the explicit statements in the Synoptics, the following items in the Markan account support the identification of the meal with the Passover. Although Jesus and his disciples had been spending the nights in Bethany, they returned to Jerusalem, the only place the Passover could be eaten. Although ordinary meals began with the breaking of bread, this one apparently began by dipping in a bowl as at Passover meals. Wine, which was mandatory at the Passover, was used at this meal, whereas it was rare, at least among

---

[48] It has been argued by Edwards, "Markan Sandwiches," 211, that 14:17–31 is another instance of interrelating accounts (see comments on 3:20ff.). The account of the Lord's Supper (vv. 22–26) is bracketed by predictions of betrayal (vv. 17–21,27–42) for the purpose of contrasting the faithlessness of one of Jesus' disciples and the covenant faithfulness of God.

[49] Josephus, *War* 5.3.1; Exod 12:18.

common folk, at other meals. The meal took place in the evening, as did the Passover meal, rather than late in the afternoon, as did most Jewish suppers. Jesus and the disciples reclined as was done at formal meals, but not necessarily at common ones. A hymn was sung at the end as at the Passover, which was not done at ordinary meals.

Other considerations, however, cast much doubt on such an identification. First, John's Gospel makes clear that the last supper took place the night before the Passover, i.e., the evening of 14 Nisan, and that Jesus died at the same time the Passover lambs were being slain, i.e., the afternoon of 14 Nisan (13:1,29; 18:28; 19:14,31). John's dating may find support in 1 Cor 5:7. Second, the *Babylonian Talmud* preserves a tradition that Jesus was executed on the eve of the Passover.[50] Third, in the Synoptic accounts there is no mention of the lamb, the bitter herbs, the explanation of the meaning of the Passover, or the singing of the first part of the Hallel. Fourth, the Synoptics use the word *artos* (bread, any kind of bread, ordinarily leavened bread) rather than *azyma* (unleavened bread). Fifth, it borders on the inconceivable that Jesus was arrested on the holiest night of the Jewish year and that he was tried and executed on an especially holy day (cf. 14:2). Sixth, it is unlikely that weapons would have been carried during the evening of Passover (14:47) or that a traveler would have been coming in from the countryside during the day of the Passover (15:21). Seventh, if the last supper had been an annual Passover meal, the observance of the Lord's Supper would likely have become an annual rather than a weekly rite.

Various attempts have been made to reconcile the two dates/identifications of the meal. One is that the meal was a Passover but that John placed it a day earlier for a theological reason, namely to identify Jesus as the Christian's Passover lamb by having him appear to die at the same time as did the lambs. This is quite possible. None of the Gospels is strictly chronological, and each has adapted the tradition for theological reasons as redaction criticism has shown. It could also be argued that the meal took place the day before the Passover and that the Synoptics describe it as a Passover for much the same reason—to identify Jesus as the Passover lamb and/or to emphasize the sacrificial and liberating effects of his death.

Another explanation is that two calendars were in use in first-century Palestine and that in them the Passover fell on different days. The Synoptics used one and John the other. There is certainly evidence for two calendars, a lunar one used by official Judaism and a solar one used by sectarian Judaism as seen in the Dead Sea Scrolls and the apocryphal book of *Jubilees*.[51] It is very

---

[50] *B. Sanh.* 43a.

[51] A variant view is that the solar calendar was used by the Pharisees as well as the Essenes at Qumran or by Galilean Jews as opposed to Judean Jews, but there is no evidence for this.

doubtful, however, that the sectarian one was used by Jesus and his disciples, by any of the Gospel writers, or in Jerusalem itself where the Sadducees were in control.

Still another explanation is that because of the throngs that crowded into the city, it was impossible for everyone to eat the Passover meal on the same night. Not only did the meal have to be eaten within the city, but it had to be eaten indoors. The city simply did not have enough rooms for thousands and thousands to eat the meal at the same time. Therefore of practical necessity, Passover-type meals had to be eaten throughout the preceding week in addition to the official night of the Passover. These earlier meals possibly did not involve a lamb, just as Passover meals today do not. This would explain the absence of any reference to the lamb in vv. 17–26. Admittedly no evidence for this view exists in the ancient sources. If such a practice did exist, one might expect Josephus to have mentioned it; but he did not. One would not expect the *Mishna* or *Talmuds* to mention it because of their late date and their idealizing tendency.

There is simply no altogether satisfactory explanation. Despite the fact that it is conjecture, we lean toward the last view. If it is correct, the last supper was a Passover-type meal a day before the official Passover. In such case both John and the Synoptic Gospels are "right" in their dating and description. A problem does arise with reconciling this view with the statement in v. 12, "On the first day of the Feast of Unleavened Bread, when it was customary to sacrifice the Passover lamb." It seems unlikely that 13 Nisan could be referred to as the first day of the Feast of Unleavened Bread. No view is without problems; and on the basis of present knowledge, the matter cannot be finally resolved. Believers simply must accept some uncertainties about exactly what happened and when. We can, however, take great assurance in the fact that the Gospels are all in substantial agreement on the *why* of Christ's death, which is the truly important question.

In the first part of the verse the word "Passover" refers to the Passover lamb, as the NIV properly interprets; but in the last part of the verse, as well as in vv. 1,14,16, it refers to the Passover meal. The preparation would have included purchasing all the necessary items, baking the unleavened bread if it could not be purchased, preparing the sauce for the bowl in which the bitter herbs were dipped, and—if it was a proper Passover meal—having the lamb slain at the temple and then roasting it.

14:13 Luke 22:8 identifies the disciples as Peter and John. A "man carrying a jar of water" would be easy to spot because water was ordinarily transported by women. For many commentators this item indicates that Jesus had friends in the city and that he had prearranged a signal (cf. the comments on 11:1–6). Secrecy may have been necessary to prevent premature arrest. Nothing is improbable about Jesus making prior arrangements, but one could question how he could expect the disciples to arrive at just the time the man was carrying the jar. Why would he not simply send them to the man's house? Probably Mark intended to suggest another instance of supernatural knowledge on Jesus' part.[52]

14:14 "The Teacher" could be translated *Our teacher*. The expression "my guest room" (a quite literal translation of the Greek) is somewhat unusual. It could mean *the one I have arranged for* (cf. NEB) or even *the one divinely appointed for me.*

14:15–16 Most Palestinian houses consisted of from one to four rooms on one level. Large upper rooms were doubtless more common in ancient Jerusalem than in the countryside. The place was perhaps a wealthy person's home or even a semipublic building. The word translated "furnished" could mean *paved* or *with a floor,* but here it probably means that the room had carpets, couches, and vessels. People who visit Jerusalem today may see the *Coenaculum* (Latin meaning *dining room*) or *Cenacle* (the Middle English form), but the building is of Crusader construction (A.D. 1099 or shortly thereafter). A tradition locating the place as the site of the supper goes back to the fourth century, but one cannot have much confidence in the tradition because of the destruction of Jerusalem in A.D. 70 and its reconstruction in A.D. 135 and following.

14:17 Some commentators have quibbled over the accuracy of the term "Twelve," claiming that two of the disciples were already in the city (v. 13). The term is a fixed expression for the disciples regardless of the exact number (note its use in 1 Cor 15:5 for a period when there were only eleven). Furthermore, the two could have returned with news that all was ready.

14:18 Verses 18–21 contrast the treachery of Judas with the graciousness of Jesus. The prediction of betrayal shows that Jesus was not taken by surprise but knew in advance his fate. Jesus' words in v. 18 contain an allusion to Ps 41:9. The psalm describes a righteous sufferer who calls upon God to vindicate him. Jesus was the fulfillment of the entire psalm. The statements here ("one who is eating with me") and in v. 20 ("one who dips bread into the bowl with me") are intended to show just how heinous was Judas's crime. In ancient Semitic society eating together was one of the most meaningful indications of friendship, and few actions were more despicable than betraying a friend at or shortly after a meal.

14:19 The question in the Greek text employs a construction that expects a negative answer, and this nuance is nicely brought out by the NIV. Mark probably wanted his readers/hearers to ask themselves whether they would betray Jesus in the face of persecution or other trial. Every modern reader of

---

[52]The instructions are reminiscent of Samuel's words to Saul (1 Sam 10:3–7). The point in both accounts is the solemnity of the occasion as part of God's plan.

the Gospel ought to ask the same question.[53]

14:20 Mark identified the betrayer as "one of the Twelve" (cf. v. 10). However, he did not name him. The bowl contained a sauce consisting of dried fruits, spices, and wine or vinegar into which the bread and bitter herbs were dipped. The best manuscript of Mark and three others of medium quality read "into one bowl." This reading further emphasizes the awfulness of the act, but it probably is secondary for that very reason.

14:21 Where Jesus' betrayal and death are prophesied Mark did not indicate, but such passages as Ps 41 and Isa 53 immediately come to mind. The use of the word "go" (*hypagō*) is unexpected. It is characteristic of John rather than the Synoptics. It may carry the idea of predestination. Some commentators think the word "woe" (*ouai*) is more an expression of sorrow than condemnation, but in view of the last statement the latter idea is more likely.

14:22 Mark suggested that at some point during the Passover meal or perhaps at its end Jesus departed from the traditional observance and instituted a new meal for his followers.[54] "Gave thanks" (*eulogeō*) here and in v. 23 is a better translation than "blessed" (KJV, NKJV, RSV; similar NRSV) because the idea is not that of hallowing or consecrating the elements but of giving God thanks for them. (Cf. "said the blessing," NEB, REB.) From the cognate Greek noun is derived the word "Eucharist" (v. 23), the most frequent term in the early church for the supper. The addition of the word "eat" after "take" (KJV, NKJV) is a scribal assimilation to Matt 26:26, where the word is original.

Much dispute has centered on the meaning of the verb "is" in vv. 22,24. Protestants are divided among themselves as to the exact meaning, but the greater divergence separates Catholics ("is really" or "is literally") and Protestants ("is figuratively"). First, in the Aramaic, in which Jesus no doubt spoke, there is no verb "is." A very literal translation would be "this—my

---

[53] Cf. the traditional prayer often offered by Morgan Edwards (pastor of FBC Philadelphia beg. 1762) at the beginning of the Supper: "Cast out of every heart the Judas that would betray thee, that would eat bread with thee, and then lift up the heel against thee."

[54] The point of transition cannot be determined. Nevertheless it may be helpful to give a description of a Passover meal, the one found in *m. Pesaḥ.* 10, even though it is difficult to be certain of the exact order of events and whether each item was observed during the first century. The meal began with the head of the family giving thanks for the Passover in general and the wine in particular. After this the first cup of wine was drunk. Then the lamb, the unleavened bread, the bitter herbs, and the *harosheth*, or sauce, were brought in to be eaten. After a while the son or someone appointed to function as such asked the father or head of the feast why the night was different from others, and the later replied by reciting the story of the Exodus. As a result those present praised God by singing the first part of the Hallel (Ps 113 or Pss 113–114) and drinking the second cup. Then the head of the house again gave thanks, a third cup was drunk, and the eating resumed. Later there was the singing of the last part of the Hallel (Pss 114–118 or 115–118) and a fourth cup. The feast had to conclude by midnight.

body" and "this—my blood." This lack of a verb in Aramaic probably rules out material identity. The fact that Jesus was physically present probably does also. Drinking blood was so offensive to Jews that something else must have been meant. Furthermore, the preceding Passover meal was full of symbolism so that one might expect the same of the new memorial meal. Still further, the underlying Aramaic word probably means *person* rather than *physical body.* Perhaps "represents" would be a better translation than "is." Compare the meaning of the Greek verb "is" in 4:15–20. There the NIV translates it "are like" and "like."

14:23 A common cup probably was used, and it likely was filled with fermented wine rather than grape juice.[55] Many modern Christians continue to use a common cup, probably because of its symbolization of the oneness of those who drink from it. An even larger number continue to use wine, although it has no symbolic or other value. Most rightly feel that neither of these is necessary for a proper observance of the rite any more than is the use of unleavened bread.

There has been some discussion about whether the cup was the third or fourth that was drunk during the Passover meal. This depends on whether Jesus interrupted the Passover meal to institute his own memorial and if so where. Information is not available to determine such things. Luke 22:17 may refer to one of the cups of the Passover meal (cf. the commentary on 10:38 for the cup as a symbol of suffering and God's judgment).

14:24 The word "new" before "covenant" (KJV, NKJV) is a scribal addition to harmonize Mark with Luke 22:20 and 1 Cor 11:25. "Covenant" is a much better translation than "testament" (KJV) as even the NKJV recognizes. The allusion is to the new covenant of Jer 31:31–34. The word does mean *will* or *testament* in classical Greek, but it is regularly used in the Septuagint to translate the Hebrew word that can only mean *covenant.* New Testament usage is dictated by that of the LXX. The translators of the LXX probably chose this word rather than the one that otherwise means *covenant* in order to convey the idea that the covenants of the Old Testament are not mutual agreements between equals but compacts, the terms of which are dictated by Almighty God—in much the same way as are the terms of a will.[56]

---

[55]Verse 25 and Matt 26:29 identify the contents of the cup simply as "the fruit of the vine." The word "wine" is not used in any of the four accounts of the institution. There is some evidence that unfermented juice was drunk in antiquity. Nevertheless the use of wine in moderation was widespread in Jewish and pagan society. Certainly the beverage at the Passover meal was real wine. In ancient times, however, wine was usually diluted with water so that its alcoholic content was much less than that of most modern wine.

[56]By the same token the component parts of the Bible ought to be known as the Old Covenant and New Covenant rather than the Old Testament and New Testament. The books of the Bible are in no sense a will or testament, but they do reflect the old covenant and new covenant respectively.

The term "blood of the covenant" reflects Exod 24:8 and Zech 9:11. The same expression appears in Heb 9:20 and 10:29. Just as the blood of a sacrificial animal sealed the covenant God made with Israel at Sinai, so the blood of Jesus sealed the new covenant God made with his new people, the church, at the cross. Just as blood confirmed the death of an animal, so the blood of Jesus confirms his death. The blood/death of Jesus provided forgiveness of sins and right relationship with God. The old covenant sacrifices anticipated the sacrifice of Jesus and depended on his death on the cross for validity. Here the blood/death of Jesus is symbolized by the wine. "Poured out" is a term that describes violent death (cf. similar expressions in Gen 4:10–11; 9:6; Deut 19:10; Jer 7:6). As in 10:45 "many" is a Semitism meaning *all who are many.*

Those who eat the broken bread indicate their desire to have fellowship with Jesus and his other disciples. Those who consume the cup indicate their commitment to the new covenant. These things are made possible by the death of Jesus Christ.

14:25 Whether Jesus referred to the period following his resurrection is difficult to decide. Although Mark recorded no resurrection appearances, certainly Jesus ate and presumably also drank with the disciples during that time (Luke 24:30,41–43; John 21:9–13). Also as a result of Jesus' death and resurrection, the kingdom of God was established in a way it had not been before. Nevertheless, the primary reference is to the final consummation of the kingdom and the messianic banquet at that time (cf. Isa 25:6–8; Rev 19:6–9).

No explicit command for continued observance of the Supper is given in Mark or anywhere else in the New Testament. (Continued observance is implicit in 1 Cor 11:26.) Except for the simple statements "this is my body" and "this is my blood of the covenant," Mark did not elaborate on the significance of the meal, that it is a remembrance of Jesus (Luke 22:19; 1 Cor 11:24–25), a means of proclaiming his death (1 Cor 11:26), a means of communion with Jesus (1 Cor 10:16), and a symbol of the oneness of God's people (1 Cor 10:17). Unquestionably Mark's readers were already observing the rite on a regular basis (probably every Lord's Day) and knew much about its significance. Mark needed only to give it a historical base by recounting its institution by Jesus himself.

14:26 The "hymn" was probably Ps 118. As previously indicated the Hallel (Pss 114–118 or 115–118) was sung in parts during the Passover meal. On the location of the Mount of Olives, see the comments on 11:1. The departure from the house seems to be in violation of Exod 12:22, but the prohibition must have been no longer observed. Leaving the city might be considered a violation of Deut 16:7, but the Mount of Olives was no doubt considered to be a part of "greater Jerusalem."

10. The Prediction of Desertion and Denial (14:27–31)

²⁷"You will all fall away," Jesus told them, "for it is written:

"'I will strike the shepherd,
   and the sheep will be scattered.'
²⁸But after I have risen, I will go ahead of you into Galilee."
²⁹Peter declared, "Even if all fall away, I will not."
³⁰"I tell you the truth," Jesus answered, "today—yes, tonight—before the rooster crows twice you yourself will disown me three times."
³¹But Peter insisted emphatically, "Even if I have to die with you, I will never disown you." And all the others said the same.

The theme of abandonment dominates 14:27–72: Jesus was abandoned by denial (Peter, vv. 66–72), indifference (Peter, James, and John in Gethsemane, vv. 37–41), betrayal (Judas, vv. 42–45), and fleeing (the Twelve and the young man, vv. 50–52). Such examples serve as encouragement and warning for readers/hearers who have sometimes abandoned Jesus or are tempted to do so in persecution.

This section shows that the unfaithfulness of the disciples was foreseen by Jesus and prophesied by the Scripture. An explanation was needed for the conduct of those who became the leaders of the early church. The setting of the account seems to be while walking from the upper room to Gethsemane.

14:27 The verb *skandalizō*, which can mean *fall away, take offense*, or *cause to sin*, is properly translated "fall away" here and in v. 29. Note its various uses in 4:17; 6:3; 9:42–47. In the present context the idea is not *lose faith permanently* but *temporarily lose courage*.

The quotation is from Zech 13:7 except that a first-person future is substituted for the second-person imperative which is in both the Hebrew and Greek texts of Zechariah. The change may be due to the use of an otherwise unknown Hebrew and/or Greek text, adaptation in a collection of messianic texts (*Testamonia*), loose quotation, or deliberate alteration. If the last, the text emphasizes that God smote the Shepherd in accordance with his will and that the Shepherd was not smitten by men contrary to divine providence. Sometimes the quotation of a brief passage is intended to recall a larger one, and that may be the case here. Zechariah 13 tells about a coming cleansing from sin and reform of existing religious institutions. As a result of being smitten, Jesus effected such things.

14:28 The verse seems to interrupt the sequence of vv. 27,29 and may be a Markan addition to the account, which he received from the earlier tradition. If so, Mark prepared for 16:7, which is quite similar, and showed that the smiting of the Shepherd (Jesus) and the scattering of the sheep (the disciples) had but temporary effect. In the present context *proagō* is translated "I will go before you" (RSV, NRSV, NASB; similarly NEB, "I will go on before you") and means *I will lead you as a shepherd leads his sheep*, not *I will precede you* (cf. "I will go ahead of you," NIV, GNB, REB).[57] Mark wanted to assure his readers/hearers that Jesus regathered the scattered disciples, forgave, and restored them. This was a reassuring word as Mark's community faced persecution in which they too would be scattered.

14:29   The claim of v. 29 is similar to that in 10:39, but the result was different. James and John did later faithfully endure persecution, but Peter quickly denied Jesus.

14:30   Here is the last use of the solemn word *amēn* ("I tell you the truth") in Mark. The word "twice" is peculiar to Mark and is awkward. It is omitted by the second-best manuscript of Mark and several others of medium quality, but this probably is due to assimilation to Matt 26:34 and Luke 22:34. The presence of the word is presupposed by a similar expression in 14:72, where, however, there is also some textual evidence for omission. Some commentators think that "before the rooster crows twice" is a proverbial expression meaning *early morning;* others think the reference is to the *gallicinium*, the Roman bugle call for the changing of the guard between the third and fourth watches, the third of which was called "the cock-crow." Probably, however, Mark referred to a literal rooster within earshot of Peter. Perhaps the first crow was to serve as a warning to Peter.

The fulfillment of Jesus' prediction is recorded in vv. 66–72. The improbability of the early church inventing a story about the cowardice of their apostles confirms the historicity of what is found in vv. 27–31,66–72.

14:31   The vehemence of Peter's affirmation of loyalty only serves to make his failure all the greater. That Mark—in this instance the other Gospels as well—did nothing to spare Peter and the other apostles is one indication of the trustworthiness of the accounts. Even so the Bible continually affirms that good can come out of bad, and the utter failure of Peter encourages later disciples who fail in a similar way.

11. The Agony in Gethsemane (14:32–42)

32They went to a place called Gethsemane, and Jesus said to his disciples, "Sit here while I pray." 33He took Peter, James and John along with him, and he began to be deeply distressed and troubled. 34"My soul is overwhelmed with sorrow to the point of death," he said to them. "Stay here and keep watch."

35Going a little farther, he fell to the ground and prayed that if possible the hour might pass from him. 36"Abba, Father," he said, "everything is possible for you. Take this cup from me. Yet not what I will, but what you will."

37Then he returned to his disciples and found them sleeping. "Simon," he said to Peter, "are you asleep? Could you not keep watch for one hour? 38Watch and

---

[57] In 16:7, however, the idea probably is to get there first.

pray so that you will not fall into temptation. The spirit is willing, but the body is weak."

³⁹Once more he went away and prayed the same thing. ⁴⁰When he came back, he again found them sleeping, because their eyes were heavy. They did not know what to say to him.

⁴¹Returning the third time, he said to them, "Are you still sleeping and resting? Enough! The hour has come. Look, the Son of Man is betrayed into the hands of sinners. ⁴²Rise! Let us go! Here comes my betrayer!"

In addition to the parallels in Matt 26:36–46; Luke 22:39–46; perhaps John 17:1–18:1, the agonizing prayer is also alluded to in Heb 5:7. Peter possibly was Mark's source. This would explain the frankness of the description of Peter's failure. The historicity of the account is rarely questioned. The early church would not have invented an account that not only puts the disciples in a bad light but also indicates that Jesus asked to be spared from death.

Mark's account emphasizes the obedience of Jesus to his Father's will and thereby sets an example of discipleship for his readers/hearers. In doing so it emphasizes the humanity of Jesus, who really did suffer, prior to the cross as well as on it. He really did fear death, just as those who were going to be called upon to die for him would fear death. Jesus agonized alone just as many of his followers would have to do. When facing crisis, he prayed just as his followers should do. Mark pictured Jesus as praying at the beginning (1:35), middle (6:46), and end of his ministry. By so doing, he indicated that Jesus' life was characterized by prayer. The clear implication is that the lives of disciples should be also. Mark's account also provides an additional example of the failure of the disciples, which could serve both as a warning to and an encouragement of other disciples who would fail in various ways.

14:32 "Gethsemane" is a transliteration of two Hebrew words meaning *oil press.* It was evidently an olive grove (only John 18:1 calls it a garden [RSV, NRSV, NASB, KJV, GNB]; but the NIV translation "olive grove" is a harmonization) where there was or had been an olive press. The exact location is not known,⁵⁸ but almost certainly it was on the lower slopes of the western side of the Mount of Olives across the Kidron Valley (John 18:1) and opposite the temple area. It is mentioned in the New Testament only here and in the Matthean parallel.

14:33 Peter, James, and John—the so-called inner circle—had been singled out previously in 5:37; 9:2; and with the addition of Andrew in 13:3. Aside from the fact that they were the leaders and were called forth on special occasions—something that alerts the readers/hearers of the Gospel to the importance of what is about to happen—here Peter may have been singled out

---

⁵⁸Today there is a Latin (Roman Catholic), Armenian, Greek Orthodox, and Russian Orthodox Gethsemane.

because of his recent boast of loyalty (v. 31) and James and John because of their claim that they would suffer with Jesus (10:38–40). As the sequel shows, they were not able to pray even for a few hours. If Jesus took them along because he needed their companionship or support, they provided none of that.

Mark's description of Jesus is shocking. Mark employed words that express the strongest possible anguish. The NEB does a better job than the NIV, NASB, and RSV in bringing out their meaning: "Horror and dismay came over him." The REB has, "Horror and anguish overwhelmed him." Matthew softened the statement, and Luke's text is most uncertain.

14:34 As if the statement in v. 33 were not enough, Mark rephrased the same thought. This statement probably alludes to Ps 42:5–6,11 and perhaps also 116:3. Mark indicated that Jesus did not die with stoic apathy as though death were of no consequence. He really hurt as he approached the cross.

That Jesus intended the three to watch out for Judas is not likely. As before, "watch" means *to be spiritually alert.* More specifically it refers to being alert against the temptation of indifference. It could also carry the idea of sharing the agony of Jesus.

14:35 Jews most often prayed standing and with uplifted hands. Prostration was the gesture of extreme urgency. The term "hour" refers to the time set by God for the accomplishment of his purpose, whether judgment or salvation. Here it is the time of Jesus' arrest, trial, and execution. Contemporary Christians should not be disturbed that he prayed for deliverance from these things. They should not try to explain away the prayer by saying that it was for ability to survive until he actually mounted the cross. The prayer is simply an expression of the real humanity of Jesus, which is as necessary a part of his nature as his deity.[59]

14:36 "Abba" is an Aramaic word, as Mark hastened to add for the benefit of his Greek-speaking readers and hearers, meaning *father* or *daddy.* The word was used primarily by little children within the family circle. There is no evidence that Jews used the word in addressing God. Such familiarity, they thought, would be irreverent. By using the word, Jesus affirmed his intimate relationship with God. By commending it to his disciples—it is the Aramaic word that lies behind the Greek *patēr* in Matt 6:9; Luke 11:2—he affirmed that they could enjoy a similar relationship. So precious was the word that it was preserved and used by the Greek-speaking, Gentile churches (Rom 8:15; Gal 4:6).

The "cup" is synonymous with the "hour" in v. 35 and 10:38–39 (see comments there). The last statement is the most important because by it Mark indi-

---

[59]The books of 1 and 2 John were written to oppose the variety of Gnosticism that refused to identify the divine Christ with the human Jesus and therefore denied the humanity of Jesus Christ. Contemporary Christians who have a very high Christology are sometimes prone to do a similar thing, in practice if not in theory.

cated that in the end Jesus was submissive to God's will. His prayer to be spared death was answered in accordance with the divine will. God gave him something better, victory over death. The same would be true for future martyrs. First death and then resurrection was the will of God, the most important thing for which Jesus prayed in Gethsemane.

14:37 The coming, finding, and sleeping here and in v. 40 may be compared with that in 13:36 as another example of Mark's tendency to use the same phraseology. For the disciples to sleep after a long, emotional day and a big meal was quite natural, but Jesus expects something more than the ordinary from his disciples. The use of the name "Simon" suggests that Peter (*the rock*) had reverted to his old self! Here the word "hour" should be taken quite literally. Jesus probably prayed for three periods of approximately one hour.

14:38 The repetition of the word "watch" is probably intended to warn the reader/hearer to do the same. To it is added a command to pray, and a reason for both is appended. The temptation could be failure to confess Jesus due to cowardice, but probably no particular "temptation" to sin or time of testing (the word could mean either) is intended.

The last sentence alludes to Ps 51:11–12. Whether the reference is to the willingness of God's Spirit or the human spirit, which wants to do right but is often frustrated by the "flesh" (literal translation of the Greek as in RSV, NASB, NEB, REB, GNB), is uncertain. Most translations and commentaries take the latter position. A similar idea is in Rom 7:14–25.

14:39–40 The disciples "did not know what to say" to Jesus (cf. 9:6) because they were without legitimate excuse for having fallen asleep each time after being commanded to watch and pray.

14:41 The threefold sleeping corresponds to the threefold denial of Peter. The statement can be taken as an imperative (KJV) or as a question (NIV and the other translations cited in the commentary). In either case it is reproachful.

Much discussion has centered on the meaning of the word the NIV and many other versions translate "enough" (*apechei*). Other possibilities include "it is settled" (there is no longer any question about Jesus dying); "it is paid" (Judas received his money to betray Jesus); and "he [Judas] is taking possession" (of me).

There is also a textual problem. A few witnesses of medium quality omit the difficult word, but a larger number, also of medium quality, add the words "the end" to it, perhaps by way of assimilation to Luke 22:37. If by any chance the second of these were the original reading, the idea would be "the end has come" or "is the end far off?" Even if "it is enough" or "enough of this" is the proper idea, as seems likely, is the reference to the disciples' sleeping or to Jesus' rebuke or to time (i.e., the time for praying is up; arrest is imminent)? The first seems the most likely. The second most likely interpretation is "it is settled." The two statements that follow, "the hour has come" and "the Son of Man is betrayed into the hands of sinners," would indicate the content of "it."

14:42 The verb translated "Let us go" cannot mean *let us flee* in the present context. It means *let us go to meet Judas and those with him*. A more literal translation of the final clause would be, "My betrayer is at hand" (RSV). Mark used the same word and tense as in 1:15, where he said, "The kingdom of God is near" or "at hand" (RSV).

12. The Arrest (14:43–52)

⁴³Just as he was speaking, Judas, one of the Twelve, appeared. With him was a crowd armed with swords and clubs, sent from the chief priests, the teachers of the law, and the elders.
⁴⁴Now the betrayer had arranged a signal with them: "The one I kiss is the man; arrest him and lead him away under guard." ⁴⁵Going at once to Jesus, Judas said, "Rabbi!" and kissed him. ⁴⁶The men seized Jesus and arrested him. ⁴⁷Then one of those standing near drew his sword and struck the servant of the high priest, cutting off his ear.
⁴⁸"Am I leading a rebellion," said Jesus, "that you have come out with swords and clubs to capture me? ⁴⁹Every day I was with you, teaching in the temple courts, and you did not arrest me. But the Scriptures must be fulfilled." ⁵⁰Then everyone deserted him and fled.
⁵¹A young man, wearing nothing but a linen garment, was following Jesus. When they seized him, ⁵²he fled naked, leaving his garment behind.

In addition to recording a necessary fact, Mark emphasized further the treachery of Judas, indicated that Jesus was no revolutionary or a man of violence, and showed the fulfillment of Jesus' words in v. 27. Still further Mark probably pictured Jesus as a model for Christian conduct during persecution.

14:43 Again Mark used the word (*euthys*), which means *immediately* but which here is rendered "just as" by the NIV. He pointed out that Judas was "one of the Twelve." There was no attempt to cover up the disgrace of Jesus being betrayed by one of his own disciples.[60] The word translated "crowd" here indicates a mob or rabble with no official status. Mark used the word "crowd" (*oxlos*) for those Jesus taught and fed (2:4,13; 3:9; 4:1,36; 6:34,45; 7:14,17; 8:1,34; 10:1; 11:18; 12:12,37). Prior to this usage in 14:43 the crowd was never hostile to Jesus. After 14:43 (15:8,11,15), the crowd was always hostile to Jesus.

It seems unlikely, however, that the "chief priests, the teachers of the law, and the elders"—i.e., the Sanhedrin or at least some of its leaders—would have employed such a group for the delicate task of arresting a popular

---

⁶⁰Some think that the repetition of "one of the Twelve" is an indication of use of an independent unit of tradition.

teacher. Furthermore, Luke 22:52 indicates that the temple police were employed, and John 18:3 indicates that they were accompanied by some Roman soldiers. Perhaps Mark's diction was not exact; perhaps he was reflecting a Christian caricature of those who arrested Jesus. More likely Mark was not clumsy and knew what he was saying. He, in a representative fashion, used this crowd to typify the larger public, which from this time forward was hostile to Jesus.

14:44 Evidently Mark understood the betrayal to consist of indicating the time and place where Jesus could be found with few others about and identifying him in the darkness. A kiss was a common way for a disciple to greet his teacher and beyond that an act of endearment between any two persons. The mention of it confirms the wickedness of Judas's act. The NIV translation "under guard" is a good treatment of the adverb, which literally means *firmly, safely, securely.*

14:45–46 Jesus was previously called "Rabbi" in 9:5; 10:51 (where a more emphatic word is used); and 11:21. Much more often, however, Mark translated the Hebrew term with the Greek word meaning "teacher." The word translated "kissed" is an intensive form of the word in v. 44 and could indicate a prolonged kiss or a very elaborate one.

14:47 Mark's account is brief in comparison with that of the other Gospels. Luke 22:50 and John 18:10 indicate that it was the right ear that was cut off, and John 18:10 identifies the assailant as Peter and the victim as Malchus. Matthew 26:52; John 18:11; perhaps Luke 22:51 contain the command to sheath the sword. Luke 22:51 indicates that Jesus replaced the severed ear. The use of the diminutive form of the word "ear" may indicate that only a portion of it was affected. Some have questioned the historicity of the account because there is no indication that the assailant was arrested, but there may have been a scuffle in the darkness during which he could not be identified or he ran off.

14:48 The Greek text reads literally, "Have you come out as against a thief?" (cf. RSV, NASB, NEB, REB);[61] but the word "thief" probably refers not to a common criminal but to a revolutionary. The NIV interpretation therefore is quite accurate.

14:49 The statement may indicate that Jesus had been in Jerusalem more than a week, as John's Gospel clearly shows. Mark emphasized that Jesus did most of his teaching in public. Therefore, there was nothing secretive or seditious about it. This fact had great significance for the Christian community in Rome at the time Mark wrote. Mark did not indicate what (Old Testament) Scriptures Jesus had in mind. Isaiah 53:12 (Mark 14:46–49) and Zech 13:7

---

[61] The sentence could also be interpreted as a declaratory statement rather than a question, but even so it would still be a protest.

(Mark 14:50) are the most likely individual passages, but it is also possible that the reference is to the teaching of the Scripture in general.

14:50 This verse indicates the fulfillment of Jesus' prediction in v. 27. For once Mark did not explicitly mention the disciples but referred to them by the word "everyone." Perhaps "everyone" includes the crowds, which earlier had protected Jesus from the Jewish leadership (11:18; 12:12). The position of the word at the end of the Greek sentence emphasizes that Jesus was left completely alone by those who might have been expected to stand by him.

14:51–52 Much speculation has taken place about the identity of the "young man." The traditional view is that he was John Mark, the author of the Gospel, and that Mark included the account as a way of confessing his own sin. The incident is so trivial—it is found only in Mark—that for some the only explanation is that it is the author's allusion to himself, his "signature in the corner of his work" or something comparable to a medieval artist painting his own face on one of the crowd.

This explanation, however, seems to be of modern origin. In the early church the young man was occasionally identified with John the apostle (Ambrose, Chrysostom) or James the brother of Jesus and leader of the Jerusalem church (Epiphanius). Furthermore, Papias (ca. A.D. 130) said that Mark "neither heard the Lord nor followed him." [62] The description may allude to Amos 2:16 and/or Gen 39:12.[63] It has also been pointed out that in 15:46 Jesus' naked body was wrapped in a linen cloth so that the present passage may anticipate the burial of Jesus.[64] Still further it has been pointed out that in 16:5 another young man, in contrast to the cowardice of this one, announced the resurrection.[65] It is probably best not to try to identify the young man. The view that the reference is an autobiographical one pointing to John Mark may be the most probable, but it is still nothing more than a possibility. Although the young man cannot be identified, the incident is of such a nature that it is most likely an eyewitness account.

If perchance the young man was Mark, he may have followed Jesus and his disciples from the upper room, which could possibly have been in the home of his mother.[66] The wearing of a linen cloth suggests a well-to-do person, and

---

[62] Eusebius, *Church History* 3.39.15. This statement, however, is not decisive against the traditional view because Papias may have been mistaken, or he may have meant nothing more than that Mark was not a regular disciple of Jesus during Jesus' lifetime.

[63] Even if there is an allusion to one or both of these passages (the first is far more likely than the second), it is farfetched to claim that someone invented the incident to fulfill the Scripture.

[64] But it strains credulity to see any association between the two pieces of linen.

[65] But what would be the point of the contrast? Furthermore, the first young man is a human being; the second, an angel.

[66] The possibility depends upon the identity of the house with an upper room of the Gospels with "the house of Mary the mother of John, also called Mark" (Acts 12:12). No upper room is mentioned in the latter, and the identification can be nothing more than a mere possibility.

Mark's mother evidently was wealthy because she had a house large enough for meetings of the church (Acts 12:12). The word translated "naked" could mean that, or it could refer to wearing only a loin cloth. The former is more likely because, although the NIV does not translate it, the Greek text reads "being clothed with a linen cloth over his naked body" (cf. NASB).[67] The incident may have been remembered because it was so unusual. Mark may also have wanted to associate "nakedness," which is an image of shame, with anyone who abandons Jesus (cf. 8:38).

13. The Jewish Trial (14:53,55–65)

[53]They took Jesus to the high priest, and all the chief priests, elders and teachers of the law came together. . . .

[55]The chief priests and the whole Sanhedrin were looking for evidence against Jesus so that they could put him to death, but they did not find any. [56]Many testified falsely against him, but their statements did not agree.

[57]Then some stood up and gave this false testimony against him: [58]"We heard him say, 'I will destroy this man-made temple and in three days will build another, not made by man.'" [59]Yet even then their testimony did not agree.

[60]Then the high priest stood up before them and asked Jesus, "Are you not going to answer? What is this testimony that these men are bringing against you?" [61]But Jesus remained silent and gave no answer.

Again the high priest asked him, "Are you the Christ, the Son of the Blessed One?"

[62]"I am," said Jesus. "And you will see the Son of Man sitting at the right hand of the Mighty One and coming on the clouds of heaven."

[63]The high priest tore his clothes. "Why do we need any more witnesses?" he asked. [64]"You have heard the blasphemy. What do you think?"

They all condemned him as worthy of death. [65]Then some began to spit at him; they blindfolded him, struck him with their fists, and said, "Prophesy!" And the guards took him and beat him.

One last time Mark resorted to bracketing/intercalation/sandwiching in order to use two accounts to help interpret each other. This instance, however, is more complicated than the previous ones. Instead of one account merely being inserted into another, both accounts are interrupted by the other. The intercalation in 14:53–72 contrasts the confession of Jesus with the denial of Peter and upholds Jesus as a role model for Roman Christians to follow when they were interrogated by the authorities. In Mark's account Peter as well as Jesus was on trial. Peter dismally failed his test; Jesus triumphed in his. In the providence of God, the passage applies to Christians of all times and all situations in which their faith is in any way challenged. The trial account also gave

---

[67]A few textual witnesses of medium quality omit the words "upon his naked body," but it is unlikely that the NIV translated this text.

Mark an opportunity to develop further his Christology and show clearly who Jesus really is.

The historical problems connected with the trial account are notorious. At various points Mark's account is in violation of the provisions of the *Mishna* tractate *Sanhedrin* 4–7. First, no trial could be held at night.[68] Second, the verdict in a capital case could not be reached until the second day, and therefore trials could not be held on the eve of the Sabbath or a feast day.[69] Third, witnesses had to be warned to relate only true, firsthand testimony.[70] Fourth, those accused of blasphemy could be convicted only if they reviled the Divine Name.[71] Fifth, trials could not be held in the palace of the high priest.[72] Sixth, the Old Testament does not specify crucifixion as a punishment.[73]

Various explanations of the irregularities have been given. First, virtually all of the evidence pertaining to what was legal or not comes from the *Mishna*. The *Mishna* was not completed until about A.D. 220 and contains a miscellaneous collection of traditions from various rabbis during the three previous centuries. Dating individual traditions is difficult and even impossible. It is unlikely that all of the *Mishna*'s "laws" were in force during the time of Jesus. Therefore the trial may not have been illegal. This claim may have some validity. Second, the trial may have involved illegalities. Illegal trials and perver-

---

[68] "In capital cases they hold the trial during the daytime and the verdict also must be reached during the daytime" (*m. Sanh.* 4.1, trans. Danby).

[69] "In capital cases a verdict of acquittal may be reached on the same day, but a verdict of conviction not until the following day. Therefore trials may not be held on the eve of a Sabbath or on the eve of a Festival-day" (*m. Sanh.* 4.1, trans. Danby).

[70] "How did they admonish the witnesses in capital cases? They brought them in and admonished them, [saying,] 'Perchance ye will say what is but supposition or hearsay or at secondhand, or [ye may say in yourselves], We heard it from a man that was trustworthy. Or perchance ye do not know that we shall prove you by examination and inquiry?' . . . They used to prove witnesses with seven inquiries. . . . The more a judge tests the evidence the more he is deserving of praise" (*m. Sanh.* 4.5–5.2, trans. Danby).

[71] "'The blasphemer' is not culpable unless he pronounces the Name itself" (*m. Sanh.* 7.5, trans. Danby). There is evidence, however, that blasphemy was interpreted much more broadly in the first century than the third when the *Mishna* was put together. Part of the evidence is in the New Testament, e.g., Mark 2:7; 3:28.

[72] "Three courts were there [in Jerusalem]: one used to sit at the gate of the Temple Mount, one used to sit at the gate of the Temple Court, and one used to sit in the Chamber of Hewn Stone . . . the Great Court that was in the Chamber of Hewn Stone, whence the Law goes forth to all Israel" (*m. Sanh.* 11.2, trans. Danby). The Great Court was the Sanhedrin before which Jesus appeared.

[73] "The Court had power to inflict four kinds of death-penalty: stoning, burning, beheading, and strangling" (*m. Sanh.* 7.1, trans. Danby). Of course the Jews did not execute Jesus. The Romans did. Crucifixion was their method. Whether the Romans gave the Jews the right to execute one of their own is a hotly debated issue about which the scholarly world still has no consensus. John 18:31, however, explicitly states that the Jews did not have the right of capital punishment. Even if they did, their leaders still may have wanted the Romans to execute such a popular teacher so they could not be blamed directly.

sions of justice have occurred throughout human history in all societies (including "Christian"), and this trial may well have been such an instance. No injustice should be excused, but first-century Jews should not be condemned beyond all others for their error. Third, not only Jews but in recent decades liberal Protestants and Catholics have contended that Mark's account reflects an anti-Jewish bias so that he pictured some things as illegal that were not.[74] Furthermore, how could Mark have known what went on in private before the Sanhedrin? Quite aside from any prejudice, he could not have had accurate information.[75] Fourth, what Mark described in chap. 14 was not a formal trial but an informal hearing. Some have compared it to a police interrogation following an arrest or to a grand jury inquiry. Therefore none of the prescriptions of the *Mishna* would be applicable. According to one explanation of 15:1, a formal trial was held the next morning. Therefore this explanation could have some validity, but confidence about it is elusive. Even so it would not account for a trial on the eve of a Sabbath and feast day or conviction on the same day.

There are difficulties with the account. Not all of them can be resolved on the basis of present knowledge. Uncertainty about various points must remain; however, there is no decisive objection to the historicity of the account.

14:53   Mark did not name the high priest. According to Matt 26:57 he was Caiaphas.[76] The "chief priests, elders, and teachers of the law" constituted the

---

[74]The charge of anti-Semitism often made against the authors of the Gospels is serious and must be faced by conscientious Christians. It is claimed that because of their bias the Evangelists shifted the blame from the Romans to the Jews. The Romans made the final decision to execute, and the ultimate responsibility was theirs. It is beyond dispute that Jesus was a threat to the Jewish establishment, and it is easy to see why the Jewish authorities would want to get rid of him. If the traditional attributions of authorship may be accepted, three of the Gospel writers were Jews, and one might expect their attitude toward their fellows to be one of sorrow like that of Paul (Rom 9:1–5; 10:1) rather than one of hatred. As a matter of fact all of the Gospel accounts are very reserved, make no accusations, and fix no blame. Later Christians have made from the accounts false inferences about Jewish responsibility. No Jew living since the first century, however, has been guilty of any injustice against Jesus. Even in the first century only a small group of leaders were involved in Jesus' condemnation. Therefore the Jews as a body should never be blamed. One of the most disgraceful aspects of Christian history is prejudice against and persecution of Jews. Such prolonged and widespread injustice is far more serious than one instance of injustice.

[75]This objection is not weighty. Within hours of the trial servants and assistants who were present likely told what had happened. Apparently two members of the Sanhedrin, Nicodemus and Joseph of Arimathea, became Christians and would have been willing to share their knowledge— knowledge they would have had even if they were not present. Jesus himself could have related the events after his resurrection.

[76]Caiaphas's appointment about A.D. 18 and deposition about A.D. 37 is mentioned in Josephus, *Antiquities* 18.2.2; 4.3. He therefore served longer than any high priest during the Roman era. John 18:13 indicates that Jesus was first taken to Annas, who is explicitly identified as the father-in-law of Caiaphas and who was a former high priest (see also *Antiquities* 18.2.1) but who was still sometimes referred to as high priest (John 18:22; Acts 4:6).

Sanhedrin (v. 55 and see comments on 11:27). Note how the statement in this verse fulfills the one in 8:31.

14:55 The statement "were looking for evidence" supports the view that Mark was describing an informal hearing, but the expression "the whole Sanhedrin" points toward a formal trial.

14:56–59 Jewish law stated that at least two, and better three, witnesses had to agree before imposing the death penalty (Num 35:30; Deut 17:6; 19:15; Josephus, *Antiquities* 4.8.15). Mark indicated that none agreed because they were testifying falsely.

Mark did not record that Jesus made a public statement about the destruction of the temple such as the one in v. 58. He did record in 13:1–2 a private prediction of the destruction of the temple, and the cursing of the fig tree and the clearing of the temple in 11:12–21 probably intimate the same. John 2:19 does record such a statement. The Jews understood the reference to be to the Jerusalem temple (v. 20), but John indicated that the reference was to the body of Jesus (v. 21).

Some interpreters think that in Mark the words "man-made" and "not made by man" are later scribal interpolations to prevent the kind of misunderstanding reflected in John's Gospel, but there is no manuscript evidence for omission and no other evidence unless it is the omission in 15:29 and Matt 26:61. That Jesus did make a statement about the destruction of one temple and the construction of another is certain. There was therefore an element of truth but also an element of untruth in the charge. Jesus never claimed that he would destroy the Jerusalem temple. He did indicate that the "temple" of his body and the literal temple would be destroyed by others.

The recipients of the Gospel no doubt realized that Jesus' death made the temple and its cultus irrelevant and to that extent "destroyed" it. This may be symbolized by 15:38. Jesus never claimed that he would rebuild the Jerusalem temple in three days or any other time period, but he did intimate that the new temple of his resurrection body would be raised in three days. The expression "not made by man" may allude to his resurrection body. Still further the early church came to look upon the individual Christian (1 Cor 6:19; cf. Rev 3:12) and the whole church (1 Cor 3:16; 2 Cor 6:16; Eph 2:20–22) as the new temple.

14:60–61 Jesus may not have answered because there was no need to do so. No charge had been sustained. Silence indicated innocence.

The silence of Jesus fulfilled Ps 38:13–14 and especially Isa 53:7. Some commentators insist that claiming to be the Messiah ("the Christ") was not a capital offense. They point to Simon bar Kosiba, who led the revolt of A.D. 132–35 and who was acclaimed as the messiah even by the famous Rabbi Akiba. Others think that to make such a claim without accompanying it with convincing credentials, such as military prowess, might have been a crime because Jewish hopes centered on a messiah who would deliver from foreign oppression.

Many commentators agree, however, that no Jew would associate the Messiah and the Son of God ("Blessed One" is a Jewish substitute for the divine name) because the Jews were expecting a human, not divine, messiah. They insist that the high priest could not have spoken the words in the last part of v. 61, that the words represent the theology of Mark and the early church. This claim overlooks the fact that on the lips of the high priest "son of God" need not signify more than "son of David." Israel's kings were sometimes called sons of God (2 Sam 7:14; Ps 2:7; 89:26–27), and the messiah was looked upon as a new king of the line of David. In fact, all of the passages just cited have messianic implications.

Jesus' association of the titles of v. 61 with "the Son of Man sitting at the right hand of the Mighty One" (v. 62) reinterpreted these potentially ambiguous titles as divine honors that make v. 61 one of two passages that constitute the climax of Mark's Christology—the other being 15:39. At the very beginning of his Gospel, Mark announced that Jesus was the Christ and the Son of God. Throughout the Gospel allusions are made to Jesus' messiahship and sonship (1:11,24; 3:11; 5:7; 8:29–30; 9:7; 10:47; 12:6,35–37; 13:26). Now near the end two of the most important titles are brought together—ironically on the lips of an opponent.

14:62 In view of the secrecy motif that has pervaded the Gospel up to this point, Jesus' answer is quite surprising. There is, however, a textual problem. Some manuscripts of medium quality read, "You say that I am." If this were the original reading, it would still constitute an affirmative answer but a much less emphatic one more in line with the "messianic secret." The textual evidence definitely favors "I am," and "You say that I am" probably is a scribal assimilation to Matt 26:64 and Luke 22:70. Since Jesus' fate was sealed, secrecy was no long necessary. Both Jesus and Mark may have intended "I am" to be more than an affirmative answer. It may be an allusion to the divine name in Exod 3:14.

"The Mighty One" is another substitute for *Yahweh.* The "right hand" is the place of honor and reward in Oriental society. Jesus' affirmation in the last part of the verse combines Ps 110:1 and Dan 7:13. "You will see" does not necessarily refer to physical sight. It could refer to realization. Jesus probably meant that his opponents would realize that he was the Son of Man in the apocalyptic sense, that he was God's Son and would sit by his side, and that he would return for judgment. He did not imply that he would return during the lifetime of those present. In fact, some commentators do not think the word "coming" refers to the second coming at all but to Jesus' exaltation. However little or much the high priest may have understood Jesus' words, Mark knew that his readers/hearers would. Ultimately the words were intended for Christians.

14:63 Tearing a garment was usually a sign of grief or alarm (Gen 37:29,34; 2 Kgs 18:37; 19:1; Jer 41:5; Acts 14:14). In the case of the high priest, it was an official act expressing indignation that later at least was regulated by the *Mishna*.[77]

14:64 Some do not think that claiming to be the Messiah would have been considered blasphemy. This may well be so, but claiming to be the Son of God (in the most intimate sense), claiming to be the Son of Man (in the supernatural sense), claiming to sit at God's right hand, predicting a return from heaven, and using the divine name "I am" could and probably would have been considered blasphemy. Mark may have intended some irony by leaving the impression that the high priest committed blasphemy by reviling the Son of God.

The last part of the verse reads like a formal vote of condemnation. The word "all" need not be taken literally. Nicodemus and Joseph of Arimathea, if present, would not have voted to condemn and then the next day identified themselves with Jesus by burying him. Of course they may not have been "invited."

14:65 In constructing this verse, Mark used words and ideas from 1 Kgs 22:24; Isa 50:6; 53:3–5; Mic 5:1. There may also be an allusion to Isa 11:1–4, which evidently was interpreted by some rabbis to mean that the Messiah would be able to judge by smell without sight or hearing. To "prophesy" in the present instance refers to Jesus' being able to identify those who struck him despite the blindfold. At least this is the way Matt 26:68 and Luke 22:64 and some manuscripts of Mark (by way of assimilation to Matthew and Luke) interpret it. Again there is irony, for the guards taunted Jesus to prophesy because they thought he could not. What they did to him fulfilled his own prophecy in 10:34 and the prophecies in Kings, Isaiah, and Micah (above).

The final statement in the verse is found only in Mark and is somewhat awkward Greek (literally, "The guards received/took him with slaps/blows," RSV; cf. NASB). The NIV conveys the right idea in good English.

14. The Denial of Peter (14:54,66–72)

[54]Peter followed him at a distance, right into the courtyard of the high priest. There he sat with the guards and warmed himself at the fire. . . . .

[66]While Peter was below in the courtyard, one of the servant girls of the high priest came by. [67]When she saw Peter warming himself, she looked closely at him.

"You also were with that Nazarene, Jesus," she said.

[68]But he denied it. "I don't know or understand what you're talking about," he said, and went out into the entryway.

---

[77]After the witnesses relate the blasphemy they have heard, "the judges stand up on their feet and rend their garments, and they may not mend them again" (*m. Sanh.* 7.5, trans. Danby).

⁶⁹When the servant girl saw him there, she said again to those standing around, "This fellow is one of them." ⁷⁰Again he denied it.

After a little while, those standing near said to Peter, "Surely you are one of them, for you are a Galilean."

⁷¹He began to call down curses on himself, and he swore to them, "I don't know this man you're talking about."

⁷²Immediately the rooster crowed the second time. Then Peter remembered the word Jesus had spoken to him: "Before the rooster crows twice you will disown me three times." And he broke down and wept.

The interweaving of the accounts of Jesus' trial and Peter's denial not merely indicates that they took place at the same time but contrasts the conduct of Jesus and Peter. Specifically the account of Peter's denial warned the Christians in Rome who would soon face persecution that if even the prince of the apostles denied Jesus they might do so also if they were not spiritually prepared. Mere profession is not enough. Constancy in all circumstances is required of true disciples. Still another emphasis in Mark may be that Jesus went to the cross alone, completely forsaken by all including even the leader of his disciples.

The historicity of the account is not questioned. One cannot conceive of the early church inventing a story that so discredits one of its most prominent leaders. What is not so widely recognized is the likelihood that Peter himself was the source of the account. It is told in a factual way without apologetic motive.

14:54–66 Although Peter followed Jesus "at a distance" (v. 54) and eventually denied that he was his disciple, at least he did stay close, something none of the other disciples did. Although Peter was not ready to confess Jesus publicly, neither was he ready to abandon him altogether. The word "below" suggests that Jesus' trial was held in another upper room. The various rooms of the high priest's palace were apparently built around a "courtyard." The fact that Peter was intimidated by a young servant girl makes his conduct all the more reprehensible.

14:67 The incidental remark about "warming himself" is quite true to life because nights in Jerusalem in March and April are very chilly. It probably shows that Peter was more concerned with his own comfort than with the fate of Jesus. The NIV's "that Nazarene, Jesus" does an excellent job of catching the contemptuousness of the girl's statement.

14:68 In the first instance Peter attempted to evade the question by claiming ignorance, by claiming that he did not even understand what the girl was talking about.⁷⁸ The word translated "entryway" (*proaulion*) might better be

---

⁷⁸It has been claimed that Peter used a legal denial. "[If the owner said,] 'Where is my ox?' and he answered, 'I do not know of what thou speakest,' . . . he is exempt" (*m. Shebu.* 8.3, trans. Danby). Again it is uncertain whether the prescription existed in the first century and, even if it did, whether Peter would have had any knowledge of it.

rendered "forecourt" (NRSV, REB) because it was the way in which the "courtyard" (*aulion* in v. 66) was approached.

As the NIV textual note indicates, some early witnesses add "and the rooster crowed" at the end of the verse. Difficult to decide is whether copyists added the words to indicate the fulfillment of Jesus' prophecy in v. 30 and to prepare for v. 72 or whether they omitted them to harmonize Mark with Matt 26:71 and to avoid the question of why Peter did not repent if he heard the first cock crowing. Thorough harmonization is not the explanation, however, because only two of the Greek manuscripts and one of the Latin manuscripts that omit the words here also omit the references to the second crowing in v. 72 (and for that matter in v. 30 as well). Where internal considerations produce conflicting conclusions, it is best to follow the earliest and best manuscripts, which here have the shorter text as in the NIV.

14:69–70a A certain amount of escalation is in the charges and denials. The first time the girl accused Peter of being with Jesus, Peter claimed he did not understand what she was talking about. The second time she purposely followed him to the forecourt and accused him of being one of an identifiable group of disciples, and Peter denied that. In v. 68 the verb "denied" is aorist (undefined action but often a single act), but here it is an imperfect, which could be translated "kept on denying."

14:70b–71 The third accusation came not from one girl but from several persons, presumably men (the article and participle are masculine, although the gender could be common). This time Peter swore that he did not even know Jesus, and he "began to call down curses on himself" if he were not telling the truth.[79] At the end of v. 70 the mass of medieval manuscripts plus a few earlier witnesses add "and your speech shows *it*" (NKJV, similar KJV). Admittedly the wording is different from Matt 26:73, and mere harmonization is probably not the explanation. Even so, the textual evidence is heavily against authenticity, and there is no explanation for the omission of the words if they were original. If Judas is excluded, Peter's denial represents the greatest failure of the disciples. It is recorded in all four Gospels. There is no attempt to cover up. The very man who confessed Jesus at Caesarea Philippi (8:29) later denied him three times.

14:72 Again a few textual witnesses omit "the second time" and "twice" in part at least to bring Mark's account into line with those of Matthew and Luke, who mention only one crowing; but there is little doubt that these words are original. Ironically, at the very moment Jesus' accusers were challenging him to prophesy (v. 65), one of his prophecies was coming true.

---

[79] The word "curse" has no object in the Greek text and could be aimed at the bystanders, but the context favors the NIV understanding. Again Mark employed irony. In attempting to escape a curse, Peter invoked one upon himself.

The meaning of the last sentence is most uncertain. "He broke down and wept" (NIV, RSV, NRSV, similar GNB), "he began to weep" (NASB), "he burst into tears" (NEB, REB), "he thought about it and wept," "he covered his head and wept," "he pulled his cloak over him and wept," "he fell down and wept," and "he ran out and wept" have been suggested as possible translations; but there is no decisive argument for any. It is hard to determine whether the NASB reading is an interpretation of the best attested Greek text or the adoption of a variant reading, which in turn may be an ancient interpretation of the original text. In any event Peter's weeping probably was a sign of sorrow and repentance.

Mark did not indicate how Peter escaped from the hostile crowd, and here and in 16:7 he merely hinted at Peter's restoration by Jesus. Inconclusive endings of accounts is a literary characteristic of Mark, which helps explain the ending of his Gospel.

15. The Roman Trial (15:1–15)

¹**Very early in the morning, the chief priests, with the elders, the teachers of the law and the whole Sanhedrin, reached a decision. They bound Jesus, led him away and handed him over to Pilate.**

²**"Are you the king of the Jews?" asked Pilate.**

"Yes, it is as you say," Jesus replied.

³**The chief priests accused him of many things.** ⁴**So again Pilate asked him, "Aren't you going to answer? See how many things they are accusing you of."**

⁵**But Jesus still made no reply, and Pilate was amazed.**

⁶**Now it was the custom at the Feast to release a prisoner whom the people requested.** ⁷**A man called Barabbas was in prison with the insurrectionists who had committed murder in the uprising.** ⁸**The crowd came up and asked Pilate to do for them what he usually did.**

⁹**"Do you want me to release to you the king of the Jews?" asked Pilate,** ¹⁰**knowing it was out of envy that the chief priests had handed Jesus over to him.** ¹¹**But the chief priests stirred up the crowd to have Pilate release Barabbas instead.**

¹²**"What shall I do, then, with the one you call the king of the Jews?" Pilate asked them.**

¹³**"Crucify him!" they shouted.**

¹⁴**"Why? What crime has he committed?" asked Pilate.**

But they shouted all the louder, "Crucify him!"

¹⁵**Wanting to satisfy the crowd, Pilate released Barabbas to them. He had Jesus flogged, and handed him over to be crucified.**

In addition to recording a necessary preliminary of Jesus' death, Mark's description of the Roman trial shows that the first Roman official who encountered anyone related to Christianity determined that its founder was innocent but was pressured by the Jewish leaders and mob to execute him. Knowledge of Pilate's favorable decision about Jesus was important for Mark's Roman readers/hearers if they had occasion to defend themselves before Roman authorities. The example of Jesus' conduct before Pilate would also prove helpful when they appeared in court. Mark's account also emphasized that Jesus died as the Messiah and King of the Jews and that this was in accordance with the will of God.

15:1 Mark divided the day of Jesus' death into four periods of three hours each ("very early in the morning," v. 1; "the third hour," v. 25; "the sixth hour . . . the ninth hour," v. 33; and "evening," v. 42). By so doing he implied that the momentous events happened by divine appointment and not haphazardly.

Interpreters of 15:1 have not been able to agree whether Mark described a separate, formal trial after sunrise to legalize the decision already reached at the informal hearing the night before or merely the conclusion of the night trial. Even if a formal trial was held after daybreak to circumvent the prohibition against night trials, there would still be the illegalities of having a trial on a feast day (or the day before a feast, as the case may have been) and passing a sentence of condemnation on the first day of a trial (cf. the introductory comments on 14:53,55–65).

Part of the problem concerns the original text and the translation of the two Greek words rendered "reached a decision" in the NIV. Both of the variant readings have good attestation. The one with perhaps the poorer manuscript support can mean only *to reach a decision* (NIV) or *to make a plan* (NEB, GNB; similar REB). The one with the slightly better support, which may also be the more difficult and more likely the original reading, could also mean *to reach a decision*; but it probably means *to convene a council* (cf. "held a consultation," RSV, NRSV, NASB). The evidence ever so slightly favors the second variant with the second meaning. Apparently Mark described in v. 1 a formal meeting and decision of the Sanhedrin. In any event the piling up of terms in the first sentence shows that the decision was a deliberate one that was made by all of Jewish officialdom and not just a few leaders.

Again Mark used the term *paradidōmi*, "handed over" or "betrayed" in the NIV, to describe Jesus' fate (also 3:19; 9:31; 10:33 twice; 14:10–11,18,21,41–42,44; 15:10,15).[80] It carries both the idea of something sinister and evil and of something done in accordance with the will of God.

Pilate was the fifth Roman governor of Judea[81] after the deposition of the client-king Archelaus (cf. Matt 2:22) in A.D. 6. He held the office from A.D.

---

[80] The same Greek word is used with reference to the fate of John in 1:14 and the fate of the disciples in 13:9,11,12. It is also used in 4:29 and 7:13.

[81] The province of Judea included Idumea to the south and Samaria to the north. The remainder of Palestine was still client kingdoms, Galilee and Perea under Herod Antipas and northeastern Palestine under Philip (cf. Luke 3:1).

26–36. His proper title was legate as is shown by an inscription found at Caesarea, the provincial capital located on the Mediterranean coast.[82] Both Josephus[83] and Philo[84] described him as being cruel and without any sensitivity for Jewish religious beliefs or practices. One of his atrocities is mentioned in Luke 13:1. By the time Mark wrote, Pilate was so well known in Christian circles that he did not need to be described. Although the governors usually resided at Caesarea, they often came to Jerusalem at festival times in order to be at the site should disorder arise among the thousands who came to the feasts.

15:2 Pilate's question is exactly the same in all four Gospels (also Matt 27:11; Luke 23:3; John 18:33). Up to this point the term "king of the Jews" has not appeared in Mark, but it appears six times in chap. 15 (also vv. 9,12,18,26,32—the last being the synonymous expression "King of Israel"). Obviously Mark emphasized that Jesus died as the king of the Jews. Although Mark did not explicitly say so, the Jewish officials doubtless brought Jesus to the Roman governor on charges of claiming to be their king.

Although Jesus is called "king" only by his enemies, Mark doubtless wanted his readers/hearers to do so as well, although in a reverential way. The kingship of Jesus is implicit in the titles "Christ" and "Son of God" because the kings of Israel were anointed and called "sons of God" (see the comments on 1:1 and 14:61). Even the title "Son of Man" may reflect Jesus' royalty because the son of man of Dan 7:13 was given "authority, glory and sovereign power" and "his dominion is an everlasting dominion that will not pass away, and his kingdom is one that will never be destroyed" (v. 14). "King of the Jews" is therefore a Christological title emphasizing Jesus' authority and greatness. For Mark and his readers Jesus was more than King of the Jews; he was King of all those who submit to him. The kingdom of Jesus is virtually identical with the kingdom of God. Both are primarily spheres of influence and dominion rather than places. Significantly, Jesus is proclaimed as King precisely in context of his service to all through his death on the cross (cf. 10:42–45).

---

[82]Tacitus, *Annals* 15.44, does indeed call Pilate a procurator, but he was merely using the terminology familiar in his day (early second century). The term "procurator" was first used by the emperor Claudius (A.D 41–54). Therefore the proper title of the governors, including Felix and Festus (Acts 23–26), during the second period when Judea was an imperial province, i.e., A.D. 44–66, was procurator.

[83]Josephus, *Antiquities* 18.3.1–2; 4.1–2; *War* 2.9.2–4. Pilate ordered his soldiers to bring their standards into Jerusalem, something the Jews considered to be idolatry. He attempted to use temple money to construct an aqueduct. He slaughtered a number of Samaritans who had gathered on Mt. Gerizim to witness the recovery of some sacred objects supposedly buried there by Moses. The last of these led to his deposition.

[84]Philo, *Embassy to Gaius* 38. Pilate attempted to smuggle into Jerusalem some golden shields bearing the image of the emperor, which the Jews interpreted as an attempt to establish emperor worship in the city.

Some claim that at the Jewish trial Jesus was charged with a religious crime; at the Roman trial, with a political crime because a Roman governor would not have considered a religious charge. There is some truth in this claim, but it is also true that "king of the Jews" is the equivalent of "the Christ" (14:61). Mark probably emphasized that both the Jews and the Romans condemned Jesus for the same reason, not different ones.

Jesus' answer, which is exactly the same here, in Matt 27:11, and in Luke 23:3, and which is similar in John 18:37, is deliberately ambiguous in the Greek. The NIV's "Yes, it is as you say" obscures this ambiguity, which was necessary because if Jesus had answered with a simple yes the trial would have ended immediately with conviction. Ironically, Jesus *was* a King, not in the political sense that the Jews and Pilate understood but in a spiritual sense.

15:3 What the other charges were, Mark did not say. Some can be gathered from the other Gospels. Some textual witnesses of medium quality add, "He gave no answer." Some have argued that this statement is presupposed by v. 4, but it is more likely a harmonization to Matt 27:12.

15:4–5 Just as he did in his account of the Jewish trial (14:60–61), Mark emphasized Jesus' silence. This may have been to picture Jesus as the fulfillment of the prophecies about the righteous sufferer (Ps 38:13–14) and the suffering servant (Isa 53:7). Mark indicated that "Pilate was amazed" in order to show that the governor recognized that Jesus was a most unusual person. Probably Mark intended to convey the idea of religious awe. Certainly the theme of amazement is a consistent Markan theme (1:22,27; 2:12; 5:20; 6:2,51; 10:24,26; 11:18; 12:17).

15:6 The accuracy of the statements in vv. 6,8 has often been denied because there is no other evidence for the practice.[85] If such a practice had existed in Roman Palestine, one might expect Josephus to have mentioned it. Josephus cannot be expected to have mentioned every item in first-century Palestinian life. The practice may have been limited to Pilate and for this reason is not mentioned elsewhere. The argument is one of silence. In the absence of any evidence to the contrary, Mark's statement, which is repeated by Matt 27:15 and attested independently by John 18:39, should be accepted.

15:7 "Barabbas" means *son of Abba* or *son of a father* or just possibly *son of a rabbi*. "Barabbas" could be a personal name, but it is more likely a

---

[85] Only two possible parallels have been cited, but neither is convincing. *M. Pesah.* 8.6 indicates that the Passover lamb may be sacrificed "for one whom they have promised to bring out of prison" (trans. Danby). The provision is related to the Passover, but of its date and circumstances there is no indication. Papyrus Florentinus 61, cited by A. Deissmann, *Light from the Ancient East*, trans. L. R. M. Strachan, reprint ed. (Grand Rapids: Baker, 1965), 269, quotes the governor of Egypt, G. Septimius Vegetus, as saying to an accused person named Phibion, "Thou hadst been worthy of scourging . . . but I will give thee to the people." There may be an allusion to release in response to popular demand, but there is no connection with a feast.

patronymic to distinguish the man from others with the same personal name. If so, it is strange that Mark did not give the man's personal name, especially since he used an attributive participle that could be translated literally "the one who is called Barabbas." The original text of Matt 27:16–17 probably is "Jesus Barabbas" (NEB, REB, GNB, NRSV, *UBSGNT*) rather than "Barabbas" alone. Although he chose not to include it—unless it dropped out of all the extant manuscripts of his Gospel—Mark may have also known this personal name, and such knowledge may have influenced the construction he used.

Mark indicated that Barabbas was not a common murderer but an insurrectionist, a nationalist who opposed Roman rule. Neither Josephus nor any other source records a rebellion about this time, but from A.D. 6 onward Judea was seething with discontent and frequent but feeble attempts to overthrow Roman rule.

15:8 Unless the Jewish officials had rounded them up for the purpose, the presence of such a large crowd for the trial of Jesus is unusual, especially since he had been arrested during the middle of the previous night. Certainly the large group of people would have been nearby and easily gathered together during the Passover celebration. Because he was a nationalist, Barabbas was probably quite popular; and the crowd may have come for the purpose of pleading for his release. If in fact the man's name was Jesus Barabbas, and if the crowd came up and cried out for the release of Jesus (meaning Barabbas), one can understand why Pilate mistakenly thought he could easily release Jesus the Christ.

15:9 Pilate's use of the designation "king of the Jews" was certainly sarcastic and shows his contempt for Jesus in particular and the Jews in general.

15:10 This verse is a separate sentence with a finite verb ("he knew") in the Greek text and in no way weighs against the suggestion made earlier that Pilate thought the crowd was asking for the release of Jesus the Christ rather than Jesus Barabbas. Pilate quickly realized that the Jews did not ordinarily deliver one of their own to him for any purpose and certainly not for claiming to be a king in opposition to Roman rule. He quickly realized that the Jewish officials had other issues probably of a religious nature against Jesus, issues in which he had no interest. His attempt to release Jesus was not likely based on principles of humanity or justice but on spite. The leaders were envious of Jesus because of such things as his piety, his popularity, and his ability to perform miracles.

15:11 If that understanding is correct, the chief priests must have incited the crowd to clearly call for the release of Jesus Barabbas rather than Jesus the Christ.

15:12 As in v. 9 Pilate's designation of Jesus as "king of the Jews" is contemptuous. It is made even more so by the addition of "the one you call."

Pilate had unconditional power of amnesty (regardless of any practice of releasing a prisoner at feast time) and could have released both prisoners. Mark seems to make the point that he did not release Jesus because of the danger of a riot if he did.

15:13 The fickleness of the crowd has often been pointed out. Crowds are just that way. Not all welcomed Jesus to the city. Not all the people heard him gladly in the temple. Although the people were much more receptive to Jesus and his message than the leaders, Jesus certainly had enemies among them also. If, however, the crowd had come for the purpose of gaining the release of their hero Barabbas, their cry to crucify Jesus is altogether understandable (cf. the note on "crowds" at 14:43).

15:14 The unwillingness of the crowd to answer Pilate's question was especially important in establishing Jesus' innocence.

15:15 Again Mark's presentation is ironic. Jesus was falsely accused by the Jews and condemned by Pilate for the very thing of which Barabbas was actually guilty. The pseudo "son of the father" was freed, but the true Son of God was executed. Mark probably pictured Jesus as a substitute for one sinner and by implication for all sinners. Mark also may have had in mind Isa 53:6,12, where in the LXX the same word is used that is here translated "handed . . . over" in the NIV (cf. the comments on v. 1).

Flogging was both a preliminary to crucifixion (perhaps to hasten death) and an independent punishment. It was a Roman punishment and must be distinguished from the much milder synagogue beatings of forty lashes less one. Bits of metal, bone, or glass were imbedded in leather thongs; and the flesh of the victim was shredded, sometimes until bones or entrails appeared. Flogging was sometimes fatal. The flogging fulfilled Jesus' own prophecy in 10:34 and perhaps also Isa 53:5.

16. The Mockery of the Soldiers (15:16–20)

¹⁶The soldiers led Jesus away into the palace (that is, the Praetorium) and called together the whole company of soldiers. ¹⁷They put a purple robe on him, then twisted together a crown of thorns and set it on him. ¹⁸And they began to call out to him, "Hail, king of the Jews!" ¹⁹Again and again they struck him on the head with a staff and spit on him. Falling on their knees, they paid homage to him. ²⁰And when they had mocked him, they took off the purple robe and put his own clothes on him. Then they led him out to crucify him.

Jesus was first mocked by the members of the Sanhedrin and others at the Jewish trial (14:65), then by the Roman soldiers after Pilate passed sentence (here), and finally by the mob around the cross (15:29–32). Mark recorded these instances of mocking to show that Jesus' prophecy in 10:34 was fulfilled and to fortify his own readers/hearers for the abuse they would soon endure.

Irony continues to dominate the account. Jesus was mocked as a pretender, but he was in fact a real King. The mocking was his enthronement; the cross, his throne. Mark wanted to emphasize that Jesus' kingship was characterized by humility and servanthood and was different from all the kingships of the world.

This mocking contains some interesting parallels. When the Jewish client-king Herod Agrippa I (Acts 12) visited Alexandria in A.D. 38, the pagan mob insulted him by dressing up as a king a demented Jew named Carabas and paying homage to him.[86] In A.D. 68 the deposed emperor Vitellius was mocked and otherwise abused before he was executed.[87]

15:16 The word translated "palace" ordinarily means *courtyard* (14:54), but the qualifying expression "that is, the Praetorium" probably refers to the building or buildings that constituted the residence and office of the governor. The praetorium was not a fixed place but wherever a high Roman official held court and conducted other business. Often it was out of doors. The question arises where this was in Jerusalem.

The traditional site of Jesus' trial is the fortress Antonia, which adjoined the northwest corner of the temple compound. At that site and within the modern Convent of the Sisters of Zion, one may observe today an impressive stone pavement (cf. John 19:13) in which Roman soldiers carved game boards and other trivia. Most archaeologists, however, think the pavement dates not from the time of Herod the Great, who built the fortress, but from A.D. 135 when the city was rebuilt following a second (or third) Jewish revolt. Josephus indicated that when the procurator Gessius Florus (A.D. 64–66) came to Jerusalem he resided in what had been Herod's palace on the western side of the city.[88] A priori it seems much more probable that the governor would reside in luxury at the palace rather than rough it with the troops at the barracks. Therefore Jesus probably was tried at Herod's palace rather than the fortress Antonia. If so, the famous *Via Dolorosa*, the "way of sadness," the route he walked to the cross, would have to be changed.

The word translated "company of soldiers" refers to a cohort. Ten cohorts were in a legion, and six centuries (one hundred men) were in a cohort. In actual practice, however, a cohort consisted of from two hundred to six hundred troops. Here the word was used loosely to refer to the soldiers stationed in Jerusalem and present at the time. These were not members of the regular army but provincial auxiliaries recruited from non-Jews in Palestine and elsewhere in the eastern part of the empire.

---

[86] Philo, *Against Flaccus* 6.35–40.
[87] Dio Cassius, *History* 15.20–21.
[88] Josephus, *War* 2.14.8; 15.5.

15:17   Purple cloth was very expensive, and a "purple robe" was popularly associated with royalty. The "crown of thorns" was not intended so much to add to Jesus' suffering as to parody the laurel crown worn by the emperor.

15:18   Here "Hail, king of the Jews!" is an imitation of "Hail, Caesar the Emperor!"

15:19   The NIV does a good job of bringing out the force of the imperfect tense of the first two verbs by prefixing "Again and again" (actually all three finite verbs in the verse are imperfect). The beating fulfills Mic 5:1; Isa 50:6; 53:4–5. Similarly the spitting, which may be a parody of the kiss of homage, fulfills 10:34 and Isa 50:6.

15:20   The mocking fulfills Ps 22:6 and Isa 53:3. The usual practice was to strip a man before he was led away to the place of execution and then to flog him along the way. Jesus, however, had already been flogged (v. 15) and probably could not bear any more. He was stripped for the flogging of v. 15 and again at the place of execution (v. 24).

17. The Crucifixion (15:21–41)

[21]A certain man from Cyrene, Simon, the father of Alexander and Rufus, was passing by on his way in from the country, and they forced him to carry the cross. [22]They brought Jesus to the place called Golgotha (which means The Place of the Skull). [23]Then they offered him wine mixed with myrrh, but he did not take it. [24]And they crucified him. Dividing up his clothes, they cast lots to see what each would get.

[25]It was the third hour when they crucified him. [26]The written notice of the charge against him read: THE KING OF THE JEWS. [27]They crucified two robbers with him, one on his right and one on his left. [29]Those who passed by hurled insults at him, shaking their heads and saying, "So! You who are going to destroy the temple and build it in three days, [30]come down from the cross and save yourself!"

[31]In the same way the chief priests and the teachers of the law mocked him among themselves. "He saved others," they said, "but he can't save himself! [32]Let this Christ, this King of Israel, come down now from the cross, that we may see and believe." Those crucified with him also heaped insults on him.

[33]At the sixth hour darkness came over the whole land until the ninth hour. [34]And at the ninth hour Jesus cried out in a loud voice, "Eloi, Eloi, lama sabachthani?"—which means, "My God, my God, why have you forsaken me?"

[35]When some of those standing near heard this, they said, "Listen, he's calling Elijah."

[36]One man ran, filled a sponge with wine vinegar, put it on a stick, and offered it to Jesus to drink. "Now leave him alone. Let's see if Elijah comes to take him down," he said.

[37]With a loud cry, Jesus breathed his last.

[38]The curtain of the temple was torn in two from top to bottom. [39]And when

the centurion, who stood there in front of Jesus, heard his cry and saw how he died, he said, "Surely this man was the Son of God!"

⁴⁰Some women were watching from a distance. Among them were Mary Magdalene, Mary the mother of James the younger and of Joses, and Salome. ⁴¹In Galilee these women had followed him and cared for his needs. Many other women who had come up with him to Jerusalem were also there.

The account is characterized by brevity, simplicity, and restraint. There is no attempt to create sympathy for Jesus or hatred for his enemies—a consideration that does not support the frequent charge that Mark is anti-Semitic. Unlike some modern sermons, no attempt is made to describe the physical sufferings of Jesus. Far more important for Mark was the significance of those sufferings.

The description of the death of Jesus in this section reveals several purposes in Mark's theology. First, he showed that all that happened was in fulfillment of Old Testament prophecy, especially Ps 22. Indeed, the main historical problem in the account is the extent to which it has been influenced by the Old Testament. Mark and his predecessors doubtless interpreted the Old Testament Christologically, saw its fulfillment in various events in Jesus' life and death, and used Old Testament language in describing these events. These admissions, however, in no way prove that the early Christians invented events to provide fulfillment. Their line of reasoning was from the events in the life of Jesus to the Old Testament, not vice versa, because many of the Old Testament texts do not at first seem to be a prediction of anything or anyone. As previously indicated, the idea of divine foreordination is also set forth by the exact time references.

Second, Mark showed that although the eleven disciples had fled and could give no firsthand report of what happened,[89] there were Christian eyewitnesses, Simon of Cyrene and the women. Third, Mark emphasized not only the utter rejection and humiliation but also the self-control of Jesus during his last hours. Particular emphasis is on the mocking, something found previously in 14:65 and 15:16–20 and here brought to a climax.

Crucifixion seems to have been invented by the Persians, who transmitted it to the Carthaginians, from whom the Romans learned it. It was the ultimate Roman punishment for slaves and provincials, but it was not used for Roman citizens.[90] It was one of the most horrifying forms of execution ever

---

[89]Mark does not record the fate of Judas as does Matt 27:3–10; cf. Acts 1:16–20.

[90]Although the Jewish priest-king Alexander Janneus crucified eight hundred of his opponents early in the first century B.C. (Josephus, *Antiquities* 13.14.2; *War* 1.4.6), the usual Jewish method of execution was stoning. The fact that Jesus was crucified rather than stoned proves conclusively that he was executed by the Romans rather than the Jews. In exceptional circumstances the Jews did hang on a tree the bodies of persons who had already been executed. They did this to expose them to shame and to indicate that the curse of God was upon such persons (Deut 21:23).

devised.[91] After having been stripped and flogged, the victim was lashed and/ or nailed to a pole. John 20:25 certainly implies that Jesus' hands at least were nailed (cf. Acts 2:23; Col 2:14). Evidently there were different styles of crosses including a single upright pole and two crossed poles in the form of an *X*, but the most common seems to have been a vertical pole and a horizontal one in the form of a *T* with the crossbar either at the top or near the top of the vertical piece. The usual practice was for the condemned to carry the crossbar to the place of execution where he was affixed to it and where it was hoisted upon the vertical stake that was permanently fixed. Death usually came slowly as a result of exposure and exhaustion. Inasmuch as no vital organ was damaged, it often took two or three days for the subject to die, although death could be hastened by breaking the legs (cf. John 19:31–33).

Archaeologists have recently discovered the bones of a man who was crucified in Jerusalem about the time of Jesus. A single spike was driven through both heels in such a way as to show that the legs supported no weight as the victim hung upon the cross. The legs may have been drawn up and bent backwards together so that the whole body resembled an *S* or drawn up and forced apart so that the legs alone resembled an *O*. The arm bones were scratched, but it could not be determined if the hands were nailed. One of the leg bones was severed and the other splintered, perhaps while the man was still alive, perhaps when the body was removed from the cross. There is some evidence that he may have been crucified upside down.

15:21   Since the fourth century a colony of Jews had lived in Cyrene North Africa.[92] Simon may have been a Gentile or a God-fearer,[93] but probably he was a Jew who had come to the feast. The statement "on his way in from the country" does not necessarily indicate that he had been working in the fields but only that he was entering the city. The obvious reason for the mention of "Alexandria and Rufus" is that Mark's readers/hearers knew them. They were probably members of the Roman church. A certain Rufus is mentioned in Rom 16:13. If the Rufus of Mark 15:21 and the one of Rom 16:13 are the same person, and if Rom 16 was written to Rome,[94] there is additional evidence for a Roman provenance for Mark's Gospel.

---

[91] Josephus, *War* 7.6.4 describes crucifixion as "the most painful of deaths." The Latin verb *cruciare*, "to crucify," and the Latin noun *crux*, "cross," have been preserved in the English adjective "excruciating" and its cognates.

[92] Josephus, *Against Apion* 2.4.

[93] The God-fearers were Gentiles who were attracted to Judaism because of its monotheism and high ethical standards. They worshiped at the synagogues and in the outer courts of the temple but did not fully convert, in part at least because of the difficult requirement of circumcision. In Acts they appear to constitute one of the most fertile fields of early Christian evangelism because Christianity could offer them the same God and the same ethical standards without circumcision.

[94] An Ephesian destination for Rom 16 has been strongly argued.

John 19:17 indicates that Jesus carried the horizontal piece of the cross. It is not a forced harmonization to suggest that Jesus began to carry his cross but soon was unable to continue to do so because of the flogging. At this point Simon was impressed to carry it. In addition to recording a factual event—this is not the kind of detail that likely would have been invented—Mark no doubt wanted crossbearing to convey the idea of discipleship (cf. 8:34).

15:22 "Golgotha" is a Grecianized form of the Aramaic word meaning *a skull*.[95] Neither Mark nor any other Gospel locates or describes the place. Inasmuch as both the Jews and Romans customarily executed outside cities but in public places, presumably the place was not far beyond the city wall and beside a road. Also Heb 13:12 says that Jesus "suffered outside the city gate," and John 19:20 says that the place was "near the city." Nowhere is it stated that Golgotha was a hill, but it may have gotten its name from being a low-lying hill in the shape of a skull. The name is not likely derived from skulls lying around because of Jewish insistence on quick burials even of enemies and criminals. Possibly the name reflects a place of unnatural death. Compare the modern use of a skull and crossbones to indicate the danger of death especially from poison.

The traditional site of the crucifixion and the burial is the site that since about A.D. 326 has been occupied by the Church of the Holy Sepulcher. Its claim has been strengthened in recent years because archaeologists have proved that it was outside the second wall on the northwest side of the city in Jesus' day. The actual site, however, cannot be determined because of the lack of data in the Gospels, the ramp the Romans built against the north wall during the siege of A.D. 70, the destructions of the city in A.D. 70 and A.D. 135, and the desecration of holy sites and the rebuilding as a pagan city after A.D. 135. The only other site with any serious claim is Gordon's Calvary and the adjoining Garden Tomb, which are a little beyond the Damascus Gate in the present north wall. Gordon's Calvary does somewhat resemble a skull in appearance, but that appearance probably is the result of medieval and even modern excavation. The Garden Tomb is Byzantine rather than ancient. The Church of the Holy Sepulcher has the better claim, but the place cannot be determined with much confidence. Mark was far more concerned with the significance of the death of Jesus than with making sure his readers knew exactly where it took place.

---

[95] Few words are more common in modern Christian vocabulary than "Calvary," and few have less justification. The word does not appear in any Greek manuscript of the Gospels or in most modern English translations. It appears in the KJV and NKJV only in Luke 23:33, where for some unexplained reason the translators used an anglicized form of the Latin word *calvaria*, which appears regularly in the Vulgate, rather than the English word "skull" to translate the Greek word *kranion*. Elsewhere they properly employ "skull" to translate *kranion*.

15:23 Neither Matthew nor Mark provides a clear antecedent for "they" (cf. "one of them," Matt 27:48; "some of those," Matt 27:47). Inasmuch as the Romans flogged their victims to make death as painful as possible, probably "they" were Jews. The *Babylonian Talmud* records a tradition that the women of Jerusalem, perhaps in response to Prov 31:6–7, provided a narcotic drink for those who were condemned to die.[96] Both "wine" and "myrrh" have pain-deadening qualities. Jesus probably refused the drink so that he could face death in complete control of himself.

15:24 Clothing was much more valuable in ancient times than it is today. The Roman practice was for the executioners to receive the garments of their victims. Although he cited no Scripture as did John (19:24), Mark and his readers/hearers probably thought of Ps 22:18.

15:25 The "third hour" would be 9:00 in the morning. This time reference has been the object of much skepticism because (1) it is difficult to believe that everything in 15:1–23 took place in just three hours, (2) the time reference is out of sequence (logically it should be at the end of v. 20), (3) Matthew and Luke omitted it, and (4) because it is difficult to reconcile with "the sixth hour" in John 19:14.

None of these objections is very weighty. If the Jewish leaders brought Jesus to Pilate within the hour after dawn, it is quite conceivable that the trial took less than the next hour and the beating much less than a third hour. (A bigger problem is to find time for what is in Luke 23:6–12.) John's figure may be "theological" rather than "historical" to associate Jesus' condemnation with the beginning of the slaying of the Paschal lambs. Both figures are approximations, not exact times, and one is as "accurate" as the other. Neither Mark nor other biblical writers always put things in what Western readers would call logical order. The reference could also have gone after v. 24a.

15:26 The Roman custom was to hang around the neck of the condemned or have carried before him on the way to the place of execution an indication of the charges; this placard was then affixed to the cross. No doubt Pilate meant this inscription as an insult to both Jesus and the Jewish leaders (cf. John 19:19–22). Again, however, he was unwittingly proclaiming the truth.

15:27 The word translated "robbers" in the present context probably means *insurrectionists* or *rebels*. They may have been two of the "insurrectionists" of v. 7. Josephus often used the Greek word with reference to the Zealots. The crucifixion between two criminals is certainly historical because the early church would not have invented such a discrediting idea. Later tradition has supplied names for the two: the old Latin manuscript Colbertinus (c/6) Zoatham and Camma in Matt 27:38 and Zoathan and Chammatha in Mark; Dysmas and Gestas in the *Acts of Pilate*; and Titus and

---

[96] *B. Sanh.* 43a.

Dumachus in the *Arabic Infancy Gospel*. Such traditions are of little or no value. The statement "one on his right hand and one on his left" recalls the request of James and John in 10:37 and gives insight into what it means to occupy places of "honor" in the kingdom of God.

[15:28] Quite probably Mark saw in the crucifixion between two rebels fulfillment of Isa 53:12, but again he did not cite a passage. What was only implicit in Mark's original was later made explicit in the majority of extant Greek manuscripts by adding what appears in the KJV and NKJV and in the NIV margin as v. 28. The textual evidence is overwhelmingly against the addition, and its language is un-Markan.

15:29–30 The word translated "hurled insults" is the verbal form of the noun "blasphemy" in 14:64. Ironically the one who was falsely accused of blasphemy became the object of blasphemy.

Shaking of the head was a gesture of contempt (Isa 37:22; Jer 18:16). The scene appears to fulfill Pss 22:2–7 and 109:25. The charge of plotting to destroy the temple (14:58) reappears. Ironically if Jesus had come down from the cross, he could not have saved either himself or others. He had come "to give his life as a ransom for many" (10:45); only by dying upon the cross could he do so.

15:31 Some have objected that "the chief priests and the teachers of the law" would not likely have demeaned themselves by attending the execution. If in fact they had long been plotting to destroy Jesus, there is every reason to think they would have come to enjoy their success. When the leaders said, "He saved others," they probably were referring to Jesus' healing miracles and just possibly to his resurrection miracles as well. The Christian reader/hearer, however, should understand the word "save" in its deeper, theological sense of *salvation from sin* and should also recall 8:35. Precisely because he refused to save himself, he was able to *save* others. The irony that pervades the accounts of the trials and crucifixion makes them even more dramatic!

15:32 The NIV translation "Let this Christ" nicely reflects the contempt of the chief priests and the scribes. It follows upon the question in 14:61. The demand to come down from the cross so they could "see" is similar to the demand for an extraordinary sign in 8:11–12. By quoting the words "that we may see," Mark probably intended to convey the truth that believing is not based on seeing external proofs but on confidence in God and his Christ. This verse and the two that precede show that just as God did not rescue Jesus, he will not always rescue Jesus' disciples. To those who would be tried and condemned, Jesus exemplifies faithfulness to God to the very end of life.

Whereas the Romans would naturally use the word "Jews," their own name for the inhabitants of Palestine (vv. 2,9,12,18,26), the inhabitants would naturally use their own name, "Israel." Therefore the use of "King of Israel" may be seen as another instance of accurate reporting. The linking of "Christ" (or

"Messiah") and "King of Israel" shows clearly that Jesus was condemned by both the Sanhedrin and Pilate for claiming to be the Jewish Messiah. Therefore the concept of Jesus' messiahship is not a later invention of the church as has been claimed.

The last sentence indicates that Jesus died utterly forsaken and alone. Only v. 40 lessens this Markan emphasis.

15:33   Here Mark recorded the first of two apocalyptic signs that accompanied the death of Jesus and showed its significance. The "sixth" and "ninth" hours were noon and 3:00 p.m., respectively. "Darkness" is often a symbol of evil, and the "darkness" here could be an indication of the apparent triumph of evil. More likely it is a sign of coming judgment (Amos 8:9–10; possibly Isa 60:2; Jer 15:9). It recalls the darkness that preceded the judgment upon Egypt (Exod 10:21–22). Mark had already quoted Jesus (and Isa 13:10; 34:4) to the effect that darkness would accompany the judgment at the end of the world.

Inasmuch as a solar eclipse is impossible at the time of the full moon, some attempts have been made to provide a natural explanation for the darkness at the crucifixion: a dust storm accompanying a sirocco and heavy rain clouds. Such explanations were foreign to the thought of Mark and his church. For them it was simply a supernatural manifestation, and that is still the best explanation. Although the Greek word *gē* often refers to the whole earth, "the whole land" is the better translation here because the darkness probably was limited to Palestine and perhaps even to Judea. There are no ancient reports of an unusual darkness elsewhere at the time.

15:34   The only saying from the cross in Mark's Gospel is undoubtedly authentic. The early church would not have invented such a potentially embarrassing statement and then attributed it to Jesus. Mark first quoted an Aramaic version of Ps 22:1 and then immediately translated it into Greek, the primary language of his readers/hearers. (The Greek, but not the Aramaic, has in turn been translated into English.)

This verse poses several problems. First, what were Jesus' actual words? Inasmuch as Aramaic was the language of the common people in first-century Palestine, one might expect Jesus to have spoken in Aramaic as Mark indicated. Nevertheless it is difficult to see how *Eloi* could have been mistaken for *Eliyoāh*, i.e., "Elijah" (v. 35). It is much easier to see how the Hebrew equivalent *Eli* could have. Most manuscripts of Matt 27:46 and a few manuscripts of Mark of medium quality do in fact have *Eli, Eli*. That Jesus spoke the words "My God, my God" in Hebrew and the words "why have you forsaken me?" in Aramaic is possible. It is also possible that the Hebrew is a Matthean assimilation to the text of Ps 22. Regardless, the early Palestinian church probably translated the Hebrew into its language, Aramaic, and this was the form passed on to Mark.